D0161390

Carmel – Thank you for your help and patience. I appreciate!

Joan N. Herber

TEACHING IN CONTENT AREAS

WITH READING, WRITING, AND REASONING

HAROLD L. HERBER
Syracuse University

JOAN NELSON HERBER
The State University of New York at Binghamton

ALLYN AND BACON
Boston   London   Toronto   Sydney   Tokyo   Singapore

Series Editor: Sean Wakely
Series Editorial Assistant: Carol Chernaik
Production Administrator: Marjorie Payne
Editorial-Production Service: Cynthia Newby, Chestnut Hill Enterprises, Inc.
Cover Administrator: Suzanne Harbison
Composition Buyer: Linda Cox
Manufacturing Buyer: Louise Richardson

Teaching in Content Areas with Reading, Writing, and Reasoning

Copyright © 1993 by Allyn & Bacon
A Division of Simon & Schuster, Inc.
160 Gould Street
Needham Heights, MA 02194

All rights reserved. No part of the material protected by this copyright notice may be reproduced or utilized in any form or by any means, electronic or mechanical, including photocopying, recording, or by any information storage and retrieval system, without the writtten persmission of the copyright owner.

---

*DEDICATION: To family, friends, students, and
colleagues who have made our lives
so interesting and rewarding.*

Herber, Harold L.
    Teaching in content areas with reading, writing, and reasoning /
Harold L. Herber, Joan Nelson Herber.
        p.   cm.
    Includes bibliographical references (p.   ) and indexes.
    ISBN 0-205-14158-7
    1. Content area reading—United States. 2. English language—
Rhetoric—United States. 3. Thought and thinking—United States.
I. Nelson Herber, Joan. II. Title.
LB1050.455.H47 1993
428.4'07—dc20   92-3173
                                                                                   CIP

Printed in the United States of America

10 9 8 7 6 5 4 3 2 1   98 97 96 95 94 93 92

___ CONTENTS ___

FOREWORD

The professionals who constitute the intended audience for *Teaching in Content Areas with Reading, Writing, and Reasoning* are present and future classroom subject-area teachers. The instructional strategies discussed in the book are applicable from intermediate grades through college; illustrative materials are drawn from a variety of subject areas and grade levels. Materials you respond to as a reader of the book illustrate applications of the instructional strategies with adults. The book is designed so that you will have direct experience in using the same kind of instructional materials that we recommend you use with your own students. Thus, you will not only study the instructional strategies and materials in an academic sense, you will also experience their effectiveness in a practical sense. You will also learn how to create similar materials to support your own students' learning.

In writing to our specified audience, we take as our first premise the belief that subject-area teachers are interested principally in teaching their course content, the substance of their disciplines. We take as a second premise the belief that these teachers also are interested in helping their students learn how to learn their course content. Thus, the major purpose of this text is to present instructional strategies by which subject-area teachers can support their students' learning of course content.

The instructional strategies presented in this book are designed to promote the processes of reading, writing, and reasoning; the contexts for the application of these strategies are subject-area classrooms. The teachers who apply the strategies are regular classroom teachers; the curricula around which the strategies are organized are regular, subject-area curricula. The resource materials used for the instruction are those normally used by the teachers and students. The students who are the beneficiaries of this instruction are all students who are enrolled in the courses taught by the subject-area teachers.

Teaching in Content Areas with Reading, Writing, and Reasoning, then, presents ways to teach the content of various subjects while *simultaneously* teaching the relevant reading, writing, and reasoning skills. It is not our wish to convert subject-area teachers into reading teachers or writing teachers. Rather, our desire is to help subject-area teachers become more proficient in teaching their subject by adding strategies for teaching reading, writing, and reasoning to their instructional repertoires.

While the book demonstrates how to integrate instruction in reading, writing, and reasoning with instruction in course content, it also shows teachers how to take advantage of the reciprocal relationships that exist among these three processes. The interrelationships among reading, writing, and thinking are well documented in the professional literature. This book shows not only how reading, writing, and reasoning relate to one another but also how these relationships can be incorporated to support the teaching of course content.

This book is based on the belief that students can be successful in learning the concepts and principles presented in the subjects they study *if* they are shown how to be successful in doing what they are required to do. It is also based on the expectation that teachers (when *they themselves* are shown how to do so) will show their students how to be successful in meeting their course requirements. It is based on the belief that when teachers expect their students to be successful in their courses and show them how to be, they really are successful. Finally, the book is based on the belief that students will be successful when they expect it of themselves and when their expectations are a reflection of their teachers' expectations for them.

Throughout this book you will find the optimism we have described and the reasons for it. Similarly pervasive is the sense of positive expectations toward teachers and teaching, toward students and learning. Undergirding the expectations is the belief in teaching as "showing how" and an operationalization of that belief in each of the chapters, in building on students' strengths, and in showing them how to do what is required to be successful in learning.

ACKNOWLEDGMENTS: During our professional careers, we have been supported by university colleagues, inspired by school teachers and administrators, and stimulated by our students. All have contributed significantly to our thinking about what to include in this book, to our determination to have the book reflect both practice and research, and to the professional environments that make such writing possible.

University colleagues with whom we have been closely associated have cared about us and about our work. Their support has been of inestimable value. Classroom teachers and school administrators have applied many of our ideas in a variety of challenging educational settings. Their work has inspired our own. Our students have been both interesting people and interested scholars. We have been stimulated by their applications, refinements, and extensions of what they have learned from us. Excerpts from some of their work are included in the book. Of particular note is the Latin unit created by Diane Mannix and included in chapter 11.

Moving ideas from mind to paper involves a variety of keyboarding on word processors. Our friend Joan Simonetta was particularly helpful to us on such tasks.

We acknowledge our professional debt to all of these good people.

Finally, we are happy to report that after spending about five years in joint authorship of this book, we are still best friends. We thank each other publicly for that fact!—Harold L. Herber and Joan N. Herber

SECTION I
Point of View

1

Rationale

Organizing idea: The why and how of instruction are of equal importance.

Reflections

Before reading this chapter, please record in your journal your responses to the following tasks. If possible, share your writing with other individuals who are also reading this book.

1. List words and phrases that you believe accurately describe your teaching.

2. Analyze your words and phrases to determine those that relate to the why of teaching and those that relate to the how.

3. Write out a synthesis statement for each of the two sets of words or phrases so you have a summary of the how and a summary of the why of your teaching.

CONCERNS EXPRESSED BY TWO science teachers give a sense of the kind of issues that this book addresses. One was a physics teacher whose students, he said, "Can't read!" and were having difficulty with the course. Inquiry was made into the ability and achievement levels of the particular class in question. No student in the class had attained less than the 95th percentile on a recently administered standardized reading test. The median ability level of the class was in the superior range, according to a standardized test. When asked how he reconciled his description of the students with this data the teacher said, "Well, you know they can read; they just don't know what to do with what they read. I ask them questions; they give me information. I ask them what the information means; they give me more information. They seem not to be able to interpret and use what they read."

A second science teacher was teaching earth science for the first time to "less than honors students" and was experiencing some frustration. She asked the reading coordinator for help saying, "These kids don't even know the words I need to use to teach them the words I want them to know! What do I do? Where do I start?"

The physics students needed help with concept development. They could acquire essential information out of the text and other sources but were having difficulty developing and applying the concepts illustrated by that information. The teacher applied instructional strategies of the sort you will be studying in this text. His students' progress raised other teachers' interest and led eventually to a long-term, comprehensive staff development program in which participants learned how to teach reading, writing and reasoning simultaneously with their content areas.

The students in earth science needed help in making connections between ideas they already possessed and ideas being taught. The students' general knowledge was different from what the teacher was used to drawing upon to teach the technical language of the course and the concepts represented by that language. Working with the coordinator, the teacher discovered that her students did have prior knowledge that was relevant to the content, even though it was not of the sort she expected. Using instructional strategies such as those presented in this text, she succeeded in helping students connect what they already knew with what they were learning in earth science. Her success led to their success in learning the language and concepts of the subject.

The concerns of these two science teachers have been shared by teachers across all curriculum areas and grade levels. Their success in meeting the instructional challenges posed by their students' needs has been experienced by teachers across all subjects and grades. A major purpose for writing this book is to share with subject-area teachers instructional strategies their colleagues have found helpful in simultaneously teaching both course content and learning processes related to that content.

Instructional strategies presented in this book are based on a rationale that is drawn from both practice and research. The practice has been long term: thirty years working in a variety of school settings with teachers from all content areas and grade levels. Much of what we present is drawn from that experience. The research has been comprehensive: our own research in schools; research of our doctoral students; research of colleagues in schools, colleges, universities, and other educational agencies.

Before we present these strategies and materials, we want to share some reasons why you, a content-area teacher, should consider teaching reading, writing, and reasoning in your content areas.

Changes in Literacy Needs

In this last decade of the twentieth century our society is confronted by a literacy need of major proportions, a need that has been evolving over the past thirty years. The literacy demands of the workplace have outstripped the literacy levels produced by the educational system (R. Brown 1991). Indeed, for those who wish to respond fully to society's obligations and to draw fully from its opportunities, literacy requirements have increased dramatically.

It is easy to attribute this situation to a failure of the educational system and many have done so (Kozol 1985). A more realistic assessment was made by Rexford Brown, of the Education Commission of the States, who said,

> *Even people who have kept their notions of literacy confined to reading and writing have steadily raised their standards for adequate performance, in and out of school. Literacy research has revealed that the concept is far more complicated than we used to think it was. Individuals can be literate with respect to some materials, and in some contexts, but illiterate or only marginally literate with respect to other materials and contexts. Levels of literacy that were perfectly adequate for a productive life fifty years ago will no longer suffice in a world that has become more dependent on information technologies (R. Brown 1991, p. 32).*

In the workplace, in the home, and in society in general, people encounter conditions, actions, and materials that require reading, writing, and reasoning at levels of sophistication not required of earlier generations. The literacy education that well served those earlier generations (the "good old days") does not serve the present generation well.

The problem is, however, that too few people have Brown's insight. Rather than recognizing that literacy requirements have increased in complexity and sophistication, critics revert to good-old-days arguments and blame schools for not delivering the same quality education they once did. Thus, with some regularity one group or another publishes various allegations of how poorly our schools are doing in the development of a literate populace. Because of their orientation to the good-old-days, such groups generally propose a return to the basics that produced the earlier results. Both the criticism and the proposed solution are off target because they are based on faulty assumptions.

Faulty Assumptions

Many estimates of current literacy needs and their causes are based on several faulty assumptions. These assumptions seem grounded in the belief that reading should be taught only in the elementary grades.

1. The present literacy need is caused by poor literacy instruction in elementary schools.
2. Literacy instruction in elementary schools should be sufficient to meet the literacy needs of secondary and postsecondary education, work, and living.

3. An appropriate way to strengthen instruction in elementary grades is by focusing on the basics, on the fundamentals of the three Rs.
4. Students with literacy needs who enter secondary grades should be placed in special remedial classes to bring them up to speed.

These beliefs are inconsistent with what is known about both the literacy accomplishments of elementary schools and the literacy requirements of secondary schools. Taking reading achievement as an example, usually the target of critics, elementary schools consistently have done well in developing students' basic reading competencies. Today's elementary school students are reading as well as or better than their counterparts of ten, twenty, thirty, and forty years ago (Farr, Tuinman, and Rowls 1975; Farr, Fay, and Negley 1978; Farr and Blomenberg 1979; Micklos 1980). Data from the National Assessment of Educational Progress (NAEP) confirm this assertion (NAEP 1988). Critics who blame current literacy needs among adults on poor reading instruction in elementary schools deny or discount this positive data. They do not accept the notion that the blame lies elsewhere.

Literacy needs that characterize secondary and postsecondary education cannot be attributed to lack of basic-skills instruction in elementary schools. Rather, the problem is this: literacy demands in secondary schools, in the workplace, in college, and in society at large, require responses that are more sophisticated and complex than are learned in basic literacy programs in elementary schools. Thus, it is erroneous to assume that elementary school reading instruction is both necessary and sufficient to meet the more sophisticated and challenging literacy-related tasks of secondary schools and beyond (Nelson-Herber and Herber 1984).

Necessary, yes; sufficient, no. Individuals need instruction in more advanced literacy processes to accomplish tasks required of them at these advanced levels of education and experience. The logical place for this instruction to occur is in content-area classes where applications of advanced literacy-related processes are both expected and required.

Data from the NAEP provide additional evidence that secondary and postsecondary literacy needs will not be met by focusing principally on so-called basic skills either at elementary or secondary levels. Since 1970 data show that secondary school students perform satisfactorily on basic skills (a tribute to both elementary and secondary schools). However, they do not do well in their use of the higher level, inferential reading/reasoning processes (NAEP 1988). Data from a study of young adults, ages 21–25, are similar to that of the secondary school students (Kirsch and Jungeblut 1986).

It is clear that our society cannot raise literacy levels without a strong emphasis on higher-order reading, writing, and reasoning processes. Competence in these processes is needed to function well in the school, home, workplace, and in society in general. Factors that contribute to and control our lives have become more sophisticated. Individuals who read, write, and reason at these advanced levels can respond successfully to these factors.

Those who have not attained advanced levels of literacy cannot. Critics who misunderstand the reasons for the difference want to do more of what we already do well rather than to do what is needed.

Response to Need

This book addresses the need for developing advanced levels of literacy. It explains and demonstrates how content-area teachers can simultaneously teach both their course content and relevant reading, writing, and reasoning processes. It discusses ways in which instruction in content and process can have an interdisciplinary, vertical articulation—across grade levels within content-area disciplines. This book also presents ways in which this instruction can have an intradisciplinary, horizontal articulation—across disciplines within grades. It shows how teachers can support students' acquisition of reading, writing, and reasoning processes at increasing levels of sophistication to deal with increasingly abstract concepts and increasingly complex materials. By these presentations, this book squarely addresses the major literacy need in our society.

Nature of Response

Secondary school students and young adults can develop higher-order reading, writing, and reasoning processes when they become involved in the study of ideas, when they come to grips with matters of substance. It is by the study of complex concepts that students have an opportunity to develop, refine, and extend cognitive processes necessary for the acquisition, analysis, and application of such concepts. The contexts in which complex concepts are formally studied are the various subjects students take during their formal education. Thus, content-area courses are logical places for instruction in higher-order reading, writing, and reasoning processes to occur.

Many content-area teachers do not accept responsibility for teaching reading, writing, and reasoning along with their course content. They believe that their students already should possess these processes at levels of sophistication appropriate to their courses. One of education's clichés reflects this view: students should learn to read in elementary school so they can read to learn in secondary school and college. Teachers want students to read, write, and reason with independence and to meet course requirements. Data already cited show that such expectations are not valid. Students generally do not function at levels of proficiency that most content-area teachers expect and want of them.

Content-area teachers react to this situation in predictable ways. Often they adopt a student-deficit mode of thinking and join the critics who blame elementary schools for their students' inability to learn their course content independently. They join those who urge the creation of special classes in which students can develop skills necessary for becoming successful in content-area classes. Meanwhile, however, current students need to be taught, so teachers look for alternative ways of delivering the course content. A common mode of delivery is for teachers to explain the text rather than have students read it (MacGinitie and MacGinitie 1986). In this manner teachers expose students to the content of the subject and avoid dealing with students' lack of reading, writing, and reasoning proficiency at levels appropriate for the study of the discipline.

However, the assumption of deficit assures deficiency in performance. Students remain intellectual prisoners of their own learning needs because teachers make inappropriate substitutions to compensate for levels of proficiency that teachers expect but students have not had the opportunity to develop. The blame for the deficit lies not in students but in programs. Many programs have failed to show students how to read, write, and reason at levels of proficiency expected of them (Nelson-Herber and Herber 1984).

In contrast, many content-area teachers do support students' learning of both their course content and the reading, writing, and reasoning processes by which that content is learned. They recognize their responsibility in showing students how to develop proficiency in these processes. They do not assume that students should start their courses at the same levels of proficiency that they finish them.

Transitional Instruction

If you want students to engage in higher levels of reading, writing, and reasoning, you have to show them how. What makes teaching interesting and exciting is that students do not come to us already able to perform independently at levels of proficiency and understanding we hope they will have when they leave us. Our jobs are to help them become independent learners—by showing them how. We use the term *transitional instruction* to describe this process of showing how. We define *transitional instruction* as "showing students how to do what they are required to do to be successful," taking the idea as the organizing principle of this book.

The purpose of instruction is to help individuals become independent learners, able to expand their knowledge and to enrich their lives through reading, writing, and reasoning. However, independence is a relative state, particularly as it pertains to learning in school. Because students encounter increasingly complicated materials and sophisticated ideas as they progress through the grades, they are always becoming independent in their learning. Thus, helping students become independent learners is a kindergarten-through-college-level task, one in which instruction in reading, writing, and reasoning plays a central role.

Learning to Read to Learn   The traditional relationship between reading and independent learning is expressed in the cliché that students learn to read so they can read to learn. The assumption is that once students have learned to read, they can read to learn independently. An effective instructional program does not make that assumption. Rather, it provides transitional instruction that helps students learn to read to learn by providing a bridge between the point where they have learned to read to the point where they can read to learn with some independence. Thus, reading instruction moves students through a recursive cycle in which they learn to read, then they learn to read to learn, and finally they read to learn.

When students learn to read they learn to crack the code; that is, they learn how to apply their knowledge of language to printed material in order to derive meaning from that form of communication. In their early years, code cracking involves recognizing that squiggles on pages represent words they use when they speak and describe familiar experiences. Later on, code cracking involves students in using various linguistic tools—grapho-phonemic clues, syntactical clues, semantic clues, and so forth—to acquire new vocabulary and new experiences. As students progress through the grades and encounter increasingly sophisticated and abstract concepts, code cracking involves students in learning technical language that represents those concepts. Thus, there is a sense in which learning to read recurs as students progress through the grades.

When students learn to read to learn, they are shown how to derive information and ideas that are explicitly and implicitly contained in various resources. What constitutes the showing how is determined by students' needs, grade level, subject area, and the kind of material being used. At early grade levels, children are shown how to derive information and ideas from simple stories. Later on, students are shown how to obtain information and develop ideas from expository materials in different content areas as well as from more complex narratives. As students progress through the grades and encounter increasingly sophisticated materials, they are shown how to derive information and ideas at increasingly higher levels of complexity and abstraction. In all circumstances, the showing how involves supporting students with instruction that enables them to learn how to do what they are required to do to be successful.

When students read to learn, they independently apply the reading processes they have attained when learning to read and when learning to read to learn. Reading to learn involves students' acquiring information and ideas on their own from text and making use of what they have acquired. The level of sophistication at which students read to learn is dictated by the level at which they have learned to read to learn. As they progress through the grades, they attain higher and higher levels.

We refer to students' movement from learning to read to learning to read to learn to reading to learn as a recursive cycle rather than a sequence because the movement is repeated over and over as students progress through the grades. If the movement were thought of as a sequence, one could easily ascribe learning to read as the responsibility of elementary grades, learning to read to learn of junior high's, and reading to learn of senior high's. Understanding this movement as cyclical rather than sequential gives purpose and meaning to the notion of teaching reading, as well as the other language arts, across the curriculum and throughout the grades and college.

Learning to Write to Learn The development and application of students' writing ability follow a similar cycle: learning to write, learning to write to learn, and then writing to learn. Young children are eager to learn to write as they are eager to learn to read. They take pencil in fist, draw their pictures, and invent a written form of language to tell stories illustrated by their pictures. Responses to their writing, from teachers and other audiences, shape students' understanding of ways that writing can be used to communicate information and ideas. As time passes, they learn the conventional forms of written language and use them to tell stories and to explain actions or conditions.

Writing to learn may seem an odd concept if you think of writing as having more to do with expressing ideas already acquired than with acquiring them. However, strong evidence points to the important contributions writing makes to the formulation and clarification of ideas (Applebee 1986).

Even as reading can prepare the mind for writing, writing can prepare the mind for reading. As you write about an idea, you consider its implications and applications. You sort through what you already know about the idea, and that helps set a context for new information you encounter related to that idea. For example, students can create group compositions, drawn from their beliefs, opinions, experiences, and knowledge sources, on clashes between individual freedom and the common good of society in general. These compositions could provide a conceptual context for a study of the Declaration of Independence. In this fashion, writing prepares students for reading and subsequently informs their reading.

Writing also can be used for responding to what you have read. After students read and discuss the Declaration of Independence (in the cited example), they can create another composition—group or individual—to reconcile beliefs, opinions, and knowledge held before and after the study. In this manner, reading informs students' writing even as their writing already informed their reading.

Writing also can be used to shape and give expression to newly created ideas. Often one hears people talk about how the process of writing clarifies conceptual development. For example, some people say that they do not really know what they think about a subject until they start writing about it. It is during the act of writing that their thoughts take shape and ideas emerge. Activities such as these constitute writing to learn: using writing for the purpose of developing, expressing, and sharing ideas and experiences that contribute to an understanding of a discipline.

Transitional instruction is as appropriate for writing as it is for reading and reasoning. Helping students learn to write to learn is similar in principle to helping students learn to read to learn. In all instances, the help lies in showing how, in supporting students' writing or reading so they become conscious of how to apply the process effectively. The how of this showing how constitutes the main subject of this book; it is the principal objective of teaching and the eventual product of instruction.

Learning to Reason to Learn The development of students' reasoning differs somewhat from the development of their reading and writing. People do not have to learn to reason in the same sense that they have to learn to read and to write. The ability to reason is innate. However, how people reason is conditioned by their experience and training. Thus, instruction that helps students learn how to use their ability to reason has an important place in formal education.

Reasoning is central to learning: to the acquisition of information; to the development of ideas; to the application of generalizations. The centrality of reasoning makes it possible to teach reasoning in, around, and through reading and writing. As teachers support students' applications of reading and writing to the study of ideas, they also support the application of their reasoning. Teachers show students how to use their reasoning to acquire information as well as to develop and apply ideas that can be derived from that information.

Central to the development and application of ideas is the process of making connections. Ideas are created when you perceive connections among the parts (information) that make up the whole (ideas) and you are able to articulate the nature of the perceived relationships. Your understanding develops when you connect what you already know with information and ideas you encounter. Teachers structure lessons to support students in their applications of various connectors—analogy, metaphor, simile, classification, categorizing, and so forth—as they read and write. As teachers show students how to apply these reasoning processes to the study of their subjects, students learn to reason to learn.

Philosophical Underpinnings

The concept of transitional instruction is central to the focus of this book. It gives purpose to the instructional strategies that are explained and demonstrated. It validates the importance of integrating instruction in reading, writing, and reasoning with instruction in course content. It gives structure to curricula and to the overall instructional program.

The philosophical underpinnings of transitional instruction have evolved from a combination of practice and research in content-area classes over many years. These underpinnings can best be discussed in the context of five contrasts:

1. Recognition versus acquisition
2. Reconstruction versus creative construction
3. Separation versus integration
4. Uniqueness versus commonality
5. Information versus ideas

Decisions related to these contrasts shape both instructional programs and teaching that occurs within the programs.

Recognition versus Acquisition

In the early stages of learning to read and write, part of the task is to connect words one already uses and understands conceptually with visual representations of those words. The connection involves the process of re-cognizing, or knowing again, but in a new form, what one knew before.

For example, most children understand the word *telephone* and use it in conversation before they can read the word in its printed form. As they develop a sense of how to make connections between sounds and symbols, they discover that the combined letters *t-e-l-e-p-h-o-n-e* have the same sound as the word they have been using to identify the telephone. In that moment they recognize the written representation of a concept and object they already know and have experienced. This is why reading to children, involving them in conversation, and providing them with conceptually enriching experiences all contribute so significantly to their success in learning how to read and write.

The process of word recognition is basic to learning to read and write. It is a process often referred to as a basic skill. It is what people have in mind when they recommend a return to the basics as an appropriate way to help students who have difficulty reading texts in content-area classes. Unfortunately, the process of word recognition does not help students deal with unfamiliar words in a content area.

> . . . *it seems too obvious to set in print that students will have difficulty using their phonics skills to recognize words that they would not recognize even if they could pronounce them.*
>
> *Take the sentence, "As we rode the old-fashioned carousel, the sounds of the calliope surrounded us." If the word* calliope *were not in the students' personal lexicons, they would not only fail to recognize it, they would most likely mispronounce it as well. While the context provides some support for the meaning of the word, it could as easily mean crowd, engine, carnival, amusement park, children.*

Further, the presence of the word calliope *in the text would probably cause students, reading orally, to also miscue on other words in the sentence because of the anxiety produced by anticipation of the unknown word (Nelson-Herber and Herber 1984, p. 235).*

Another example is found in this sentence:

The tendency of materials to fracture upon repeated stress is called fatigue.

If the concept of fracture were not known by students, the word would not help them understand how fatigue is being defined, even if they were able to pronounce the word *fracture.*

Here, then, is a reason that students have difficulty reading content-area texts: many of the concepts and the words representing the concepts are unfamiliar. Thus, when students encounter the words in print, they have no basis for re-cognizing them. Rather than being a deficit in reading or writing, it is a deficit in knowledge of content, a deficit to be expected from students who have not yet learned the content. What students need for successful performance in content areas are ways to acquire new vocabulary for use in their reading and writing activities. Content-area teachers can organize instruction in the following ways:

1. Provide experience with the new vocabulary of the content area before students are expected to re-cognize it in their reading.
2. Provide positive strategies for the acquisition of new vocabulary within the context of the content.

Content-area teachers know the value of enriching students' background to create a conceptual context for the content they are studying. The value of this background development is enhanced when teachers couple it with work on word-acquisition processes. Teachers can teach students how to make connections between background knowledge and words representing concepts that are imbedded in that background. We provide a variety of suggestions for ways in which teachers can help students create linkages between what they know and what they are about to learn. Teachers also can teach students how to use their knowledge of syntax, semantics, and etymology to derive definitions and meanings of new terminology.

The distinction between word recognition and word acquisition is important to the organization of an instructional program for teaching reading, writing, and reasoning in content areas. Word recognition is part of learning to read and write. Word acquisition is part of reading and writing to learn.

Content-area teachers devote a substantial amount of their instructional time to the presentation of specialized terminology. With modest restructuring of that time, they can show students how to gain control over the technical language of their disciplines through the application of word-acquisition processes. Section III deals directly and peripherally with ways to provide this transitional instruction.

Reconstruction versus Creative Construction

The contrast between reconstruction and creative construction deals with processes and products of comprehension. In many respects it addresses issues similar to those addressed by the recognition versus acquisition contrast. The pivotal issue is the influence of prior knowledge on the comprehension process.

To help children learn to comprehend written text, elementary school reading programs use materials that are certain to present information, ideas, actions, or conditions already familiar to the children. As noted in the previous section, children re-cognize words that represent this familiar knowledge and experience. As they string the words together, children can reconstruct from the text information and ideas that are already familiar to them.

Thus, they attribute meaning to the text. It is a reconstruction process in that students are building from the text a representation of information and ideas they had developed previously through experience and other sources of knowledge. Children can use the familiar words to reflect in oral and written form the meanings they have reconstructed from the text.

A major implication to be drawn from the concept of reconstruction is that reconstruction of meaning is difficult for information, ideas, actions or conditions around which one has neither acquired prior knowledge nor had previous experiences. This implication is particularly important for content-area teachers who wonder why students have such difficulty comprehending their texts. Expecting students to reconstruct meanings for what they have not previously known is the same as assuming students can successfully read "... textbooks that contain uncommon vocabulary, unknown facts, unfamiliar concepts, and unusual values ..." (Nelson-Herber and Herber 1984, p.237) without instructional intervention.

Take, as an example, the following sentence: "There's a bear in a plain brown wrapper doing flip-flops around 78 and passing out green stamps." This is a perfectly good English sentence. It has nouns, verbs, adjectives, phrases, clauses, etc. The words are all familiar. However, anyone not familiar with CB radio language would be very unlikely to comprehend the author's message, no matter how well he or she had learned the basic reading skills. To understand the **message,** *both the context of the message and the technical vocabulary must reside in the experience of the reader. The reader must recognize the sentence as a Citizens Band (CB) radio communication,*

*both experientially and syntactically, and must recognize the special and un-
usual meanings of the words when used within this context. The reader who
can tap this experience can readily comprehend the message as meaning: A
state trooper in an unmarked car is cruising back and forth on the highway
around mile marker 78 and issuing tickets to speeders. The reader without
this CB experience cannot comprehend no matter how well he or she applies
decoding or basic comprehension skills (Nelson-Herber and Herber 1984, p.
237).*

Students need instructional intervention when they are given texts that
use new vocabulary to present new facts and concepts. Students need to be
shown how to construct meaning from text. This involves teachers in building appropriate background with students and in guiding the students'
comprehension process as they read. Content-area teachers who do not
know how to provide such intervention will find that students have difficulty reading their texts successfully. Often these teachers substitute their
own explanations for the reading and don't assign readings from the text
(Hinchman 1987). They operationalize the distinction articulated by MacG-
initie and MacGinitie (1986) between helping students understand the content of the text and helping them understand the text. Rather than show
students how to derive an understanding of the text, teachers substitute
their explanations of the content. Thus one observes what the MacGinities
call Ruth's Law: "The more obvious or painful the student's lack of comprehension, the more likely that the teacher will explain the content rather than
the text" (MacGinitie and MacGinitie 1986).

Unfortunately, the less students read, the less their teachers expect that
they can read successfully. As teachers lower their expectations for students'
success in reading, they raise their efforts to substitute their own explanations of the course content. The level of expectation for students' reading
performance continues to spiral downward (MacGinitie and MacGinite
1986).

Separation versus Integration

This contrast has two applications to the rationale for this book. One
application has to do with the place in which reading and writing instruction takes place; the other, with the operational definitions of reading and
writing.

In elementary school programs, reading and writing have been taught
traditionally as separate subjects. While the reading and writing processes
are used as tools in other subjects, they typically are not taught as part of
those curricula. This traditional view of where reading and writing should
be taught influences the thinking about program organization in secondary
schools.

To many content-area teachers and curriculum supervisors, secondary school students who need help in learning how to read or write should enroll in reading and writing courses designed for that purpose. Thus, instruction in reading and writing is separated from the contexts in which students need to read and write in order to perform successfully.

Strategies for transitional instruction presented in this book are based on the premise that instruction in reading and writing can be integrated with instruction in course content, to the benefit of both and to the detriment of neither, by content-area teachers in content-area classes. The purpose of this instruction is

> *to help students acquire the skills they need for adequate study of all the materials required in their subjects. Using subject-related material, regularly assigned, as the vehicle for this instruction, content teachers can provide for the simultaneous teaching of reading skills and course content. Neither has to be sacrificed to the other (Herber (1970, v.).*

All of the chapters in the book deal directly or peripherally with ways in which this instructional integration can be provided by content-area teachers for their own students in their own classes.

The other application of the separation versus integration contrast relates to operational definitions of reading and writing. Representing one half of the contrast are those who view reading and writing as the coordinated application of a multiplicity of separate skills. Representing the other half of the contrast are those who view reading and writing as holistic, integrated entities that are not separable into discrete subentities.

Many elementary schools organize their reading programs according to the separate skills point of view. They use instructional materials and tests to present these separate skills in prescribed sequences. These materials seem to work reasonably well in developing students' basic reading achievement. However, applying the separate-skills point of view to reading and writing instruction in content areas has negative implications, particularly as it affects the issue of practicality.

Realistic attempts to teach reading in content-area classes have to account for the practical factors of time and curriculum coverage. Content-area teachers do not have the time to teach lessons on specific skills, nor are the materials they have students read organized to support such instruction. Rather, students require reading processes that are more holistic in nature, requiring instruction that is based on an integrated view of reading and is natural to the materials being read. Thus, if one adopts the perspective of reading as a holistic process, it is both more possible and more likely that content-area teachers can integrate the teaching of reading and writing with the teaching of course content. This entire book, both directly and indirectly, is based on the holistic perspective of reading and writing processes and on the belief that these processes can be taught simultaneously with the course content in any subject area.

Uniqueness versus Commonality

The contrast of uniqueness versus commonality has to do with the kind of reading and writing processes required across various subject areas. There is some debate over whether differences in how people read and write in different subjects is dictated by the nature of the subject matter or by the nature of the reading and writing processes inherent in each subject. An analysis of descriptions of reading processes attributed to different subject areas showed that most differences were semantic rather than substantive (Herber 1970). When semantic differences were discounted, a high degree of commonality among reading processes was found across disciplines.

Focusing on commonality rather than uniqueness of reading and writing processes across disciplines has two useful implications for instructional programs. First, students benefit from a consistency in terminology used and instructional strategies employed across disciplines as their teachers show them how to learn to read and write to learn. Second, teachers from various disciplines benefit from the same consistency when they come together in staff-development programs to study how to show students how to learn to read and write to learn. Focusing on the facets of reading and writing that are common across their disciplines, teachers can be more cooperative in their instructional planning and mutually supportive in their teaching of students whom they have in common.

This book takes the perspective that reading, writing, and reasoning processes have more commonality than difference across disciplines. Instructional strategies explained throughout the book are, therefore, equally applicable across subject areas and grade levels. Where modest adjustments have to be made because of the nature of the content-area's resource materials, examples are given and adjustments explained. In the main, however, the commonality of recommended strategies and processes holds, and examples are given to illustrate the applications of the common strategies.

Information versus Ideas

The very title of this book identifies one of its main objectives: to teach the content of various disciplines within the curriculum. Modest debate is held on what information should be taught in each of the disciplines. Extensive debate is held on how this information should be organized and delivered to students. Part of the debate has to do with whether the curriculum should stress information or ideas. While discussions involve professionals from classroom teachers to curriculum designers to textbook publishers, the decision as to which direction to take is in the hands of teachers who provide the instruction. Their decisions have a profound influence both on what is taught and how it is taught.

The information base in most curriculum areas is expanding at an increasingly rapid pace. Keeping abreast of the knowledge growth in a given field is difficult. Moreover, what is learned during the years of formal education becomes dated rather quickly. A curriculum that focuses principally on current information is not sufficient for students' future needs. Of greater use is a curriculum that focuses on concepts and principles illustrated by current information but still applicable and illustrated when the knowledge base changes in the future. Thus, a curriculum that focuses on ideas illustrated by information in the curriculum seems more appropriate than a curriculum that focuses exclusively on the information itself.

Focusing on ideas does not require abandoning information. After all, current knowledge makes a current curriculum unique. The current knowledge base is taught, but in such a way that students understand the broad concepts and general principles that are illustrated by that knowledge. Thus, students learn both the information and the related ideas. Understanding relevant principles makes it possible to keep current in the future. As new knowledge is discovered in a given field, those who understand the broad principles and concepts of that field know how that new knowledge fits into the whole and what information can be discarded. When new knowledge is discovered and serves to illustrate new concepts, people who are used to fitting new knowledge into old concepts can also create new concepts from new knowledge. Teaching that is focused on ideas educates participants for both the present and the future. Understanding the concepts and principles of a discipline is what prepares an individual to engage in life-long learning.

Consequences of Response

The instructional strategies presented in this book have positive impact on what content-area teachers teach, how they teach it, and how students learn it. Consider some of the consequences.

Conceptually Based Curriculum

A conceptually based curriculum is one that uses information to develop and illustrate principles and concepts. Instruction that operationalizes the conceptually based curriculum stresses the development of concepts and an application of principles. A curriculum, thus, can be comprised of principles, concepts, and information.

Principles of a curriculum are broad generalizations illustrated by concepts within the same discipline as well as by concepts found in other disciplines and in students' background knowledge. For example, a principle explored in literature could be:

Perspective is influenced by knowledge and experience.

Concepts of a curriculum are ideas illustrated by information within the discipline as well as by information found in other discipline as well as in background knowledge. For example, a concept related to the principle given above could be:

Time has both quantitative and qualitative dimensions, and people experience both dimensions differently.

Information in a curriculum presents details about the field of study. Information provides examples of concepts being studied even as those concepts serve as examples of principles being studied. For example, information illustrating the concept listed above could be drawn from a variety of literary works that deal with time.

The principles-concepts-information relationship in a curriculum can be top-down or bottom-up or interactive. When you teach inductively, you use the bottom-up relationship. When you teach deductively, you use the top-down relationship. When you teach conceptually, you use the interactive relationship.

This book is oriented toward conceptual teaching and the interactive relationships among principles, concepts, and information. You start conceptual teaching with principle or concept so you can tap into students' relevant general knowledge and use it as a context for studying specific examples of the concept. As specific representations of the concept are studied, they are related to the experiential context to show how previously known information and ideas fit with the new. In this manner you can help students connect the known with the new, showing them how, where, and why old and new information and ideas fit together.

As taught through instructional strategies presented in this book, curriculum is thought to be conceptually based rather than informationally based. Relationships across principles, concepts, and information are interactive rather than linear or hierarchical. The instructional focus of curriculum is on teaching ideas rather than on dispensing information.

Curriculum Analysis

Creation of a conceptually based curriculum and the instruction that flows from it start with subject-area teachers' analysis of their curricula. Teachers analyze the content of their disciplines to determine its principles, concepts, and information. They create units around principles and lessons around concepts. For example, a literature unit could be organized around the general principle identified in the previous section:

Perspective is influenced by knowledge and experience.

Sets of lessons could be constructed around different concepts, each illustrating the influence of knowledge and experience on perspective. One such set of lessons could be constructed around the concept identified in the previous section:

Time has both quantitative and qualitative dimensions, and people experience both dimensions differently.

Different literary pieces could be used to illustrate the quantitative and qualitative dimensions of time and the variability of their impact on people. For example, you could use these poems: "The Day" by Theodore Spencer, "Eight O'Clock" by A. E. Housman, and "The Sprinters" by Lee Murchison. Each, in its own way, contrasts quantitative and qualitative dimensions of time.

Curriculum analysis provides teachers with a basis for selecting instructional materials. For example, having identified the principles to be taught, they can examine different texts to determine whether the presentation of concepts is sufficiently comprehensive to allow readers to perceive the overriding principles. Similarly, having identified the concepts to be taught, teachers can then examine different texts to determine whether sufficient information is presented for readers to develop these concepts.

Curriculum analysis also facilitates the use of a discipline's structure for teaching. If teachers consciously perceive how ideas in their disciplines are organized, they will be more likely to use that structure to teach the content of the discipline. If students learn how the concepts and principles of a discipline are formulated, interrelated, and illustrated, their understanding of the discipline is likely to be deeper and more abiding.

Finally, curriculum analysis often leads to curriculum change—from a curriculum that is informationally based to one that is conceptually based. As one studies the interaction among principles, concepts, and information, it does not take long to discover which are the more enduring and universally applicable. In our era of rapidly expanding and changing knowledge, our students are better served by focusing on principles and concepts than on information. The information they do study are momentary examples of principles and concepts. Another generation may use a different set of details but may deal with many of the same concepts and principles nonetheless.

Organizing Idea

A consequence of creating a conceptually based curriculum is the utilization of an organizing idea in one's teaching. An organizing idea is a declarative statement that identifies a targeted relationship among details or among concepts. The organizing idea usually contains a key word or phrase that identifies the conceptual focus of the lesson. For example, the lesson using the poems related to time was based on the following organizing idea:

> Time has both quantitative and qualitative dimensions, and people experience both dimensions differently.

The key term in this organizing idea is *time*, and this idea serves as the conceptual focus for the lesson. As will be seen in subsequent chapters, an effective lesson is driven by an organizing idea and relevant instructional materials are designed to support students as they develop an understanding of that idea.

Typically, the organizing idea for a unit is a principle expressed as a declarative statement. It usually contains a key word or phrase that identifies the conceptual focus of the unit. For example, the unit referred to earlier was based on the following organizing idea:

> Perspective is influenced by knowledge and experience.

The key term in this organizing idea is *perspective,* and this idea serves as the conceptual focus for the unit. Lessons for this unit, with each having its own organizing idea, would be designed to develop an understanding of this broad principle. Subsequent chapters in this text show how an organizing idea for a unit can be used to capture students' interest, to motivate their participation in the study of relevant materials, and to help them make connections between what they are learning and what they already know about the principle under consideration. Creating organizing ideas for lessons and units is relatively easy to do. You can do it in two steps, and we show you how in Chapter 2. Organizing ideas have two characteristics:

1. They are sufficiently narrow to be obviously relevant to the particular content you are having students study.
2. They are sufficiently broad to encompass other, relevant information that may be in students' prior knowledge and experience.

Organizing ideas having these two characteristics allow you to use students' prior knowledge and experience as a valuable resource and to help them discover that they already know a lot about what they are about to study. For example, we used the following organizing idea for a lesson on unionism:

> Protests take many forms and produce many outcomes.

We organized the lesson around the key word *protests*. Even though students did not have particular knowledge about unionism, they did have general knowledge and experience related to protests. We drew on students' general knowledge about protests to set a context for the study of the development of unions as a particular form of protest. Thus, students were conceptually and experientially involved in the lesson from its start. They could make connections between what they already knew and what they were learning.

As you go through this book, you will see how organizing ideas work. They serve as conceptual umbrellas under which students can bring together relevant information and ideas from their prior knowledge and make connections with information and ideas derived from their current study. Organizing ideas provide a place for the synthesis of information from a variety of sources: students' prior knowledge, teacher's knowledge and experience, basic texts, supplementary texts, audiotapes and videotapes, laboratory experiments and field experiences, and so forth.

One additional benefit from the instructional use of organizing ideas must be mentioned. In the context of a conceptually based curriculum, students discover the commonality of ideas that exists across disciplines within grade levels even as they discover the conceptual connections that exist among ideas within disciplines across grade levels. For example, relationships between the concepts *illusion* and *reality* can be found across various subjects and within subjects across grades. An important outcome of formal education should be an understanding that conceptual relationships exist among various subjects. Instruction based on the use of organizing ideas within the context of a conceptually based curriculum helps to produce that outcome.

Clearly identifying organizing ideas for units and lessons helps teachers to clarify the substantive intent of these units and lessons and increases the likelihood that the intent will be translated into learning by the students. In your early attempts to formulate organizing ideas for your units and lessons, you may use the well-known behavioral objective format. This format will not be useful if it causes you to focus on descriptions of the activities you want students to perform to the exclusion of the ideas you want them to acquire. You can express the organizing ideas behaviorally if you identify them as being what students *will learn* or *will experience* or *will understand.* Some teachers create two sets of objectives for their units: content and process. Content objectives for a given unit reflect the organizing ideas for various lessons that comprise that unit. Process objectives reflect the various activities that are to be taught and experienced.

Your own teaching style as well as agreements among colleagues in your department and/or grade-level team will help determine whether you frame your organizing ideas as objectives or not. The important issue is that you take the time to identify organizing ideas for units and lessons and that you use them to organize your instruction and to design your supporting materials and activities.

A Positive Approach to Instruction

Instruction that enables students to learn both the content of their courses and the means by which that content is learned is empowering to both students and teachers. A consequence of that empowerment is a sense of optimism toward teaching which, in turn, creates a positive approach to instruction.

Teachers manifest a positive approach to instruction when their teaching is designed to capitalize on students' strengths rather than to compensate for students' weaknesses. In a context that focuses constructively on students' strengths, teachers can eventually help students deal with their weaknesses. In a context that focuses on means to compensate for students' weaknesses, teachers find it difficult to get around to building on their strengths.

Students bring numerous strengths to content-area classrooms:

1. Relevant prior knowledge
2. Ability to reason
3. Ability to communicate with others
4. Understanding of language
5. Awareness of differences between cooperative and competitive endeavors

Prior Knowledge

Students' prior knowledge is a rich resource for content-area teachers to use. The organizing idea of a unit and/or lesson is the perfect vehicle for drawing on that resource. When teachers frame the concept to be studied in broad enough terms, students have relevant prior knowledge that can serve as a context for understanding new information that is presented. When students learn how to use this strength, they develop confidence in their ability to deal with new information and ideas they are studying. Throughout this book we discuss ways in which teachers can make use of students' prior knowledge.

Ability to Reason

Reasoning is natural to the human species and is what distinguishes human beings from other forms of animal life. When teachers, often in exasperation, say, "These students can't think!" they do not mean it literally. What they are expressing is a feeling that students are not thinking clearly about information and ideas related to course content. When you watch students function in what Robert Hogan (1971) called the "nook and cranny curriculum" (activities students engage in between classes as well as before and after school), you understand that they can engage in some rather sophisticated reasoning. The problem teachers face is being able to capture that reasoning ability and help students learn to apply it to their subjects. Ability to reason is a strength that students already possess. Teachers can build on that strength to enable students to develop insights into the concepts of their courses, insights that come only by application of reasoning power. Throughout this book we discuss ways in which teachers can make use of students' reasoning abilities.

Ability to Communicate

Communication is another observable strength that students bring to the study of any content area. We know from research and practice that understandings of concepts are enhanced by the act of expressing them in either written or spoken form. Undoubtedly, you have experienced the clarifying effect of explaining something to another person and have discovered how your understanding of that idea or activity is enhanced even as you are engaged in the explanation. This phenomenon can and does occur in the study of relevant concepts in various content areas, if students are given opportunity to engage in appropriate discussions and explanations. Their natural ability to communicate can be used for this purpose. One needs to provide some structure for the communication and some criteria by which the participants can judge whether or not the discussion is relevant and effective. However, one does not have to teach students to communicate. Throughout this book we discuss ways in which teachers can make use of students' ability to communicate.

Understanding Language

Language is central to the ability to communicate and is a strength that students bring to their study of various content-area curricula. When you listen to their communication, it is clear that they understand the use of language at a rather sophisticated level. They have their own "technical" vocabulary and, thus, understand the importance of using precise and appropriate terminology to describe people, places, objects, and events. They operationalize the differences between explicit and implicit expressions of information and ideas. Thus, by experience, they know what impact the subtleties of expression have on communication; they understand what importance the use of correct terms has on description, explanation, or appeal. This understanding of language is a strength that content-area teachers can utilize in the study of their disciplines. Instruction must include ways to help students see relationships between language they use for everyday communication and language they need to communicate within the conceptual frameworks of various subjects they study. Throughout this book we discuss ways in which teachers can help students perceive these relationships and make use of students' understanding of language.

Cooperative versus Competitive Awareness

Awareness of the difference between cooperative and competitive endeavors is a strength that students bring to content-area classes. Probably they have more direct experience with competitive endeavors than with cooperative ones. However, even within competitive endeavors there is a need for cooperation among colleagues, and students understand cooperation in that sense. Thus, students have a strength that can be utilized by teachers who wish to take advantage of what is known about cooperative learning experiences in education. Throughout this book we discuss ways teachers can draw on students' strengths in this area and derive the advantages of instruction based on cooperative learning.

Teachers' Expectations

Literature, including research literature, is replete with examples of how expectation influences performance and accomplishment. Expectations of teachers have a profound influence on the accomplishments of students, both negatively and positively. Teachers who expect the worst from students are rarely disappointed. Teachers who expect the best from students also are rarely disappointed.

A sense of optimism toward education, a recognition of the nature and quality of students' strengths, and a sense of positive expectation toward students and their learning all combine to create a wonderful environment for learning. Years ago Goethe said, "If you treat a man as he is, he will remain as he is. If you treat a man as though he already were what he ought to be and could be, he will become what he ought to be and could be."

This is positive expectation, and it can be practiced by every teacher in every classroom.

Summary

Students' literacy needs focus on the development of reading, writing, and reasoning at levels of sophistication sufficient to support their study of sophisticated concepts as presented in complex and, sometimes, abstract materials. Content-area teachers can serve these needs by providing instruction that integrates the teaching of course content with the teaching of appropriate literacy skills. The instruction teachers provide has several characteristics:

1. It supports students to show them how to apply the reading, writing, and reasoning skills that are appropriate to the concepts they are studying and the resources they are using.
2. It supports students to show them how make use of the information and ideas they acquire through their study.
3. It is conceptually based, driven by an organizing idea.

4. It respects the conceptual integrity of each subject but also helps students understand the conceptual linkages that are possible across subject matter areas.
5. It is optimistic and positive in its outlook, building on students' strengths rather than compensating for their weaknesses.

REACTIONS

Journal Entries and Discussion

In your journal, record your analysis of the relationship between the concepts *transitional instruction* and *teaching as showing how.*

Record your thinking on which of the five philosophical underpinnings is of greatest concern to you as you consider how you might incorporate reading, writing, and reading instruction in your content area.

Record your thinking on the relative importance of the organizing idea to the instructional integration of reading, writing and reasoning with course content.

Analysis and Discussion

Now that you have completed this chapter, consider the statements shown below. Check the numbered lines for statements you believe reflect the point of view of the authors. Circle the numbers of statements with which you agree. In writing, explore reasons for differences on any statements between your point of view and what you perceive to be the point of view of the authors. Please share and discuss your writing with colleagues who also are reading this book.

_____ 1. There is a significant and substantial difference between instruction that helps students learn to read and instruction that helps students learn to read to learn.

_____ 2. To become independent learners, students must have the means for independently acquiring new vocabulary relevant to what is to be learned.

_____ 3. If students are to be thoughtful users of the knowledge to which they are exposed in academic settings, they must be able to create ideas from information gained and not just reproduce the information.

_____ 4. If students acquire course content but not the means by which that content is learned, it is unlikely that they will advance their knowledge beyond information gained in their formal education.

_____ 5. Lessons that focus on information deal with the present; lessons that focus on ideas deal with both present and future.

_____ 6. A single idea may be illustrated by information from several disciplines while a single piece of information usually is restricted to its presence in a single discipline.

_____ 7. Teaching that builds on students' strengths is more positive than teaching that compensates for students' weaknesses.

_____ 8. The learning processes of reading, writing, and reasoning can be taught simultaneously with course content by content-area teachers.

SECTION II
Resources for Instruction

2

Students' Diversity: An Instructional Resource

Organizing idea: Students' diverse minds and memories constitute an important resource for content-area teaching.

Reflections

Before reading this chapter, please record in your journal your answers to the following questions. If possible, share your writing with other individuals who are also reading this book.

1. What is your prediction about the instructional importance given in this chapter to the concept of an organizing idea? What do you anticipate that importance to be? On what do you base your prediction?

2. What kind of prior knowledge do your students usually bring to your subjects that you find useful as a resource to draw upon for your teaching?

3. Given a choice, would you find it easier to help students connect what they know about an idea to what they are learning about that idea or what they are learning to what they know?

RETURNING TO HIS OFFICE from a satisfying conversation with teachers working on a curriculum-development project, an administrator was savoring the quiet of the school building on a lovely summer day. "Ahhh," he said jokingly, "school would be great if it weren't for the kids!"

Anyone who has taught for a while knows what the administrator meant by that statement. When you are teaching or administering in a school, students' intensity fills your time; their proximity fills your space. Students are an ever present consideration in your schedule, your curriculum, your selection of resources, your classroom instruction, your extracurricular activities, your digestion. An occasional escape from their ubiquity seems a wonderful moment of relief, but then the restlessness starts and you get anxious "to get back to the kids."

The intensity of focus on students reflects the fact that their education constitutes the principal purpose of the educational enterprise. Providing students with the best service possible within the constraints of available resources is the function of every school district. Attention is given to students' intellectual development, their physical growth, their social adjustment, their sense of cooperation and fair play, their acceptance of responsibility, their productivity, and so forth. Most professionals would agree that students occupy most of their time and consideration.

Dealing with Diversity

An important question to consider is whether schools, in their concern about students, are focused on students in a generic and conceptual sense more than they are on students in a specific and operational sense. Any enterprise that attempts to serve a whole category of people tends to focus on the category in the abstract rather than on individuals who comprise the category. This is done, normally, in response to a need for convenience and efficiency. We all know how much easier it is to deal with people in the abstract than with people in particular. Attention is shifted to individuals within the category of people mainly when some form of deviation occurs, either negative or positive. Convenience and efficiency are reduced when deviations occur. Therefore, attempts are made to minimize deviations either by ignoring them or by changing causes of the deviations.

How applicable is this to schools? Are schools occupied with students as a category or with students as individuals?

Curricula are designed for students in a generic sense. Disciplines of science, math, literature, social sciences and the like are divided into subdisciplines and distributed across the grade levels as locations for study. Requirements are set at each level within each subdiscipline based on how students as a group have been described for the levels and how their competencies have been defined for the subdisciplines. Tests are administered and criteria are established by which competencies and performances of students as a group are defined for grade levels and subdisciplines. Texts are written and other resources are created for students in a conceptual sense who have been defined by grade level and subdiscipline criteria. Instructional units are created and lessons are prepared for students in a generic sense for whom curricula were written, requirements established, tests administered, and texts written. These units and lessons are delivered, then, to students as a category by teachers as a category.

Even though the educational system is organized to serve students as a category, teachers can be aware of their students as individuals. Many secondary school teachers meet with 150 to 200 different students during a teaching day, and yet they really get to know their students quite well—their academic achievements, their intellectual abilities, their personality quirks, their social activities, and their goals and ambitions. Teachers are aware, then, of the great diversity that exists among the individual students that make up the category of students.

Ironically, when it comes to teaching units and lessons, diversity among students is viewed as a problem rather than an opportunity because lessons and units are prepared for students as a category rather than for students as individuals. Teachers try to compensate for the diversity as though it were a negative factor, rather than taking advantage of the diversity as positive factor.

A common recommendation for responding to diversity among the body of students is to provide individualized instruction. Attempts are made to tailor objectives, activities, materials, and assessments to the ability and achievement levels of participating individuals. The student load that most subject-area teachers carry precludes serious and protracted attempts to individualize instruction. Neither time nor energy nor resources are sufficient for most teachers to sustain an individualized program of instruction in their subject areas.

Where individualized instruction is applied successfully, the diversity that exists among individual students is not used; rather, it is neutralized. Individualized instruction is designed to move students along at their own pace, and this leads eventually to isolation of individuals from one another. While individuals within the category of students meet learning objectives, they have little impact on one another, and the category remains essentially unchanged. Student diversity is neither valued nor used. The spirit and gestalt of classes taught in this manner are an example of a whole being *equal to* the sum of its parts.

Thus, there are two principal responses to teaching in an educational system organized to deal with students as a category:

1. Teach to the category, and ignore the diversity that exists among the individuals.
2. Teach to the individuals that comprise the category and neutralize the diversity.

This book offers a third response: *use the diversity* among individuals that comprise the category of students so that both the category and the individuals are changed by the interaction. The spirit and gestalt of a class taught in this manner serve to illustrate the principle that the whole is *greater than* the sum of its parts. Factors that comprise this diversity and ways to make positive use of the factors are presented in the balance of this chapter and reinforced in the remainder of the book.

Diversity in Ethnicity and Culture

The ethnic and cultural diversity of this country has been increasing at a rapid rate in the past two decades. Particularly in large urban areas, schools serve students from a wide range of ethnic and cultural backgrounds and interests. Demographic projections are that the diversity will continue and factors that contribute to this diversity will probably increase to the turn of the century. "It is estimated that, by the year 2000, one out of every three Americans will be non-White, and that one out of every five students in the nation's public schools will be non-White" (Cooper 1989, 103).

Whether schools view this increasing diversity as a problem or an opportunity will determine whether the educational enterprise will attempt to neutralize the impact of diversity or attempt to take advantage of its potential. Because of this diversity, classrooms are filled with students representing a wide range of background and experience as well as different kinds of knowledge. The combination of these factors has the potential for enriching the study of various disciplines if the factors are incorporated into the instructional procedures used by content-area teachers. The influence of ethnic and cultural diversity on instruction is accounted for in the section below on students' prior knowledge and experiences. Suggestions for ways to take positive advantage of ethnic and cultural diversity among students are included in the discussions of instructional strategies presented throughout this book.

Diversity in Ability

Diversity in students' abilities traditionally has constituted a potential problem for instruction in most content areas. The problem is to find ways to serve the learning needs of individual students in a class when its members reflect a range of intellectual ability. The traditional assumption has been that when the range of ability represented in classes is broadened, the difficulty teachers face in meeting the learning needs of the students is increased; when the range is narrowed, the difficulty teachers face is diminished. Given that assumption, the tendency in schools has been to place students in classes homogeneously grouped according to ability, with the range as narrow as practicable. Factors of students' interests and schedules, parental pressures, curriculum offerings, and the like influence the application of constrictive criteria for assigning students to classes. These factors help determine just how narrow the range will be in certain classes for certain subjects.

In recent years, political considerations have taken priority over educational ones in the matter of dealing with diversity in ability among students, particularly in newly integrated schools in major urban areas. Application of criteria for assuring homogeneity in ability tended to resegregate content-area classes within newly integrated schools. Such classes often were designated as being for non-college-bound students. Activists who had labored to integrate schools were compelled to bring suits against school districts to rectify such situations. They argued that the resegregation of students by the application of current ability indices reflected an inherent bias in the indices. They argued successfully, for the most part, for elimination of current IQ tests as the criteria for assigning students to classes—particularly content-area classes in the college-bound curriculum. In the judgment of most participants in these shifts and changes, this resolution to the problem—the elimination of IQ as a criterion for assigning students to classes—increases diversity in ability among students in most classes. This, in turn and in their judgment, adds to the instructional burden of the teachers of these classes.

But is this a valid judgment? Arguments about using IQ scores to increase or decrease the ability range of students in a class usually are based on the operational assumption that intelligence can be represented by a single number. By this reasoning, a student with an IQ of 100 is similar in intelligence to other students who have IQs of 100. By this reasoning, that same student with an IQ of 100, then, is dissimilar in intelligence to students who have IQs of 116, for example. This reflects the beliefs of

> *those who view all intellect as a piece . . . [who] believe in a singular, inviolable capacity which is the special property of human beings: often, as a corollary, they impose the conditions that each individual is born with a certain amount of intelligence, and that we individuals can in fact be rank-ordered in terms of our God-given intellect or I.Q. So entrenched is this way of thinking—and talking—that most of us lapse readily into rankings of individuals as more or less "smart," "bright," "clever," or "intelligent" (Gardner 1983, 7).*

In contrast to this set of beliefs, Gardner presents arguments for a different view of the composition of intelligence. He believes that rather than there being a singular intelligence represented by a single number, there are really multiple intelligences within individuals. Gardner's list of multiple intelligences includes the following:

1. Linguistic intelligence
2. Musical intelligence
3. Logical-mathematical intelligence
4. Spatial intelligence

5. Bodily-kinesthetic intelligence
6. Personal intelligence

Differences in relative strength of these intelligences vary among individuals, creating the range of abilities one can find across individuals within any group.

By way of definition, Gardner says that "it is helpful to think of the various intelligences chiefly as sets of know how—procedures for doing things" (Gardner 1983, 69). A careful reading of Gardner's book is recommended for those wishing to learn more about this view of intelligence.

The idea of multiple intelligences has strong instructional implications, particularly in reference to decisions about the assignment of students to classes. The strongest implication is that no matter what criterion one uses to assign students to classes, a range of abilities will exist among the members of the class. If only one of the intelligences were used as the criterion for placement, students might be matched on that one but they would vary in strength across the other five. If a composite score were created for the six intelligences and students were placed according to that score, the relative strengths among students so placed would still vary greatly. So it doesn't really matter whether you believe in single or multiple intelligences. Students assigned to most content-area classes have considerable variance in intellectual strengths and weaknesses.

It is safe to say that most schools are governed more by a belief in a singular intelligence than in multiple intelligences and that they use intelligence as one of the criteria for assigning students to academic tracks and classes. Class assignments are made to minimize diversity in students' ability within classes. Such placement, it is reasoned, facilitates instruction because the teacher can teach to the group and not have to be concerned about individuals who cannot keep up with the group or who move way ahead of the group because of a different level of intelligence. While such placement may facilitate instruction if one is teaching students as a category rather than students as individuals. Minimizing diversity in ability among individuals in a class precludes interactive learning that is stimulated by diverse levels of acquisition, analysis, and application of ideas.

Other class assignments are made so individualized instruction can neutralize diversity in abilities. Such instruction, it is reasoned, facilitates students' learning because the teacher can teach to the individual and not have to be concerned about dealing with a diverse group. While such instruction may facilitate the learning of individual students, neutralizing diversity in ability among students for instructional purposes precludes interactive learning that is stimulated by diverse levels of acquisition, analysis, and application of ideas.

What if Gardner is correct and individuals do possess multiple intelligences rather than a singular intelligence? The idea of multiple intelligences certainly helps explain the relative strengths and weaknesses reflected in the performance of individuals we know. It helps explain the variability in performance among students who have been "homogeneously grouped" and placed in classes by ability. It helps explain the adjustments that have to be made in individualized programs for students who were presumed to be of the same level of intelligence. If Gardner is right, it seems fruitless to try to minimize or to neutralize the influence of ability on the organization of classes for instructional purposes. In that case, it seems more productive instructionally to utilize—rather than attempt to neutralize—diversity among students. By the interaction among diverse students, the learning of each and of all is enhanced, with students deriving benefit individually and collectively from the interaction.

The orientation of this book is toward Gardner's idea of multiple intelligences. Instructional recommendations are predicated on the value of intellectual diversity that is present in a class. Instructional strategies that are discussed and illustrated were conceptualized for and applied in classes where intellectual diversity was present and valued. The orientation of this book is toward acknowledging the presence of intellectual diversity and toward turning it into an advantage for instructional purposes.

Diversity in Achievement

As with intelligence, when achievement is used as a criterion for placing students in classes, considerable variability in achievement is found across the members of any given class. Let's consider scores from standardized reading tests as an example.

The reading level of an individual student for a reading test is usually reported in a percentile score and/or a grade equivalent score for the total test. These indicated reading levels are usually composite scores, derived in one way or another from the subtests that comprise the total test. In some tests, the median score for all of the subtests becomes the basis for comput- ing the total test score through use of tables created for that purpose. Other tests use the mean score of all of the subtests as the basis for computing the total test score. Whether median or mean, the derived score does not repre- sent a definitive indicator of a student's level of achievement in reading. This, of course, is because the score is a composite drawn from several subscores.

Differences can occur among students with respect to their levels of reading achievement, *even when those students all have the same composite score.* Student A can score high on all subtests on which student B scored low. Student A can score low on subtests on which student B scored high. The median score for each student would be the same so the derived grade- equivalent score would be the same. The relative strengths and weaknesses of the two students would be the opposite. If one extrapolates this situation to a full class, one can infer the probable diversity that could exist among students, even when they are assigned to classes according to relatively similar total-test scores.

Differences can also occur among students with respect to accuracy in their reading performance, *even when those students all have the same composite score.* Some students work slowly and accurately; others work rapidly and less accurately. Subscores on many standardized tests are derived from the total number of items correct out of the total number of items attempted. Student A could attempt all of the items on each of the subtests and get half of them correct. Student B could attempt half of the items on each of the subtests and get them all correct. Students A and B would receive the same total score on the test but actually perform quite differently in their applications of the reading process.

Clearly, composite scores on achievement tests mask diversity in performance among students, even among those with scores that are similar or the same. Thus, it is futile to attempt to minimize the presence of diversity in achievement in a class by assigning students to classes according to similar achievement-test scores. Considerable diversity in achievement still exists. It is unrealistic to believe it has been minimized to the extent that all students can be taught as though they were one.

Attempts to neutralize diversity in achievement by individualizing instruction also are futile, particularly if attention is not given to the diversity that is masked by using total scores from achievement tests. Accounting for true diversity among students within an individualized program adds immeasurably to the work involved in planning, applying, and evaluating individualized lessons and related materials.

The orientation of this book is toward acknowledging the presence of diversity in achievement and toward turning such diversity into an advantage for instructional purposes. Accepting and utilizing diversity in achievement, rather than acknowledging but attempting to minimize or neutralize it, enhances instruction.

Diversity in Prior Knowledge and Experience

Prior Knowledge as Resource

Content-area teachers draw on a variety of instructional resources to support their teaching. First and foremost among them is the teachers' own knowledge and expertise in their fields. Basic texts and other reference materials are used as resources. Helpfully instructive videotapes and computer simulations support the teaching of concepts in various subjects. In both quantity and quality, available resources are varied.

Students themselves—their minds and their memories—are not often included in the list of resources available to teachers. This is understandable in view of the fact that students generally are thought to be recipients of, rather than contributors to, instruction. Unfortunately, being principally recipients of instruction leads to passivity in learning which, in turn, leads to a limited engagement of the mind.

A principal objective of teaching in content areas should be to engage students' minds in the study of ideas; and there are two reasons for this objective.

1. Ideas are the "stuff" of curriculum. To teach curriculum on a conceptual level rather than on an informational level, teachers have to engage students' minds in the study of ideas.

2. Students need to develop increasingly sophisticated levels of proficiency in reading, writing, and reasoning as they progress through the grades. Students attain such proficiency when they are shown how to apply the processes of reading, writing, and reasoning to increasingly sophisticated materials during the study of increasingly sophisticated ideas. Such study requires an engagement of students' minds.

Students become diverse resources for instruction when their minds are engaged and when their prior knowledge and experience are utilized in instruction. The prior knowledge and experience students bring to the study of concepts in any subject area constitute a rich resource on which content-area teachers can draw. When this diversity is used, rather than minimized or neutralized, instruction is enriched and students' learning is enhanced.

Schema Theory

Over the past two decades, considerable research has focused on schema theory, on studying the influence of prior knowledge on students' reading, writing, and reasoning (Anderson 1985; Applebee and Langer 1983; Perkins and Salomon 1989). What has been affirmed is particularly important to content-area teachers who want their students to acquire, assimilate, and apply the ideas found in their curricula. What has been found also supports the need for acknowledging and utilizing the diversity we find among students, not only in background knowledge and experience but also in ability, achievement, and culture.

How do individuals store and retrieve representations of experiences they have had and knowledge they have acquired? Research out of cognitive science suggests that the answer to that question lies in the function of schemata (the plural of schema). Rumelhart defines schemata as follows:

> *the building blocks of cognition . . . , the fundamental elements upon which information processing depends . . .*
>
> *Schemata are employed in the process of interpreting sensory data (both linguistic and non-linguistic), in retrieving information from memory, in organizing actions, in determining goals and sub-goals, in allocating resources, and, generally, in guiding the flow of processing in the system (Rumelhart 1980, 33–34).*

Schemata can be thought of as units in which knowledge is stored and from which knowledge is retrieved. These units can represent generic actions, conditions, agents, situations, events, objects, sequences, institutions, organizations, and so forth. Schemata also contain networks of interrelated parts that comprise the actions, conditions, situations, events, objects, sequences, institutions, or organizations. For example, one can have a broad schema such sports, education, politics, or transportation. One can have a narrower, related schema such as tennis, college, elections, or automobiles. One can have an even more specific, related schema such as racquets, WILLIAM and MARY, voter registration or Jaguar.

Drawing from the example above, one can see how specific schemata contribute to networks that comprise narrow schemata which, in turn, contribute to networks that comprise broad schemata. Jaguar plus other types of automobiles contribute (as subschemata) to a conceptual network that comprises the schema automobiles. Automobiles plus other means of transportation contribute (as subschemata) to a conceptual network that comprises the schema transportation.

Schemata and their networks are not developed in a linear fashion, however. One does not learn about Jaguars and all other models of cars before one grasps the concept automobiles. Similarly, one does not learn about automobiles plus all other means of conveyance before one grasps the concept transportation. Likewise, schemata are not recalled in a linear fashion. It is not necessary to recall the concept transportation and then the concept automobiles before one can recall a car called the Jaguar.

Rumelhart (1980) suggests that both the development and recall of schemata is *interactive* rather than linear. One may experience riding in a car before or after one acquires information about types of cars, before or after one becomes aware of types of cars, before or after one becomes aware that cars are only one means of conveyance, before or after one becomes aware that means of conveyance is only one dimension of the concept of transportation. Knowledge can be added to schemata at a macro level before or after knowledge is added at a micro level. The knowledge finds its place as one acquires understandings appropriate to schemata and the networks they support as well as understandings appropriate to the networks by which the schemata are supported.

The term *instantiation* is used to describe the placement of a schema (or concept) in memory, along with its related network of schemata (Rumelhart 1980). *Instantiation* also describes the placement of knowledge in the network of schemata that support a schema (or concept).

Schemata hold not only the knowledge itself but also information as to how the knowledge can be used (Rumelhart 1980). Let's return to our Jaguar-automobile-transportation example. Among the schemata that form the network for the Jaguar schema, one might find instantiated knowledge about how to drive the car. Among the schemata that form the network for the automobiles schema one might find instantiated knowledge about how to select, purchase, maintain, and resell cars. Among the schemata that form the network for the transportation schema one might find instantiated knowledge about when and how to use public and private means of conveyance, how to invest in corporations that provide public and private transportation, or how to use political means to influence the kind of public transportation that is provided in a community.

As instantiated knowledge and experience increase relative to a given schema, so does the likelihood of its retrieval for use. For well-instantiated schema, an associational stimulation of the concept can produce a stream of related subschemata. For example, given a word-association activity related to the concept transportation, students who are well grounded in the concept could produce such varied responses as those listed in the preceding paragraph. Their instantiated knowledge and experience would allow them to make many more associations than if their instantiated knowledge and experience were limited. Even if students could not make a particular association that the teacher planned to emphasize, the teacher would nevertheless know that students did have some knowledge about the concept. S/he could build on that knowledge and show students how new knowledge being explored connects with related knowledge they already possess.

In terms of retrieving information, as there is an increase in the complexity and comprehensiveness of subschemata that students possess for a given schema, there is a decrease in the amount of cuing needed to stimulate retrieval of information about that schema. For example, a person with comprehensive knowledge about Jaguars needs only to glimpse a small portion of a fender, a headlight, a trunk ornament, or a bumper to know that the objects belong to a Jag. Instantiated knowledge fills in the gaps, completing the picture. Thus, when students have rich networks of schemata related to a concept being taught, the teacher has a comprehensive resource upon which to draw. On the other hand, students may have some instantiated knowledge generally related to a targeted concept but yet lack specific knowledge that could be associated with the concept. In such cases the more general knowledge can serve as a context in which specific knowledge is explored. Let's look at the Jaguar example once again. Students may have general knowledge about automobiles but not particular knowledge about Jaguars. If they understand that the specific car they are studying (the Jag) has features similar to their schema for automobiles, they discover that they already know a lot about the Jag. Connecting what they know about automobiles to what is new about a specific car facilitates their learning the new information.

In this same manner, students' general knowledge about conflict can be used to understand causes of the Civil War as a particular form of conflict. Students' general knowledge about protest can be used to understand how unions were created as a special kind of protest. Students' general understanding of the process of change can be used to understand the particular kind of change represented by metamorphosis. In all such instances, teachers draw on students' prior knowledge and use it as a means to illuminate and understand new knowledge. Thus, comprehension and understanding involve connecting what is known with what is new.

Influence of What Is Known on Learning

We see, then, that students have stored in their memories an accumulation of knowledge and experience, which can be recalled if their memories are sufficiently stimulated. As relevant new information or experience is acquired, it is instantiated in the appropriate schemata and subschemata. As the mind is engaged in the examination of an idea, relevant schemata and subschemata are stimulated, and what has been accumulated therein is recalled and used. From the perspective of schema theory, the process of education involves adding to the accumulation of information and ideas within already-established schema, creating new schemata, and using both old and new schemata in the acquisition and creative application of ideas.

Knowing about schemata is important to the teaching of reading, writing, and reasoning across the curriculum. The comprehension process, for example, involves the reader in the active construction of meaning by making connections between what is known and what is new (Anderson 1985). Meaning does not reside in the text being read but, rather, in the mind of the person doing the reading. Langer (1985) calls this "inside-out reading" (in contrast to "outside-in reading" in which meaning is dictated by the teacher or the text). She says,

> We now know that knowledge is, to a certain extent, idiosyncratic; it is built from the inside out. Knowledge is based on individual experiences and shaped as learners fit these experiences into their own individual frameworks for understanding the world. People continually make sense of the world using their existing knowledge to interpret new information. Being able to make sense of the world involves not merely using terse language to frame a definition, but describing and elaborating concepts by linking them to other understandings. If a student has had no experience with a particular concept, a definition will make no real sense unless it can be linked to what is already known. These links help learners make sense from the inside out, from their home-talk world of personal language and experience to the school-talk world of academic thought and technical language (Langer 1985, 55–56).

Readers construct meaning by perceiving relationships between the information being read and the relevant information and ideas held in their prior knowledge and experience. As meaning is constructed, it finds a place in the reader's relevant schemata and is available for helping to construct meaning from other text.

Using Diversity of What Is Known in Teaching

How, then, do students' schemata become a useful instructional resource for content-area teachers? Clearly, students' comprehension and composition is influenced by what they already know about what it is that they are about to study. Two issues are involved here: (1) the richness of prior knowledge and (2) the relevance of the prior knowledge.

The issue of richness is quite obvious. Let's look at the process of inferencing, for example. Inferencing, as part of comprehension, requires one to read between the lines by supplying information or ideas that authors assume one already knows and then by connecting it with what the authors provide. Students with a rich background knowledge and experience are more likely to make connections between what is known and what is new and, thereby, read between the lines than are students with limited background knowledge and experience. Students who have been shown how to use their prior knowledge and experience to make connections between what is known and what is new are more likely to read between the lines than students who have not been shown how.

Composing also requires writers to make connections between what is known and what is new. Writing an exposition on some topic, for example, often involves the use of metaphors, similes, or some other form of analogy to explain features of some object, consequences of some action, and so forth. Rich backgrounds of knowledge and experience increase the likelihood that individuals can create appropriate analogies for use in their compositions. Students who are shown how to use their knowledge and experience to create analogies for use in their writing will be more successful than students who have not been shown how.

The issue of relevance of schemata is more subtle than the issue of richness, and it holds profound implications for instruction. By what process do students learn to make connections between what is known and what is new? In what ways can students learn to perceive the content of what they are reading or writing as elaborations on what they already know?

Helping students learn how to identify relevant schemata starts with teachers' selection of an organizing idea for their units and lessons. Teachers identify an idea that is illustrated by the particular information students are to study in a lesson or unit and that also can be illustrated by information from other domains of knowledge and experience. Using activities illustrated throughout this book, teachers encourage students to draw upon what they already know to give examples of the idea being discussed. Teachers show students how to connect their own examples of the idea with course-based examples of the idea. They do this by using students' examples from their prior knowledge, by pressing students for reasons for the connections they have made, and by asking students to recall other relevant experiences. In so doing, teachers develop and reinforce students' perception of how relevant their experience is to what is being studied. Also, in so doing, teachers build students' confidence in tying what is relevant to the concept being studied.

Consider two examples of how this can be done.

1. A science teacher started the initial unit on the circulatory system by having students discuss the statement *What goes around comes around*. Students recognized the statement as having something to do with cause/effect or action/reaction relationships. They shared relevant experiences that illustrated the idea. In this manner the circulatory system became an elaboration on the previously known idea of what goes around comes around.

2. A history teacher started a lesson on the development of unionism by exploring the idea of protest. After discussing the word *protest* and its etymology he asked students to do some brainstorming around two related categories: types of protest and results of protest. Students then discussed generalizations about the agents, actions, conditions, and consequences of protest, drawing from prior knowledge and experience to support or reject the generalizations. The teacher then asked the students to read about the development of unions and to decide whether the participants in that development would agree with the same generalizations. In this manner, the development of unions became an elaboration of the previously known idea of protest.

In the section on organizing ideas that appears later in this chapter, more examples are presented for reinforcing the relevance of students' schemata.

At the heart of the relevance issue is showing students how to make connections between what is known and what is new. The issue speaks to the organizing principle for this book: The essence of good teaching is to show students how to do what they need to do to be successful. Langer says, quite rightly,

> The students themselves must make the connections; no one else can make them for the students because no one else shares the personal knowledge used to make sense of the world. Thus, hard as we try, no one but the students can fashion the links that will be meaningful (Langer and Purcel-Gates 1985, 56).

However, even though students must themselves make the connections, teachers can support their doing so in ways that raise their consciousness about making relevant connections. A principal purpose of any subject is to increase participating students' knowledge and experience relative to its curriculum. As students gain in knowledge and experience, their schemata are elaborated and enriched and the usefulness of their schemata as resources for learning additional concepts is enhanced.

Diversity of prior knowledge and experience among students in a given class compounds the resource. Diversity in intellect, education, achievement, and cultural background all come together to influence the nature, substance, and comprehensiveness of students' knowledge and experience. In classes characterized by a high degree of interaction among students in cooperative learning settings, diversity in students' prior knowledge and experience is a strong asset to be utilized. As students explore the relevance of their own knowledge and experience to the concept being studied in a content area, they learn from one another. The learning includes both the process of determining relevance and the substance of what has been determined relevant, adding to the elaboration and enrichment of schemata of all participating parties.

Order of Relationship between What Is Known and What Is New

Research on schema theory affirms a long-standing belief about teaching: the importance of making connections between what is known and what is new. Content-area teachers typically apply a variety of methods to help students make connections between the ideas being studied and what students already know. The fact that connections should be made is not the issue. What is the issue, one not often considered, is the order in which the connections should be made. While the order of connection is usually described as connecting what is known with what is new, in actual practice the order is connecting what is new with what is known. The difference is highly significant.

Content teachers want their students to learn the subject matter as rapidly and thoroughly as possible. Being experts in their fields, most of what they teach is old hat, comfortable, familiar, and straightforward. To these teachers, connecting new information with old information is not a big deal. That's what review is for; it sets a context for the new information and fits it into place. The focus is on the new, on what students do *not* know. As a consequence, it diminishes the known that students *do* know.

This order, connecting the new with the known, seems comfortable for teachers because they already know what is new to their students. However, the order is difficult for students for whom the new truly is new.

It is difficult for students to connect what is new with what is known unless they first understand the new information so they can see how it fits with information that is known. Of course, if they really understand the new information, it is no longer new. Furthermore, if they really understand the new information, what's the point in their spending time making a new-known connection? Focusing on the new information first with perfunctory connections with what is known results in segmented learning. Content is learned in chunks that are isolated from one another. Students do not develop a sense of interrelationships among ideas or of how new ideas are often elaborations on ideas they already possess.

Teaching that focuses principally on what is new diminishes the value of what students already know. In such teaching, students have very little by which to deal with the new concept. They are kept constantly on the edge of ignorance.

The recommended order, *connecting the known with the new,* seems more comfortable for students because they know what they know. The order may be less comfortable for teachers because they have to think differently about the new. They have to think of the new information as an illustration or elaboration of ideas and experiences that their students already possess. They use organizing ideas for lessons to help students establish what they know and then perceive the relevance between what is known and what is new. With the known information established, students perceive analogs to the new information as the new ideas are presented, analyzed and applied. A result of these connections is that students develop a sense of interrelationships among ideas that comprise the curriculum.

For example, a teacher started a lesson on the *Declaration of Independence* with a word-association activity focused on the word *freedom.* Students clearly were connecting with what they knew; because among the words produced by the groups were *flower, leaf, tree, sky, boy, baby, waterfall,* and so forth. Also included were more "history/social studies" words, drawn from previous years of study. The class discussed the words, looked for relationships among the words and then labeled the relationships. In so doing they identified categories of agents, actions, institutions, and the like. They discussed how freedom related to the ideas implicit in the categories they identified.

The teacher then invited them to evaluate the behavior of hypothetical group of people who were interested in separating themselves from a larger group to which they belonged. The separating group wanted the larger group to know what was motivating them to separate. The teacher posed the question, "What would you say to the larger group?" He then gave them the statements shown in Example 2-1 and asked them to indicate whether they would say any of them to the larger group. The students responded to the statements and discussed them in their groups.

After students discussed their responses to the statements and the reasons for their responses, the teacher distributed copies of the Declaration of Independence. Students, in their groups, decided whether the writers of the document would have agreed with the same set of statements. They were asked to cite evidence from the document to support their decisions.

After a full-class discussion on several of the statements from Example 2-1, the teacher then asked the students to respond to the statements found in Example 2-2. As you can see, these statements focused on broad principles related to history, social science, and citizenship.

EXAMPLE 2-1 ━━━━━━━━━━━━━━━━━━━━━━━━━━━━━━

Freedom I: Would You Say This?

_____ 1. Sometimes certain people are better off being separated from one another than being together.

_____ 2. When one group of people separates from another, both groups are then equal.

_____ 3. If one group decides to leave another group, it should give the reasons for its decision.

_____ 4. Reasons for groups being separate and equal are really very obvious. Here are some of them:

    a. All individuals and groups are equal.

    b. These individuals all have the right to live, to be free, and to enjoy life.

    c. These rights are made possible when a group organizes itself and puts people in charge of protecting these rights for the group.

    d. When the people in charge of a group do not protect these rights, the group has the right to put new people in charge and to tell them how things should be run.

_____ 5. A group should separate from other groups or change people in charge of itself only for the most serious reasons.

_____ 6. However, when it seems necessary to take action, a group should do so even though it seems strange to them to do so.

EXAMPLE 2-2 ━━━━━━━━━━━━━━━━━━━━━━━━━━━━━━

Freedom II

_____ 1. Belief is as much a part of freedom or slavery as is action.

_____ 2. You may get freedom without working for it, but you cannot keep it that way.

_____ 3. Separation of people brings equality among them.

_____ 4. Independence occurs more in a person's mind than in his or her daily living.

_____ 5. Freedom is more a state of mind than a condition of body.

In this lesson the teacher started with what students knew and showed them how to connect it with the new information.

Organizing Idea

Critical to the order of moving from what is known to what is new is the identification of an organizing idea for lessons and units. An organizing idea is a declarative statement that identifies a targeted relationship among information or among concepts. The organizing idea usually contains a key word or phrase that identifies the conceptual focus of the lesson.

Organizing Ideas for Lessons

Organizing ideas for lessons express concepts sufficiently narrow to be illustrated by the particular information to be presented in the lesson yet sufficiently broad to be illustrated by other kinds of information and ideas. For example, the lesson on unions that focused on protest, discussed earlier in this chapter, was based on the following organizing idea:

Protests take many forms and produce many outcomes.

The key term in this organizing idea is *protest*, and this idea served as the conceptual focus for the lesson. Teachers often use the key term as the stimulus for word-association activities. As students generate word lists related to the stimulus word, they draw on their prior knowledge and experience and discover that they already know a lot about the idea being studied. In this lesson, students eventually discovered how the development of unions is an elaboration on the idea of protest, which they already understood. In this manner the organizing idea was used to help make connections between what was known and what was new.

As will be seen in subsequent chapters, effective lessons are driven by organizing ideas and relevant instructional materials are designed to support students as they develop an understanding of those ideas.

Organizing Ideas for Units

An organizing idea can be used for units as well as for lessons. Usually, the organizing idea for units is more abstract and inclusive than one for lessons. It serves to identify the conceptual focus of the entire unit. Lessons within the unit have their own organizing ideas. The organizing idea for a lesson is less abstract and inclusive than it is for a unit.

For example, consider again the organizing idea for a particular literature unit discussed in Chapter 1:

Perspective is influenced by knowledge and experience.

The key term in this organizing idea is *perspective,* and it serves as the conceptual focus for the unit. Each lessons for this unit, has its own organizing idea, and is designed to develop an understanding of this broad principle. For example, one lesson focuses on various perspectives of time, drawing on different poems to reflect those perspectives. The organizing idea for this particular lesson is as follows:

> Time has both quantitative and qualitative dimensions, and people experience both dimensions differently.

In that lesson, students read the following poems and relate their own experiences with time to those expressed by the poets: "The Day" by Theodore Spencer, "Eight O'Clock" by A.E. Houseman, and "The Sprinters" by Lee Murchison.

Another lesson in this unit on perspective focuses on fate. Its organizing idea is as follows:

> Attempts to gain a perspective on fate are sometimes grounded in reality, sometimes in imagination.

Students read the following poems and relate their own considerations of fate to those expressed by the poets: "Ozymandias" by Percy Shelly, "The Road Not Taken" by Robert Frost, and "Limited" by Carl Sandburg.

Subsequent chapters in this text show how the organizing idea for units can be used to capture students' interest, to motivate their participation in the study of relevant materials, and to help them make connections between what they already know about the principle under consideration and what they are learning.

Illustrative Organizing Ideas

Teachers from many subject areas have created organizing ideas for units and lessons they teach. Example 2-3 includes a sampling. In parentheses ( ) following some of the statements are original versions of the organizing ideas. You can see that the revisions raise the level of abstraction and generalization. In brackets [ ] following some of the statements is listed the specific subject area or topic to which it is related.

Creating Organizing Ideas

Creating organizing ideas for lessons and units is relatively easy to do. You can do it in two steps. First, make a conceptual analysis of the resources you are going to have the students study. Second, formulate a generalization that is both *sufficiently narrow* to be obviously relevant to the particular content you are having your students study and *sufficiently broad* to encompass

---

EXAMPLE 2-3 _____

Illustrative Organizing Ideas

1. While change is inevitable, it has both a positive and a negative impact on society. (Eighth-grade history)
2. It is possible to attain one's objective by making "what is not" seem like "what should be." (Tenth-grade literature)
3. The development of new systems impacts negatively and positively on societal and environmental issues. (The development of the American factory system created undesirable social and environmental consequences.)
4. Differences among people cause conflicts among nations. (Wars between and among nations often can be traced to religious differences.)
5. A picture is worth a thousand words. (Curve sketching: introductory calculus)
6. Art is a lie that makes us realize the truth. (Junior high art)
7. People without internal control are subject to external control. (Social studies: freedom and discipline within the law)
8. The individual is an instrument of creativity. (General health)
9. Loss of our treasures often leads to discoveries of even greater worth. (Since the end of the Civil War, the United States has contributed to progress both at home and abroad.)

---

other, relevant information that may be in your students' prior knowledge and experience.

Having organizing ideas with these two characteristics allows you to use students' prior knowledge and experience as a valuable resource and to help them discover that they already know a lot about what they are about to study.

Modeling Time

Following is an example of how to use the two steps to create an organizing idea for a particular reading selection that could be used in a course on auto mechanics. The unit is focused on internal combustion engines; the lesson is on turbocharged engines.

First, you should read the text selection, which is shown below as Practice 2-1. Read it for the gist of its content. This provides the basis for your making a conceptual analysis of the material. Write out the conceptual analysis, and then think of a broad concept or principle that could be illustrated by the content of your conceptual analysis.

PRACTICE 2-1

Turbo Charging

When you think of a turbocharged engine, do you picture a high-powered "muscle car"? Lots of folks do. Many people also imagine that a turbocharger makes incredible demands on an engine, and uses great quantities of gasoline.

These preconceptions are often misconceptions. A turbocharger does boost available power. But it does so efficiently and economically.

The power you get when you step on an accelerator comes from the ignition of air that is pumped into engine cylinders. The more air that can be forced into the cylinders, the greater the power you can generate. That is where a turbocharger comes in.

A turbocharger is actually a marvel of efficiency. It is basically a fan driven by exhaust gases that would otherwise be wasted, monitored by an electronically-controlled computer system. When you call for power, the turbocharger fan (impeller) spins, compresses the air and feeds it to the cylinder. But overstuffing the cylinder is only half of the formula; the computer then takes over and provides the extra fuel. You get the power you need, when you need it.

Before turbo technology, the "traditional" way to increase power was to increase engine size. This meant greater weight, higher fuel consumption and less efficiency. That big engine had to be fed, even when it was "loafing." With a turbo, you get increased power without increased engine size.

What about durability and reliability? A turbocharger's shaft can spin at incredible speeds... up to 130,000 RPM! That can generate lots of heat, but turbocharging systems now use the twin weapons of engine oil and coolant to fight friction and dissipate heat. The result is rugged, long-lasting performance.

Some people think turbocharged engines need special care and feeding. They do not. In fact, it is no harder to maintain a turbo engine than a normally-aspirated one. Just make sure to **check your oil and coolant regularly.** Replace them in accordance with a maintenance schedule.

Here is our conceptual analysis made of the reading selection:

For its size and weight, a turbocharged engine produces more power than a conventional engine.

Here is the organizing idea we created for the lesson:

Appearances can be deceiving.

You can see how it works. Organizing ideas serve as conceptual umbrellas under which students can bring together relevant information and ideas from their prior knowledge and connect them with information and ideas derived from their current study. Organizing ideas provide a place for the synthesis of information from a variety of sources: students' prior knowledge, teacher's knowledge and experience, basic texts, supplementary texts, audiotapes and videotapes, laboratory experiments and field experiences, and so forth.

Clearly identifying organizing ideas for units and lessons helps teachers clarify the substantive intent of these units and lessons and increases the likelihood that the intent will be translated into learning by the students. The time that you invest in identifying organizing ideas for units and lessons is time well spent. Using the ideas to organize your instruction and to design your supporting materials and activities enables your students to share the benefits of your investment.

Practice Time

It's now time for you to try your hand at creating an organizing idea for a lesson. First read the article presented in Practice 2-2. Then write out a conceptual analysis as we did for Practice 2-1. Finally, write out an organizing idea for the material. You may wish to review the features that should characterize an organizing idea. You will find the conceptual analysis and organizing idea that we created for this article in Appendix A.

Summary

Students' knowledge and experience constitute an excellent resource upon which teachers can draw. This chapter makes clear how this resource is renewable and ever expanding.

While teachers draw on students' schemata to help them connect known ideas with new ones, such use does not diminish the resource. The more opportunities students have to perceive elaborations of ideas they possess and understand, the richer their schemata will become. In turn, the richer will be this special resource that teachers will have to draw upon for their instruction.

Helping students learn how to use what they already know to understand and to learn more is the heart of the educational process. The content of your curriculum provides the substance for expanding and enriching what students know. The processes of your curriculum provide the means by which students can expand and enrich what they know. The instructional strategies presented in this book enable you to help students be successful in this learning experience.

PRACTICE 2-2

Sand Art, on a Deadline

The young man arrived on the Massachusetts beach early carrying a portable radio, a shovel and an odd assortment of tools. There were a bricklayer's trowel, a palette knife, spatulas, spoons and a spray bottle.

He walked down near the water—the tide was out—put down the radio and tuned it to soft rock. Then he shoveled wet sand into a pile nearly four feet high and as many feet across. The took up the trowel and used it to slice large hunks off the pile, creating a rectangular shape.

After that, he set to work with palette knife, spatulas and spoons. He shaped a graceful tower, topped walls with crenelated battlements, fashioned elegant bay windows and carved out a massive front gate.

The man knew his sand. With deft strokes, he smoothly finished some surfaces, embroidered baroque designs on others. As delicate shapes began to dry, he gently moistened them with water from the spray bottle, lest they crumble in the breeze.

All this took hours. People gathered, commenting to each other and asking questions of the sculptor. Lost in concentration, he gave only perfunctory replies. At last he stood back, apparently satisfied with a castle worthy of the Austrian countryside, or Disneyland.

Then he gathered his tools and radio and moved them up to drier sand. He had known for a while what many in the rapt crowd still overlooked: the tide was coming in. Not only had he practiced his craft with confidence and style, he had done so against a powerful, immutable deadline.

As the spectators looked on, water began to lap at the base of the castle. In minutes it was surrounded, a miniature Mont-St.-Michel. Then the rising flood began to erode the base; chunks of wall fell, the tower tumbled, finally the gate's arch collapsed. More minutes passed, and small waves erased bay windows and battlements—soon no more than a modest lump was left.

Many in the crowd looked distraught; some voiced dismay. But the sculptor remained serene. He had, after all, had a wonderful day, making beauty out of nothing, and watching it return to nothing, as time and tide moved on.

Source: "Sand Art; on a Deadline," The New York Times, August 13, 1989, sectn 4, p 22.

REACTIONS

Journal Entries and Discussion

Analyze your prediction concerning the instructional importance of the organizing idea as discussed in this chapter. How close were you to what was actually developed? How do you account for the proximity, or distance, of your prediction?

Using Congress as a metaphor for students in your institution, speculate on who are the senators, the representatives, the pages, and the lobbyists. What does the product of your speculation tell you about the kind of diversity that exists among your students?

Analysis and Discussion

Now that you have completed this chapter, consider the statements shown below. Check the numbered lines for statements with which you agree. Circle the numbers of statements you believe reflect the point of view of the authors. In writing, explore reasons for differences on any statements between your point of view and what you perceive to be the point of view of the authors. Please share and discuss your writing with colleagues who also are reading this book.

_____ 1. At the beginning of the study of a new unit, students already know quite a lot about the general principles and broad concepts that are related to its content.

_____ 2. Students are much more motivated to participate in the study of a concept when they are able to connect it with something they already know.

_____ 3. Comprehension involves an active construction of meaning, which involves drawing on prior knowledge to connect known information and ideas with new ones.

_____ 4. Students' relevant prior knowledge of a given concept is at a fairly abstract level at the beginning of their study of that concept.

_____ 5. Teachers' activation, organization, and review of students' prior knowledge of a given concept is at a fairly general level at the beginning of their study of that concept.

_____ 6. When using students' prior knowledge as a resource, connecting what is known with what is new is preferred over connecting what is new with the what is known.

_____ 7. Individual students can be lost in an environment that deals with students as a generic whole.

_____ 8. Ideas can be lost by an overemphasis on information.

3

Texts

Organizing idea: Workers know their tools and understand how to use them well.

Reflections

Before reading this chapter, please record in your journal your responses to the following tasks. If possible, share your writing with other individuals who are also reading this book.

1. Make a list of features and factors that should characterize instructional resources used by students in the content areas you teach. What generalizations about instructional materials can you draw from your list?

2. For a typical lesson or unit taught in your field, calculate the percent of information students derive from their text compared to what they derive from your lectures and other resources.

3. Identify and discuss the criteria used in the selection of basic texts used in your subject area.

WHEN YOU TAKE a trip into unfamiliar territory, you usually take a map along to help you find the way. Technology has been developed for displaying computerized maps on a screen in a car so that as the car travels across a given terrain, its location is shown on the map (Cushman 1990). The probability is high that when you buy your first car in the twenty-first century, this technology will be available as an option. The road maps we now use will become quaint artifacts found in museums.

What does this have to do with texts? Texts have built-in "maps" that can give directions to readers and let them know where they are located midst the developing information and ideas. Some of the "maps" are explicit, visible guideposts that you can use to find your way through the text.

Other "maps" are implicit, invisible signals that tell you where you are located within the developing ideas. The explicit maps are provided through text organization. The implicit maps are provided through text structure.

Text Organization

Texts have organizational clues that are visible and predictable. Some of these clues are general in nature and are found in texts used in most subject areas. Other clues are specific in nature and are dictated by the kind of subject matter presented in the text. Helping students learn how to use these visible and predictable organizational clues helps them make more efficient and effective use of their texts.

General Organizational Clues

The general organization of most texts is predictable. Clues to the organization are the presence of a preface or foreword, a table of contents, separate sections and/or chapters, appendixes, references, a glossary, and an index. These parts are found in most texts, thus providing a predictable organization.

The prevalence of this text organization can easily lead you to assume that your students are sufficiently familiar with the form and function of various parts of the text and need no further instruction in that regard. On the contrary, they need reminders of functions served by each of the parts. The functional distinction between a table of contents and an index needs to be reinforced, for example, with a focus on how each can be used to discover what information and ideas authors emphasize. Students need reminders of how a glossary works and when it is best used.

These reminders are profitable early in a school year or whenever a new text is introduced. Reminders can take the form of a tour of the book. For example, you can have students work together in groups on a text tour of the type that follows. Part A (Example 3-1) of the tour deals with explicit knowledge of the parts and their functions. Part B deals with implicit knowledge of the parts and their applications.

Specific Organizational Clues

The specific organization of most texts, while generally predictable in function, is not as predictable in form. Clues to this characteristic are the presence of titles for chapters as well as the presence of headings and subheadings within chapters. Titles and headings are predictable in function in that they serve to signal the start of sections or subsections of the text.

EXAMPLE 3-1 ━━━━━━━━━━━━━━━━━━━━━━━━━━━━━━━

Text Tour—I

Directions: Using your text, *Physical Science,* answer the questions in Part A and Part B. Questions in Part A focus on the locations of parts of the books. Questions in Part B focus on the kind of information contained in different parts of the book. Work together with other members of your group as you complete this tour of your text. Write your answer in the space that follows each question.

Part A

1. What book part is located on page 593? _____
2. What book part is located on page vii? _____
3. What book part is located on page 580? _____
4. What book part is located on page 567? _____
5. What book part is located on page 258? _____
6. On what page do you find the name of the book part that tells you how the book is organized? _____
7. On what page do you find the name of the book part that tells where specific information is located in the book? _____
8. On what page do you find do you find an example of a book part that identifies a major section of the book? _____
9. On what page do you find the name of the book part that provides definitions of words used in the book? _____
10. On what page do you find the name of the book part that presents information that is essential but cannot be placed in major sections of the book? _____

Part B

1. Do the authors deal with the topic of electromagnetic waves? _____
2. How many subtopics do they present? _____
3. How did you find the answers? _____
4. In how many locations in the book do the authors deal with the topic of radiation?
5. How did you find the answer? _____
6. How have the authors defined the word galaxy? _____
7. How did you find the answer? _____

Titles and headings are unpredictable in form in that they vary in size, placement, and levels of subordination. Subordination can be signaled by type size, type style, or the amount of indentation. Understanding interactions among these more specific organizational clues gives students insight into the relative importance among ideas presented by authors as well as relationships that exist among the ideas.

The presence of titles and headings, as well as interrelation- ships that exist among them, can be pointed out in the general tour of the text. Example 3-2 shows how that part of the text tour can be organized.

Titles and headings can be used by students as aids to more independence in comprehending the text. Chapter 12 presents instructional strategies for teaching students how to use titles and headings as study aids. Essential to the strategies is students' familiarity with the purposes for the use of headings and the significance of their placement in the text. Activities such as the one in Example 3-2 can help develop that familiarity and can serve as the basis for the study strategies.

Text Structure

In contrast to the organization of text, the structure of text is not readily visible. Text structure reflects the manner in which the authors' have arranged the information they present. According to Meyer and Rice, the term text structure is used

> to refer to how the ideas in a text are interrelated to convey a message to a reader. Some of the ideas in the text are of central importance to the authors message, while others are of less importance. Thus, text structure specifies the logical connections among ideas as well as subordination of some ideas to others (Meyers and Rice 1984, 319).

EXAMPLE 3-2 ─────────────────────────────

Text Tour—II

Directions: Using your text, *Physical Science,* answer the following questions. Work together with other members of your group as you complete this tour of your text. Write your answer in the space that follows each question.

1. Locate the beginning of Chapter Ten. Determine the numbering system used to identify major headings in the chapter?_____
2. How many major headings does Chapter Ten have?_____
3. How are subheadings identified?_____
4. Which major headings in Chapter Ten have subheadings?_____
5. Does the table of contents list major headings of chapters?_____
6. Does the table of contents list the subheadings of chapters?
   _____

The structure of texts can be classified into two broad areas: exposition and narration (Muth 1989).

Exposition

Exposition is the principle structure used by authors of text in most subject areas. Slater and Graves provide a broad definition of expository text, saying it

> is prose in which an author presents information to a reader. Good expository text is explanatory in that the author provides the necessary explanations to enable readers to understand the information being presented. Good expository text is also directive in that the author actively engages readers in a dialogue that highlights information and tells readers what is and is not important. Finally, much good expository text incorporates narrative elements to give life to the prose and to portray people in a more compelling and comprehensible manner (Slater and Graves 1989, 144).

The purposes of exposition used in content texts essentially are to explain and illustrate objects, actions, agents, or conditions that contribute to an understanding of the curriculum. These expository texts also serve as a means for exploring and interpreting curriculum-related values, ideas, motives, missions, concepts, or principles. From their review of research, Slater and Graves conclude that "students' knowledge and understanding of expository text structure in prose is crucial for the comprehension of the information in texts" (Slater and Graves 1989, 146). In their review of relevant research, Nelson-Herber and Johnston state:

> To put it simply, we have evidence that students who have prior knowledge of text structure use it in understanding and recalling information. Furthermore, the research suggests that teaching students to be aware of the ways that ideas are organized will aid them in comprehending expository text. Thus, it is important for teachers to use strategies that show students how to use their background knowledge of both content and structure to support their comprehension of expository text (Nelson: Herber and Johnston 1989, 271).

Authors generally develop their exposition by presenting their ideas and information in an hierarchical order (Meyer 1979). Major ideas are set forth and supported through the presentation of subordinate ideas. Subordinate ideas are developed through the presentation of more detailed information. Researchers who study the organization of text describe three levels in this hierarchy:

> The first is the sentence or micropropositional level, which is concerned with the way sentences cohere and are organized within a text. The second is the paragraph or macropropositional level, which pertains to issues of logical or-

ganization and argumentation. The third is that of the top-level structure of the text as a whole (Meyer and Rice 1984, 325)."

The top-level structure in this hierarchy can be described broadly in terms of organizational patterns. Niles (1965) identified these patterns as cause/effect, comparison/contrast, time order, and simple listing. Meyer (1977) uses the term *enumerative order* to describe Niles's term *simple listing*. To help you identify what these patterns "look like," Examples 3-3 through 3-6 present four brief expository passages, each representing one of the patterns. As you will see, the patterns are not all that obvious. In some cases you can see evidence for more than one possibility. Choice is made based on which pattern seems to reflect the more controlling, or overarching, relationships present in the passage. Following each passage we identify what we think is its organizational pattern and our reasons for the choice.

Example 3-3 compares differences between an arch and a beam. Cause-and-effect relationships are pointed out in the discussion of each. Moreover, a sequence (time order) is implied in the ordered discussion of two demonstrations. Even so, the thrust of the passage is a comparison of the two architectural devices.

Example 3-4 (see page 61) gives background for understanding over-feeding of algae. Comparisons are made between the solubility of sugar,

EXAMPLE 3-3 ━━━━━━━━━━━━━━━━━━━━━━━━━━━━━

Comparison/Contrast

The important difference between an arch and a beam is this: A loaded arch cannot sag downward unless the materials in it move outward first. This outward force is directed not only against the structural members of the arch itself but also against the point of attachment. To visualize this effect, consider the following two demonstrations. In the first, we have constructed two arches of thin, weak, metal rod and attached them both firmly to a block of wood. Now let us push down on one until it starts to collapse and leave the other alone for comparison. We can see in the second photograph that as we push downward, the metal bends outward.

To perform the second demonstration, sit in an armchair, place each elbow on an arm of the chair, and clasp your hands together, thus forming a simple arch. Now have someone push down hard on the top of your arch. Since your bones are strong enough not to bend appreciably, under the load, this arch will not fail like the thin metal rod. But if your friend pushes down harder, you will hear the sides of the armchair creak, and if the downward force is great enough and the chair is weak, the arms of the chair will break outward.

Source: Turk and Turk, *Physical Science, (Philadelphia: W.B. Saunders Company, 1977), 307–308.*

EXAMPLE 3-4

Cause/Effect

The use of modern detergents has contributed to overfeeding of algae. To appreciate this somewhat complex situation, it will be helpful to understand something about the nature and mode of action of detergents. We mentioned earlier in this chapter that the ease with which a foreign substance can dissolve in a liquid depends on how strongly the molecules of the two different substances attract each other, relative to the mutual attractions of like molecules. Sugar dissolves in water, and if your hands are sticky with honey or lollipops they can be washed clean by rinsing them in pure water. Vegetable oil and animal fat, however, are insoluble in water, and the pure water that rinsed away the honey will leave any grease on your hands behind. It was known in ancient Rome that heating a mixture of animal fat and wood ashes produces a substance that could dissolve both in water and in grease and that could somehow bring these two otherwise incompatible substances together. Therefore, if you rinse your greasy hand with a mixture of water and this new substance, which we now all soap, the grease can be washed away. Soap functions in this manner because it is made up of long molecules that have, on one end, separated regions of positive and negative electrical charge that are strongly attracted to water molecules and, on the other end, a hydrocarbon character that is attracted to grease molecules. This action of the soap molecule is called detergency.

Source: Turk and Turk, *Physical Science,* (Philadelphia: W.B. Saunders Company, 1977), 164–165.

vegetable oil, and animal fat, and the impact of soap and water on each. However, the thrust of the passage is on the effect of detergency.

Example 3-5 (see page 62) presents a sequence of events related to water-pollution control. Effects of these events also are discussed. However, the thrust of the passage is on the order in which the events occurred.

Example 3-6 (see page 62) presents a listing of ways that rivers carry rock materials: solution, suspension, and bed load. A comparison among the three is implicit in the listing. Moreover, some effects of each way are identified. However, the thrust of the passage is on describing each way that rivers carry rock material without concern for consequence, comparison or order.

Skilled readers use their knowledge of text structure to aid their comprehension. They are aware of the hierarchical relationships that characterize expository material and that these relationships fall into discernable patterns. They use this knowledge to identify the particular pattern(s) being used in materials they are reading. They use their understanding of the structure of the pattern(s) to interpret relationships and connections that authors make across the information and ideas they present. Each pattern

EXAMPLE 3-5 ━━━━━━━━━━━━━━━━━━━━━━━━━━━━━━━━━━━━

Time Order

In 1956 Congress passed the Federal Water Pollution Control Act. One of the chief provisions of this act was to grant federal money to 2,746 municipalities to help them build water-treatment plants. Six years later Congress amended this act to give more money for building water-treatment plants and to give the federal government more powers to enforce the act's regulations. The amended act also increased research for solving water pollution problems and gave federal assistance to interstate pollution control programs. In 1965 additional congressional legislation was passed to help in the construction of solid-waste disposal plants in our nation's cities.

All this congressional legislation started with the federal government's desire to help American cities build water-treatment plants. Within nine years, congressional legislation had been enacted which affected many aspects of water pollution control in American cities.

Source: Daniel Goldberg, *Challenges in our Changing Urban Society*, (Palo Alto: Laidlaw Brothers, 1969), 323.

EXAMPLE 3-6 ━━━━━━━━━━━━━━━━━━━━━━━━━━━━━━━━━━━━

Simple Listing

Rivers carry rock material in three ways. Some mineral matter is carried in solution. Most of this comes to the river in the ground water that seeps into it. The most common minerals carried in solution are compounds of calcium and magnesium, especially in limestone regions.

When river water looks muddy, it is carrying rock material in suspension. Suspended material includes clay, silt, and fine sand. Although these are heavier than water, they are stirred up and kept from sinking by the *turbulence* of stream flow. Turbulence means swirls and eddies resulting from friction between the stream and its bed and banks. The faster the stream flows, the more turbulent—and muddy—it becomes. A rough bed also increases turbulence.

Sand, pebbles, and boulders that are too heavy to be carried in suspension may be carried as bed load, especially during floods. Boulders and pebbles roll or slide on the river bed. Large sand grains are pushed along in jumps and bounces, like grins of sand in a sandstorm.

Biologists estimate that the rivers of the United States carry about one-fourth of their load in solution, about one-half in suspension, and about one-fourth as bed load.

Source: Samuel N. Namowitz and Donald B. Stone, *Earth Science*, (New York: American Book Company, 1978), 112-113.

has verbal clues that indicate its presence in a text. Skilled readers use these clues to identify the predominant pattern being used by the authors of what they are reading. Use of the patterns helps them interpret what is being presented. Example 3-7 presents a listing of verbal clues for each of the patterns (Vacca and Vacca 1989, 189).

Each pattern establishes a particular kind of relationship among the major ideas and supporting information presented in the writing. It is rare to find extended exposition that is organized exclusively by a single pattern. As you have seen, more than one pattern may be present in a given section of text. Sometimes cause/effect explanations are given within material that is organized around an over-all chronology. Sometimes passages mix comparison/contrast with time order or with cause/effect. When showing students how to comprehend passages with mixed patterns, it is useful to focus on the predominant pattern rather than on both. The decision as to which one to emphasize often is determined by the conceptual focus you have given to the study of the material. The conceptual focus, of course, is reflected in the organizing idea that you have established for the lesson to which the materials are related. Having identified the organizing idea for the lesson, you emphasize the pattern that most clearly supports the conceptual thrust of the lesson. This becomes the predominant pattern and is the one around which comprehension activities are organized.

Chapter 8 includes discussions and examples of ways to guide students' use of the patterns as they read required materials in your lessons.

EXAMPLE 3-7 ▬▬▬▬▬▬▬▬▬▬

Signal Words for Patterns

Cause / Effect	Comparison / Contrast	Time Order	Simple Listing
because	however	on (date)	to begin with
since	but	not long after	first
therefore	as well as	now	second
consequently	on the other hand	as	next
as a result	not only . . . but also	before	then
this led to	either . . . or	after	finally
so that	while	when	most importantly
nevertheless	although	also	
accordingly	unless	in fact	
if . . . then	similarly	for instance	
thus	yet	for example	

These activities show students how patterns work, how they facilitate comprehension, and how they can be used for more independent reading of text material. Chapter 12 presents a variety of study strategies that help students make use of their knowledge of these patterns to set purposes for reading, to analyze what is being read, and to summarize and review what was read. The organizational pattern for a passage, whether it be long or short, is not always easily discernible. You will find it helpful to practice identifying the patterns found in expository materials in your subject area. Your own facility with their identification will be helpful as you support your students' use of the patterns as aids to comprehension.

Placed at the end of this chapter are four passages with which to practice (Practices 3-4, 3-5, 3-6, and 3-7). Examine each and determine what organizational pattern predominates. If the decision depends on what the organizing idea would be for a lesson in which the materials were being used, first state the organizing idea and then identify the pattern. You will be using these excerpts for work you will be doing in Chapter 12, so be certain to record and preserve your decisions. Our opinions on the organizing ideas and predominant patterns are in Appendix A.

Narrative

The second kind of text structure is narrative. Simply put, narrative is telling a story. Mandler and Johnson call it story structure and define it as "an idealized internal (mental) representation of the parts of a typical story and the relationships among those parts" (Mandler and Johnson 1977, 111). Most children and adults have a sense of story (Stein and Glen 1979). There is a general, predictable order to stories that is relied upon by both tellers and listeners. The reliance comes because the knowledge of story structure is imbedded in readers' and listeners' memories as a story schema. The knowledge helps "them understand, predict, recall and create stories" (Nelson-Herber and Johnston, 1989, 263). Understandably, some aspects of story are strongly affected by cultural influences. However, there seem to be regularities in other aspects of story that cut across cultures (Meyer and Rice 1984).

Researchers who study story or narrative have developed what they call story grammars (Colby and Cole 1973; Mandler and Johnson 1977; Rumelhart 1975; Stein and Glenn 1979; Thorndyke 1977).

"These grammars describe the hierarchy of rules which govern the occurrence of the different categories of story content . . ." (Meyer and Rice 1984). They provide a way to systematically identify relationships that exist among the various parts of a story. "Although they use different terminology, they all include character, setting, a problem one or more attempts to overcome the problem, a resolution, and an ending" (Nelson-Herber and Johnston 1989, 264).

Differences exist among researchers as to the elements that comprise a story, though "results of studies using story grammar tend to show that settings, beginnings, attempts, and outcomes are very central to people's ideas of what belongs in stories" (Fitzgerald 1989, 17).

For our purposes, we discuss setting separately and include the rest under the general category of plot.

Setting

Settings of stories establish the context(s) for the events that will take place. In various ways, authors let readers know when and where the story is taking place. Also in various ways, authors let readers know who the people are who play out the story and how they relate to one another. Depending on the complexity of the story, settings may be single or multiple; and the number of characters may be few or many, with interrelationships among them being simple or complicated.

Plot

Plots of stories are made up of episodes. Episodes spin a sequence of actions or events that usually have causal relationships to one another. Depending on the complexity of the story, there may be one episode with a causal sequence of events that is straightforward and linear or there may be multiple episodes with causal sequences of events that are complex and interactive. Whether interactive or linear, the sequence of events create a "causal chain." Drawing from Mandler and Johnson's (1977) work, Vacca and Vacca suggest the following elements in a causal chain:

1. *An initiating event: either an idea or an action that sets further events into motion.*
2. *An internal response: the protagonist's inner reaction to the initiating event, in which the protagonist sets a goal or attempts to solve a problem.*
3. *An attempt: the protagonist's efforts to achieve the goal or alleviate the problem. Several attempts, some failed, maybe evident in an episode.*
4. *An outcome: the success or failure of the protagonist's attempts.*
5. *A resolution: an action or state of affairs that evolves from the protagonist's success or failure to achieve the goal or alleviate the problem.*
6. *A reaction: an idea, an emotion, or a further event which expresses the protagonist's feelings about success or failure of goal attainment/problem resolution or which relates the events in the story to some broader set of concerns (Vacca and Vacca 1989, 192).*

Using this causal sequence, you can map out the structure of a story as you prepare to teach it. You also can show your students how to trace the story structure as they read and, thereby, enhance their comprehension and understanding of a story. Vacca and Vacca suggest the following possibilities:

For the teacher, establish key elements.

- *Setting (time, place, main character)*
- *Problem/goal (the problem or goal of the story are intertwined since most stories represent attempts of the character to achieve a goal based on a problem that has arisen)*
- *Major events (the set of attempts to achieve the goal)*
- *Resolution (the attainment of the goal and alleviation of the problem)*

For the students, prepare questions similar to the following that derive from the story structure:

Beginning-of-Story Questions

Setting: Where did the story take place? When did the story take place? Who is the main character? What is _____ _____ like?
Problem: What is _____'s problem? What did _____ need? Why is _____ in trouble?

Middle-of-Story Questions

Goal: What does _____ decide to do? What does _____ have to attempt to do?
Attempts/Outcome: What did _____ do about _____? What happened to _____? What will _____ do now?

End-of-Story Questions

Resolution: How did _____ solve the problem? How did _____ achieve the goal? What would you do to solve _____'s problem?
Reaction: How did _____ feel about the problem?
Why did _____ do _____? How did _____ feel at the end? (Vacca and Vacca 1989, 196)

An analysis of the plot and setting gives students a sense of when and where who did what to whom. With that information in mind, students are then able to deal with the why question. This question moves them into addressing the theme of the story.

Theme

The theme of a story addresses the concept, principle, or moral that is illustrated by the plot and setting of the story. Organizing ideas of lessons that are constructed around stories usually reflect the stories' themes (see Chapter 2). Thus, themes (as organizing ideas) provide the conceptual focus for stories and lessons that are structured around the story. It is important to guide students' response to the story so they are able to encounter and reflect upon the theme. This response is critical to the adequacy of students' study of literature. It is also critical to the refinement of their ability to analyze, synthesize, and apply what they read. Chapters 6 through 10 deal with various ways to provide students with this guidance.

Considerate Texts

A common complaint about content-area texts is that they are too hard. This complaint comes both from teachers ("This book is too difficult for my students.") and from students ("This book doesn't make sense!"). Teachers' complaints are intensified when suggestions are made that they teach their students how to read the texts.

What is it about textbooks that brings this response from teachers and students? What can be done with texts to make them less difficult to read? Are textbooks really necessary for instruction in content areas? If readable texts are necessary for content-area instruction, are they sufficient in and of themselves for developing students' understanding of the concepts contained therein?

When required texts are used for independent reading rather than instructional reading, they are inevitably "too hard." Independent reading of texts requires a reader to have a well-grounded prior knowledge of relevant concepts as well as knowledge of the technical vocabulary being used in the text. Independent reading also requires an ability to develop concepts out of the information presented in the text and to apply those concepts in ways appropriate to the purposes for reading. Most students enrolled in your courses cannot, nor should they be expected to, read their texts independently. Were they able to, they would already know so much about your course that you would need to question the appropriateness of their being enrolled in your course in the first place.

Difficulty levels of texts are reduced when the texts are used instructionally. When using texts instructionally, teachers develop students' relevant prior knowledge to serve as a context for what is to be read. They present and teach technical vocabulary used in the passages to be read. They guide students' actual reading to support their comprehension of the text and their application of concepts derived from their reading.

Texts are made less difficult when they are written to be considerate of their readers (Anderson and Armbruster 1984). Considerate texts are well organized, presenting their information and arguments with sufficient headings, subheadings, graphs, charts, pictures, and other appropriate adjunct aids to elucidate, illustrate, and support an understanding of the content of the text. Moreover, the content of considerate texts is well structured. That is, information is presented in a logical and well-ordered manner. Relationships between main ideas and subordinate information are clear. Concepts are fully developed rather than just mentioned. Diversions and the inclusion of extraneous information are omitted or kept to a bare minimum. New terminology is presented through contexts that support readers' acquisition of definitions and meanings of the words. The cohesion of the text is sufficiently strong that pronominal antecedents are clear, not leaving readers guessing as to who or what the *it* or *them* or *they* might be.

But even when you have a considerate text to work with, it is important to provide students with instruction that shows them how to read the text. Part of the purpose of that instruction is to support students as they read so they will successfully develop an understanding of both course content and relevant reading and reasoning processes. In other words, even basic texts in content-areas that are considerate of their readers should be used for instructional reading, not for independent reading.

Unfortunately, the probability of your students' having what could be called a considerate text is quite minimal (Anderson and Armbruster 1984). Many content-area texts are inconsiderate and poorly written. Some authors, in an attempt to make their texts easier, have "dumbed them down." That is, they have shortened sentences, abbreviated content, omitted more difficult technical language, and added graphic aids. Instead of making the texts easier, these adjustments make the texts more difficult (Pearson 1984). Short sentences often limit or omit clarifying linkages in explanations, requiring more inferencing by the reader than would be required with longer sentences. Abbreviation of content omits bridges between and among concepts and requires more inferencing. Omission of technical vocabulary limits readers' capabilities for explaining and/or understanding important concepts.

Substantial evidence suggests that content-area teachers often use their own explanations of course content as a substitute for the text (Hinchman 1987; MacGinitie and MacGinitie 1986). Teachers doubt their students' ability to read their texts with the level of understanding sufficient for being successful in the course. Teachers feel pressured to get their students "through the content" of the course in the prescribed period of time. The most efficient course of action for them, given the limitations of students and texts, is to explain the course content in lecture-type format and avoid reading-related problems by not assigning readings from the text. While expedient in the short term, it is detrimental to students in the long term. As students pass through the grades under the rule of expediency, they do not have the opportunity to improve their reading and reasoning proficiencies. In addition, the skills that they do have will deteriorate over time for lack of use (MacGinitie and MacGinitie 1986). Students remain dependent on teachers for the presentation of course content and do not develop the skills by which they eventually can acquire new knowledge independently.

How much better it is for students when their teachers take time to show them how to read their required texts, even when those texts are inconsiderate of the students. Such texts can be made usable when they are used instructionally. Section III of this book focuses on instructional strategies that enable your students to read texts in your course.

Assessment of Texts

As a content-area teacher, you can judge the considerateness of the text you use in your courses. The visible, supporting structures are clearly discernable. The presence of cohesion and coherence is less easily judged, requiring a close reading of the text; but it is discernable nevertheless.

Readability Formulas

Additional information about the difficulty level of your texts can be obtained through the use of readability formulas. Researchers originally developed readability formulas to have some objective means of estimating the level of difficulty of reading materials used in their experimental studies of reading. In their formulas they incorporated such factors as sentence length and complexity, number of syllables or the presence of certain frequently used words, and the like. They produced rough indicators of how readable various texts are to average readers at various grade levels. However, the formulas do have limitations (Nelson 1975; Klare 1974–75).

Readability formulas do not generally consider such variables as levels of abstraction, conceptual density and complexity, or variability of meanings within the general, technical, and scientific vocabulary. Furthermore, readability generally use averages to indicate reading difficulty within text materials. They draw samples across the text and average the results in a single estimate for the total text. Thus, the readability estimate does not reveal the variance in levels of difficulty often encountered as one progresses through a content-area text; and it is this variability that causes problems for less accomplished readers, not the averages (Estes and Vaughan 1978). Finally, readability formulas do not measure interest, motivation, language competence or experiential background of readers, particularly as these factors relate to the conceptual focus of the text under consideration (Nelson 1975).

Recognizing the limitations of readability formulas, you can use them as general indicators of text difficulty. The Fry Readability Formula is widely used and illustrates the purpose, use and value of such scales. Based on a graph, Fry's formula involves plotting the results of several calculations applied to a targeted text.

Fry suggests the following steps in the use of his formula:

1. Randomly select three 100-word passages from near the beginning, middle, and end of the book. Do not count numbers. Do count proper nouns.

Graph for Estimating Readability—Extended

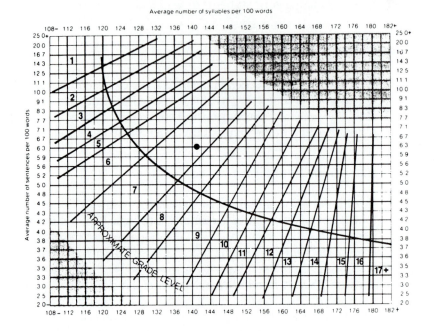

Average number of syllables per 100 words

2. Count the total number of sentences in each 100-word passage (estimating to the nearest tenth of a sentence). Average these three numbers.

3. Count the total number of syllables in each 100-word sample. There is a syllable for each vowel sound. For example: cat (1), blackbird (2), continental (4). Do not be fooled by word size. For example, *polio* has three syllables; *through* has one. Endings such as *-y*, *-ed*, *el*, and *-le* usually make a syllable. For example, the *-dy* in *ready* is the second syllable, the *-ed* in *complicated* is the fourth syllable. (2). To simplify the counting, Fry suggests that in multisyllabic words you place a mark above each syllable starting with the second syllable. Count all the marks and add 100. Adding 100 covers all of the single-syllable words plus the first syllable in the multisyllabic words in the 100-word sample.

4. On a graph, plot the average number of sentences per 100 words and then the average number of syllables per 100 words.

5. From the graph read the approximate grade level for your book or selection, using the lines that lie perpendicularly to the curved line.

6. Should you find a wide range of variability among your original three samples, select and process additional sample to stabilize your averages.

Three 100-word excerpts drawn from a text are given in Practice 3-1. Using the the first five steps listed above, calculate the reading level for this

PRACTICE 3-1

Selected Passages

Excerpt One

Agricultural Revolution. The job of gathering berries and plants was usually left to the women. They used sticks to dig up the earth in search of edible plants. However, they still had to look for their vegetables. A great moment came when it was learned that the shoot of an edible plant could be planted and would then grow into edible food. What did this mean? Man could now grow his own food in what was really a kind of vegetable garden. He could depend on this garden to give him a continual supply of some of his food. (p. 28)

Excerpt Two

Commerce and Industry. Chicago's position on the Great Lakes and its rail-roads have made it important in trade and industry. As we have seen, foodstuffs were important in early trade. Later, meat packing and wood products became important. Chicago's trade has consisted, to some extent, of taking raw materials and processing them into finished goods to be sold throughout the country, and even to other nations.

Today, Chicago has many industries and manufactures numerous products. Most important among these products are various metals, railroad equipment, and chemicals. Meat packing and food production are still important industries in Chicago. (p. 143)

Excerpt Three

New York City, however, proved to be a staunch supporter of the Union during the Civil War. It contributed about 300 million dollars to the war effort, and over eighty thousand men from New York City served in the Union Army. But as the war progressed, the federal government found it necessary to introduce the draft system in order to get a sufficient number of soldiers. This was the first time in America's history that the draft was used and, in July, 1863, anti-draft riots broke out in New York City. During the riots many buildings were burned and several hundred people were killed or wounded. (pp. 62–63)

Source: Goldberg, D. (1969) *Challenges in our Changing Urban Society.* (River Forest, IL, Laidlaw Brotheres, Publishers), pp. 28, 143.

Goldberg, D. (1969) *New York State and New York City.* (River Forest, IL, Laidlaw Brotheres, Publishers) pp. 62, 63.

text according to the Fry formula. Look in Appendix A to compare your answer to our calculation.

The reading level derived from the Fry formula is an estimate of the level of the reading performance a person must have in order to comprehend the targeted material at 50 percent to 75 percent accuracy. This, of course, is a rather loose criterion and is based on the assumption that the text is being read independently. That is, the reader is neither being prepared to read the text nor being instructed in how to read it. It is always important to remember that "instruction, not a readability formula, [is] the key to comprehension of subject matter material." (Nelson-Herber 1978, p. 624).

Other Readability Estimates

Directly involving readers in estimates of text difficulty can take two forms: (1) a cloze test and; (2) a content-reading inventory. Both estimates involve having readers actually read excerpts from the target text. The combination of these two readability estimates provides you with useful information about how well your students handle the text you use for your course.

Cloze Test

The reading selection in Practice 3-2 has every fifth word deleted. Read the selection and fill in the missing words. The complete text appears at the end of this chapter. Words that were deleted are underlined in the complete text.

What you have just experienced is a cloze test, a measure of how well you can read from a text entitled *Private Pilot Manual.* You can check your answers at the end of this chapter. According to researchers who have worked with this kind of test, if you scored 60 percent or higher (that is, if you chose the correct words for 60 percent or more of the blanks), the text is on your independent reading level. If you scored between 40 percent and 60 percent, the text is on your instructional reading level. If you scored below 40 percent, the text is on your frustration level. Let's talk about this test. its origins, its construction, its administration, its results.

Wilson Taylor created this test format in 1953, conceptualizing it as a way of determining how well students can read specific text material. To develop the test, he drew on the psychological phenomenon of closure, the need to close out something that is incomplete or to supply elements that are missing. He also drew on the principles of cohesion and coherence, relying on knowledge of natural language to determine the missing linguistic elements. Through his studies, Taylor determined that deleting every fifth word provides an appropriate test of a reader's ability to handle that material. There is sufficient text remaining after the deletions to provide a context for inferring appropriate words to fill in the blanks. There is sufficient text removed to require readers to draw on their previous knowledge of the

PRACTICE 3-2

Changing Angle of Attack

You have direct control over angle of attack. During flight at normal _____ speeds, if you increase _____ angle of attack, you _____ lift. Anytime you move _____ control column fore or _____ during flight, you change _____ angle of attack. At _____ same time, you are _____ the coefficient of lift. _____ **coefficient of lift** (CL) _____ a way to measure _____ as it relates to _____ of attack. CL is _____ by wind tunnel tests _____ is based on airfoil _____ and angle of attack. _____ airplane has an angle _____ attack where maximum lift _____.

A **stall** is caused _____ the separation of airflow _____ the wing's upper surface. _____ results in a rapid _____ in lift. For a _____ airplane, a stall always _____ at the same angle, _____ of airspeed, flight attitude, _____ weight. Since training airplanes _____ do not have an _____ of attack indicator, the _____ point to remember is _____ you can stall an _____ at any airspeed, in _____ flight attitude, or at _____ weight.

Stall characteristics vary _____ different airplanes. In most _____ airplanes, the onset of _____ stall from a level _____ attitude is gradual. The _____ indications may be provided _____ a stall warning device _____ a slight buffeting of _____ airplane.

All you have _____ do to recover from _____ stall is to restore _____ smooth airflow. The only _____ to do this is _____ decrease the angle of _____ to a point below _____ critical angle.

Although the _____ or critical angle of _____ does not vary with _____, the stalling speed does. _____ increases slightly as the _____ of the airplane increases _____ decreases as weight decreases. _____ means you need slightly _____ airspeed to stay above _____ stalling speed in a _____ loaded airplane. If you want to fly an airplane at a given weight, there are many combinations of airspeed and angle of attack which will produce the required amount of lift.

conceptual focus of the text, on their innate understanding of linguistic constructions and redundancies, and on their ability to read between the lines and make intelligent guesses about missing information and ideas. To strengthen the context of the test, both the first and the last full sentences of the target selection are left intact.

The test is easily administered, as you have already experienced. However, if your students are unfamiliar with the format of the test (as you may have been), you should provide an opportunity to practice on one or more selections before giving them the target passages.

Estes and Vaughan suggest the following steps as appropriate for administering a cloze test:

1. *Provide directions which might read: "You are to fill in the blanks in the following selection with the word that has been left out. Try to supply the exact word the author used. Only one word has been deleted from each blank. You will have as much time as necessary to complete this exercise."*
2. *If the students are unfamiliar with the task, show them some examples prior to handing out the test.*
3. *The students are not to use any books or materials when completing the test.*
4. *Let students know that they should try to use context clues to determine what word fits each blank.*
5. *Allow them as much time as necessary to complete the test (Estes and Vaughan 1978).*

The test is also easily scored. Several researchers have developed substantial data showing that the most valid scoring of the cloze test is exact word replacement (Ruddell 1964; Bormouth 1966; Miller and Coleman 1967). Another way of saying this is that you do not allow any substitutions for the word that has been replaced (except for misspellings if there is an obvious intention to replace the deleted word). The number of correct replacements is divided by the total number of deletions, and the percentage score for the test is derived. Now that you have experienced taking a cloze test and have come to understand its purpose and function, you should create a cloze test of your own for your own students.

Estes and Vaughan suggest the following steps:

1. *Select a reading passage that your students have not yet read. It should be approximately 300 words in length.*
2. *Type the first sentence intact. Starting with the fifth word in the second sentence, delete every fifth word until you have fifty deletions. Replace each deletion with an underlined blank fifteen spaces long.*
3. *Finish the sentence in which the fiftieth deletion occurs. Type one more sentence intact (Estes and Vaughan 1978).*

Content-reading Inventory

A straightforward way to determine whether the difficulty level of a text seems appropriate for your students is to have them read from it. Among professionals in reading instruction, this procedure is called an informal reading inventory and it has been used for many decades. More recently, and as applied to reading in content areas, it has been called a content-reading inventory.

The content-reading inventory can be as simple or as complex as you want it to be. Estes and Vaughan suggest the following steps in constructing a simple content-reading inventory:

1. *Select a passage from the material that the students have not previously read. Choose a length that is complete in itself and will approximate the length that they might be expected to read as an assignment.*
2. *Ask the students to read it.*
3. *Administer a ten-question test based on:*

   a. *Main idea*
   b. *Factual information*
   c. *Inferences*
   d. *Vocabulary*

4. *Go over the text with them. Discuss the answers and determine through your intuition and their opinions how well they will be able to learn from this material (Estes and Vaughan 1978).*

You have to set your own criteria for judging the adequacy of your students' responses. You will need to consider the specific level of performance you require for that particular material as well as the general level of performance you require for any material your students read for your course. You may need to give different weight to the categories of questions according to how you value the kinds of responses they elicit. If you value acquisition of information highly, you may wish to give more weight to factual questions. If you value synthesis and conceptual development, you may wish to give more weight to the main idea or the inferencing questions. Your expected outcomes from students' reading of assigned texts should produce the criteria for judging their response to your informal inventory.

Practice 3-3 on pages 76–78 contains an example of a content-reading inventory. It was constructed for a text used in flight schools for pilot training. This gives you opportunity to have first-hand experience with a content-reading inventory written on your reading level. Possible answers are listed in Appendix A.

Ubiquity and Utility of Texts

Content-area texts are permanent fixtures in the education process. A significant portion of education budgets is expended texts. How, or even whether, they are used by students depends largely on the teacher.

Some teachers doubt their students' ability to fully comprehend the text. Consequently, they substitute their own explanations of the content for students' reading of the text. Realizing this fact, students rarely read the text.

PRACTICE 3-3 ━━━━━━━━━━━━━━━━━━━━━━━━━━━━━━━━━━

Content-Reading Inventory: Predicting Performance

Directions: Answer the following questions after you read the selection from the text entitled "Predicting Performance." You may refer to the reading selection as you respond to the questions. Make your answers as complete as possible. Write them out on a separate piece of paper.

1. What performance is discussed in this reading selection?
2. What factors determine whether an airplane is flying at its maximum level flight speed?
3. The acronym *FAR* appears in the third paragraph of the reading selection, but without its definition. What do you think the initials might stand for, and why?
4. What is the difference between service ceiling and absolute ceiling for an airplane?
5. What is the difference between maximum endurance speed and maximum range speed?
6. If a pilot has to clear obstacles at the end of the runway on takeoff, should he or she use the best angle-of-climb airspeed or the best rate-of-climb airspeed? Why?
7. Which works better when a plane is at absolute ceiling, best angle-of-climb airspeed or best rate-of-climb airspeed? Why?
8. If a pilot is low on fuel and over territory unsuitable for landing, should he or she be concerned more about maximum endurance speed or maximum range speed? Why?
9. How do the factors of thrust and drag contribute to the flight of an airplane?
10. What knowledge comes from being able to predict the performance of an airplane?

Text for Predicting Performance

Your ability to predict the performance of an airplane is extremely important. It allows you to determine how much runway you need for takeoff, if you can safely clear obstacles in the departure path, how long it will take you to reach a destination, how much fuel is required, and how much runway you'll need for landing.

In addition to predicting performance, you must also observe the airplane's **operating limitations**. These limits establish the boundaries within which the airplane must be flown. They are often referred to as the flight or performance envelope. Operating within the envelope is safe, while operating outside the envelope may cause structural damage or even failure. If you understand an airplane's operating limitations, you are unlikely to fly outside its performance envelope.

(continued)

PRACTICE 3-3 Continued ━━━━━━━━━━━━━━━━━━━━━━━━━━━━

According to FARs, operating limitations may be found in the approved airplane flight manual; approved manual materials, markings, and placards; or an combination of these. For most light airplanes manufactured in the U.S. after March 1, 1979, the pilot's operating handbook is the approved flight manual, and a page in the front of the handbook will contain a statement to that effect. This section emphasizes the performance data and limitations of typical training airplanes. Before you operate any airplane, be sure you consult the pilot's operating handbook or other approved documents for the specific operating limitations, systems information, and performance figures that apply to that airplane.

Performance Speeds

In determining performance speeds, airplane manufacturers must consider many factors. To compute maximum level flight speed, engine power is compared against total drag. For climbs, excess power and thrust are the important factors; for range and endurance, speeds that result in minimum drag or require minimum power are important.

Maximum Level Flight Speed

In level flight, the maximum speed of the airplane is limited by the amount of power produced by the engine and the total drag generated by the airplane. If thrust exceeds total drag when you apply full power, the airplane accelerates. This continues until the force of total drag equals the force of thrust. At this point, the airplane is flying at its maximum level flight speed.

Climb Speeds

The pilot's operating handbook for the airplane you're flying will list airspeeds for a variety of climbing flight conditions. Two of the most important are the **best angle-of-climb airspeed** (Vx) and the **best rate-of-climb airspeed** (Vy).

The best angle-of-climb airspeed normally used immediately after takeoff for obstacle clearance. Because of the increased pitch attitude at Vx, your forward visibility is limited. If you happen to lift off prematurely during takeoff, you should accelerate the airplane while you are still in ground effect to at least the best angle-of-climb airspeed before attempting to climb. This technique is often used by pilots when taking off from soft fields.

Normally, you use Vy after you have cleared all obstacles during departure. In addition, you may use a cruise climb after traffic pattern departure when climbing to cruising altitude. You can also use it during the cruise

(continued)

PRACTICE 3-3 Continued ━━━━━━━━━━━━━━━━━━━━━━━━━━━━━━━━

portion of a flight to climb to a higher cruising altitude. Normally, the cruise-climb speed is higher than Vx or Vy, and the rate of climb is slower. The advantages of higher indicated climb speed are better engine cooling and improved forward visibility.

Before an airplane can climb, it must have a reserve of power or thrust. At a given speed, more power is required for a sustained climb than for unaccelerated level flight. Since propeller-driven airplanes lose power and thrust with increasing altitude, both the best angle-of-climb and best rate-of-climb speeds change as you climb. When the airplane is unable to climb any further, it will have reached its **absolute ceiling**. Another important altitude, known as the **service ceiling**, refers to the altitude where a single-engine airplane is able to maintain a maximum climb of only 100 feet per minute. This altitude is more commonly used than absolute ceiling, since it represents the airplane's practical ceiling.

As altitude increases, the speed for best angle-of-climb increases, and the speed for best rate-of-climb decreases. The point at which these two speeds meet is the absolute ceiling of the airplane.

Cruising Speeds

In selecting your cruising speed, you usually want to cover the distance to be traveled in the shortest period of time. However, just as an airplane can only fly so fast, it can only go so far and stay up only so long before it runs out of fuel. When range or endurance are important factors, you must select the proper speed for the flight.

Maximum endurance speed is the speed which allows the airplane to remain aloft while using the least amount of power necessary to sustain level flight. The minimum power setting provides the lowest rate of fuel consumption. In contrast, the **maximum range speed** provides the greatest distance for a given amount of fuel. Your can think of it as getting the most miles per gallon out of the airplane. To determine this speed, you must consider the speed and rate of fuel consumption for any given power setting. The setting which yields the greatest distance traveled per gallon of fuel burned is the power setting which provides maximum range speed. As you may recall from the discussion of drag in Chapter 1, this speed produces the minimum total drag. It is where the lift-to-drag ratio is the greatest, and it is referred to as L/D max.

━━━

It does not seem practical to them to make the effort to read what is going to be explained fully anyway. Earlier in this chapter, this phenomenon and its consequences were explored.

In contrast, texts can be used as tools for learning both content and process. Students can be guided in their reading of texts so they learn both the imbedded concepts and the relevant reading, writing, and reasoning processes. Texts are natural vehicles for instruction that integrates the teaching of reading, writing, and reasoning with the teaching of course content. Chapter 5 sets a framework for this instruction. Section III explains how to provide this instruction.

Cautions about Texts

Two important cautions about texts need to be kept in mind:

1. Content-area texts are inherently complex resources, and little can be done to reduce their complexity.
2. The meaning of texts does not reside in the text itself but in the mind of the reader.

One well-intentioned person seriously suggested that the way to make content-area texts easier to read was "to get rid of all those difficult words!" Without the technical vocabulary used in a subject area, a text would have little substance.

Complexity and difficulty are endemic to resources used in content-area classes. As discussed in this chapter, there are ways to write complex texts that are considerate of the reader. However, even considerate texts are complex. Many ways are available to teachers for heightening students' awareness of graphic and structural aids that enable readers to deal with complex texts more effectively, but these aids do not reduce the complexity. One can apply readability formulas to texts to determine their relative difficulty level, but these formulas do not change the level of difficulty or degree of complexity of the resources to which they are applied. A difficult and complex text remains so even after reading formulas have been applied.

It is helpful to acknowledge the appropriateness of the complexity of content-area texts. Such an acknowledgement eliminates a fruitless search for texts that are both uncomplicated and useful repositories of appropriate, content-related concepts. Such an acknowledgement leads one inexorably to considerations of ways to support students' use of available texts, complex though they may be.

The second caution about texts has to do with their meaning. It is important to remember that texts take on meaning as readers give them meaning. As noted, meaning resides in the minds of the readers, not in the text itself.

The belief that meaning resides in texts can lead to futile and frustrating uses of them. If a text is distributed under this belief, it is hoped that students will read it, acquire its meaning, and develop an understanding of the relevant course. This hope is not realized because what students bring to the text is what determines its meaning. If students are unprepared for the reading and bring little or nothing to the text, they will derive little meaning from the text. If teachers do not show students how to make connections between what they already know (what they bring to the text) and what is presented in the text, they will derive little meaning from the text.

In contrast, careful preparation of students for their reading of texts raises the probability that they will derive meaning and understanding from the experience. Likewise, careful guidance of students as they read the text will support their comprehension and reasoning about the information, enable them to connect prior knowledge with new knowledge, and produce an understanding of the content presented in the text. Subsequent chapters in this book explore instructional conditions and instructional strategies that make possible this productive use of texts.

Summary

As with workers in any field, students need to develop proficiency in the use of their tools. Their job is learning, and one of their major tools is the text. This chapter presents ways to determine how well the tool fits students' needs and proficiencies. The chapter also presents ways to develop and refine students' understandings of how the tool works.

Students do not become independent learners independently. They have to be shown how. Merely assigning reading from the text is not showing how. Acquainting students with both the organization and structure of their texts is an important first step.

REACTIONS

Journal Entries and Discussion

Write a brief essay on the comparative impact on students' academic success of teachers' explanation of text versus students' reading from text. Ask a colleague for feedback on the ideas you present with a view toward refining their presentation. If you wish, repeat the request for feedback for subsequent drafts. Also if you wish, edit the piece carefully and then submit it for publication to a place of your choice.

Review the generalizations you drew from your list of features and factors related to instructional resources. What additions or deletions are you making after having read this chapter? Why?

Analysis and Discussion

Now that you have completed this chapter. consider the statements shown below. Check the numbered lines for statements you believe reflect the point of view of the authors. Circle the numbers of statements with which you agree. In writing, explore reasons for differences on any statements between your point of view and what you perceive to be the point of view of the authors. Please share and discuss your writing with colleagues who also are reading this book.

_____ 1. The organization of a text provides visible clues to the arrangement and presentation of the information contained therein.

_____ 2. The structure of a text provides invisible clues to the type arrangement and presentation of the information contained therein.

_____ 3. Organizational patterns are more characteristic of expository text than of narrative text.

_____ 4. For a given piece of exposition to be well written, it should follow a single organizational pattern rather than incorporating a combination of patterns.

_____ 5. A teacher who did not want to guide his or her students' reading of exposition in their social studies text because such action "would ruin the story" didn't understand the function of exposition.

_____ 6. Considerate texts may be difficult for students to read but may be so for the right reasons.

_____ 7. Inconsiderate texts may be easy for students to read but may be so for the wrong reasons.

_____ 8. Teachers who know their students and texts probably can assess the appropriateness of their texts as well as can cloze tests or informal reading inventories can.

Complete Text for Changing Angle of Attack—Practice 3-2

You have direct control over angle of attack. During flight at normal operating speeds, if you increase the angle of attack, you increase lift. Anytime you move the control column fore or aft during flight, you change the angle of attack. At the same time, you are changing the coefficient of lift. The **coefficient of lift** (CL) is a way to measure lift as it relates to angle of attack. CL is determined by wind tunnel tests and is based on airfoil design and angle of attack. Every airplane has an angle of attack where maximum lift occurs.

A **stall** is caused by the separation of airflow from the wing's upper surface. This results in a rapid decrease in lift. For a given airplane, a stall always occurs at the same angle, regardless of airspeed, flight attitude, or weight. Since training airplanes normally do not have an angle of attack

(continued)

PRACTICE 3-2 Continued ———————————————————

indicator, the important point to remember is that you can stall an airplane at any airspeed, in any flight attitude, or at any weight.

Stall characteristics vary with different airplanes. In most training airplanes, the onset of a stall from a level flight attitude is gradual. The first indications may be provided by a stall warning device or a slight buffeting of the airplane.

All you have to do to recover from a stall is to restore the smooth airflow. The only way to do this is to decrease the angle of attack to a point below the critical angle.

Although the stalling or critical angle of attack does not vary with weight, the stalling speed does. It increases slightly as the weight of the airplane increases and decreases as weight decreases. This means you need slightly more airspeed to stay above the stalling speed in a heavily loaded airplane. If you want to fly an airplane at a given weight, there are many combinations of airspeed and angle of attack which will produce the required amount of lift.

Source: *Private Pilot Manual* (Englewood, CO: Jeppesen Sanderson, Inc., 1988), 1-16–1-18

PRACTICE 3-4 ——————————————————————————

Complete Text for Ignorance, Ignorantly Judged

The past few years have seen a dirge of statistics testifying to the depth of ignorance of Americans. There seems to be no end to what we do not know, be it history, geography, but especially science. Is that really the case?

In one survey, 75 percent of U.S. respondents believe antibiotics are effective against viruses. In another, one of six respondents could not identify DNA. Were such a question posed, I'm certain that Walt Whitman would just as likely be identified as a left fielder for the old Brooklyn Dodgers as a poet.

A recent survey by the International Association for the Evaluation of Educational Achievement compared ninth grade general science students in 16 countries. Americans ranked next to the bottom, outscoring only students from Hong King. Advanced chemistry pupils (grade 12) in the U.S. finished 12th of 14, ahead of Canada and Finland, and far behind England, Singapore, Japan, Hungary, Australia, and Poland.

Surveys that plumb the depth of our ignorance and that of our students are methodologically suspect. More importantly, the interpretation of these statistics in isolation is questionable. One needs an accompanying discussion of the social, cultural and economic environment in which these supposedly ignorant individuals function as members of a productive society.

(continued)

PRACTICE 3-4 Continued

The methodology used in these surveys typically compares American high school students with their foreign counterparts. This fails to take into account the continued elitism of foreign educational systems. Although European children are no longer shunted out of a university-bound track at age 11 on the basis of a single examination, the educational pyramid narrows much more steeply everywhere else.

The study that compares a 12th grade student in Finland or Hong Kong with one in the U.S. is not satisfactory: We have many more people in our educational pipeline. Yet this study, as well as similar "statistics of ignorance," are superficially used as certain indicators of the decline, first educational, then economic and technological, of our country. The Japanese are far ahead, the South Koreans and Taiwanese not far behind. As a nation, we're doomed.

It's not so simple. Most will agree America was clearly a leader, not only in wealth and power, but in science and the arts from 1945 to 1969. Were there a clear, causal tie between level of education, knowledge and economic success of a country, then there should have been a recorded superiority of American youth in the years preceding that period. I've never seen a shred of evidence for that and suspect that surveys of our state of knowledge would have shown us years behind Europe.

It is impossible to make a connection between statistics of ignorance and past or future status of a country without consideration of society as a whole. One has to look at the economic system, the history of the country, patterns of immigration and the psychological forces at play.

Let's look at the countries ranked ahead of the U.S. in the survey. Perhaps Hungarian and Polish students know more, but the tragedy is what the Soviets' ineffective and social and economic system does (or did) to them.

England has traditionally had a first-class educational system, but one that is elitist. Furthermore, the superior English system has not stemmed the economic decline of this former colonial power. And as for Japan, I doubt if we'd want to subject our children to the psychological pressures, the exam fever and the tension of Japanese schools.

In America, if you are not as motivated toward learning as your peers in high school, you can still get a diploma. After working for a while, there are no barriers to studying at a local community college. The strength of our system is the multitude of paths to an education.

The ways to national economic and political power are manifold. A country certainly requires a basic level of scientific and technological literacy and fundamental skills on the part of its population. But after that the litical system needs to provide an open, mobile society, a superstructure of higher education and industry into which people can move, a society which encourages hard work and creativity. With all our faults, this is what we have.

(continued)

PRACTICE 3-4 Continued

Moreover, we have managed to build such a system with a heterogeneous population, with immigrants from hundreds of cultures, from incredibly divergent family structures and work ethics. Compare this to the homogeneous societies of, say, Norway or Japan.

Yes, we've missed out in part on fairness. And, yes, we've got a long way to go on access to education for some segments of our population. And, yes, we have this terrible, wide range of incomes—real poverty coexisting with immense wealth. But we've done pretty well.

What concerns me about scientific, or humanistic, illiteracy is the barrier it poses to rational democratic governance. Democracy occasionally gives in to technocracy—a reliance on experts on matters such as genetic engineering, nuclear waste disposal or the cost of medical care. That is fine, but the people must be able to vote intelligently on these issues. The less we know as a nation, the more must rely on experts and the more likely we are to be misled by demagogues. We must know more.

Source: Roald Hortman (1981 Nobel Prize in Chemistry) *New York Times*, September 14, 1989.

PRACTICE 3-5

Complete Text for Passing Down Murphy's Law

It wasn't my fault that the door of my father's new 1967 Mercedes caught fire.

It wouldn't have happened, I told my father, if some jerk hadn't turned left right in front of me, causing me to swerve violently around him and accidentally drop my cigarette into the pocket on the door.

It wouldn't have happened if Dad himself had not used that very same pocket to store a pack of matches.

"It wouldn't have happened if you hadn't been driving my car," said Dad. He had a point, I suppose. After all, he had told me before he left town for a few days that I was not, under any circumstances, to drive his car.

He had a point, I suppose. After all, he had told me before he left town for a few days that I was not, under any circumstances, to drive his car.

Bizarre as it was, however, I should have expected something like that would happen.

Somehow, if the needle came off my father's stereo or one of the speakers blew out or a power tool burned up, it usually happened while I was using it without permission or against direct orders not to.

Although he was not otherwise superstitious, my father maintained that some corollary to Murphy's Law dictated that a mysterious force

(continued)

PRACTICE 3-5 Continued

caused such things to happen when we were doing things we were not supposed to do.

In the years since, however, I have come to agree with Dad that it is an immutable law of nature, or perhaps a self-fulfilling prophecy. Either way, it made me think twice and twice again about doing something I knew was wrong.

What's more, it has carried on to a new generation, much to my daughter's chagrin.

At 13, Laura suddenly has friends who have friends or brothers or sisters with driver's licenses. So I thought it was time to set rules and regulations about with whom she could or could not accept a ride.

As an example of someone with whom she was not to ride, I specifically named one boy, a friend of a friend. Laura assured me he was a nice fellow and a good driver. But I didn't know him so his car was off-limits.

Two nights later, when Laura was late coming home from a friend's house, I went after her and discovered the reason she was late was that she had accepted a ride home form the very boy with whom I had expressly told her not to ride.

And they had run out of gas after driving only a mile.

After we had dealt with her transgression, I passed along the corollary to Murphy's Law that had caused me so much frustration so many years ago.

Just like her father, of course, she scoffed at my warning. She said she didn't believe a word of it.

But if there is any justice at all, she will.

Source: Ray Recchio "Passing Down Murphy's Law," *Syracuse Herald American*, August 27, 1989.

PRACTICE 3-6

Complete Text for The Blunderers of June

In one of the most moving elegies in the English language, the poet Thomas Gray speaks of a summer night where "all the air a solemn stillness holds, save where the beetle wheels his droning flight." Another poet, William Collins, was moved by the same sentiments to write, "Now air is hushed save where the beetle winds his small but sullen horn." Both lines capture the essence of June—warm, still evenings, serenity, and gentle lulling song.

What a contrast to the advent of spring when the shrill piping of peepers proclaims the end of winter while the fanfare of spring birds and the drumming of April showers herald the bursting buds of May flowers. Surely

(continued)

the serenity of the first month of summer merits a harbinger of refinement and delicacy. Instead, June is proclaimed by boisterous, rowdy blunders that bang on the screens, thump at the doors, and whirl around porch lights as though intoxicated by the import of their message. these crude, hardheaded heralds, so out of tune with the character of this gentle month, have been summoned from a long winter sleep in the soil by the warm nights of late May and early June. They answer to many names: May beetle, June bug, cockchafer, dor beetle. It is they that drive through the gloaming in humming flight, content to "wind their small but sullen horns" until the lights in our houses draw them hypnotically from the fields. Then, too aerodynamically unstable to execute sharp turns, they crash into whatever lies ahead, be it foliage or building. Thus is June announced and summer begun.

A June bug begins life as an egg in the soil, having been placed there by its mother just before her death. During the first summer of life, until the first frost, the small grub hatched from that egg chews on fine rootlets just beneath the surface of the ground. As winter approaches and the land gives up its heat, the grub burrows ever deeper until it lies safely below the frost line. Not until spring does it crawl back to the thick nutritive mat of roots. Here it passes the entire second summer in total darkness, grazing so effectively that large populations of grubs can kill entire pastures, fields, lawns, and gardens.

For three years each generation lives out its subterranean existence. At the end of the third summer the grubs transform into beetles. Winter may symbolize old age for us, but for June bugs it signals the beginning of adult life.

As the end of May of the new year approaches, those beetles that have not been rooted out of the soil by skunks and crows stir in their galleries. On the first warm, still night they swarm forth into the dusk. By early June the emergence has reached its peak. Throughout the night ravenous hordes gorge on the succulent foliage of leafy trees. With dawn they hasten back to the soil like the spirits of the dead, to be called forth by the next twilight.

As long as the weather is warm, they make their nightly appearance, knocking at the doors, summoning us out to enjoy the night. By Midsummer Night, life, hardly begun, is nearly ended. The grubs have labored in the soil for three years to live as adults for a single June. In equivalent human terms it is as though a person spent a childhood of 68 years in order to enjoy as an adult a mere two summers. Perhaps it is worth it.

Source: Vincent G. Dethier. "The Blunders of June." *Yankee*, June 1985, p. 160

PRACTICE 3-7 ────────────────────────────────

Complete Text for Graphic Organizers

Graphic organizers can be used following the reading of the assigned passage for reinforcement and review. The following procedures for this postreading are suggested:

1. Analyze the vocabulary of the reading/learning task and list all the terms you feel are necessary for the students to understand.
2. Arrange (rearrange) the list of words into a schema or diagram which depicts key relationships among the terms.
3. Add to the schema terms you believe are understood by the students to clarify relationships between the learning task and the course (or discipline) as a whole.
4. Type each of the words included in your structured overview on a ditto master.
5. Following the students' reading of the passage or the material to be learned, introduce the idea behind the graphic organizer to the class with an example at the blackboard.
6. Place the students in groups of two or three and distribute the list of terms and a packet of 3" × 5" index cards to each group.
7. As the students work, circulate about the room to provide assistance.
8. Terminate the activity and provide feedback.

──

4

Contexts

Organizing idea: Expectations influence outcomes.

Reflections

Before reading this chapter, please record in your journal your responses to the following tasks. If possible, share your writing with other individuals who are also reading this book.

1. Make a list of personal qualities that contribute to teachers' instructional environments. Group items in your list that seem to fit together, and label the groups. With your colleagues, compare the categories you developed and discuss the qualities listed therein. Develop a group essay on the topic.

2. Make a list of roles that teachers play in creating an instructional environment that is cooperative and supportive. Group items in your list that seem to fit together, and label the groups. With your colleagues, compare the categories you developed and discuss the roles listed therein.

3. Make a list of roles that students play in contributing to a learning environment that is cooperative and supportive. Group items in your list that seem to fit together, and label the groups. With your colleagues, compare the categories you developed and discuss the roles listed therein.

VARIOUS STUDIES OF TEACHING have shown that when teachers expect students to succeed in their classes, students generally are successful. Similarly, when teachers do not expect students to succeed, students generally are unsuccessful. Expectations do, indeed, influence outcomes (Leu and Kinzer 1991; Rosenthal 1968; Rosenthal and Jacobson 1968).

Expectations of success are stimulated and supported by a variety of personal and professional contexts. These contexts contribute to the overall learning environment. Most of the contexts are created by teachers in the classroom and are under teachers' control. Students contribute to the contexts by the manner in which they respond to what their teachers have created.

This chapter discusses some of the personal and professional contexts that stimulate expectations of success and establish positive climates for learning. The balance of the book deals with instructional strategies that help fulfill the expectations. It is important not only that you read this chapter now, but that you refer to it later while you read chapters that deal with the supporting instructional strategies.

Personal Contexts

Teachers, as people, establish contexts. The kind of people teachers are determines the kind of classroom environments they create. This personal context is reflected in their work and in the relationships they establish with others. Our purpose is not to engage in psychoanalysis or deep introspection. Rather, our purpose is to stimulate your thinking about how you, as a total person, influence the learning that occurs in your classroom.

Polarities

Certain attitudinal and behavioral polarities can be used to describe some of the components of personal contexts we create. While few of us would locate ourselves at the extremes of either end, it is useful to consider where we fall and how that positioning influences our work.

Optimistic—Pessimistic
A person's weather can be partly sunny or partly cloudy. A person's work can be full of opportunities or full of obligations. A person's glass can be half full or half empty. To be totally optimistic is to be Pollyannaish and unrealistic, but to be totally pessimistic is to be paranoid and suicidal. Most teachers fall somewhere between the two extremes. Where they fall influences their responses to the students and the curriculum they face each day. Their responses create a climate that characterizes their classrooms. If their responses lean toward optimism, the tone of their classrooms is more optimistic. If their responses lean toward pessimism, the tone of their classrooms is more pessimistic.

Students are influenced by environments in which they learn. When the environment is optimistic, cheerful, and upbeat in nature, students tend to be more comfortable and confident in their participation and performance. Teachers also are influenced by the environments in which they work, especially since they have so much to do with creating the environment in the first place. When the environment is optimistic, cheerful, and upbeat in nature, teachers tend to be seen as supportive of students' participation and performance. The consequence of the comfort, confidence, and support is mutual and reciprocal expectations of students' and teachers' success, each for themselves and each for the other. Because expectations influence outcomes, students' success is more probable in this optimistic learning environment.

Initiating—Reactive

How is work done in teachers' working environments (their classrooms) and principally under whose auspices? Teachers have little or no control over some aspects of their work. In those situations, they are in the position of reacting rather than of initiating. However, in many instructional facets of their work, teachers can either initiate or react. Either they can be involved more in initiating actions or conditions that influence and shape their instruction, or they can be involved more in reacting to such actions or conditions that are initiated by others.

When instructional activities are determined principally by the personal initiative and decision of separate individuals within a faculty, something close to instructional chaos and anarchy can be created. Yet, when instructional activities principally are reactions to externally imposed mandates, outcomes may be dull and stultifying experiences for both students and teachers. Most teachers fall somewhere between the two extremes in terms of the control they exert over their instructional activities. Where they fall on this continuum influences their responses to the students and curriculum that they face each day. Their responses create a climate that characterizes their classrooms. If their responses lean more toward exercising initiative and control, the tone of their classrooms is more creative. If their responses lean more toward reacting to external dictates and control, the tone of their classrooms is more pedestrian.

Students are influenced by the environments in which they learn. When the environment is filled with creative learning opportunities, students tend to be more stimulated and interested in participating and performing. Teachers are influenced by the environments, too. When teachers fill the environment with creative and interesting instructional opportunities (the reciprocal of learning opportunities), teachers tend to be seen as supportive of students' participation and performance. A consequence of the stimulation, interest, and support is both mutual and reciprocal expectations of students' and teachers' success, each for themselves and each for the other. Because expectations influence outcomes, students' success is more probable in an environment in which teachers initiate.

Flexible—Rigid

How easily do some teachers modify what they do? Specifically, how easily do they modify their instructional resources or their instructional strategies? How easily do they modify the organization and presentation of their curriculum? How easily do they follow productive but tangential lines of reasoning that their students raise?

Applications of curriculum and instruction can be so flexible as to be devoid of both substance and organization. On the other hand, applications of curriculum and instruction can be so rigid as to be both unimaginative and unresponsive. Most teachers fall somewhere between flexibility and rigidity in terms of both what and how they teach. Where they fall on this continuum influences ways that they deal with their students and curriculum and creates a climate that characterizes their classrooms. If what they do leans toward flexibility in the application of curriculum and instruction, the tone of their classrooms is more stimulating and exciting. If what they do leans toward rigidity in the application of curriculum and instruction, the tone of their classroom is more restrictive and constraining.

Students are influenced by the environments in which they learn. When the environment is flexible and responsive to unanticipated learning opportunities, with a certain tolerance for ambiguity, students tend to be more creative and proactive in their participation and performance. Teachers are also influenced by the classroom environment they create. When teachers are sensitive to the "teachable moment," encouraging divergent as well as convergent thinking, they are seen as supportive of students' participation and performance. A consequence of this support is both mutual and reciprocal expectations of students' and teachers' success, each for themselves and each for the other.

Because expectations influence outcomes, students' success is more probable in a flexible learning environment.

Collaborative—Confrontational

When some teachers are called upon to interact with colleagues, is it a case of them with the world or them against the world? Do some teachers accomplish important elements of their work because of or in spite of the work of others? When confronted with professional problems, do some teachers circle the wagons with colleagues for a collective response or do they ride off in their own wagon and deal with the issues themselves?

The need for collaboration and consensus can be so strong that it renders a group impotent and leaves it without accomplishment. On the other hand, the need for confrontation and individualization can be so strong that it isolates individuals and leaves them without influence. Most teachers fall somewhere in between collaboration and confrontation in terms of their interpersonal relationships. Where they fall on this continuum influences how they deal with their students and colleagues and creates a climate that characterizes their classrooms. If they lean toward collaboration in the sharing of information and development of ideas, their classrooms are more inviting and comfortable. If they lean toward confrontation in the presentation of information and ideas, the tone of their classrooms is more tense and threatening.

Students are influenced by the environments in which they learn. When the environment is inviting and inclusive, students tend to feel less at risk while exploring new ideas. Teachers also are influenced by the environment in which they work, especially when they create much of it themselves. When teachers create an environment that invites collaboration in learning, they tend to be seen as supportive of students' participation and performance. A consequence of the feelings of collaboration is safety and support. It also is both the mutual and reciprocal expectations of students' and teachers' success, each for themselves and each for the other. Because expectation influences outcomes, students' success is more probable in this learning environment.

A Safe Place to Learn

What description best typifies a classroom as a context in which effective instruction is taking place? We think it is a safe place to learn. This does not mean that learning should be risk free. To the contrary, the type of learning that we advocate in this book is risky. We advocate learning that goes beyond literal comprehension and rote memorization, learning that engages students' minds in the exploration of ideas, learning that encourages consideration of alternative explanations of phenomena.

Learning that involves students in the processes of conceptual development and application is anything but intellectually risk free. Participants examine alternative data and make choices, and they are called on to give reasons for their choices. Learners engaged in conceptual development and application must have a high tolerance for ambiguity, in contrast to learners engaged in rote memorization and literal comprehension. In the latter, choices need not be made; what one is to memorize and recall is clear. In the former, however, choices—and decisions—are multiple.

Criteria have to be established for judging the importance and worth of available information and for determining whether more information is needed. Relationships across significant sets of information have to be perceived and classified to infer reasonable and appropriate conclusions. Applications of the inferred conclusions have to be tested for reasonableness, given the actions, conditions, or agents to which the applications are made. No, instruction that engages students in the active pursuit and development of ideas certainly is not risk free.

However, such instruction can occur in classroom environments that provide a safe place to learn, a place where intellectual risks can be taken without fear of damage or destruction. In such environments, both students and teacher have achieved a tolerance for ambiguity. They have developed an attitude of acceptance for the right to hold differing opinion. They have come to understand the value of marshalling convincing evidence before drawing conclusions as well as for withholding judgment until sufficient evidence is obtained.

This environment can be misunderstood. Some people think that because the classroom is safe it also is soft, that it is a place where anything goes, a place lacking in intellectual rigor. Not so. What makes it safe is not that no thinking takes place. Rather, the environment is safe because, while it encourages careful thinking about concepts under consideration, it also provides time and room for that thinking to take place. Careful thinking about a concept requires time for:

1. Reflection on its relevant issues and information
2. Time to formulate and fashion expressions of the concept
3. An audience on which to test the expressions
4. A place in which one can interact with the audience about the concept thus expressed

By providing an accepting environment for the exploration and exchange of ideas, a classroom can be a safe place to learn. By providing an audience of minds responding to proffered ideas, a classroom can be a safe place to learn. By giving students room to talk out ideas that are dawning in their consciousness, a classroom can be a safe place to learn. By providing a challenge to the intellectual quality and reasonableness of ideas presented for discussion, while supporting the presentation itself, a classroom can be a safe place to learn.

Teachers create and orchestrate this safe environment. Students participate and are beneficiaries of what this context offers. Of central importance to this safe place to learn is the use of small groups in the classroom to facilitate cooperative learning.

Cooperative Learning

The terms cooperative grouping and cooperative learning are both used in the literature on classroom instruction and management to describe intraclass grouping. While the terms are often used interchangeably, important differences exist between the two concepts.

Cooperative grouping deals with the organization of students into groups for the purpose of instruction. The work of the participants in groups is cooperative in nature because they all work toward the accomplishment of specific objectives and support one another in that work.

Cooperative learning deals with students' working together in the pursuit of knowledge. Teachers create lessons that call for students to interact with one another, mutually pursuing an understanding of particular concepts and mutually applying specific reading, writing, and/or reasoning processes to facilitate that understanding. Activities students engage in and materials that support those activities are designed to develop students' understanding of the organizing ideas of lessons and units.

The important distinction between cooperative grouping and cooperative learning is that the former is a means for instruction and the latter an end of instruction. Cooperative grouping does facilitate cooperative learning, but cooperative learning can occur when students interact in a full class as well as when they interact in small groups.

The experiences of content-area teachers with whom we have worked over the past thirty years confirms the value of cooperative learning through intraclass grouping. They have found it possible to extend the principles and practices of cooperative learning from small-group contexts to full-class contexts. Their experiences have been affirmed by researchers who focus on cooperative grouping as a means for learning rather than as an end of learning (Johnson and Johnson 1987).

We feel strongly about the value of cooperative learning, and you will find both the concept and the practice deeply imbedded in the instructional strategies we present in this book. Throughout the book we use the term *cooperative learning* rather than *cooperative grouping* because we want to keep reminding you that intraclass grouping itself, while important to students' learning, is a means to an end and not an end in itself. Intraclass grouping greatly facilitates cooperative learning, so we strongly advocate that you organize your instruction accordingly. Keep in mind that learning cooperatively is a constant, whether students are working in small groups or as a full class.

Facilitating Conditions

In the first part of this chapter we talk about the kinds of contexts we create as teachers and how they influence our work. Those contexts are included among the conditions that facilitate cooperative learning and intraclass grouping in your classrooms. Other facilitating conditions to consider are the following:

1. A cooperative spirit among the participants
2. A supportive administration
3. Willing teachers
4. A well-structured curriculum
5. Well-organized lessons
6. Clearly defined tasks, rules, and procedures

The influence of these conditions is considered throughout the discussion on cooperative learning and in later sections of the book where we deal with instructional strategies that make use of intraclass grouping to promote cooperative learning.

Purposes for Intraclass Grouping

Cooperative learning is facilitated by organizing your class so students can interact with one another in small groups. This intraclass grouping serves several interrelated purposes.

Stimulation

Placing students in small groups provides them with "legitimate" access to one another for purposes of study. Recall the discussion of how important it is to have a conceptually based curriculum if you want students to learn not only the course content but also the relevant reading, writing, and reasoning processes (see Chapter 1). A contributing factor in the development of concepts is the opportunity to discuss the relevant information and ideas with other individuals engaged in the same study. The thinking of all participants is stimulated as the discussions take place and the exploration of the concepts is more fulsome. One participant elaborates on the point of another participant and a third elaborates on the point of the second.

The conceptual product derived by the total group is more comprehensive than what each of the participants might produce individually. Well-structured intraclass grouping provides both the means and the context for stimulating such discussions.

Clarification and Refinement of Ideas

You know how clarifying it is to be able to talk through an idea with a sympathetic, supportive audience, particularly when you are not quite certain what or how you think about a certain issue. As you discuss the information and talk through the relevant ideas, your understanding of the issues becomes clearer. Members of the small group provide the audience for this clarifying and refining process. You, of course, serve as audience for other members of your group, and you help to clarify and refine their thinking on the ideas being discussed.

Mutual Support

In an earlier section of this chapter we talked about providing students with a safe place to learn. The small-group setting is the focal point of that safe place. Students who rarely, if ever, volunteer to speak in full-class discussions often are strong participants in small-group discussions. They feel safer in the smaller setting and derive a sense of support from the cooperative enterprise. They see themselves as legitimate participants in doing whatever task the group has been given to complete. They eventually recognize that the support among participants is reciprocal.

Practice

The instructional focus of this book is on the simultaneous development of course content and related reading, writing and reasoning processes. Intraclass grouping provides a setting in which the concepts of the curriculum can be acquired and refined. In this same setting, content-related reading, writing, and reasoning processes can be practiced and refined.

Several decades ago, Donald Durrell (1966) stated that intraclass grouping provides opportunities for "multiple recitation." He argued that students' acquisition and refinement of learning processes depend, in part, on the frequency with which they have opportunity to use the processes in meaningful settings. Placing students in small groups and structuring assigned tasks so the participants are involved in applying targeted learning processes increases the number of opportunities for each participant to recite. As the frequency of recitation increased, so does the students' practice on the processes. As applications of the targeted learning processes increase, so do participants' understanding of and facility with the processes. In the group setting, each member has many more opportunities to participate than s/he would have in a full-class setting; hence, intraclass grouping increases opportunities for multiple recitation.

History of Intraclass Grouping

Intraclass grouping for instruction in elementary school has a long history. Formation of reading groups in the primary grades has been part of the traditional way to serve the range of students' learning needs during early reading instruction. Small groups are used for extending learning by providing practice on reading skills already acquired.

Small groups are used in intermediate grades in most subject areas to facilitate students' completion of curriculum-related projects. Social studies and science projects often are accomplished by students working together in groups. These work groups (Miles 1967) focus on the completion of particular tasks, not on the development of skills or understandings. Groups provide opportunities for practice on or refinement of concepts and/or skills that are taught in other settings.

In secondary schools, two influences have limited the use of intraclass grouping for instructional purposes: individualized instruction and competitive learning. Individualized instruction has a strong hold on curricula that focus principally on reading, writing, or reasoning. A variety of programs exist that embrace mastery learning and/or behavior-modification models of instruction and are based on a medical model of diagnosis and prescription. Tests are given to students to determine their learning needs. Instruction is prescribed based on the test results, with the prescription being individually focused. Because the diagnosis and prescription are individualized, the instruction is isolated. That is, students wind up working alone, in isolation from other students. Cooperative learning is not part of the instructional program. These students miss advantages that are available from cooperative learning through intraclass grouping.

A strong influence in secondary and postsecondary education lies in what can be called the tyranny of the normal curve. Students constantly are being compared with one another for grades, for praise, for recognition, and for general accomplishment. The consequence of this constant comparison is the development of a spirit of competition rather than cooperation. While it is true that competition does not negatively effect the top achievers in a school, it can have a debilitating effect on students with lesser academic abilities. This is particularly true when expectations for high academic performance are not accompanied by instruction that shows students how to perform at the expected levels of competence. Unfortunately, top achievers in competitive settings may fail to discover the possibility of maintaining a high level of performance while still contributing to the knowledge and well-being of others.

Cooperative learning through intraclass grouping can overcome the negative aspects of competitive learning. Specifically, research affirms the following outcomes from cooperative learning:

1. Increases students' motivation
2. Facilitates students' communication
3. Improves students' academic achievement
4. Enhances students' self-esteem
5. Improves students' interpersonal and intergroup relationships (Johnson and Johnson 1987)

Focus of Group Work

The purpose of intraclass grouping is to facilitate students' learning of course content and related reading, writing, and reasoning processes. You don't organize your class into small groups just to provide variety in your students' day. Thus, intraclass grouping serves as a means to an end, not as an end in itself.

The focus of group work is on facilitating the study of course content. All activities that groups are given to do should be designed to develop students' understandings of the organizing ideas of lessons and units that comprise the curriculum. Small-group activities that divert students' time and attention from the study of the curriculum are unproductive and unnecessary, making intraclass grouping an end itself rather than a means to an end.

Each lesson and each unit should have an organizing idea that provides a substantive focus to all of the instructional activities. The particular learning processes of reading, writing, and reasoning, emphasized during the lessons and units, are derived from resource materials being studied. Teachers show students how to apply learning processes while studying the organizing ideas. The showing how is facilitated by students' cooperative interaction in small groups.

The chapters in Section III of this book present a variety of activities that facilitate students' interaction and support their learning in small groups. The activities focus students' attention on the organizing ideas of lessons and units. The activities also support students' application of relevant reading, writing, and reasoning processes. Thus, students simultaneously learn both course content and relevant learning processes.

Forming Groups

When forming small groups and keeping them in operation throughout the school year, two general principles are applicable:

1. Heterogeneous grouping supports a more comprehensive learning environment than does homogenous grouping.
2. Rotating membership of groups maintains a more stimulating learning environment than does fixed membership.

Types of Groups

Heterogeneous classes exist when members possess an array of abilities, achievements, and backgrounds. Some educators believe that education can be more comprehensive when classes are heterogeneous in nature (Otto, Wolf, and Eldridge 1984). Other educators believe that education can be more efficient when classes are homogeneous in nature, when the members are more similar in their abilities, achievements, and backgrounds (Otto, Wolf, and Eldridge 1984). Since both efficiency and comprehensiveness are appropriate goals, it is important to understand the values inherent in both positions.

Homogeneous grouping supports efficient learning when it favors the development of the product over the acquisition of process. When students are assigned to homogeneously grouped classes according to their proficiency with learning processes, teachers can focus principally on the acquisition and application of course content. It is assumed that instruction in and refinement of learning processes are not necessary. Thus, teaching homogeneously grouped classes may seem more efficient.

We believe that heterogeneous grouping supports comprehensive learning when it focuses on both product and process. When students are assigned to heterogeneously grouped classes according to their proficiencies with learning processes, teachers can focus attention both on the acquisition of course content and the acquisition of appropriate learning processes. It is assumed that students need instruction in both course content and learning processes. Thus, teaching heterogeneously grouped classes may seem more comprehensive.

Placing students in small groups within heterogeneously grouped classes provides more opportunity to apply the principles of cooperative learning. Participating students are more likely to possess a range of ability, achievement, experience, knowledge, interests, motivations, proficiencies, and deficiencies. In this diverse context, opportunities abound for students to learn from one another and to help one another learn. Structures that teachers create to support students' work in groups take advantage of students' diversity and facilitate their small-group teaching and learning (see Section III).

Assignment to Groups

When you assign students to small groups within a heterogeneously grouped class, you want to preserve the advantages of heterogenous grouping. It is important that the distribution of variables—ability, achievement, interest, experience, motivation, and prior knowledge—among members of each small group be essentially the same as it is among members of the full class. This comparability of variables between small groups and the full class can be accomplished rather easily by randomly assigning students to groups. Having students count off by a given set of numbers is a simple way to accomplish random assignment. For example, if you have thirty students in your class and you want five students in each group, have the students count off by sixes. Have all of the ones work together as a group, all the twos, and so on through the sixes. In this manner, the probability is high that each group will be similar to the whole class in its range of variables.

Because students become comfortable with one another after a while, they may not engage in the discussion of ideas and application of learning processes as seriously as they did when their present group was originally formed. Because of their familiarity with one another's thinking, they may assume that they already know the other students' views on whatever is being discussed. Thus, it becomes useful to rotate the membership of groups to bring fresh perspectives to their discussions and interactions. A simple way to regroup students is to have them count off within each group, moving from group to group until each student has a number. Students with the same numbers form their groups.

We suggest using groups of five for your intraclass grouping. An odd number seems to facilitate the search for consensus in discussions. Three people usually do not constitute a sufficient body for a group. Because you want students to be able to draw on background knowledge and experience for many tasks, limiting the group to three also limits that resource. Seven people, another odd number, is usually too many for a group to work efficiently. Typically, two subgroups evolve from a group of seven because it is difficult to communicate with everyone in the larger group. Five, then, seems workable, comfortable, and reasonable. This group size satisfies the odd-number criterion. It has sufficient body by having backgrounds of five people to draw upon, and it is small enough that each member can interact comfortably with the other four. The physical layout in most classes can most comfortably incorporate groups of five without a major disruption of the environment. So, we recommend that you start with five students per group and see how it works for you. You can always make adjustments as appropriate to suit your circumstances.

Management Issues

For content-area teachers who rarely, if ever, have placed their students into small groups for instructional purposes, even the thought of intraclass grouping produces anxiety. The anxiety, of course, comes from lack of familiarity with procedures and practices that make intraclass grouping work. We discuss these procedures and practices in the context of selected management issues.

Time on Task

Much has been written on the importance of learners' time being focused on the task at hand (Rosenshine and Berliner 1978; Brookover et al. 1978; Berliner 1981; Leu and Kinzer 1991). How *time on task* is defined and interpreted depends on the tasks, who is teaching, who is learning, and who is observing. In the main, however, studies show that the more time students' spend doing tasks designed to produce the intended learning, the more likely it is that they will learn what the tasks were designed to teach.

To the uninitiated, intraclass grouping seems to be antithetical to promoting students' time on task. To them, the potential for straying off task seems greater if students are working together than if they are working separately. However, what certainty is there that students are spending any more time on task when working alone than when working together in a group? It is easier to observe deviations from time on task when students are in a group because you can hear what they are saying as well as observe their task-oriented behaviors. When students are working separately, you can observe their task-oriented behaviors but you cannot know what's going on behind their eyes! Is their thinking on task all of the time? Might not their minds drift off to other considerations as they work alone, even though to outward appearances they seem to be focused on the task at hand? Most of us recognize that our minds occasionally drift off task even though our outward behaviors would suggest otherwise. If this happens to us, it must also happen to our students. They are, after all, real people!

What keeps students truly on task is investment in the task. The purpose of group work is to acquire, analyze, synthesize, refine, and apply ideas that comprise the curriculum of the course in which the group work is taking place. We assume that concepts worthy of study in a curriculum can be presented in such a way that students will want to invest themselves in such study. Using organizing ideas to drive lessons and units, as discussed in Chapter 2, facilitates such a presentation of concepts.

Tasks students perform in the groups are applications of reading, writing, and reasoning processes relevant to ideas being studied. Structure given to tasks is found in the Instructional Framework, discussed in Chapter 5. Tasks that prepare students for the study of ideas are facilitated by group interaction. Tasks that guide students as they respond to the resources used to study ideas are facilitated by small-group work. Tasks that support students' independence in refining, extending, and sharing what they have learned are facilitated by intraclass grouping.

Students become invested in study when all of the following factors merge:

1. Pursuit of significant ideas
2. Opportunity to interact with peers in the reading, writing, and reasoning about these ideas
3. Lesson structure that clearly delineates the tasks
4. Support mechanisms that enable students to perform the tasks successfully

Such investment keeps students on task.

We all recognize that when people work together in groups, they occasionally talk about things other than the task at hand. We do it in our professional and social contexts. We should recognize this phenomenon for what it is, a natural act of the human species, and not be upset when it occurs on occasion. When instructional conditions offer no competition to off-task interests, off-task behaviors will result. However, when instructional conditions promote on-task interest and guide on-task activities, then on-task behaviors will result.

The more students engage in intraclass grouping, the more value they find in it and the more they are able to take advantage of the support it gives to their learning. Teachers who are experienced with intraclass grouping say that they can tell immediately which students have had previous experience working in small groups. A high school English teacher observed,

"I have noticed over the past few years that as students come through from the junior high, that have worked in groups prior to coming to high school, they have a much easier attitude toward working in groups."

The cumulative effect of well-structured intraclass grouping is something every faculty and administration should carefully consider.

Outcomes

Of what value is intraclass grouping to teachers and their students? Here are some comments from teachers who have studied the instructional strategies presented in this book, including intraclass grouping. All of these teachers use intraclass grouping in their teaching, though many of them did not before they participated in the long-term staff-development program conducted in their districts.

High School Teacher: French

> *I very often have students who are very inhibited about speaking out in class. You try to call on every student so many times per class. Sometimes that's not always possible, or you might feel as if you don't want to pressure them. In a group situation, those more shy students are able to work with other students . . . so they are totally involved more of the time.*

High School Teacher: Algebra/Calculus

> *When students are working individually, some of those individuals may discover certain things when they are working on it. And so maybe out of a group of twenty kids, two or three may discover certain things that you are looking for. But when they're working in groups, if one student in two or three different groups finds it, then two or three groups are making that discovery, and they're relaying that to each other. So as normally two or three individuals would get out of the lesson what you want, you are multiplying that factor by the number of people that you have in the groups. So, you're reaching more people.*
>
> *My attitude toward students working together has always been that I don't want students working together on homework; and I still don't. But, seeing them work together in the room in their groups and hearing some of the things they are saying to each other, it's what I have been looking for as far as using the vocabulary and helping each other out are concerned. It's also teaching students how to help one another; and that applies to a lot of different things, not just to school work.*
>
> *In the group work, comments by the students will quite often bring in things that you never planned on. You can have the materials there, but that's not like a script because you never can tell what some of these kids are going to come up with in a group. They'll ask questions applying to other situations, to related situations; and this is one of the things that you are hoping to accomplish.*

Middle School/Junior High School Teacher: Music

> *I look a lot to the amount of participation I get from the kids, from the beginning to the end. I had a situation with a new class that started about six days ago. One of my students is a learning disabled boy, and he was very,*

very quiet the first day—offered nothing. All of the strategies I used to bring out certain responses from students were met with very strong hesitancy. So I put them into groups and had them work together on their first assignment. As I was watching, he was doing a lot of listening—had trouble writing it down, but he knew what was going on. I found that after about three or four days of some group work and that sort of thing, this boy was raising his hand because he knew what was going on. And after that, he felt much more confident and comfortable, I think, with me and with the other students in the class. He felt, "I know what's going on and I have something to offer and it's OK!".

High School Teacher: Social Studies/Psychology

In twelfth grade social studies we have heterogeneous grouping; everybody is mixed together. And I think it's really exciting when students from what we call the "B track" are in a group with "A track" students and are taking part, are demonstrating that they have something to offer and are being accepted by the rest of the group. I think that's an important assessment of how effective the program can be; and you get to see that as students work in their groups.

High School Teacher: Chemistry

By encouraging student interaction and more opportunity to evaluate what the kids are doing, every day, you as a teacher have a better handle on your progress and you don't have to wait for the chapter test or the unit test or the Regents exam before you discover that the students have—or haven't— learned the concepts.

The more student interaction I have, the more opportunity I have to go around and get a sense of what the students understand. And this is more time-efficient for me because I don't have to correct 30 homework papers from every class every day.

High School Teacher: English

Kids do feel more secure in groups. Talking in front of each other, expressing their opinions, they don't feel that their thoughts are dumb and don't count. Once you start this group discussion, they are willing to lay themselves on the line to express something.

The experiences of these teachers are consistent with what we have already noted as outcomes from research on cooperative learning.

Roles of Participants

The success of intraclass grouping is determined by both teachers and students. Both teachers and students have particular roles to play. How well and conscientiously the parties play their roles determines how much the intraclass grouping contributes to teaching and learning processes that are occurring in the classroom.

Teachers' Roles. About eighteen content-area teachers and administrators spent a three-day retreat analyzing teachers' roles in the effective use of intraclass grouping for teaching reading, writing, and reasoning in content areas (Herber and Nelson-Herber 1984). The teachers had participated for several years in a staff-development program, studying strategies that support the instructional integration of content and process. All were experienced in the use of intraclass grouping, and all believed that it contributed positively to the learning environment of their classes, to students' academic achievement, and to students' reading, writing, and reasoning abilities. During this retreat they studied videotapes of lessons they and others had taught using intraclass grouping. From the analyses of these tapes, from their reading of relevant literature, and from the related discussions, they identified four essential roles teachers play in successful intraclass grouping:

1. Directing
2. Monitoring
3. Probing
4. Supporting

1. *Directing.* Directing involves organizing students in groups and helping them to define the task. Directing involves modifying group activity that is under way or starting an entirely new course of action.

Directing involves making certain that students understand the directions for tasks they are to perform. Implicit in those tasks are reading, writing, and reasoning processes that are essential for students to apply in order to develop an understanding of the concepts being studied. The tasks and related materials are designed to support students' application of these learning processes. However, students will only be successful in learning both concepts and learning processes if they do the tasks as they were designed to be done. Directing, therefore, includes modeling how to respond to assigned tasks. Modeling is done by walking students through actions indicated by the directions for the task and by doing so for enough of the task that students can see what they are to do and can understand why they are doing it.

As students gain competence and confidence in their group work, they need less and less direction. They become more self-directed and self-managed. Teachers' directing roles diminish in relative importance to other roles they need to play.

2. *Monitoring.* Monitoring involves careful observation of the quality and effectiveness of students' interactions within their groups. As noted further on in this chapter, students have roles to play in the intraclass

grouping. Part of the monitoring should focus on how well they are doing and what the teacher might do to enhance their performance.

Monitoring requires a high level of self-discipline on your part. You will be constantly tempted to intervene in group activities, particularly when it appears that a group is pursuing a line of reasoning that may prove fruitless or when students are applying a process in a way that is inefficient. You need to give them room to discover the fruitlessness of their current reasoning and to recover from their current inefficiency. A principal value to be derived from group interaction is for students to apply themselves to both content and process within the structures you provide for these purposes. You can easily suspend or terminate productive interaction among students by too quickly inserting yourself into a group's discussions.

We recommend that in your monitoring you be carefully quiet in the main, particularly as students are talking through ideas and working to resolve differences among themselves. Once they have reached some consensus on issues under consideration, it is appropriate for you to interact with them, as noted below.

In Chapter 12, we discuss assessment as it relates to teaching reading, writing, and reasoning across the curriculum. We refer to *functional assessment* as an important dimension of the complete process of assessment. Functional assessment is close and careful observation of students actually applying reading, writing, and reasoning processes to the study of curriculum-related concepts. Your monitoring of students' group work contributes to this functional assessment. Based on what you observe, you can make adjustments in subsequent group activities and in individual assignments for students who evidence particular needs.

3. *Probing.* Probing involves direct interactions between yourself and groups as a whole or individual students within the groups. The objects of the probing are the concepts being explored by the groups and the learning processes being applied by the groups. Probing can be used to do the following:

    a. Clarify information.
    b. Refine understanding.
    c. Elaborate issues.
    d. Apply findings.
    e. Anticipate outcomes.
    f. Synthesize ideas.
    g. Communicate results.

Probing is more than questioning. We don't call probing "questioning" because questioning as a rule carries too much instructional baggage. Questions usually are used in a testing mode; that is, questioners already know the answers to the questions being asked, and answerers may or may not know. Answerers often are reduced to guessing what questioners have in mind and, as such, lose track of the impact or import of ideas that prompted the question in the first place.

Questions can serve as probes when they are open ended, when they invite reflection, and when they make room for alternative responses. Questions can serve as probes when they require rigorous analysis of resources for evidence to support positions taken on issues under consideration without requiring that specific positions be adopted on those issues. Questions can serve as probes when they prompt speculation and encourage elaboration on possible applications of issues being studied.

Probing can take many forms:

a. Sharing examples of concepts being studied drawn from different contexts to encourage synthesis and elaboration
b. Sharing of your own thought processes on a problem to encourage analysis and interpretation
c. Wondering aloud about possible alternative explanations for conclusions already drawn
d. Encouraging reexamination and refinement of understandings

4. *Supporting.* Supporting involves both overt and covert interaction between yourself and the groups. Open words of praise and approbation are important aspects of support, if applied judiciously. If everything is "excellent" or "wonderful," students have difficulty knowing when they are improving and really doing well.

Teachers can support students in a variety of ways.

a. Words of encouragement support students in their work. Your students may have reached a point of mental fatigue as they deal with a problem or issue and may be looking for a way out. "Hang in there...," "Keep at it...," or similar comments acknowledge their fatigue and/or frustration but also tell them you expect them to continue and to complete the tasks. This encouragement provides support that students recognize and value.
b. Empathetic responses support students in their work. They may be struggling with a complex task or an abstract concept and they are at some distance from a resolution to the struggle. "This is a tough one...," "This really stretches the mind...," or similar comments let your students know that you understand the difficulty the task; but the comments also let them know that you have confidence in their ability to complete the task and you expect them to do so. This constitutes strong support on your part.
c. Nonanswers to questions support students in their work. They may be having difficulty resolving some problem or issue related to the tasks they have undertaken. As you approach the group,

the students turn to you as a resource that can immediately solve their problem. If you give a direct answer, you short-circuit their reasoning processes and minimize the value to be derived from the task you have given them to do. Acknowledge the question without answering it. "You want to know . . . [repeating the question]" reflects back to them what they asked you without answering it. When they confirm that that is, indeed, the question, encourage them to continue seeking the answer. You can then discuss with them the implications of the question and ways that the answer may be found, but don't answer that question.

d. Answers to some questions support students in their work. Sometimes students need specific information to continue their tasks, and they ask you for it. In this situation, a direct and immediate response is called for and you give it. The answer supports their work and makes it possible for them to continue. When questions from students relate to the mechanics of tasks they are being asked to perform, direct answers are appropriate and should be forthcoming.

e. Nonverbal behaviors support students in their work. Many covert, indirect means of supporting students' work are an important part of the teacher's role during intraclass grouping. Your nod or a smile of commendation or approval gives a feeling of support after a student has completed an extended commentary on the issue under consideration in the group. You do not have to speak to support your students in their work. They will be with you only a short while before they learn to read your body language. Be certain that your gestures, posture, and demeanor are supportive of them in their work. Your nonlinguistic communication contributes strongly to the total learning context that you create in your classroom. Make certain that this communication is positive and supports students in their work.

Students' Roles As we noted earlier in this chapter, both teachers and students have particular roles to play when engaged in intraclass grouping. How well and conscientiously the parties play their roles determines how much the intraclass grouping contributes to the teaching and learning processes that are occurring in the classroom. Now we turn to a discussion of students' roles.

A colleague of ours, Dr. John Wrape, has found value in extending the modeling aspects of teaching to the formation and operation of intraclass groups. He explains students' roles and responsibilities for cooperative learning to his class. Together he and the students organize a checklist containing these roles and responsibilities. He then forms one group, with himself as a member of the group and with each member serving in one of the roles (discussed below). The group then engages in a task that is typical of the group work that will be occurring in the class. Remaining members of the class observe the work of the group to determine how well members perform in their roles. Observers use the checklist of rules and responsibilities as the criteria for making their judgments. When the group work is completed, the observers offer feedback to group members and they make suggestions for ways in which the group work could be improved. In this manner, students internalize an understanding of the purpose and function of intraclass grouping. Periodic repetition of this modeling reinforces this understanding and sharpens the work of students in the groups.

We have found the following five roles to be important in the successful application of intraclass grouping. With five-member groups, each person has a responsibility during a specific working session. You probably will want to rotate these responsibilities among members within groups so each student has repeated experiences of filling each role. In time, the formal assignment of roles will not be necessary. All students will understand all roles and will see to it that all are filled.

1. *Leader.* The group leader initiates activities to be undertaken, makes certain that group members understand the directions to be followed, and generally keeps the group on task. The leader may be appointed by you; the leader may be formally elected by the group itself; the leader may emerge, informally established by group consensus.

2. *Recorder.* The group recorder writes for the group, keeps records of ideas generated and/or discussed, and lists decisions made by the group. Groups will be discussing vocabulary-development materials (Chapter 7), comprehension materials (Chapter 8), or reasoning-development materials (Chapter 9). They also will be engaged in the development of group compositions (Chapter 10). In each type of activity, recorders keep track of groups' decisions and are ready to report on decisions to the full class when called upon to do so.

3. *Checker.* The group checker asks for clarification if there appears to be doubt or ambiguity with respect to tasks to be performed or responses by individuals to tasks. The checker reminds participants of the need for evidence and examples to support decisions they make on ideas being generated and/or discussed. The checker makes certain that directions are being followed and that all aspects of the task are completed.

4. *Encourager.* The encourager is the cheerleader of the group. S/he promotes the participation of each member in the current activity. The encourager finds ways to support contributions of each member and to identify their contributions to the overall work of the group. S/he makes and solicits encouraging comments about contributions of group members.

5. *Shusher.* The "shusher" is sensitive to the decibel level generated by the group activity. If you have five or six groups operating in your classroom, the noise factor can become a problem. Typically, you will be bothered

by this noise more than your students. When they are immersed in their group work, they are not aware of what is going on around them. However, they will raise their voices to be heard within the groups, and as sound from other groups interferes with their hearing, they will raise their voice levels again. If unchecked, the sound level can reach a pain-inducing level! So, the "shusher" notes the sound level of the group and encourages the use of softer voices.

Rules

Several rules govern the organization and operation of the groups. If followed, they contribute to the efficiency and effectiveness of intraclass grouping. They all are self-explanatory. We list them for your consideration and recommend that you discuss them with your students as part of their orientation to intraclass grouping. Even if they have had prior experience with cooperative-learning activities, it is useful to review the rules as well as to discuss the roles presented earlier.

1. Get into groups quickly and quietly; time is an important commodity that should not be squandered.
2. Stay with your group; don't wander.
3. Use quiet voices; pay attention to your "shusher."
4. Use an individual's name when speaking to one another; don't allow any group member, by default, to be an anonymous participant.
5. Encourage everyone to participate; give people time to do so, remembering that some people are inclined to reflect before speaking while others are inclined to reflect while speaking.
6. Have one person speak at a time; do not allow increased volume or aggressive speakers to "talk over" less assertive participants.
7. Look at and listen to the speaker; really attend to what the person is saying rather than spend that time composing what you will say as soon as this person stops talking.
8. Keep your hands and feet to yourself; the interaction among group participants is to be intellectual, not physical.
9. Do not use put-downs; the small-group context is to be a safe place to learn and, as such, is governed by a spirit of mutual respect and acceptance of the right to differ in opinion and conclusion.

Rewards

What motivates students to participate in cooperative learning activities? What is the reward?

We believe the reward is the developing sense of competence that comes from work students accomplish in cooperative-learning settings. Recall that in these settings students are acquiring both an understanding of course content and competency with relevant reading, writing, and reasoning processes. They are learning course content. They are learning how to learn. They are learning how to be successful in doing what their current role requires them to do. Competence provides the intrinsic motivation that sustains students' interest and participation in cooperative-learning activities.

Some who study the effectiveness of cooperative grouping recommend the use of grades as rewards. Extrinsic motivations, such as grades, reinforce the impression that the primary reason for participating in grouping is to learn about grouping and to be successful with activities designed to facilitate cooperative efforts in group settings. Such extrinsic rewards shift students' attention away from the real purpose for intraclass grouping, which is learning course content and relevant learning processes.

Grading and other means of evaluating students' work are discussed in Chapter 12. Certainly it is appropriate to give students feedback on your estimates of the quality of their work and the efforts they are applying to the work. But this feedback serves as a means to an end, not as an end in itself. Feedback serves to promote and enhance learning and to provide information on how that learning can be advanced and improved. A grade, which can be used to communicate estimates of the quality of the work, can be abused by subverting its use to a means of controlling behavior or of focusing attention on a particular activity. Thus, we distinguish between grading the product of cooperative learning and grading the process of cooperative learning. We believe that the former is appropriate but the latter is not.

Apparent Benefits

Cooperative learning benefits both students and teachers in multiple ways. We have already listed beneficial outcomes of cooperative learning as evidenced by research. These outcomes are affirmed by everyday practice, and everyday practices suggest even more benefits. Following are some we have observed in our work with content-area teachers in a variety of educational settings.

1. Working in groups multiplies opportunities for students to receive explanations on matters that have caused them problems.
2. Small-group discussions facilitate the clarification of ideas and, in so doing, clarify understandings of technical vocabulary used to express the ideas.
3. Small-group interaction facilitates the use of multiple resources in a class.
4. Cooperative learning provides opportunities for discovering sources of error in problem solving, without having to wait for personal conferences with the teacher.
5. Cooperative learning provides a collegial experience with the excitement that true learning generates in its recipients.
6. Intraclass grouping provides an opportunity to accommodate differences in learning rates among students.

7. Cooperative learning provides multiple opportunities for participants to receive immediate feedback on the quality and appropriateness of their work.
8. Cooperative learning provides an opportunity for students to learn from one another. Natural forms of peer tutoring can occur within the groups.
9. Through cooperative learning, information is acquired and ideas are clarified as students engage in discussions with one another. The small group provides the environment for the discussion, and the guide materials provide the vehicle.
10. Cooperative learning provides an opportunity for a person to derive benefit from interacting with other participants who represent a range of ability, achievement, motivation, and interest.
11. Writing activities during cooperative learning can promote collegial relationships.

Regarding item 11, when students have several pieces of writing in their folders, they can trade folders and write letters to each other suggesting one or another piece as a likely candidate for further development. Asking students to identify classmates' ideas that they would like to read more about sets up a collegial relationship in the classroom (Mamion 1988).

Summary

Teachers' own views of the world and their opinions of the roles they play in that world influence how they work and how they feel about what they do. Teachers' personal and professional self-concepts influence the classroom environments they create and the quality of learning that takes place in those environments.

Teachers can create an instructional environment that is both disciplined and caring, a safe place in which learners can explore ideas and stretch their intellectual wings. The environment operationalizes the principles of cooperative learning both through small-group and full-class interactions among students. Teachers and learners play complimentary roles in their mutual explorations of concepts being studied. They develop respect for one another, respect for the content of what they studying, and respect for the processes by which they study.

REACTIONS

Journal Entries and Discussion

With the reading of this chapter, you have completed Sections I and II of this text. Review the focus of these chapters, and develop an essay that highlights the interplay among the concepts presented. Share this essay with others who are reading this book. Ask if you can serve as an audience for their essays as well.

The text distinguishes between cooperative grouping and cooperative learning. What do you understand the differences to be? How important is this distinction to your teaching?

Analysis and Discussion

Now that you have completed this chapter, consider the statements shown below. Check the numbered lines for statements with which you agree. Circle the numbers of statements you believe reflect the point of view of the authors. In writing, explore reasons for differences on any statements between your point of view and what you perceive to be the point of view of the authors. Please share and discuss your writing with colleagues who also are reading this book.

_____ 1. An experienced professional can enter a classroom, sense its tone, and estimate with some accuracy the affective qualities of what occurs therein.

_____ 2. How one behaves toward one's colleagues and students often reflects how one feels about one's self.

_____ 3. Good intentions are necessary but not sufficient for creating positive and supportive instructional environments.

_____ 4. Conditions within teachers' spheres of influence but outside their realm of control contribute significantly to instructional environments.

_____ 5. Cooperation and competition are different means to the same ends.

_____ 6. Rules can serve as criteria for self-assessment as well as the means of control.

_____ 7. Students need opportunity and receptive ears to "think out loud" about issues and ideas and thus discover what they really think about what they are studying.

_____ 8. One can have cooperative learning within a class without having students organized into small groups.

SECTION II

Processes of
Instruction

5

A Framework for Instruction

Organizing idea: Organization and structure make teaching manageable.

Reflections

Before reading this chapter, please record in your journal your responses to the following questions. If possible, share your writing with other individuals who are also reading this book. The ideas that emerge will establish a context for this chapter.

1. Most teachers have an identifiable organization or structure to their lessons. What are the divisions or parts in your lesson structure? What descriptive labels can you give to these parts? Arrange the labels you identify into a display that portrays your lesson structure.

2. What instructional strategies do you rely on most heavily in your teaching? What is there about those strategies that make them so reliable? Do you ever add to this repertoire?

3. What thoughts do you now have about ways to integrate the teaching of your course content with the teaching of reading, writing, and reasoning? What is your estimate of the importance of a strongly grounded theory of teaching relative to the instructional integration of content and process?

TEACHING IS BOTH science and art in action. The science of teaching deals with logic and order that exists in both the content and process of teaching. The art of teaching deals with the manner in which the content and process are translated into action. The action is what teachers and students do separately and interactively to accomplish their learning objectives. How much organization and structure are necessary to support the action is a point of debate among teachers.

Some teachers lean more toward defining teaching as science. They rely on their knowledge of subject matter and its structure to prepare lessons. They rely on teacher-centered classrooms to teach them. They feel at loose ends when asked to attend to the affective aspects of teaching and learning or to include student interaction and cooperative-learning activities in their teaching.

Other teachers lean more toward defining teaching as art, as creative endeavor. They rely on inspiration, intuition, and reflection, coupled with their knowledge of subject matter, to prepare lessons. They rely on student-centered classrooms to teach them. They feel constrained by efforts to impose specific structures and formats on how they teach their lessons.

Still other teachers define teaching as both science and art. Flexibility within structure characterizes their teaching style. They use the structure of their disciplines to organize lessons and draw on their intuitions to teach them. They value both cognitive and affective aspects of teaching. They incorporate both teacher-centered and student-centered activities in their teaching.

Variability in teaching style is a clear characteristic of participants in our profession. However, they do seem to have something in common. Ask them to describe what they include when they teach lessons, and you will find that they mention the following three categories of activities:

1. Activities that get students ready to learn
2. Activities that direct and support students in their learning
3. Activities that give students an opportunity to demonstrate what they have learned

Using these categories, we have developed a framework for lessons (and units) that accommodates the organizational and managemental needs of teachers with different teaching styles. We call it the Instructional Framework. The components of the Instructional Framework reflect the three categories of activities mentioned above: preparation, guidance, and independence.

This chapter has three purposes:

1. To explain the derivations of the Instructional Framework
2. To define the components of the Instructional Framework
3. To preview the instructional strategies that are applicable within the various components of the Instructional Framework, strategies that are explained and demonstrated in Chapters 6 through 10 of Section III.

Derivations of Framework

The Instructional Framework has two major functions:

1. To facilitate the teaching and learning of course content

2. To facilitate the teaching and learning of content-related reading, writing, and reasoning processes

The Instructional Framework is derived from curriculum. Instruction in the content (or substance) of the curriculum is organized by the framework. Instruction in the process (or means by the which substance is learned) of the curriculum is facilitated by the framework.

Curriculum as Context

Curriculum is the context in which the Instructional Framework operates. Curriculum is comprised of content and process (see Figure 5-1).

The content of your curriculum—its substance—defines your teaching and your association with the teaching profession. We believe strongly in the importance of the curriculum content. For that reason we stress the importance of having organizing ideas for lessons so there is always a substantive focus to content-area teaching.

The process of your curriculum—the means for learning its substance—enables your teaching and your students' learning of the content. We also believe strongly in the importance of curriculum process. For that reason we stress the importance of showing students how to acquire, understand, and apply the substance of curriculum.

The Instructional Framework provides a vehicle through which instruction in content can be joined with instruction in process. Instructional strategies imbedded in components of the framework make possible the simultaneous teaching of content and process. Operationalizing connections between content and process is what this book is all about.

Content

Content of curriculum is its substance. Content is comprised of interrelationships among principles, concepts, and specific information. Principles of a curriculum are broad generalizations illustrated by concepts within the same discipline. Principles in one discipline also are illustrated by concepts

FIGURE 5-1

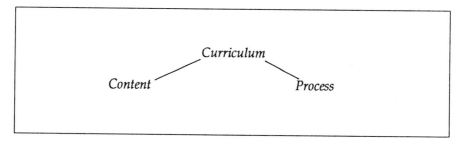

found in other disciplines as well as by concepts found in students' prior knowledge and experience.

Process

Process of curriculum is the means by which content is learned. Three learning processes constitute the major means by which students acquire and demonstrate their understandings of curriculum content. These learning processes are reading, writing, and reasoning.

Reading is applied to resource materials for purposes of acquiring information and developing ideas. Writing is applied to information and ideas for the purpose of reflecting, analyzing, communicating, and clarifying. Reasoning is applied to reading and writing for the purpose of giving power to each. Reasoning also is applied independently of reading and writing for purposes of reflecting, creating, analyzing, refining, extending, and sharing.

The particular reading, writing, and reasoning processes applied in the study of a given concept are determined by the conceptual focus of the lesson and the particular materials being used. As Parker and Rubin (1966) said, "Content determines process." That is, the substance of the material being studied, the manner in which it is organized, and the nature of the concepts to be developed all dictate the kind of reading, writing, and/or reasoning to be emphasized as part of the lesson or unit. Section III of this book presents ways to identify and teach these reading, writing, and reasoning processes.

Organizing Idea

The organizing idea for lessons brings content and process together instructionally (see Figure 5-2). The organizing idea, as defined in Chapter 2, is a declarative statement that expresses targeted relationships between or among targeted concepts. Learning processes are acquired as relationships are explored. Concepts are developed as relationships are applied.

The organizing idea serves as the conceptual focus for the instruction. It articulates particular aspects of the content to be studied in units and lessons. It is a vehicle for bringing content and process together so students learn both simultaneously. The organizing idea drives lessons and units and is a derivative of the Instructional Framework (see Figure 5-3).

Instructional Framework

The Instructional Framework is comprised of three main parts: preparation, guidance, and independence (see Figure 5-4).

FIGURE 5-2

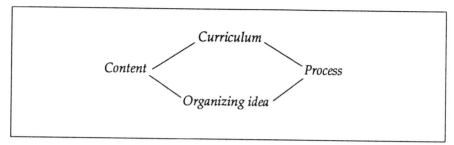

These three parts follow the generally accepted logic of teaching. That is, students are prepared for the study of a specific concept. They are guided in the acquisition of information and ideas related to that concept. They are then given opportunities to apply independently what they have learned relative to that concept.

Each of the three parts of the framework include instructional strategies that content-area teachers have found successful in their own practice, strategies that have been affirmed by research. Generic forms of these strategies are applicable across subject areas, grade levels, and teaching styles (Misulus 1988). The strategies are explained in general terms in this chapter. They are then explained and illustrated in detail in subsequent chapters in Section III. The chapters in Section III are organized around the Instructional Framework to make clear the relationships that exist between the strategies and the framework.

FIGURE 5-3

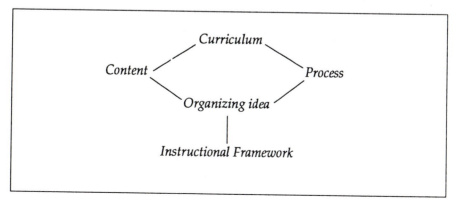

FIGURE 5-4

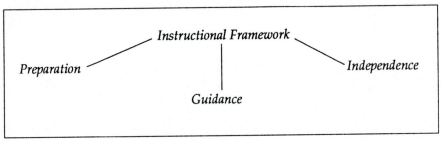

Preparation

The Instructional Framework includes activities and materials that prepare students to study the content of the curriculum and to apply appropriate reading, writing, and reasoning processes. Figure 5-5 identifies purposes for the preparation phase of the framework.

Making Connections

Learning involves making connections between what is known and what is being learned. Extensive research and practice has revealed the powerful influence that prior knowledge has on learning in general and on comprehension in particular (Bartlett 1932; Ausubel 1960, 1978; Herber 1970, 1978; Bransford and Johnson 1972; Anderson and Pearson 1984; Anderson 1985;

FIGURE 5-5

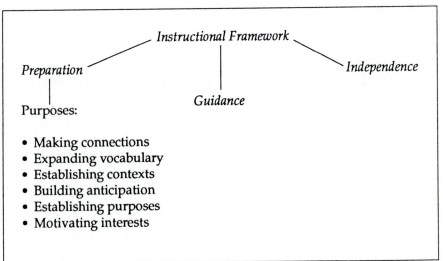

Langer and Nicolich 1981). Indeed, comprehension has come to be operationally defined as connecting what is known with what is new.

Students come to the study of a concept already possessing a certain amount of relevant prior knowledge and experience. How useful that knowledge and experience is depends on how broadly conceived the organizing idea is for the lesson. For example, if a teacher starts a social studies lesson on the concept of checks and balances by discussing specific aspects of the branches of federal government, students probably will have little to contribute because they do not yet know the particular information. In contrast, if the teacher starts this lesson with a general discussion of kinds of power, he or she can then lead the discussion to a consideration of political power and then to the idea of balance in political power. It is likely that students can illustrate applications of power and political power and balance of political power when they are given opportunity to draw examples from their everyday experiences. Their own experiences and prior knowledge serve as a context for studying a particular feature of the United States federal government, one that promotes a balance of political power among the three branches of government: the concept of checks and balances.

Thus, a central purpose in preparing students for learning a new concept is helping them discover that they already know a lot about what it is they going to study and then showing them how to use it. Information taught in a conceptually based curriculum is usually only one example of the particular concept being studied. The concept usually can be illustrated by other kinds of information as well, information that already exists in students' prior knowledge and experience. This means that organizing ideas have to be sufficiently comprehensive and abstract to be illustrated by more than just the specific information being studied in the lesson. This is why the articulation of organizing ideas for lessons or units is so important.

When organizing ideas are too narrow and specific, students' prior knowledge and experience become less relevant and useful for what is being studied. When organizing ideas are sufficiently broad and comprehensive, students' prior knowledge and experience become more relevant and useful. From students' perspectives, learning new information seems more possible when it is tied to a concept for which they already have acquired an understanding. Learning new information seems less possible when students are unable to make connections between what is known and what is new. The preparation part of the Instructional Framework establishes a basis for making connections between what is known and what is new by identifying the relevant known information that exists in students' prior knowledge and experience.

Traditional review activities help students connect with the relevant known information. Word-association activities, focused on the key word or words of the organizing idea, also reveal relevant experience and knowledge. When students have an opportunity to sort through what they already know about they are going to study, they have a stronger basis for making intellectual connections with what is new about what they are going to study.

Expanding Vocabulary

Each subject has its own technical language. Learning concepts within a discipline requires knowledge of vocabulary through which concepts and information are communicated. Preparing students to study a concept includes acquainting them with technical language needed to acquire basic information about the concept. Selected words are taught and other words are presented as part of the initial acquisition of technical language. (See Chapter 7 for a discussion of differences between teaching and presenting words.) Vocabulary is expanded and refined during the entire study of a concept, but the process begins in the preparation phase of the lesson. Chapter 7 presents a variety of ways to expand, extend, and refine students' technical language in various subjects.

Establishing Contexts

Providing conceptual contexts for what students are to study is an important purpose for preparing students for that study. Ausubel (1960) coined the term *advance organizer* to describe expository materials he designed to expose students to concepts they were to study. His materials were written at a higher level of generality and inclusiveness than the materials students actually were going to study. The rationale was that the more general and inclusive materials would serve as a context for the more specific information and ideas about to be studied. Since Ausubel's work, other vehicles have been devised and used for the same purpose.

Earle and Barron (1973) coined the term *structured overview* to describe the kind of conceptual context they created. Using technical vocabulary that comprises a concept, they construct a visual representation of that concept. They recommend that teachers identify technical vocabulary used to describe the concept under consideration. Teachers arrange that vocabulary in a visible display (on an overhead projector, chalkboard, oak tag, and so forth) so that students can see interrelationships that exist among the words that comprise the concept. While creating a structured overview, teachers draw known words from students, pointing out relationships among words as the concept develops. Teachers add appropriate information about the relationships so students acquire a sense of how the concept is organized and the structure relative to the concept. In this manner, students' develop a sense of the important information and ideas related to the concept, and they understand how the concept is organized. Figures 5-1 through 5-8 in this chapter are structured overviews of the concept *Instructional Framework* and its various derivations and components.

Technical vocabulary can be used in various other ways to establish conceptual contexts, such as graphic organizers, semantic maps, semantic webs, and semantic-feature analysis. These serve to prepare students for the study of concepts (see Chapter 7). They also can be applied in the independence phase of the Instructional Framework (see Chapter 12).

Building Anticipation

When students look for something as they study, they usually find it. When they look for nothing, they usually find it too! Methods and materials discussed thus far give students something to look for: showing relevance between students' prior knowledge and experience and concepts they are about to study, acquainting students with language they need to study the concept, and using technical vocabulary to portray the structure of a concept. These activities, plus others yet to be mentioned, combine to develop a sense of anticipation relative to the concept students are studying. This anticipation can be heightened by having students sort through their own beliefs about some specifically stated ideas relative to the concept and by having them subsequently make judgments about whether various authorities hold the same views on those same ideas. The anticipatory use of reasoning guides as part of the preparation phase of the Instructional Framework is discussed in Chapter 10. Also discussed is the use of reasoning guides in both the guidance and independence phases of the Instructional Framework.

Establishing Purposes

Establishing purposes for lessons is part of the preparation phase of the Instructional Framework. Some teachers like to use objectives to express their purposes; others like to have the purpose revealed as they progress through the lesson. Whichever approach is used, it is important to establish clearly your purposes for instruction. Purposes can be established when you identify the organizing idea of a lesson; when you identify relevant content from available resources; or when you identify the reading, writing, and reasoning processes to be emphasized while teaching the organizing idea. Purposes established in these contexts often are dependent upon teachers' expertise and thus are more teacher-centered. Purposes also can be established when you have students respond to word-association activities, anticipation guides, structured overviews, or journal writing. Purposes established in these contexts often are conditioned by students' prior knowledge and thus are more student-centered. The orientation and timing of the purposes established for your lessons are conditioned by your teaching style and your perception of your students' needs.

Motivating Interest

Preparation activities discussed thus far capture students' interests and motivate their study. Motivation for study is strongly related to students' intellectual and emotional investment in the concept under consideration. When they invest their own experiences, feelings, or ideas in a lesson, they are more interested in how that lesson progresses and in how their investment is used. As you progress through this book, you will see how the instructional strategies can prompt such investments by students.

Guidance

The Instructional Framework includes activities and materials that guide students' study of the content and application of reading, writing, and reasoning processes. Figure 5-6 identifies purposes for the guidance phase of the framework.

In Chapter 1 we discussed transitional instruction, defining it as showing students how to do what they need to do to be successful. The Instructional Framework provides the structure within which this showing how occurs. While a certain amount of showing how is present in the preparation phase of the Instructional Framework, much more is found in the guidance phase.

We use the word *guidance* in the Instructional Framework because it is the phase in which students are shown how to apply reading, writing, and reasoning processes that are natural to the concepts and materials they are studying.

Guiding students' reading, writing, and reasoning involves a variety of instructional options. What you select from these options for a particular lesson depends on the organizing idea being explored, the resources being used, and the level of proficiency students exhibit in the use of such resources and in the exploration of such ideas.

The guidance phase of the lesson includes the following general provisions. Ways to include these provisions in instruction are presented throughout the book.

FIGURE 5-6

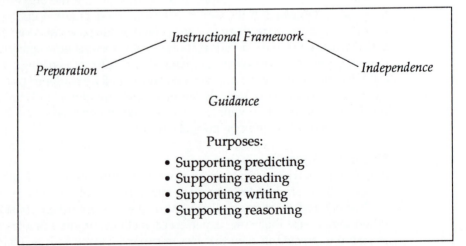

1. Giving careful directions for the tasks to be performed
2. Modeling and illustrating reading, writing, or reasoning processes needed to perform the tasks
3. Showing students how to apply the reading, writing, or reasoning processes
4. Monitoring of students' work and provision of feedback to them on what has been observed
5. Using intraclass grouping so students' work on tasks is facilitated by cooperative learning

Specific instructional strategies for guiding students' predicting, reading, writing, and reasoning are discussed and illustrated in Chapters 8, 9, and 10. Several of these instructional strategies are briefly mentioned in this section to give you a sense of what occurs in the guidance phase of the lesson.

Supporting Predicting

An important facet of guidance is prediction. Through some of the preparation activities already discussed, students develop a conceptual context for making predictions about actions, conditions, or attitudes they may discover or confront.

You can guide students so they learn how to base predictions on what is known and how to determine what, therefore, are reasonable expectations. They can be shown how to use evidence from relevant resources to confirm or disconfirm their predictions.

Supporting Reading

The most critical aspect of reading is comprehension. Without comprehension reading has little point. Years ago William S. Gray, the father of "Dick and Jane," defined *comprehension* as reading the lines, reading between the lines, reading beyond the lines (Gray 1960). It is possible to use these three descriptors to guide students' reading of various resource materials.

When students are shown how to read the lines, they learn how to acquire essential information from their reading. When they are shown how to read between the lines, they learn how to analyze information to determine its meaning and to develop ideas. When they are shown how to read beyond the lines, they learn how to apply the ideas to new situations and draw generalizations. You can create materials to guide students in this comprehension process, to show them how to comprehend the resource materials used in your subject (see Chapter 8).

Another major dimension of comprehension is the use of organizational patterns (see Chapter 3) found in most expository materials: cause-effect, comparison-contrast, time order, and simple listing (Niles 1965). What pattern you use is dictated by the organization of materials being read. Students can be shown how to use appropriate patterns as they read required resource materials. You can create materials to guide students' use of these patterns to show them how to comprehend resource materials used in your subject (see Chapter 8).

Supporting Writing

The composing process contributes importantly to students' learning. The interface between the composing process and the comprehension process is a critical one. The interaction between the two is mutually supportive and instructive. It is well known that reading informs one's writing (Smith 1984; Squire 1984; Tierney and Pearson 1984). It is less well known that writing informs one's reading (Smith 1984; Squire 1984; Tierney and Pearson 1984). It is possible, therefore, to use writing to prepare students for the reading they will do as well as to use reading to prepare them for their writing. In either or both cases, students can be guided so their understandings of both composing and comprehension are enhanced. Materials and instructional strategies can be devised to show students how to compose and comprehend for such purposes (see Chapter 9).

Supporting Reasoning

Reasoning encompasses a range of cognitive processes, from those that are analytical in nature to those that are elaborative.

1. Analytical reasoning is often constrained by specific contexts, with attempts being made to derive meanings and to draw conclusions from specific information and ideas.
2. Elaborative reasoning often spins off from given information and ideas, with attempts being made to develop new applications of the ideas or to synthesize resources and create new ideas.

Using both kinds of reasoning, students can derive more from resources they are exposed to and can make more interesting use of what they learn. Materials can be designed to guide students in the application of these reasoning processes to show them how to reason analytically and elaboratively (see Chapter 10).

Independence

The Instructional Framework includes activities and materials that encourage and support students' independence in their application of ideas and learning processes. Figure 5-7 identifies purposes and strategies for the independence phase of the framework.

Independence is the third phase of the Instructional Framework. Chapter 12 includes a comprehensive discussion of issues related to developing independence. However, a few of the issues should be considered at this juncture as well.

The term *independence,* as it is used in the Instructional Framework, describes an objective more than an accomplishment. That is, the purpose of instruction is to show students how to become independent rather than to assume that they are already independent.

Teaching independence is almost an oxymoron. As long as you are showing students how to be independent, they are not truly independent. But the answer to this dilemma is not to throw them completely on their own. Rather, it is to apply the idea of becoming independent to our instructional purposes, remembering that independence is a relative condition.

Given that independence is part of the Instructional Framework, it follows that independent applications of the content and process being taught are themselves being taught. Students do not function with complete independence when they are learning how to be independent. Just as students are supported in the preparation and guidance phases of the Instructional Framework, so they are supported in the independence phase. While some students can learn academic independence independently, most students benefit from being shown how to function independently. Thus, the showing how of instruction extends to the objective of developing students' independence.

Developing independence is a logical extension of carefully structured instruction. Students are shown how to apply and assess what they have learned about the content and the reading, writing, and reasoning processes. They are given opportunities to practice different applications of the content and the processes. They refine their application of the processes by analyzing how they work. They extend their use of the processes by applying them to related-but-different materials, ideas, or subjects. With sufficient showing how, combined with refinement and extension through practice, students

FIGURE 5-7

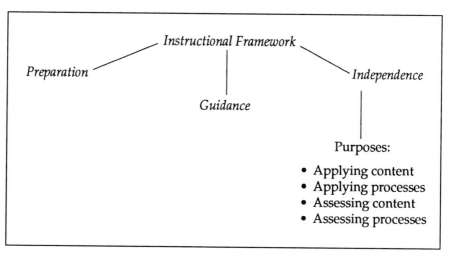

can attain new levels of independence in the process of becoming independent.

It is important to remember that independence is a relative state. You may develop independence in a given field, but if the knowledge base changes, if the job requirements change, or if the applications of the knowledge change, you lose your independence. You have to learn how to become independent in that new setting, with that new knowledge base, or with that new application. So it is with students as they progress through the grades. For them, independence in the application of reading, writing, and reasoning processes is a relative condition—always an objective but rarely a full accomplishment—because they move on to new levels of sophistication and abstraction in each curriculum area they study. Understanding the relative nature of independence increases one's understanding of the need for instruction in reading, writing, and reasoning.

Combining the Phases

The three phases of the Instructional Framework logically combine to create a lesson structure. There is logic and common sense to a structure that prepares students to perform a particular task, shows them how to perform it, and gives them an opportunity to practice using what they have learned. It is useful to think of these three phases as interactive as well as sequential. As is illustrated in discussions of the instructional options presented in this book, some aspects of guidance occur in the preparation phase of the lesson. Similarly, some preparation is involved in the guidance phase of the Instructional Framework. Equally so, some aspects of independence can be found in both the preparation and guidance parts of the lesson.

The Instructional Framework provides a structure for lessons that is sufficiently specific to be functional and sufficiently flexible to be practical. It serves well the concept of teaching as showing how. Figure 5-8 pulls together the purposes of all three parts of the framework. Instructional strategies that teachers can use to accomplish these purposes are presented in the Chapters in Section III.

Consequences

What are the consequences of using the Instructional Framework as a means for organizing your lessons? This depends on how you have organized your lessons to date. Most teachers include preparation and independence activities, whether or not they call them by such names. Fewer teachers include guidance activities in the sense that the term has been used in this Chapter. Our experience in working with content-area teachers over the years is that they find it beneficial to think through how they have been preparing and

FIGURE 5-8

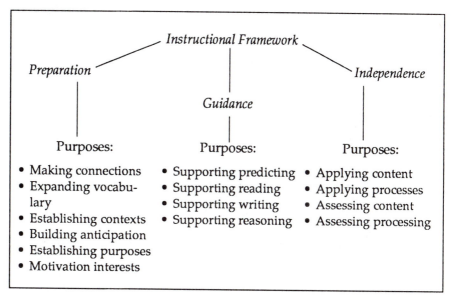

guiding their students and the extent to which they have shown their students how to become independent in their study of course concepts. Through this review, they often resurrect activities that once were useful but have been forgotten out of disuse. Then, as they study the instructional strategies presented in this book, they add to their repertoire those that work for them in the classroom—and most of them do.

Teachers who apply the Instructional Framework, or their version of it, generally discover the following:

1. The organizing idea drives lessons and keeps them focused on concepts, with information used to develop ideas rather than taught for its own sake.
2. Students gain immediate access to the organizing idea of a lesson when teachers frame the idea with sufficient breadth and comprehensiveness that it can be illustrated by ideas and information from students' prior knowledge as well as from the new material to be studied.
3. Preparation improves performance, especially as teachers prepare students for comprehending and composing.
4. An increase in preparation usually results in an increase in performance. Thus, time spent in the preparation part of a lesson or unit is time well spent.
5. Careful preparation of students for doing required tasks motivates their interest by building a sense of anticipation, a sense of purpose, a sense of direction, and a sense of confidence.

6. Guiding the development of students' reading, writing, and reasoning competencies is both a demanding and stimulating aspect of teaching.

7. Guiding the development of students' reading, writing, and reasoning involves modeling the processes in action.

8. The guidance part of the lesson structure develops students' confidence in their acquisition and use of technical vocabulary, comprehension of various resource materials, and communication of information and ideas in written form.

9. The independence part of the lesson structure also is part of instruction in that students are shown how to function independently.

10. The independence part of the lesson structure refines, expands, and extends students' understandings of the concepts acquired in the lesson and their use of reading, writing, and reasoning processes.

Summary

Integrating instruction in course content with instruction in reading, writing, and reasoning requires an overarching structure by which to manage all of the components. This structure needs to be sufficiently comprehensive to provide organization and direction to the instruction. However, it cannot be so complex as to make the preparation for and application of lessons burdensome, restrictive, and inefficient. The Instructional Framework provides the requisite structure. It is uncomplicated and has clearly identifiable components that can be applied efficiently and flexibly.

Instructional integration of content and process does not just happen. It requires thoughtful application of a theory of instruction that is well grounded in both practice and research. The Instructional Framework reflects such grounding. By its application, concepts and skills to be taught are easily selected and applied. Students are supported in their learning of concepts and skills in ways that raise the probability of their successful acquisition of both content and process.

REACTIONS

Journal Entries and Discussion

Review the display you prepared in response to Reflection 1 at the beginning of this Chapter. Compare it with the diagram in Figure 5-8. Analyze the similarities and differences with respect to both explicit and implicit instructional strategies. Include in your analysis your thoughts on why these similarities and differences exist.

Analysis and Discussion

Now that you have completed this chapter, consider the statements shown below. Check the numbered lines for statements with which you agree. Circle the numbers of statements you believe reflect the point of view of the authors. In writing, explore reasons for differences on any statements between your point of view and what you perceive to be the point of view of the authors. Please share and discuss your writing with colleagues who also are reading this book.

_____ 1. The purpose of the Instructional Framework is to facilitate the instructional integration of course content with related learning processes.

_____ 2. The label given to the organization of lessons doesn't really matter. What matters is that the lessons prepare students to perform required tasks, show students how to perform those tasks, and give students an opportunity for practice and application of what they have learned.

_____ 3. If a lesson structure omits the showing how, it may be an example of form without substance.

_____ 4. A lesson structure should be sufficiently firm to give a sense of purpose and direction yet sufficiently loose to allow for individuality and divergence.

_____ 5. Instruction should remain simple unless it would serve students better to make the instruction more complex.

_____ 6. When teachers focus on the presentation of information, they teach for the present. When teachers focus on how to develop and apply ideas, they teach for both the present and future.

_____ 7. If we want students to grow, we have to give them room to expand.

_____ 8. Just as the content in curriculum areas increases in sophistication through the grades, so does the process by which that content is learned. Students need to be taught how to handle both.

6

Teaching as Showing How

Organizing idea: The essence of good teaching is to show students how to do what is required to be successful.

Reflections

Before reading this chapter, please record in your journal your responses to the following questions. If possible, share your writing with other individuals who are also reading this book. The ideas that emerge will establish a context for this chapter.

1. What substitutes do you use for the textbook when that resource seems to be too much for your students to handle? How effective have these substitutes been?

2. In most occupations, special devices are used to support workers in their work in some way. What supporting devices do you provide your students?

3. What is there in the materials you construct for your teaching that provides for the showing how required for effective teaching?

THE ORGANIZING PRINCIPLE for the entire book was identified in the first chapter as "The essence of good teaching is to show students how to do what is required of them to be successful". Most chapters in the book discuss and illustrate some aspect of showing students how to read, write, or reason in various content areas. The organizing principle for the book also serves as the organizing idea for this chapter.

The purpose of this chapter is twofold:

1. To present a rationale for the showing-how aspect of teaching
2. To discuss and illustrate the following ideas:

   a. Content and process of a curriculum area can be taught as a unified whole; there need not be a dichotomy between content and process.
   b. Reading, writing, and reasoning processes that are taught in a content area are functionally derived from the organizing idea of the lesson as applied to the resources being used for the lesson.
   c. Reading, writing, and reasoning processes are taught through simulation and explicit instruction.
   d. Students' independence in their use of reading, writing, and reasoning processes is developed *over time* through repeated cycles of simulation, explicit instruction, and practice.
   e. The showing how of teaching requires a structure within lessons as well as a structure *of* lessons.

Practice

Before exploring this set of ideas, we want you to do the tasks presented in Practice 6-1 and Practice 6-2. Your experience with these activities will serve as a context for studying the concept of teaching as showing how. Please read the article entitled *When to Lie to Yourself* and then do the activity that follows the article, referring back to the article as you feel the need.

Now, please read the brief article in Practice 6-2 (see page 136), and then respond to the statements that follow, as specified in the directions that precede the statements.

Your response to the article in Practice 6-1 was guided by a set of questions. Your response to the article in Practice 6-2 was guided by a set of declarative statements. Did the statements guide your response in ways that were different from ways that the questions guided your response? Make a list of the differences you perceived. In a written analysis, identify factors that seem to have contributed to the differences and explain why. We will be drawing upon this experience later in the chapter.

Teaching Content and Process

This book is predicated on the substantiated belief that the processes of reading, writing, and reasoning can be taught simultaneously with course content in any subject by any subject-area teacher. This instruction occurs by applying the principle that "content determines process" (Parker and Rubin 1966). Instructional programs that incorporate this principle successfully develop students' proficiency in reading, writing, and reasoning in content-

PRACTICE 6-1

When To Lie to Yourself

"Sorry, but I lost track of time".... "I must not have heard you".... "The dog ate it." Everybody knows it's wrong to make up excuses to get off the hook when something goes wrong. But the fact is, excuses work. When we have failed to live up to our own or someone else's expectations, excuses help preserve our self-image and sense of control.

Indeed, recent research by psychologists C. R. Snyder and Raymond Higgins at the University of Kansas shows that people who offer themselves plausible excuses have greater self-esteem and better health and perform better on all sorts of cognitive, social and physical tasks than individuals who put the blame on themselves when things go wrong.

Making excuses is a distancing process according to Snyder and Higgins; it lays the blame for failure on external causes rather than on our own lack of intelligence or competence. Although distancing rarely absolves us completely from a particular failure, it does help explain failures in less troubling terms. It's easier to walk away from a mishap, for example, if you can say, "I flunked the exam because I didn't study" rather than "I flunked because I'm dumb." . . .

Snyder and Higgins say that excuse making is part of "reality negotiation"—a conflict between the "development, maintenance and nurturing of a positive personal theory of what we are" and the commentary, in the form of failures, that life is continually making about us.

Excuses are one way of resolving these inconsistencies. They "slow down the rate of change involved in reacting to threatening events" and give us time to marshal additional psychological resources.

Our own version of reality, the researchers point out, often bumps up against the way others see the same situations. Excuses bridge the gap between the two versions. Fortunately for the excuse maker, even skeptical listeners are normally reluctant to challenge or deny directly what we say. Snyder and Higgins say that an audience "collaborates" with an excuse maker to keep his or her selfesteem intact. And our friends are among our closest conspirators.

Excuses, according to Snyder and Higgins, are necessary illusions, far from the "simple, silly and ineffective ploys" most people consider them. The selfimage that excuses bolster enhances happiness and contentment. The fault, say the happy few, lies not in ourselves, but in our stars.

Source: Nick Jordan, "When To Lie to Yourself," *Psychology Today*, June 1989, vol. 23, No. 6, p. 24.

Directions: Listed below are ten questions. Answer each question with a statement that can be supported directly or inferentially with information

(continued)

PRACTICE 6-1 Continued ━━━━━━━━━━━━━━━━━━━━━━━━━━━

found in the article entitled "When to Lie to Yourself." With your group members, discuss the evidence you used to support each of your answers.

1. Why is it that excuses work even though they are wrong?
2. How does the health of excuse makers compare with the health of nonexcuse makers?
3. What is the safety factor that excuse making provides?
4. What constitutes distancing and how does it relate to excuse making?
5. Why do Snyder and Higgins advocate excuse making?
6. How does excuse making relate to reality negotiation?
7. Do Snyder and Higgins believe that life's "commentary . . . about us" is generally negative or generally positive?
8. Is reality absolute or relative, and what makes it so?
9. How do friends and mirrors relate to excuse makers and excuse making?
10. How would Snyder and Higgins fit Caesar and Brutus in a conspiracy theory of excuse making?

━━━

area classes. *Content determines process* means that the reading, writing and reasoning processes taught in a subject area are dictated by two factors:

1. The focus and complexity of the concepts being taught
2. The sophistication and organization of the resources being used to teach the concepts

For example, suppose that a concept being taught in history or science involves the study of some comparative relationships. Suppose also that the resources being used are organized to present such comparisons. As students use the resources, they are guided so two things occur:

1. They learn the concept.
2. They also learn how to perceive and apply comparative relationships.

Content and process are learned simultaneously because both are imbedded in the resources being used. Instruction in how to read, write, or reason for comparative relationships should not be separate from instruction in the substance of those relationships. By such a separation, instruction in how to apply the processes of reading, writing, and reasoning to a text are disconnected from instruction in the concepts contained in the text. Such a separation inverts Parker and Rubin's principle and makes it process determines content where resources are selected to teach a process rather than processes selected to teach course content.

PRACTICE 6-2

Bedtime Story

Have you ever noticed that when you are sleeping happily and the telephone rings, the voice at the other end always says, "Did I wake you up?" And have you ever noticed how you immediately and invariably reply? You lie. "Of course not," you say. "I've been up for hours."

For some reason, to sleep peaceably in your bed is looked upon as a deed so degrading that people are ashamed to confess it over the telephone. Why? And how does the caller always know that he has awakened his victim? Through decades of being telephoned out of sleep, I recollect not one case in which the caller did not know instantly that he had awakened me.

I believe the question, "Did I wake you up?" is maliciously framed to give the caller powerful psychological advantage over his victim. Since he obviously knows he has awakened you, why does he bother to ask? He could do the civilized thing and immediately hang up with a quiet, "Sorry, I'll phone later when you are awake." Instead. he takes the opportunity to subject you to a humiliating cross-examination. He knows you will lie.

This tendency to lie about sleeping probably reflects some ancient American belief in the virtues of early rising. Benjamin Franklin held that, coupled with early bedding, it made you healthy, wealthy and wise. The early bird gets the worm, goes another aphorism, and I suppose all Americans sleeping after 6 a.m. may feel subconsciously guilty about enjoying themselves instead of getting worms.

This does not explain, however, why most people are just as quick to lie about being asleep when the phone goes off at three o'clock in the morning and the inevitable question comes out of the earpiece, "Did I wake you?"

"At three o'clock in the morning?" you reply. "You must be kidding. I've been up since midnight getting worms."

Witty reply, however, is never possible from a mind summoned out of sleep. Even if it were, the caller would almost certainly turn out to be Aunt Isabel phoning in tears to report that Uncle Norman had been gravely stricken with the boll weevil.

So we lie. Wake me up? Not a chance. Everybody is wide awake here in the U.S.A. Twenty-four hours a day.

Source: "Bedtime Story," *Reader's Digest*, September 1989, 153 (from Russell Baker in *The New York Times*).

Directions: Listed below are ten statements. On the numbered line before each statement, place a check if you believe it represents ideas that can be supported by information in the article entitled "Bedtime Story".

(continued)

PRACTICE 6-2 Continued ━━━━━━━━━━━━━━━━━━━━━━━━

With your group members, discuss the evidence you identified that caused you to accept or reject each of the statements.

_____ 1. Most people believe that it is undesirable to be caught sleeping.

_____ 2. A lie is not a lie when both parties know it is not the truth.

_____ 3. Not being indolent is more virtuous than not being truthful.

_____ 4. Ancient virtues can control modern behavior.

_____ 5. Unwanted intrusion can lead to unwarranted prevarication.

_____ 6. Efforts to gain psychological advantage over others are maliciously motivated.

_____ 7. Management of wit is highly correlated with alertness of mind.

_____ 8. Early to bed and early to rise makes a person healthy, wealthy, and wise.

_____ 9. If your diet consists principally of worms, your best time for meals is in the early-morning hours.

_____ 10. Feelings of vulnerability are highly correlated with sudden arousal from somnolence.

Functional Teaching

Derivation of Processes

The principle *content determines process*, is operationalized by "functional teaching" (Herber 1970, 1978). In functional teaching, the particular learning processes you teach are dictated by the resources students use in the lesson and by the organizing idea that drives the lesson. Functional teaching of reading, writing, and reasoning involves the following steps:

1. Establish the organizing idea for the lesson.
2. Identify resources to be used to help students develop an understanding of the organizing idea.
3. Analyze the resources to determine what reading, reasoning, and writing processes students will need to use in order to acquire the essential information and to develop and apply the relevant concepts, including identification of:

   a. The technical vocabulary that should be taught or presented
   b. How the organization of the material can be used to support the comprehension of its content
   c. The levels of sophistication and abstraction of concepts contained in the material

4. Create materials to support students as they apply the reading, writing, and reasoning processes so identified.
5. Organize the lesson using the Instructional Framework or a similar plan.

By following these steps, the conceptual focus of the lesson is assured because the organizing idea drives the lesson and is based on the content objectives of the curriculum. The process focus of the lesson is assured because the processes to be emphasized are functionally derived from the resources being used to study the organizing idea of the lesson. Thus, an instructional unity is created between content and process. Separation of the two is unnecessary.

Showing How

Once you have identified both the content and the learning processes to be taught, how do you teach so the content and processes of the lesson are learned together? If the essence of good teaching is to show students how to do what is required of them to be successful, then the essential question is "How do we show our students how?"

Instructional Scaffolding

The showing how of teaching requires support of students while they are learning required content and process. A useful metaphor for describing this support is instructional "scaffolding" (Applebee 1986; Applebee and Langer 1983; Vygotsky 1962, 1978). In his definition of instructional scaffolding, Applebee defines learning as

> *a process of gradual internalization of routines and procedures available to the learner from the social and cultural context in which the learning takes place. Typically, new skills are learned by engaging collaboratively in tasks that would be too difficult for the individual to undertake alone but that can be completed successfully in interaction with parent or teacher. In this interaction, the role of the parent or teacher is to provide the necessary support, or scaffolding, to allow the child to complete the task and in the process to provide the child with an understanding of the problem and of the strategies available for its solution (Applebee 1986, 108).*

Scaffolds allow workers to perform tasks they could not otherwise complete. Scaffolds provide a place to work, a position from which workers can accomplish what they are expected to do. Scaffolds also provide workers access to places they could not reach on their own. In these otherwise inaccessible places, they can complete tasks they could not otherwise perform.

Teaching as showing how is building the scaffold for the students to use so they derive the benefits of such support. It contrasts with more conventional teaching which, in essence, is giving lumber to the students and saying, "Build your own scaffold."

Applebee suggests the following features that characterize instructional scaffolding:

1. *Student ownership of the learning event.*

   The instructional task must allow students room to make their own contribution to the activity as it evolves, giving them a sense of ownership of what they are doing. In writing instruction, this means that writing activities must serve real language functions (informing, persuading, telling a story, or the like) beyond the simple desire to please the teacher.

2. *Appropriateness of the instructional task.*

   Tasks should build upon knowledge and skills the student already possesses but should be difficult enough to allow new learning to occur. Sequence in instruction thus becomes as much a function of the psychology of the learner as of the logic of the subject matter. In Vygotsky's (1962) words, instruction should focus not so much on the ripe as on the ripening functions.

3. *A structured learning environment.*

   The instructional interaction should provide a natural sequence of thought and language, thus presenting the student with useful strategies and approaches to the task. Through this structure, the student learns new skills in the process of doing the task in a context where the instruction provides the scaffolding or support necessary to make the task possible. This structure is at the heart of learning: it is the mechanism by which social knowledge is shared with young learners, enabling them to participate in their common culture and eventually to claim it as their own.

4. *Shared responsibility.*

   Tasks are solved jointly in the course of instructional interaction; the role of the teacher in this process needs to be more collaborative than evaluative. The teacher's task must be conceived as helping students toward new learning, rather than just as testing the adequacy of previous learning.

5. *Transfer of control.*

   Over time, as students internalize new procedures and routines, they should take a greater responsibility for controlling the progress of the task. Some tasks will simply be completed independently; others will evolve into dialogues in which teacher and pupil become more equal partners in the problem-solving effort. The amount of interaction may actually increase as the student becomes more competent, with the interaction shifting from simple questions or directives toward a more expert exploration of options and alternatives (Applebee 1986, 110).

Instructional strategies presented in this book, based on the notion of teaching as showing how, operationalize these features of instructional scaffolding. However, it is important to note that instructional strategies you already know and use can be part of the scaffolding, if adapted for that purpose. As Applebee says about the features noted above,

they provide a new way to think about familiar teaching routines, rather than demanding the wholesale abandonment of the past. Any teaching technique will be appropriate to the extent that it provides useful scaffolding for a particular task; and given a particular new problem facing a student, any technique chosen will be seen as only one of a variety of possible ways to address that same problem (Applebee 1986).

Simulation

Creating the scaffolding that shows students how to apply specific processes is probably the most difficult part of teaching. By comparison, it is relatively easy to identify the information and ideas you want your students to acquire. It is relatively easy to assign students materials to be read and to lead a discussion to determine whether or not students have acquired the information and ideas. It is relatively easy to test students to determine what they have retained from what you taught and at what levels of sophistication and abstraction they have done so. It is much more difficult to show students how to apply various reading, reasoning, and writing processes that are required for a successful response to all of those required tasks.

Showing how essentially involves a form of simulation that is a kind of scaffolding. For the purpose of showing how, *simulation* can be defined as "an artificial representation of a real experience; a contrived series of activities which, when taken together, approximate the experience or the process that ultimately is to be applied independently" (Herber and Nelson 1975).

In other words, simulation involves walking students through processes we want them to apply independently some day. The process of walking through helps students develop a feel for how their minds work as they apply the reading, reasoning, and writing processes they are learning. Simulating a physical process can be complicated, but generally easier than a cognitive process. Most people are familiar with driving simulators, or flight simulators which can replicate specific physical conditions people experience while driving or flying. Through these simulators, trainees develop an understanding of the forces and conditions that influence their performance. They develop the physical skills needed to respond to the various replicated conditions, to the point of automaticity. Thus, when trainees actually drive their cars or fly their planes, the forces and conditions they experience are already familiar to them and they can function satisfactorily.

Simulating cognitive processes such as reading, reasoning, and writing, is much more difficult. Chapters 7 through 10 discuss and illustrate ways to simulate applications of reading, writing, and reasoning. To illustrate simulation in this chapter, we focus on the process of interpretation. We do so by using your responses to the two articles you read at the beginning of this chapter.

Your response to the article in Practice 6-1 was guided by questions. Most of the questions involved some form of interpretation. That is, in order to answer the questions, you had to analyze the information given in the article, determine what pieces of information seemed to relate to one another, and formulate an idea that seemed to emerge from those relationships. Then, in your own words, you had to express those ideas and/or describe the nature of the relationships you found. Because you already are a skilled reader, you probably did not have much difficulty reading the article and answering the questions. But how successful you would have been if you were not already a skilled reader? You might have experienced difficulty perceiving the logical relationships across pieces of information presented in the article. You might have experienced difficulty inducing ideas that flow from the relationships you perceived. You might have experienced difficulty expressing your answers in written form.

So if you were a reader having trouble interpreting expository material, would a set of questions that require you to interpret the article independently show you how to interpret the article? Probably not, even if the intended purpose in giving you the questions were to help you learn how to interpret. The task would be requiring you to do independently what you had not yet learned to do. If the task were part of an instructional activity designed to improve your interpretive skills, you would be a recipient of "assumptive teaching" (Herber 1970, 1978). Assumptive teaching occurs when a teacher gives students tasks that require students to do independently what the teacher intended to teach them to do. The assigned task assumes competence in what supposedly is being taught.

Suppose, once again, that you were a reader having some difficulty interpreting expository material. Suppose that your teacher decided to help you with this problem and gave you the material in Practice 6-1 so you could learn how to interpret expository material. If you could articulate what is happening to you, you might well think, "Wait a minute, please. I'm having trouble here. I need to have someone show me how to do this work. I need to learn how to interpret this material and answer these questions." However, suppose that the teacher, despite noting your difficulty with the material, just gave you more of the same kind of material? How long would it be before you decided that learning how to interpret expository material was not a fruitful experience for you?

This is an example of assumptive teaching. The questions require you to apply the very interpretive processes that the teacher, by using this article and related questions, is trying to teach you. Giving you more of the same kind of activity and increasing the frequency of your exposure to the materials does not increase the likelihood that you will learn how to interpret. Someone needs to show you how to interpret and how interpretation works for you.

You may well be wondering, "But who would teach so assumptively? Surely this is not what happens in schools. Teachers *must* be teaching students *how* to interpret expository materials as well as other comprehension processes."

Your response is logical—the reality is not what you think it should be. Assumptive teaching of reading, writing, and reasoning processes is prevalent. Close examination of materials used to guide students' responses to resource materials, both published and teacher made, reveals an implicit presence of assumptive teaching. For the most part, teachers who are engaged in assumptive teaching are unaware that they are doing it. Their attention has not been called to what they are doing and, because their use of questions is consistent with our teaching traditions, they do not perceive a problem.

Another way to clarify assumptive teaching is to note the contrast between teaching students *how to do* something and providing students with *practice* on something they previously have been taught to do. Many activities that purport to *teach* a reading, writing, or reasoning process are better used to provide *practice* on that process after it has been acquired. The materials in Practice 6-1, for example, provide practice on the process of interpretation. If students had previous instruction in how to interpret expository material, they could apply their knowledge of interpretation as they respond to the questions. The practice experience could help students refine interpretive skills they already possess.

Prequestioning Strategies

Assumptive teaching is avoided and teaching as showing how is operationalized through the use of prequestioning strategies. Prequestioning strategies support students while they are learning a new process or while they are learning how to apply a known process at a new level of sophistication. Prequestioning strategies contrast with strategies that provide refining practice on processes already known at levels of sophistication already acquired.

Implicit in the notion of prequestioning strategies are two factors:

1. An acknowledgement of the importance of questions to teaching

2. A recognition that students ultimately need to be able to respond independently to questions to demonstrate both the content and the process of what they have learned.

We discuss the importance and usefulness of questions later in this chapter, in Chapter 4, and also in Chapter 12.

Declarative Statements

Declarative statements form the centerpiece of prequestioning strategies. Typically, declarative statements are just that: well-crafted, complete sentences that express a point of view, an idea, hypothesis, or an understanding relative to the organizing idea of the lesson and to the particular resource materials being used. Your response to the article in Practice 6-2 was guided by declarative statements. The statements focused on ideas related to the article. Responding to the statements involved you in a discussion of issues related to the organizing idea for the lesson, which was

Unwanted intrusion leads to unwarranted prevarication.

You were involved in learning the content of the lesson. Your response to the statements also involved you in applying the process of interpretation. You selected statements that you could support with evidence from the text. You actually identified that supporting information. You discussed how the information fit together to support the statements. Thus, you interpreted the text in a simulated form, not in an independent form.

Simulation

How is this response to declarative statements a simulation? In what way is it teaching by showing how?

To interpret text you identify important information in the text, look for logical relationships across that information, draw inferences or conclusions from the relationships, and create statements that reflect the inferences or conclusions you have drawn. Using declarative statements to guide readers' response to text inverts this procedure. Readers are given possible inferences or conclusions in the form of declarative statements. They determine if there is evidence in the text to support the statements. If they find evidence, they discuss how the evidence fits together to support the statements. In responding to statements in this manner, readers are walked through the process of interpretation. The experience simulates interpretation.

Selecting evidence to support (or reject) a statement is the obverse of selecting information from which to create a statement. Evidence is required in both instances. However, using evidence to create a statement of interpretation requires higher levels of independence and sophistication in the use of interpretive skills than does using evidence to support a preexisting statement. Nonetheless, as students analyze information to find evidence to support or reject a preexisting statement, they develop a feel for determining how information fits together conceptually. They also develop a feel for what it is like to create a statement that reflects the concept derived from an analysis of information.

Understanding how information can be gathered and interrelated to support a declarative statement leads to an understanding of how information can be gathered and interrelated to create an answer to a question. The two experiences are sufficiently similar to allow students to perceive the connection and to be used by teachers to help students make the transition to writing their own statements as answers to questions. *Declarative statements, then, serve transitional instruction operationalizing teaching as showing how.* Consequently, the use of declarative statements provides a distinct instructional advantage in the development of both content and process.

Answers before Questions

Another way to consider this use of declarative statements is to think of using answers to guide students' reading rather than using questions. Thinking of the statements as answers is particularly helpful when you design your guide materials. For example, if students' response to a resource should be interpretation, as was the case for the article presented in Practice 6-2, then you create statements that reflect your own interpretation of the material. You do this by asking yourself questions about the material, questions such as "What is the significant information? What are the significant relationships across this information? What ideas emerge when I examine these relationships? What meaning do I give to these ideas?" You create the guide by writing out your answers to these and other appropriate self-questions in the form of declarative statements. You give these statements to your students to guide their response to the same resource materials.

Because your statements are answers to questions you ask of the material, you naturally will expect that students will find evidence in the material to support the statements. Don't be surprised when students sometimes disagree with you and with one another about whether there is sufficient evidence to support some statements. Such independent thinking should be encouraged. Unless you are dealing with absolutes, the important criterion is evidence, not rightness or wrongness.

You can use differences in students' responses to encourage modest writing activities. Ask students who disagree with a statement to rewrite it to the point at which they feel there is sufficient evidence from the text to support it.

Designing Guide Materials

Designing the guide materials becomes a relatively straightforward and uncomplicated task.

1. You establish the organizing idea for the lesson and select the resource materials to be used.
2. You determine what reading or reasoning processes students must apply to the resources in order for them to develop an understanding the organizing idea.
3. You create statements that simulate the processes you identified.
4. You give students the declarative statements in a format that is appropriate to the process you are simulating and supporting. (See Chapters 7 through 10 and Appendix B for examples.)
5. You include directions that clearly explain what students are to do and fully support the reading or reasoning process they are to apply.
6. You give the material you have created to students to use as they respond to the resource materials you have assigned.

Encourage your students to respond to your guide materials in the same way that you responded to the article and guide material in Practice 6-2. That is, have them identify statements for which they can find support in the article itself. Encourage them to cite specific information as evidence to support their decisions for accepting or rejecting statements. Have them work with other students in the class, usually in a small-group format, to discuss the reasons for their decisions.

Access and Sophistication

The use of declarative statements to guide students' response to resource materials has two important side benefits. The first benefit has to do with providing all students with access to ideas being discussed in a lesson. When ideas being discussed are derived principally from reading the text, students with reading problems have only limited access to the ideas. However, when declarative statements in the guide materials are used to represent ideas possibly found in the text, all students have access to the ideas. Through their interactions in small-group discussions, all students participate in the exploration and application of the ideas. Equity in access to ideas is an important students' right. Use of declarative statements helps to assure the realization of that right.

The second benefit derived from the use of declarative statements has to do with the level of sophistication of ideas to which all students have access. Use of declarative statements makes it possible for students to deal with ideas at much higher levels of abstraction and sophistication than would be possible if students were restricted to discussing their own answers to questions. A learning principle involved here is that *it is easier to recognize the relationship between an idea and the relevant information than it is to create an expression of the idea that can be induced from that information.* Many students cannot independently conceptualize and express sophisticated and abstract relationships that exist across pieces of information. However, they can recognize information that fits together to support an abstract or sophisticated idea when that idea has been conceptualized and expressed in written form. They can learn what their minds "feel" like when they put information together as evidence to support their response to the statements. Such feelings serve as the experiential basis for eventually putting information together to create written statements of their own.

Teachers with whom we have worked over the years, from a wide range of school settings, consistently have been impressed by the number of students who enthusiastically participate in the discussion of sophisticated and abstract ideas even though the students themselves could not independently create such ideas. These same teachers report that over time, as students gain confidence and experience in responding to such ideas and in finding evidence to support or refute the ideas, they develop an ability to conceptualize such ideas themselves. Instruction that uses declarative statements is responsive to students' potential levels of accomplishment rather than being restricted to their current levels of accomplishment. Such instruction stretches students' minds in a nonthreatening manner and involves them in the exciting part of learning: the discussion of substance the exploration of ideas that make a difference.

As you will see in Chapters 7 through 10, declarative statements can be used in a variety of forms and represented in a variety of ways to simulate various aspects of reading, writing, and reasoning. Because the statements are driven by the organizing idea of the lesson and because the resource materials being analyzed are selected to help develop that idea, the information and ideas that students discuss are central to what it is that teachers want students to learn. Thus, students learn the content of the lesson. Because they are responding to statements that are products of particular reading and/or reasoning processes, students develop a consciousness about how those processes work. Prequestioning strategies provide continued support for students as they respond to resources in subsequent lessons, and their competence in the application of reading and reasoning processes grows. Eventually, they will be able to respond independently to questions for which they themselves must construct the answers.

Before then, however, they are shown how to develop those answers. And in that showing how, they are learning relevant processes along with course content.

Explicit Instruction

Consistent with the definition of teaching as showing how is the concept of explicit instruction, a concept supported by recent research in teaching (Baker and Brown 1984; Pearson 1984, Pearson and Leys 1985). Explicit instruction is intended to raise students' consciousness about the strategies for learning they apply while learning. In reference to reading, for example,

> *the use of a reading strategy helps a reader experience the sense of a text and learn what it means to make sense of text. A reading strategy is a means for cultivating this experience, but is not a means for directly teaching the experience. What is directly taught is the use of the strategy. The effective use of strategies over time helps the student learn to experience the sense of text (Mosenthal 1989, 245).*

As noted earlier, one does not teach students how to interpret materials just by requiring them to do so. This is assumptive teaching. One must teach them *the use of* interpretation as a means of making sense of what is being read. Using the nomenclature of this text, the focus of what students are taught in explicit instruction is *how to do what is required of them to be successful,* how to perform the learning tasks that are needed in order to acquire an understanding of the organizing idea of the lesson. Several factors are involved in this explicit instruction:

1. Explaining the process to be applied
2. Modeling the application of the process
3. Giving directions in how to apply the process
4. Monitoring students as they apply the process
5. Providing feedback to students on what was observed during the monitoring
6. Extending the explaining, modeling and directing as needed

Remember Mosenthal's distinction between *teaching (about)* a learning strategy (process) and *teaching the use of* a learning strategy (process). This is a fine, but important, distinction that is easily blurred. The *explaining* that is done in explicit instruction is not *about* a learning process *per se;* rather, it is *about the use* of the learning process. Spending time explaining about a learning process is appropriate if you are teaching teachers who themselves will be teaching that process; but it is not necessary if you are teaching students who need to learn how to use the process. The explanation to students focuses on its use.

Similarly, the modeling, the directing, and the monitoring that are part of the explicit instruction are concerned with the *use of* the process. Raising students' consciousness about the use of a process, then, is the purpose of explicit instruction. Given that the processes being emphasized are functionally derived, students develop a consciousness about how to use learning processes essential to the study of disciplines in which they are enrolled.

Researchers who have focused their professional attention on students' use of learning processes use the term *metacognition* to describe this consciousness-raising (Brown 1980; Brown, Campione, and Day 1981;

Baker and Brown 1984). In brief, metacognition involves one in developing knowledge about the thinking one is doing while engaged in a task. Applied to explicit teaching of the uses of reading, writing, and reasoning, metacognition involves one in developing knowledge about how these thinking processes work. Particularly it does so *as* one learns the content of the disciplines in which the processes are being used. The factors fundamental to explicit instruction (explaining, modeling, directing, monitoring, providing feedback), are metacognitive in nature. That is, teachers' applications of these factors raise students' consciousness about what they are doing when they read, write, and reason. These factors get students thinking about the thinking required by the application of these learning processes.

Questions and Control

The ultimate aim of our instruction is for students to be able to function with independence in the acquisition of new knowledge. In Chapter 1 we talked about how transitional instruction is cyclical in nature and how students are moved from the point where they need a high degree of structure and support to the point where they can function with a high degree of independence. The goal for our students is that they eventually become self-monitoring learners. We learned from the discussion of transitional instruction that students' movement to independence, or to being self-monitoring learners, is not accomplished in one once-and-for-all shift. Indeed, there is some question as to whether one ever reaches the state of being a totally independent, self-monitoring learner. Nonetheless, we should expect students to make progress toward independence. As they progress through the grades, they learn to use learning processes at increasingly higher levels of sophistication. They become more and more able to function independently, requiring less and less time for metacognitive instruction. The relative roles of teachers and students in this cycle are important. A useful metaphor to describe these roles is the ebb and flow of the tides. There cannot be a ebb of the tides on the shore lines without there being a concomitant heaping of water at mid ocean. So, too, there cannot be an increase in teacher management of learning without a corresponding diminution of student management. Logically, there cannot be an increase in students' self-management of learning without a corresponding diminution of teacher management. Making this transition involves a shift in control, from teacher control over the learning to student control (Pearson and Leys 1985). Applying the tidal metaphor, we move students toward being self-monitoring learners by having teachers control the ebb while students control the flow.

The interaction between statements and questions, as a means for guiding students' response to resources, is an important one. In that statements are used as a *prequestioning* strategy, statements are used before questions. But the order of use is not static; rather it is recursive. You do not start with statements and then shift permanently to the use of questions. Rather, as you guide students through concepts and materials at increasingly higher levels of sophistication and abstraction, you can shift back and forth between statements and questions. When moving to a new level of sophistication and abstraction, you can use statements to simulate the learning processes and to develop awareness and knowledge of how the processes are used at that level. You then can use questions to practice, extend, and refine the processes that have been learned at that level of sophistication (see Chapter 12). When you move to the next level of sophistication, you repeat the cycle.

Questioning is a hallmark of teaching. Socrates is imbedded in the professional psyche of most teachers, and the Socratic method of teaching underlies much of our methodology. In an educational context, the person asking the questions usually is the person in control of the instruction. That person usually is the teacher. Eventually, as students become self-monitoring learners and take more control over their learning, *they* ask the questions. Let's review how this can work.

Recall the Instructional Framework (see Chapter 5) and its three parts: preparation, guidance, and independence. When teachers are in control of the instruction, they use questions to prepare students for the work to be done. Through questioning they probe students' prior knowledge relative the organizing idea of the lesson. Through questioning they help students make predictions about what it is they will be learning, which helps students develop a sense of anticipation to carry with them in their study. Through questioning they help students develop knowledge about how to use these *preparation* strategies. When teachers are in control of the instruction they use self-questioning to create declarative statements to *guide* students' reading of resource materials. They use the equivalent of declarative statements to guide students' writing and reasoning about the organizing idea of the lesson (see Chapters 9 and 10). Through subsequent questioning of students about their reasons for accepting or rejecting various statements, teachers help students develop knowledge of how the reading, writing, or reasoning process works and how to use it to develop an understanding of the organizing idea of the lesson.

When teachers are in control of the instruction, they use questions to help students develop *independence* in the application of what they learned in the preparation and guidance phases of the lesson structure (see Chapter 12). Through questioning teachers provide students with practice on the use of the reading, writing, or reasoning processes they were exposed to in the preparation and guidance phases of the lesson. Through questioning, teachers provide students with opportunities to refine their understanding of the organizing idea of the lesson as well as to apply the knowledge they have gained relative to that idea.

As time passes and students' knowledge increases with respect to how to use various reading, writing, and reasoning processes, teachers can let their control over the learning begin to ebb and the students' control begin to flow. It is important to note that this shift in control is gradual, not abrupt; it is accomplished by design, not by chance. Teachers begin this shift in control by a calculated expansion of the factors already identified as being important in explicit, metacognitive teaching:

- Explaining
- Modeling
- Giving directions
- Monitoring
- Providing feedback
- Extending the explaining, modeling, and directing as needed

Teachers' *explanations* of learning processes are expanded to refine students' understanding of their use and how such processes facilitate learning the content of the lesson. The teachers' *modeling* of the application of the processes is expanded to demonstrate both how to think about the processes as they are applied and how to actually apply them. Teachers' *monitoring* is expanded to probe students' thinking as they apply the processes and thereby demonstrate what eventually can become the students' self-monitoring of their own applications of the learning processes.

As more time passes, teachers can provide students with opportunities to practice the procedures that eventually will make them self-monitoring learners. Working in small groups, students take turns assuming the role of the teacher to direct the group's study of a segment of the lesson. The student in charge applies teaching procedures similar in nature and purpose to those used by the teacher: explaining, modeling, directing, monitoring, and so forth. In so doing, the student in charge refines his or her metacognitive knowledge and application of the reading, writing, and reasoning processes. Other students in the group benefit from the instruction both by learning the content of the lesson and by reinforcing their own metacognitive knowledge and application of the reading, writing, and reasoning processes. Researchers who have focused their professional attention on the development of students' metacognitive knowledge and application of learning processes use the term *reciprocal teaching* as a descriptor for this student-as-teacher procedure (Manzo 1969; Manzo and Manzo 1990; Palincsar and Brown 1984). A careful reading of this literature will benefit those wishing to develop additional insight into ways to help their students become self-monitoring learners. The small-group work that is discussed in Chapter 4 and advocated throughout this book serves as the perfect context for helping students take this step toward attaining their independence in learning.

One more procedure needs to be mentioned, this one more specifically focused on reading, as a means for helping students become more independent in their learning. The descriptor for this procedure is QAR, which stands for "question-answer relationship" (Raphael 1984, 1986). Raphael (1984) based this procedure on a question-answer taxonomy devised by Pearson and Johnson (1978). Pearson and Johnson argue that one cannot assign a level of cognition to a question until one can see the kind of answer that the question elicits. A question that was intended to stimulate an inference but that in actuality provokes a literal response is in fact a literal question and not an inferential one. Thus, they argue, that any taxonomy derived from an assignment of cognitive levels to questions has to take into account not only the questions but also the answers that the questions provoke. The result, then, is a question-answer taxonomy.

Raphael (1984) extended this idea of question-answer relationships and created a procedure for developing students' ability to engage in self-questioning as they read. The procedure includes the factors of explaining, modeling, monitoring, and so forth that we now associate with the development of metacognitive knowledge and the application of learning processes. Use of QAR is a logical follow-up to the use of declarative statements for guiding students' reading of content-area resource materials. QAR provide an excellent means for moving students along the path of independence and toward the goal of becoming self-monitoring learners. Chapter 12 discusses this use of QARs in more detail.

Structure of and within Lessons

As noted in Chapter 5, the Instructional Framework constitutes an efficient and effective way to organize units and to structure lessons. The structure of lessons, reflecting this framework, is comprised of preparation, guidance, and independence.

In this chapter we have discussed how it is possible to teach reading, writing, and reasoning by showing students how to apply these processes as they study the content of the various disciplines in which they are enrolled. We can prepare them to study the materials; guide them in the study so they learn both process and content; and provide opportunity for them to refine, extend, and apply what they have learned in ways that move them toward more independence in learning. In this chapter we have examined ways that teachers can gradually turn over the control of learning to students so they eventually become self-monitoring learners. We have noted that the critical part of the lesson structure is the guidance we provide students. The showing how of this part of teaching requires careful organization and management so that it is effective and not perfunctory. The organization of the guidance part of the framework constitutes a structure within lessons. This is an important consideration in the design of materials and related instruction that support the showing how. In the remaining chapters of this section of the book, we make reference to and illustrate the structure within lessons.

This structure within lessons is central to teacher-monitored learning *for* students that leads eventually to self-monitored learning *by* students.

Summary

In addition to helping students learn the content of courses, subject-area teachers help students learn to read to learn (the content), learn to write to learn (the content) and learn to reason to learn (the content). Central to all this learning is the instructional process of showing how. Teachers show students how to read, write, and reason in ways that enable them to acquire and apply concepts at appropriate levels of abstraction and sophistication. The showing how develops students' metacognitive awareness of the learning processes and how they can be applied. The showing how supports the transition from teacher-directed to student-directed learning as appropriate and practicable for students. The ultimate objective for the showing how is that students become "self-managed learners" (Stauffer 1969).

REACTIONS

Journal Entries and Discussion

Some people say that the use of declarative statements to guide students' response to resources is just another form of questioning. Given your understanding of and experience with the use of declarative statements, do you agree or disagree with this view? Why?

　　Try your hand at a bit of creative writing, and play with the metaphor of instructional scaffolding. Let your ideas flow, and see where they take you. Find out what your mind has to tell you about this topic. If you wish, please share writing with some colleagues, preferably some who also are studying this book.

Analysis and Discussion

Now that you have completed this chapter, consider the statements shown below. Check the numbered lines for statements with which you agree. Circle the numbers of statements you believe reflect the point of view of the authors. In writing, explore reasons for differences on any statements between your point of view and what you perceive to be the point of view of the authors. Please share and discuss your writing with colleagues who also are reading this book.

_____ 1. Showing how in instruction involves providing a scaffold for students to use rather than giving them lumber and asking them to build their own scaffold.

_____ 2. If a process is experienced through simulation over a sufficiently long period of time, eventually that process can be applied independently.

_____ 3. To simulate a reading or reasoning process, one must start with the idea to which the process is to be applied. Otherwise. one has process but no content.

_____ 4. If students are properly placed in school, they probably will experience some difficulty in reading the texts that are assigned in their courses.

_____ 5. Emerson's apology for writing a long letter because he did not have time to write a short one has some bearing on the issue of whether to rewrite texts in order to make them easier.

_____ 6. Questions are particularly useful for providing practice on skills and content that students already possess but are not as useful for teaching new skills and content.

_____ 7. Simultaneously teaching course content with related reading processes requires the careful preparation of students for the reading they must do and the careful guidance of students while they do that reading.

_____ 8. Students' discussion of items on a reading or reasoning guide is an essential part of the simulation of the reading or reasoning processes.

_7_

Developing Vocabulary to Support Content Learning

Organizing idea: Mastering the technical language of a discipline allows mastery of the discipline itself.

Reflections

Before reading this chapter, please record in your journal your responses to the following tasks. If possible, share your writing with other individuals who are also reading this book.

1. Most subjects have a special vocabulary for communicating significant information and ideas. Given what you know about the importance of vocabulary, what words would you guess to be particularly significant to the topic on developing vocabulary? Make a list of words, and then draw from the list to arrange a diagram that shows how the words relate to one another. Discuss the arrangement and the relationships with a colleague.

2. What has been your practice in the past for determining what words you should teach your students related to a given unit of instruction?

3. What influence does vocabulary have on comprehension? Can one be taught exclusive of the other?

THE APPROPRIATE USE of language often serves as a vehicle by which people gain entry into a particular group or organization. Foucault (1977) uses the term *speech communities* to describe groups of people who come together because of common interests or needs and who use a particular form of speech and language to communicate their needs, interests, and ideas. Becoming part of a speech community includes, in part, learning the language of that community and developing facility in communicating in that language.

In many respects, the different disciplines that comprise the curriculum in our schools are types of speech communities. Each discipline has a technical language that distinguishes it from other disciplines. Individuals who are fully involved in the work of a discipline usually are fluent in its technical language. The language allows members of the discipline to record a history of what has been accomplished, to share current information and ideas, and to speculate on future possibilities.

An important dimension of the study of a discipline, then, is learning its technical language. Thus, a basic and fundamental part of instruction in any content area should be a strong emphasis on vocabulary development.

The purpose of this chapter is to discuss and illustrate ways in which content-area teachers can effectively teach the technical language of their disciplines to their students. Consistent with the central purpose of this book, this chapter discusses and illustrates how the technical language of a discipline can be taught so students simultaneously learn both the ideas represented by the language and the processes by which technical language is acquired, enriched, and applied. In this book, the term *vocabulary development* is used to describe these processes.

There are three motivations for teaching the technical vocabulary of a discipline.

1. The technical vocabulary and the concepts represented by the words constitute the building blocks of the discipline. When students understand the words, the concepts the words represent, and the interrelationships among the concepts, they understand the discipline.
2. A solid grasp of the technical vocabulary of a discipline facilitates the comprehension of resources used in the study of that discipline. Resources usually are printed materials, but resources also include the teachers' lectures, various audio and visual aids, laboratory activities, and so forth. Comprehending all of these resources is inextricably related to understanding the technical vocabulary of the relevant discipline.
3. A thorough understanding of both definitions and meanings of the technical vocabulary of a discipline is essential for communicating with others about that discipline. This need is relevant to both the receptive (listening and reading) and the expressive (speaking and writing) modes of communication. If you want students to communicate comprehensively in your discipline, you need to help them develop a comprehensive grasp of its technical language.

Though knowing the technical vocabulary of a content area is critically important to developing an understanding of the subject matter of the discipline, students often experience difficulty in acquiring the vocabulary. This is true for several reasons.

Technical vocabulary causes difficulty for the learner not only because it is unfamiliar and multi-syllabic, but also because it must be learned in relation to concept clusters of similarly unfamiliar and multi-syllabic words. For example, one can memorize a definition of photosynthesis, *but there is no way to understand the concept without understanding the meaning of* chlorophyll, oxygen, carbon dioxide, chloroplast, catalyst, glucose, *and others. One can memorize the definition of* economics, *but understanding requires knowledge of the relationships among* investment, production, employment, consumption, *and* equilibrium.

Technical vocabulary also causes difficulty for the learner because it is rarely used outside of the class in which it is taught. Students do not have opportunities to hear, see, and use the vocabulary in a variety of settings to refine and reinforce meanings as they do with general vocabulary. Unless they have multiple in-class experiences with given words, and unless they are shown how the various words relate to each other in concept clusters, students will have difficulty retaining words and meanings and will have difficulty in comprehending related materials (Nelson-Herber 1986).

This chapter presents methods for overcoming these difficulties in ways that support your interest in teaching the content of your discipline and in ways that move students toward the independent acquisition of vocabulary.

Confirmations from Research

Vocabulary development has been the focus of considerable attention among researchers and practitioners over the years. Of particular interest to these professionals is the relationship between vocabulary and comprehension. The following generalizations can be drawn from their work:

1. *Knowledge of vocabulary is strongly related to reading comprehension (Bormuth 1966; Davis 1944, 1968; McKeown et al. 1983).*
2. *Vocabulary knowledge can be acquired through incidental learning of word meanings from context (Jenkins, Stein, and Wysocki 1984; Nagy, Herman, and Anderson 1985).*
3. *Direct instruction is more effective than incidental learning for acquisition of specific vocabulary and for efficient comprehension of related material (Beck, Perfetti, and McKeown 1982; Jenkins, Stein, and Wysocki 1984; Kameenui, Carnine, and Freschi 1982; McKeown et al. 1983; Omanson et al. 1984).*

4. *Instruction using contexts may be more effective for teaching new vocabulary than instruction using definitions (Crist 1981; Crist and Petrone 1977; Gipe 1979).*

5. *Instruction that relates new vocabulary to existing knowledge structures may be more effective than instruction using definitions (Eeds and Cockrum 1985; Gipe 1980).*

6. *Vocabulary instruction is more effective when it involves the learner in the construction of meaning through interactive processes rather than in memorizing definitions or synonyms (Beck, Perfetti, and McKeown 1982; Draper and Moeller 1971; Stahl 1983).*

To put it simply, extensive reading can increase vocabulary knowledge, but direct instruction that engages students in construction of word meaning, using context and prior knowledge, is effective for learning specific vocabulary and for improving comprehension of related materials (Nelson-Herber 1986, 627).

Vocabulary Features

As a content-area teacher, you know the technical vocabulary of your discipline and have had experience in teaching it to your students. Nonetheless, it is useful to refresh your memory about some of the general features of vocabulary as well as to consider some features you may have not considered before.

Dimensions of Word Knowledge

Two dimensions of word knowledge that have significance to content-area teachers are receptive vocabulary and expressive vocabulary. Knowledge of *receptive vocabulary* "is demonstrated when one is able to associate meanings with labels that are given" (Kameenui, Dixon, and Carnine 1987, 132). Knowledge of *expressive vocabulary* "is demonstrated when one is able to produce labels for meanings" (Kameenui, Dixon, and Carnine 1987, 132).

Receptive vocabulary includes words you attend to while reading and listening. The words serve as labels to describe various objects, actions, or conditions. To the extent that you can give meaning to the labels being used as you read and listen, you are able to understand what meaning and significance to give the objects, actions, or conditions that are being described.

Expressive vocabulary includes words you use while writing and speaking. The words serve as labels to describe information, ideas, objects, actions, or conditions. To the extent that you can produce labels that accurately portray the information, ideas, objects, actions or conditions you have in mind, you are able to create a message as you write and speak.

The richness of students' vocabularies influences their comprehension and composition (Nagy and Herman 1987, Nagy 1988; Graves 1987a; Duin 1984). The richness has both quantitative and qualitative dimensions. The more words that students' hold in their available vocabularies, the more likely they are to be able to comprehend and compose well. Also, the more nuances that students understand about the words they hold in their vocabularies, the richer the meanings they can give to what they comprehend and compose. The richness of students' vocabularies, then, is reflected both in the number of words known and in the extensiveness of their knowledge about particular words (Kameenui, Dixon, and Carnine 1987).

The quantitative dimension of vocabulary is straightforward: the number of words known. The qualitative dimension of vocabulary is more varied than the quantitative and describes the extensiveness of students' knowledge of words: unknown knowledge, acquainted knowledge, and established knowledge (Beck, Perfetti, and McKeown 1982).

Unknown words are unknown words. There is not much that a person can do with them. For example, if you don't know the word *prestidigitator*, you can't do much with it except to pronounce it (if your word attack is working for you). Even if you pronounce it but can attribute neither definition nor meaning to it, you have to pretend that the word is not there. How unknown words actually interfere with comprehension is discussed later in the chapter.

With respect to acquainted knowledge of words, a person has some awareness of target words, some sense of their definitions and a modest feel for their meanings in particular contexts. For example, if you are acquainted with the word *prestidigitator*, you can define it in a context that discusses magic and magicians. You understand the relationship of *presti* meaning "quick" and *digit* meaning "fingers" to the performance of slight-of-hand tricks. You know what the person in the story, so described, is doing.

With established knowledge of words, a person has a rich understanding of target words and an extensive grasp of their meanings and nuance. For example, if you have a extensive understanding of the word *prestidigitator*, you can enrich the context in which it is found. You can draw on shades of meaning to discern or describe the intentions or reputation of the person practicing the legerdemain: words such as *conjurer, illusionist, trickster, enchanter, wizard, sorcerer, necromancer,* and *witch.*

Types of Word Knowledge

Types of word knowledge are similar to qualities of word knowledge. There are two types: definitions and meanings. Definitions parallel the quality of acquainted knowledge of words. Meanings parallel the quality of established knowledge. Definitions and meanings are important, both separately and interactively.

Because definitions of words are easier for teachers to present, for students to memorize, and for teachers to test, a significant portion of vocabulary instruction has been definitional in nature—often to the exclusion of an appropriate emphasis on meanings. "Traditionally, much vocabulary instruction has involved some variety of a definitional approach: students learn definitions or synonyms for instructed words" (Nagy 1988, 4).

If you have not thought much about the distinction between definitions and meanings of words, you can easily believe that you are teaching meanings when actually you are only presenting definitions. An example of how easy it is to make this assumption is the frequency with which teachers tell their students to look up the meanings of the words in a dictionary or in the glossary. Dictionaries or glossaries present definitions of words, not their meanings. If not attuned to this distinction, teachers can spend time on the presentation of definitions of words with little effect on students' understanding of the concepts represented by these words. This can cause considerable frustration.

What is it about definitions that contribute to this frustrating experience? Definitions do not tell you how words should be used, and it is the uses of words, after all, that give them meaning. Acquiring only the definitions of words makes it difficult for students to respond in any qualitative way to the timeworn assignment: "Look up the words in the dictionary, find their meanings, and use them in sentences." As Nagy says, "it is difficult to write a sentence for a truly unfamiliar word, given only the definition, [because] definitions do not effectively convey new concepts" (Nagy 1988, 6).

Vocabulary instruction has little value when it focuses principally on definitions of words and relatively little on their meanings. Such instruction does relatively little to facilitate either students' reading or their writing.

Meanings for words are derived from their use. Vocabulary instruction that develops word meanings includes some explanation of the concepts represented by the words and how the concepts, hence the words, fit with other concepts that are being studied. The instruction also provides an opportunity for students to use the words in ways that reinforce, refine, and expand their understandings of how the words can be used in different contexts and relationships. (Examples are given later in this chapter.) Vocabulary instruction that emphasizes word meanings serves students well in their reading and writing.

> *Knowledge of definitions is not adequate to guarantee comprehension of text containing the words defined: reading comprehension depends on a wealth of encyclopedic knowledge and not merely on definitional knowledge of the words in the text (Nagy 1988, 7).*

Emphasis on meaning provides the encyclopedic knowledge that serves both the comprehension and the composing processes. Knowing the meanings of the words you read enables you to understand the message in what you are reading even as knowing the meanings of the words you write enables you to create a message that is understandable. You positively influence the development of your students' comprehension and composition by the extent to which your vocabulary instruction helps them understand the meanings.

Dimensions of Meaning

When vocabulary instruction is focused on developing an understanding of word meanings, it contributes more to students' learning than when it is focused primarily on the acquisition of word definitions. As you endeavor to give more emphasis to word meanings in your vocabulary instruction, it is important to take into account the different dimensions of meaning that students confront as they learn the technical vocabulary of your content area. The dimensions are made up of two factors:

1. Whether the word is familiar ("old") or unfamiliar ("new") to students
2. Whether the concept to which the word is applied is familiar ("old") or unfamiliar ("new") to the students

Four dimensions of meaning derive from these factors:

1. New words for new concepts
2. Old words for new concepts
3. New words for old concepts
4. Old words for old concepts (Goodman 1970; Herber 1978; Nagy, Herman, and Anderson 1985; Graves 1987b)

In terms of levels of difficulty for teaching and learning, these four dimensions are listed in descending order.

New Words for New Concepts
Helping students develop meanings for unfamiliar words that stand for new concepts is a major instructional challenge as you teach your content-area course. Meaning comes from making connections with what is already known. The broader the connection, the richer the meaning. When neither the word nor the concept it represents is part of students' prior knowledge, the basis for making meaningful connections is virtually nonexistent. Thus, your tasks for this dimension of vocabulary development are to:

1. Build background knowledge for the concept.
2. Show students how the concept connects with information and ideas they already know.
3. Show students how the definition of the target word fits the target concept and how its meaning connects the concept to the information and ideas they already know.

EXAMPLE 7-1

Frayer Model

1. Define the new concept, giving its necessary attributes.
   Temerity is a characteristic of a person. A person demonstrates *temerity* when he or she exercises reckless boldness, ignoring serious dangers.

2. Distinguish between the new concept and similar but different concepts with which it might be mistaken. In doing so, it may be appropriate to identify some accidental attributes that might falsely be considered to be necessary attributes of the new concept.
   Temerity differs from *foolishness* in that *temerity* necessarily involves some element of danger. *Temerity* also differs from *foolishness* in that the deed that demonstrates *temerity* needs to be somewhat admirable. It is usually the case that the danger involved is physical; however, the danger need not be physical.

3. Give examples of the concept, and explain why they are examples.
   A person who wrestles a bear would be demonstrating *temerity* because (assuming that the bear isn't drugged) there is some element of danger and the practice at least could be admired.

4. Give nonexamples of the concept, and explain why they are nonexamples.
   a. Someone who fishes for marlin with a flyrod is not demonstrating *temerity* because there is no danger involved.
   b. Someone who drives after drinking too much is not demonstrating *temerity* because there is nothing admirable here.

5. Present students with examples and nonexamples, ask them to identify which are and are not instances of the concept and to state why, and give them feedback.
   a. Riding a motorcycle on the freeway without a helmet (nonexample)
   b. Crossing the Pacific in a one-person sailboat (example)
   c. Eating a whole watermelon (nonexample)
   d. Standing on the wing of a stunt plain in midair (example)

6. Have students present their own examples and nonexamples of the concept, have them discuss why they are examples or non-examples, and give them feedback.

Source: Graves, Slater, and White (1989).

Example 7-1 presents Graves, Slater, and White's application of the Frayer model (Frayer, Fredrick, and Klausmeier 1969) to developing this dimension of meaning.

Old Words for New Concepts

Helping students expand their understanding of a word and apply it to a new concept also is a major instructional challenge.

> *Whether teaching old words for new concepts is more difficult instruction-ally than teaching new words for old concepts is debatable. Old labels for new ideas may be more or less or just as difficult to handle as new labels for old ideas. In synectics terminology (Gordon 1973), labels for new ideas in-volve "making the strange familiar" and new labels for old ideas involve "making the familiar strange" . . . To some teachers it may seem more diffi-cult to help students enlarge their vocabulary relative to ideas they have held for some time. To other teachers it may seem more difficult to help students to conceptualize a new idea and then see how words used to describe familiar ideas can also describe the new idea (Herber 1978).*

Because you are teaching a new concept, you have to help students make connections between it and relevant ideas they already posses. While doing so, you use the familiar word and help students expand their under-standing of its meaning and use.

One activity that works well for this dimension of meaning is the semantic-feature analysis (see Example 7-2). Suggested by Johnson and Pearson (1978), the semantic-feature analysis helps students explore various attributes of words. The semantic-feature analysis takes the form of a grid, with a set of related words on one axis and a set of possible attributes on the other. Students work in groups to determine which attributes are appropri-ate for each of the words. By your selection of attributes when you construct

---

EXAMPLE 7-2 ───────────────────────────────────

Semantic Feature Analysis

Directions: On the line following the word *protest* are six words representing possible features of the concept of protest. Listed below the word *protest* are seven possible forms of protest. The pluses and zeroes indicate an opinion on which of the features characterize each of the forms of protest. In your groups, decide whether you agree or disagree with the opinions and why. Be ready to provide support for your decision.

			Typical Features			
Protest	Formal	Informal	Social	Economic	Political	Religious
Strike	+	0	0	+	+	+
Embargo	+	0	0	+	+	+
Sit-in	+	+	+	+	+	0
Boycott	+	+	+	+	+	+
Union	+	0	0	+	0	0
Sanction	+	0	+	+	+	+
Lockout	+	+	0	+	0	0

the matrix, you can support students' exploration of new meanings for familiar words.

You should initiate students into the use of the semantic-feature analysis by giving them one that is completed, as in Example 7-2. Later on students can add both words and attributes to matrices that you create. Still later, you may want to have students (in groups) create semantic-feature analyses of their own.

Additional ways to enrich this dimension of word meanings are included among the activities presented later in this chapter.

New Words for Old Concepts

When the concept under consideration already has a place in students' prior knowledge and experience, your task focuses more on conceptual recall than on conceptual development. You can remind students of the concept and the connections that it has with relevant information and ideas being studied. You can then enrich the concept by providing the new word, teaching the word carefully so as to demonstrate why the new word is needed and thereby develop an understanding of its meaning and use.

Semantic mapping (Johnson and Pearson 1978; Heimlich and Pittelman 1986) is useful for expanding vocabulary that can be associated with old, familiar concepts. As displayed in Example 7-3 (see page 164), the word representing the familiar concept is presented in the middle of the map. Students working in groups list words that they associate with the target word. They organize the words into related sets and give labels to the sets. Some of the words they list may serve as labels for sets of words. Labels may need to be created for some sets.

Students discuss the relationships that exist between the word sets and the target concept as well as the relationships that exist among words within the sets. Use of the semantic map enables students to enrich a familiar concept with applications in some heretofore undiscovered dimensions. Additional ways to enrich this dimension of word meanings are included among the activities presented later in this chapter.

Old Words for Old Concepts

For this dimension of meaning, the concepts are part of students' schemata and the labels used to identify and give meaning to the concepts are understood. The means for enhancing this dimension of meaning are review and refinement. Opportunities to use words in a variety of contexts that have meaning and substance enable students' to review their understanding of the words and their appropriate use. Opportunities to consider appropriate shades of meaning of known words used to describe known concepts enable students to refine their understandings of both the concepts and their labels.

One activity that is particularly useful with this dimension of meaning is the use of categorizing. As shown in Example 7-4 (see page 166), students

EXAMPLE 7-3 ─────────────────────────

Semantic Mapping

(From a computer fundamentals class. The organizing idea for the lesson is "The whole is greater than the sum of its parts.")

Memory	*Register Array*	*Control*
stack	registers	data bus
address	accumulator	fetch
data	instruction set	instruction
segment	flip-flops	
volatile	flags	
stack		
trace		*ALU*
bit		
byte		crash
word		iterate
word length		invoke
binary		decoder
RAM		opcode
ROM		operand
megabyte		operation
k	*Hardware*	execute
	(machine)	assembly

Editor

code
modify
batch   COMPUTER SYSTEM
verification
friendly   *Software*
call   (programs)
subroutine   *Input*
source code
object code   tape
compiler   hard drive
interpreter   *Output*   floppy disk
mnemonic   scanner
breakpoint   register   keyboard
disassemble   file   buffer
pseudocode   echo   disk
parameter   garbage   drive
statement   hard copy   disk drive
syntax   disk   punch card
ASCII
assembly language
machine language
bug

are given a set of words followed by three or four categories. The words and the categories are familiar to the students. Students place the words in the list under the categories with which they associate the words. They work together in groups as they categorize the words, discussing the reasons they have for their decisions. Additional ways to enrich word meanings through categorization are included among the activities presented later in this chapter.

Influences on Vocabulary Acquisition

You have considered the dimensions, qualities, and types of word knowledge related to vocabulary development in content areas. You also have considered various dimensions of meaning to be accounted for in that vocabulary development. Before considering instructional issues and applications relative to vocabulary development in content areas, it is important to think about some of the influences that bear on students' ability to acquire new vocabulary and your ability to teach it.

Prior Knowledge and Experience

Prior knowledge strongly influences both comprehension and composition. What you already know so strongly influences what you acquire from your reading that comprehension has come to mean connecting what is known with what is new. The more relevant knowledge you have about a topic, the more you will understand as you read about the topic. The words you use as labels for what you already know obviously influence what you communicate through your writing. The more extensive the vocabulary over which you have control (readily recalled and rich with meanings), the more effective your written communication will be. Prior knowledge, then, is inextricably linked with effective comprehension and communication. In the same way that a knowledge of words and an understanding of their meanings are essential elements of both comprehension and composition, prior knowledge also is inextricably linked with vocabulary development.

Three of the four dimensions of meaning discussed earlier involve prior knowledge: new words for old concepts, old words for new concepts, and old words for old concepts. Effective vocabulary instruction helps students use what they already know to understand what they are about to learn in a way that expands and refines what they already know. The fourth dimension, new words for new concepts, involves the acquisition of new knowledge. Effective vocabulary instruction also helps students to acquire new knowledge and to find a place for it within what they already know and understand.

Given the importance of prior knowledge to vocabulary development, comprehension, and composition, it is useful for you and your students to

EXAMPLE 7-4 ━━━━━━━━━━━━━━━━━━━━━━━━━━━━━━━

Categorizing

(From seventh-grade science unit on food and nutrition. The organizing idea is "As supply increases, demand decreases; as demand increases, supply decreases.")

Direction: Below are six sets of word and letter groupings. Four of the five in each set are related. For each set, draw a horizontal line through the one word that does not fit with the others in the set. On the line at the top of the set, write the word or phrase that explains the relationship that exists among the remaining words.

1. _____   2. _____
   carbohydrates   iron
   fats   calcium
   proteins   carbon
   pastries   iodine
   minerals   phosphorus

3. _____   4. _____
   meats   spinach
   eggs   carrots
   milk   squash
   beans   cabbage
   apples   sweet potatoes

5. _____   6. _____
   butter   A
   rice   K
   lard   Z
   margarine   D
   corn oil   C

discover what they already know about a topic as you begin to study it. A simple but effective way to obtain that information is through word association (see Example 7-5 on page 167).

To be effective for learning the content of a topic, prior knowledge needs to be organized. The organization should be such that students can perceive relationships among the information and ideas that comprise the knowledge. The organization should also be such that students can find places for relevant new information and ideas they encounter. A simple but effective way to support the development of that sense of organization is to help students organize what they produce in the word-association activity (see Example 7-6 on page 168).

Other ways to capitalize on the influence of prior knowledge in vocabulary development are presented later on in this chapter.

EXAMPLE 7-5 ───────────────────────────────

Word Association

An eleventh-grade chemistry teacher introduced the new concept of *nuclear power* in an on-going study of nuclear chemistry. She did so by organizing her class into four groups and giving them one minute to list words or phrases they associate with the words *nuclear power*. When the time limit was reached, she asked the groups to count the number of words each produced. She asked the group with the longest list to read its words while the other groups crossed off from their list any words that were read. Then, each succeeding group read words from their lists that had not yet been given. In the order given, the following words were listed by the groups:

uranium, chill rods, meltdown, control rods, abundant, Chernobyl, modera-tor, graphite, water, Reagan, shielding, coal, light, Three-Mile Island, oil, Zion, death, iodine, pollution, safe, unsafe, energy, atoms, neutrons, protons, electrons, molecules, matter, cost efficiency, radiation, lead, X-rays cancer, nuclear generators, protests, "no nukes," nuclear-free zone, nuclear weap-ons, China syndrome, fallout, acid rain, power plant

───

Context for Instruction

The substantive context in which vocabulary instruction takes place shapes both what teachers emphasize and what students perceive. Teachers are committed to teaching their disciplines. They use the technical language of their subjects to teach its substance. Even in cases in which common words exist across disciplines, content-area teachers stress the use and meaning peculiar to their individual subjects. For example, all teachers of English, science, history, economics, political science, and business math include the word *work* in their technical vocabularies. The substantive context of each of these disciplines dictates a different use and meaning of the word.

The English teacher uses the word *work* to describe something pro-duced by the application of creative talent. (For example, students study Shakespeare's *works*.) The science teacher uses *work* to describe the transfer-ence of energy (For example, *work* occurs when electricity runs a motor that turns a machine that grinds corn for cattle feed.) The social science teacher uses *work* to describe the labors or duties performed by people in pursuit of their livelihood. (For example, *work* is performed by secretaries, ministers, professors, physicians, bus drivers, and tennis players.) The shop teacher uses *works* to describe the moving parts of a mechanism. (For example, the clock maker installed the *works* of the clock in the new clock case.) The engineering professor uses *work* to describe structures in engineering or mining. (For example, the engineers designed the *works* for the mining shaft lift.)

EXAMPLE 7-6 ———————————————————————

Organization of Word Association

As the students read from their lists of words related to nuclear power (see Example 7-5), the teacher wrote the words on the board. As she wrote the words she placed them in following groups:

List 1	*List 2*
uranium	meltdown
chill rods	Chernobyl
control rods	Three-Mile Island
abundant	Zion
moderator	death
graphite	iodine
water	pollution
shielding	unsafe
atoms	radiation
neutrons	X-rays
protons	cancer
electrons	nuclear weapons
molecules	China syndrome
matter	fallout
lead	
nuclear generator	
power plant	

List 3	*List 4*
coal	Reagan
light	protests
oil	"no nukes"
safe	nuclear-free zone
energy	
cost efficiency	
acid rain	

When all the words had been read from the lists and the teacher had placed each with a group of words, the teacher asked the class to conceptualize labels for the word groups. The students came up with the following labels:

List 1: Operation of nuclear power plant

List 2: Disadvantages of nuclear power

List 3: Advantages of nuclear power

List 4: Miscellaneous

While each of the teachers knows the use and meaning of the word in the other disciplines, each teacher emphasizes the particular meaning and use applicable to his or her discipline. Students have to adjust their thinking as they move from subject to subject and make certain that they apply the appropriate, content-specific use and meaning of such common language as they move. In other words, students need a mind-set for math when they go to math, for science when they go to science, and so forth. As they enter the subject-area classrooms, they become involved in a situational context (Drum and Konopak 1987) that sets substantive parameters around their thinking, behaviors, and expectations.

The control exerted by this situational or substantive context has both positive and negative features. Expectation serves an important function in the learning process. When students go to science class, they expect to be studying and talking about science. The expectation provides focus to their work, and this is good. When they encounter the word *work* as in our example, they give it the meaning as used in science and use it accordingly, and this is good. The focus provided by the situational context is positive in the expectation that it builds for learning content-specific information and ideas.

Elaboration and synthesis also is important in the learning process. A situational context created by a content area is restrictive because of its focus on that subject. An important aspect of vocabulary development is the acquisition of in-depth understandings of the meanings of words. Few words have just one meaning that fits every context. When students learn the technical vocabulary of a subject, they often learn the specific content-area-related meaning of a word without exposure to meanings that fit other contexts. On the one hand, this is understandable, given time pressures to complete the curriculum requirements. On the other hand, such restrictive instruction inhibits the development of an encyclopedic sense of meanings for words that enriches students' minds and broadens their perspectives. This is the negative feature of content-specific use of vocabulary. Many of the vocabulary-development activities presented later in this chapter will enable you to help students develop this encyclopedic understanding of word meanings without jeopardizing your coverage of the curriculum.

Explicitness of Instruction

An important influence on vocabulary acquisition is how important you think it is and, consequently, how important you make it be for your students. You know from your own teaching experience that what is important to you becomes important for your students. If acquisition and control of the technical vocabulary is important to you, it will be important to your students.

Evidence of how important you consider vocabulary acquisition to be is demonstrated, in part, by the amount of instructional time you devote to it. Related evidence is the explicitness of the instruction you provide. As noted earlier in this chapter in the third generalization about vocabulary development drawn from research, direct instruction is more effective than incidental learning for the acquisition of content-area vocabulary. Because it is not possible to teach students explicitly every word they will encounter in their use of resources in their subjects, there has to be a degree of dependence on incidental learning of some vocabulary. Students do acquire some vocabulary incidentally through their use of various content-area related resources. Later in this chapter we present specific instructional strategies for the explicit teaching of technical vocabulary in content areas. We also present ways to enhance opportunities for the incidental learning of vocabulary in your subject.

Purposes for Instruction

The reason that you teach vocabulary has a strong influence on the kind of vocabulary development that occurs in your classes and the kind of vocabulary that your students acquire. Some teachers teach vocabulary because their curriculum includes a list of words that students should know. Words from the list are presented, taught, memorized, and assessed. Minimal concern is given to the question of whether students acquire the meanings of the words as opposed to their definitions. The purpose is to acquaint students with the words. Little is done to teach students processes by which they can acquire vocabulary independently.

Some teachers teach vocabulary because they want their students to learn ways to acquire new words independently. Words are selected for emphasis because of their value in teaching word-acquisition skills. Sets of words with common traits are used to teach particular skills. While some emphasis is given to the acquisition of both definitions and meanings of these words, little is done to use the words to develop an understanding of a concept. Indeed, because the words being used cluster around skills rather than ideas, it is difficult to use them to teach a concept. The purpose is to teach vocabulary-acquisition skills, not ideas that combinations of words can represent. Example 7-7 shows a set of words selected for the purpose of emphasizing common roots. This set was used in a lesson focusing on structural analysis of words.

Still other teachers teach vocabulary because they want their students to learn the ideas contained in their disciplines. They see the technical vocabulary as a means by which the ideas are acquired and communicated. Words that cluster around particular ideas are selected for emphasis so that as the words are presented and taught students develop an understanding of the ideas. Words contained in the clusters are examined to determine

EXAMPLE 7-7 ──────────────────────────

Common Roots of Words

Words Using the Root From	*Words Using the Root From*
testare *(to witness)*	specere *(to look, look at)*
testify	spectacles
testament	spectator
testimony	inspect
testimonial	respect
protest	prospect
protestation	inspection

what word-acquisition skills can be emphasized while the words are being presented and taught. Thus, these teachers are able to accomplish two objectives simultaneously:

1. Teach ideas that comprise their curriculum.
2. Teach processes by which students can acquire and use the technical vocabulary of a discipline.

This purpose for teaching vocabulary is the one subscribed to in this book. Ways to accomplish the simultaneous objectives are presented later in this chapter.

Use of the Language

A strong influence on the acquisition of vocabulary is the frequency of its use. When it comes to learning and retention, there is truth in the saying that "what you don't use, you lose." Words that you know best are the words you use most frequently and vice versa. If you want your students to be facile in their use of the technical vocabulary of your subject, you need to find ways to encourage their use of the language both in its receptive modes (listening and reading) and in its expressive modes (speaking and writing).

Three factors facilitate students' use of the technical language of your subject:

1. Creating a classroom environment that supports active pursuit of ideas
2. Using principles of cooperative learning to promote interaction among students
3. Using materials designed to support and mediate students' interaction as they focus on the definitions and meanings of selected technical vocabulary.

Your own interest in exploring ideas that comprise your discipline sets an intellectual tone for your classes. Students come to understand that mere memorization of information is not sufficient to really understand your subject. They discover how ideas emerge when interrelationships are explored across pieces and sets of information. They also discover the importance of precision in the use of technical language that represents information and explains ideas. Thus, an environment that encourages the pursuit of ideas also encourages the acquisition of relevant technical language.

You know from personal experience how ideas that you are exploring become clearer as you talk them out with colleagues who listen, analyze, and question. You also know that through the discussion that ensues, you become more precise in your use of the technical language related to the idea you are exploring. You can provide the same experience for your students by organizing your class so students can work cooperatively in small groups. Given well-defined tasks, students in these groups use the technical language of the subject to clarify their understandings of relevant concepts. How cooperative-learning groups are organized and managed is discussed in Chapter 4.

If students' group work is to be productive, it needs to be focused substantively. Group work can easily degenerate into gossip sessions or random discussions of nonessential information. Materials can be designed to mediate and monitor students' discussions and keep them focused on the organizing ideas of the lessons. Materials used for vocabulary refinement serve this purpose. These materials are presented and discussed later in this chapter.

Expanding Vocabulary

Helping students gain control over the technical vocabulary of your subject involves expanding their vocabularies or enlarging their personal lexicons. This is done in two ways:

1. Directly, by exposing students to selected sets of words that, when considered together, comprise the major concepts of your course
2. Indirectly, by teaching students ways to acquire vocabulary independently and, thus, enable them to engage in a lifelong expansion of their vocabularies

You can expand your students' vocabularies by applying the following interrelated tasks:

1. *Select* the words to be emphasized.
2. *Teach* some of the words drawn from the selected list.
3. *Present* the remainder of the words from the selected list.

Selecting Words

As a content-area teacher you have to reconcile the conflict between extensiveness of the technical vocabulary in your subject and limitations of time available for teaching the vocabulary to your students. Undoubtedly there are more words than you have time to present and teach. So, you have to make some choices.

A convenient way to select words for emphasis is to create "word clusters" that contribute conceptually to the organizing idea of the lesson (Nelson-Herber 1986). The organizing idea of lesson is supported by a variety of contributing concepts, and these concepts are, in turn, supported by sets of related vocabulary. Word clusters, then, are sets of words that support concepts which, in turn, contribute to the organizing idea of a lesson. Example 7-8 (see page 174) shows the word clusters that were formed by the selection of the vocabulary.

Formulation of word clusters is facilitated by the application of four criteria for selecting words (Herber 1978): key concepts; relative value, students' background, and facilitating independence. The purpose in applying these criteria is to reduce to some manageable number the words you need to emphasize in a given lesson. As you apply the criteria in the order given, the number is progressively reduced.

Key Concepts

The organizing idea of a lesson is comprised of one or more key concepts. The concepts are key because they contribute to an understanding of the organizing idea. Each of these concepts is represented by a combination of technical vocabulary. The combinations of vocabulary that form the key concepts constitute the word clusters. Application of the key-concepts criterion produces comprehensive and extensive sets of words that should be emphasized.

Relative Value

Not everything that we teach is of equal importance. Some concepts are more significant to an understanding of the subject than are others. Some information contributes more significantly to an understanding of specific concepts than does other information. It is also the case, then, that some words in the technical vocabulary of your subject are more important than others. You can reduce the number of words produced by the key-concepts criterion by applying the relative-value criterion. You do this by examining the words in the clusters to determine those that absolutely must be emphasized for students to understand the key concepts. Example 7-9 (see page 175) presents a list of words produced by applying the first two criteria (key concepts and relative value).

Students' Backgrounds

Some of the words produced by the relative-value criterion may already be known by your students. Words that are important to developing an under-

EXAMAPLE 7-8

Word Clusters

(From a lesson in social studies (Western Hemisphere history and geography). The organizing idea is "Where we live affects how we live.")

Land and Water Forms	_Food_	_Plants_	_Animals_
prairie	buffalo	berries	buffalo
flatlands	venison	conifers	prairie dog
bluffs	bear	birch	deer
headwaters	fish	nut trees	bear
		deciduous forest	beaver
lakes	beans		
rivers	squash	crops	
streams	berries		
hills	nuts		
valleys			

Clothing	_Transportation_	_Shelter_
buffalo skin	horse	permanent long-house
deer skin	travois	
woven material	foot paths	wigwam
	birch canoe	temporary tepee

standing of one concept may well be related to another concept that students already understand. The emphasis given to such known words is less intense than to words your students have not previously encountered. Thus, by knowing your students' background knowledge relative to words in the clusters—the third criterion—you can reduce the number to be emphasized by omitting those they already know.

Facilitating Independence

Even after you have progressively narrowed the vocabulary list by applying the first three criteria, a fairly extensive list of words still remains. Substantively, all of the words on the list contribute importantly to an understanding of the organizing idea of the lesson. You can't really narrow the list further based on substance, but you can narrow the list based on process, thus applying the fourth criterion for vocabulary selection, facilitating independence. You do this by selecting words that allow you to teach vocabulary-acquisition processes. As these words are taught, students learn not only their substantive relationships to the organizing idea of the lesson but

EXAMPLE 7-9

Words Produced by Key-Concepts and Relative-Value Criteria

(From tenth-grade American history vocabulary-development material for unit on immigration. The organizing idea is "For every action there is an equal and opposite reaction.")

Words to Present	*Words to Teach*
feudalism	immigration
absentee landlord	emigration
domination	migration
famine	new immigrants
tariff	old immigrants
autocracy	forty-eighters
oppression	old country
mechanization	utopia
liberalism	transplanted societies
emancipation	unskilled labor markets
opportunity	tenements
Darwinism	nativists
minority	quota system
prejudice	literacy tests
discrimination	know-nothing
segregation	anarchists
nationalism	principalities
nationality	influx
mercenaries	exodus
assimilation	
melting pot	
cultural pluralism	

also the particular vocabulary-acquisition processes that are appropriate to these words. In this manner, then, you are able to teach content and process simultaneously.

Teaching Words

When you teach a word, you help students develop two understandings:

1. The meanings of the word relative to the organizing idea of the lesson
2. The processes for word acquisition that can be used to derive the definition and meanings of the word

Remember, words actually *taught* are identified by applying the fourth criterion for selecting words, facilitating independence. Because all of the words on the list contribute substantively to students' understanding of the organizing idea of the lesson, any that are taught help develop students' understanding of the concept. So, from this substantively important vocabulary, you identify words that can be used to teach students how to acquire vocabulary independently: use of context; use of word parts; use of resource and reference materials. You can code words on your list to indicate which vocabulary-acquisition process you will emphasize as you teach the words (see Example 7-10).

Context

Use of context is one commonly applied means of acquiring word meanings. Because meanings of words are derived from their relationships with other words, use of context is a natural and easily used tool for determining word meanings. Students can be taught how to use different context clues for determining the meanings of specific words. In doing so, teachers use the resources students are about to read, resources to which the criteria for word selection have been applied.

It is important to point out that use of context serves additional purposes to that of deriving meanings of target words. Use of context enables students to read with understanding even though they cannot derive the meaning of a particular word in that context. Nagy attributes this to "redundancy of text." He says that

> *readers can tolerate a certain proportion of unknown words in text without comprehension being disrupted. . . . readers may be able to tolerate texts in which as many as 15 percent of the words are not fully known . . . [though the exact percent] depends on the nature of the text, the role of the unfamiliar words in the text, and the purpose for reading (Nagy 1988, 29).*

The important point to take from this is that

> *students do not have to know all of the words in a text to read it with a high level of comprehension. The teacher need not set the unrealistic goal of giving intensive instruction on every unfamiliar word in a text (Nagy 1988, 29).*

You can let your students in on this secret and show them how to use words that they *do* know in the text to develop an understanding of the concepts being presented, even though there are some words whose meanings are not revealed by the context. Meanwhile, not teaching all of the new words your students will encounter in a given lesson is a response to reality, not an abrogation of your teaching responsibility. Your helping them understand the use of context enables them to fill in the gaps or go around the

EXAMPLE 7-10 ─────────────────────────────

Coded Words from Example 7-9

(The lists from Example 7-9 were coded and are listed below.)

Words to Present	*Words to Teach*
feudalism (1)	immigration (3, 4, 5)
absentee landlord (1)	emigration (3, 4, 5)
domination (1)	migration (3, 4, 5)
famine (1, 2)	new immigrants (4)
tariff (1)	old immigrants (4)
autocracy (1)	forty-eighters (4)
oppressive (1)	old country (4)
mechanization (1, 2)	utopia (4, 5)
liberalism (1)	transplanted societies (3, 4)
emancipation (1)	unskilled labor markets (4)
opportunity (1, 2)	tenements (4, 5)
Darwinism (1)	nativists (3, 4)
minority (1, 2)	quota system (4)
prejudice (1, 2)	literacy tests (3, 4)
discrimination (1, 2)	know-nothing (4)
segregation (1, 2)	anarchists (4, 5)
nationalism (1)	principalities (4, 5)
nationality (1)	influx (4, 5)
mercenaries (1)	exodus (4, 5)
assimilation (2)	
melting pot (2)	
cultural pluralism (2)	

1 = previously encountered in reading
2 = experiential, may be brought into discussion
3 = structural analysis
4 = contextual analysis
5 = dictionary

obstacles without jeopardizing their understanding of the concepts under consideration.

Structure

Use of structure of words is a second means of facilitating independence in the acquisition of vocabulary. Some words lend themselves to structural analysis, that is, analysis of the parts of words to derive clues to their definitions. Principally, this involves the use of prefixes, roots, and suffixes of words. A comprehensive dictionary serves appropriately as a resource when you prepare for this instruction. In actually teaching a word, you draw on students' knowledge of word parts to the fullest extent possible. Make use of their responses, even when they are off the mark so that you encourage the intelligent hypothesizing that is part of the value of this means for deriving word meanings. For example, Dialogue 7-1 shows how the word *protest* was taught in the lesson on the development of union discussed in Chapter one.

This instruction shows students how to use their knowledge of word parts as clues to the definitions of specific words. Consistently applied over time and as appropriate to words selected for a lesson, such instruction adds to students' knowledge of word parts and contributes to their independence in vocabulary acquisition.

References and Resources

The third way of helping students acquire vocabulary is with the use of references and resources. This often constitutes a means of last resort for students' gaining access to the definitions and meanings of words. This, of course, is because of the extra effort it takes to locate the appropriate resource and to look up the desired information on the target word. As an experienced reader you know how much more frequently you rely on context or etymology for dealing with new words than you do on a dictionary, glossary, encyclopedia, or thesaurus. Even so, you do make use of these resources and find them useful. It is important to share with your students the value you hold for these resources. It is also important to show students how to use these resources appropriately, both by modeling their use in your own work and by providing instruction in their use as *appropriate* to the lessons you teach.

As you model the use of these resources, you should include regular reminders about the importance of three factors:

1. Remind students about the operational principles of alphabetizing words, refreshing them on how to locate words by the second, third, fourth, or even fifth letter.
2. Remind students about the use of guide words (where they are used) to facilitate the location of the target word. You may want to provide your students with periodic practice on identifying the guide words within which specific target words would be located.
3. Remind students that when they find multiple definitions for a target word, they need to select the one that is appropriate to the context from which they have drawn the word. The first definition given is not always the appropriate one to use. Periodic practice on using context to select appropriately among multiple definitions constitutes a valuable learning experience for your students.

DIALOGUE 7-1

Exerpt from Lesson on the Development of Union's

(From a lesson on the development of unions. The organizing idea is "Protests take many forms and produce many outcomes.")

The teacher writes the word *protest* on the board.

Teacher: Can anyone pronounce this word for us?

Students: (Several volunteers, one of whom pronounces the word accurately.)

T: Let's talk a little bit about what this word means. It's an important word in today's lesson. What other words come to you mind when you hear the word *protest*?

S: (Several responses) Argue. Fight. Picket. Strike. Object.

T: These are all good responses that reflect ways that the word is used and its shades of meaning. Let's take a look at the origin of the word to see what it can tell us about its meaning. When you look at the word and consider its parts (prefix and root), is there anything about the word that is familiar to you?

S: Yes, sir. *Pro* in *protest*. It has to do with sports, you know, like being a pro in basketball or football.

T: I see the similarity in sound and appearance. Interestingly, this is an abbreviation for the word *professional* (a pro is a professional). But this *pro* that we are talking about is a different one. Any other thoughts on this?

S: I think I heard that *pro* has something to do with being "for" something, like in a debate or argument.

T: That's a good possibility. Let's keep it in mind and see how it fits with the root of the word. (Teacher underlines *test* in the word *protest*.) What ideas do you have on what *test* might mean? Are there words you know that might have the same root?

S: What about *testify* . . . or *testimony* . . . or *testament*?

T: Yes, all these words have the same root. Good job! Let me show you the origin of this root. It comes from the word *testare*. *Testare* means "to witness." So, if you put "to witness" with the "for" or "before" of *pro*, what kind of meaning does this give you?

S: It means to witness for something, doesn't it? That fits with what people are doing now in their protests about school integration and stuff. Aren't they witnessing for their beliefs about equality?

T: Indeed they are. And we're going to study about a particular kind of protest that was created at a particular time in our history.

(The lesson continued.)

Presenting Words

It is clear from the discussion of structure, context, and references and resources as vehicles for teaching words, a significant amount of time goes into the careful *teaching* of a word. Given limitations of time, the number of words from a cluster that you can actually teach is quite limited; yet, the remaining words in the cluster also need to be emphasized in some fashion so students perceive their connection with one another and with the organizing idea of the lesson. While you do not have time to *teach* all of the words in the cluster, you probably do have time to *present* most of the ones that you do not teach. You will note in Example 7-10 that the word list is separated into words to be presented and words to be taught.

Presenting words involves displaying them in some fashion so students focus their attention on them for a brief period of time. The mode of presentation will vary widely, depending on the resources being used. The purpose for the presentation remains constant: to provide a *definitional* basis for recognizing target words when they are encountered subsequently in print.

Many teachers have their students keep a vocabulary notebook. As new words are presented in class, students enter them and their definitions in the notebook. This is a form of presentation. Whether or not you have your students keep a vocabulary notebook, you probably follow the practice of writing new words on the board as you discuss their definitions. This also is a form of presentation unless you carefully teach the meanings of each of the words you write on the board. You probably do teach the meanings of some, but you probably present the definitions of many more.

Example 7-11 shows another form of presentation. Students are given a set of word pairs. The first word in the pair is one that you have selected for presentation. The second word in the pair is a more familiar word that may or may not be related to the target word. Students work together in groups to decide whether the two words in each pair are related or unrelated and why they think so. Often someone in the group will be familiar with either the target word or its pair so intelligent guesses can be made. They can use a glossary in thir text to confirm their guesses. By this means you can determine which of the words require more explanation on your part in subsequent discussions. The consequence of the activity is that students have attended carefully to each of the target words, have secured some form of definition, and have increased the likelihood that they will recognize the words when they subsequently come across them in the text. This recognition plus the use of context will facilitate their acquisition of meaning as well.

You undoubtedly have experienced the fact that after a new word has been called to your attention, for whatever reason, you begin to notice its presence in different materials you read. This, of course, is because the word is now familiar to you, and you recognize it as one you have seen before.

EXAMPLE 7-11 ───────────────────────

Word Pairs

(From a resource unit on the Greek and Roman civilizations. The organizing idea for the unit is "The roots of Western culture can be found in the Greek and Roman civilizations.")

Directions: Decide whether or not the words in each of the following pairs of words are closely related. If they are closely related, write the letter *R* on the line between the words. If they are not related, write the letters *NR* on the line. Be ready to discuss the reasons for your answers.

1. gladiators	_____	Greece
2. amphitheater	_____	colosseum
3. spartan	_____	courageous
4. Parthenon	_____	games
5. acropolis	_____	defense
6. Augustus	_____	honored
7. Pax Romana	_____	Persian Wars
8. chariot	_____	Circus Maximus
9. aqueduct	_____	drama
10. Justinian Code	_____	law

This familiarity increases the likelihood that you will be able to use the context to determine a meaning. If the context is not sufficient, at least you will have recognized the word and can judge whether you need to take the time to use the glossary or a dictionary to determine its definition.

Using Structured Overviews

The term *structured overview* (coined by Barron 1969, and Earle 1969) is a useful vehicle for both teaching and presenting the vocabulary from a word cluster. The structured overview also serves as a means for displaying the interrelationships that exist between and among words in the cluster. As a result, the structured overview provides a visual display of the organizing idea of the lesson. Example 7-12 (see page 182) presents the structured overview used in the unit on the Greek and Roman civilizations referred to in Example 7-11.

Structured overviews were conceived as part of a search for alternative applications of Ausubel's (1963) notion of *advance organizers*. Ausubel suggested that before students read an assigned text, they read a teacher-prepared paragraph that presents the concept to be studied at a level of generality and inclusiveness that is higher than what is found in the assigned text. Ausubel's belief is that the more general and inclusive paragraph activates reader's prior knowledge about the concept and provides a

EXAMPLE 7-12

Structured Overview

(From a resource unit on the Greek and Roman civilizations. The organizing idea for the unit is "The roots of Western culture can be found in the Greek and Roman civilizations.")

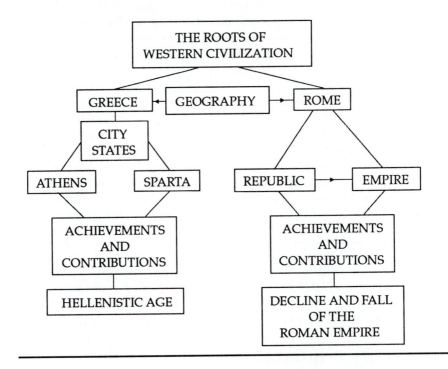

context for information and ideas about to be studied. Barron (1969) and Earle (1969) hypothesize that the technical vocabulary related to a concept being studied can serve the same purpose. By displaying relationships among words that support key concepts in the lesson, teachers provide a structured overview of that idea. As teachers talk through the display, students develop a sense of the structure of the idea and are able to make connections with relevant prior knowledge.

The structured overview communicates the structure of key concepts of the lesson. It helps students make connections between what they are studying and what they already know about it.

The value of structured overviews for teaching and presenting technical vocabulary across subject areas has been demonstrated in a variety of school settings (Herber and Nelson-Herber 1984). Additional research on the use of structured overviews for reviewing the content of lessons and units resulted in the creation of "post graphic organizers" (Barron and Stone

1973). Barron and Stone suggest the following procedures for using the post graphic organizer:

1. *Type the key words (to be included in the organizer) on a ditto master.*
2. *After reading and studying the material to be learned, place students into small groups of about two or three students each.*
3. *Distribute the list of terms and a packet of three-by-five inch index cards to each group.*
4. *Students write each word from the list on a card. They then work together to decide upon a spatial arrangement among the cards which depicts the major relationship among the words.*
5. *As students work, provide assistance as needed.*
6. *Initiate a discussion of the constructed organizer (Barron and Stone 1973).*

An important factor in the use of the post graphic organizer is that you also create one. When students complete theirs and make comparisons across groups, you can participate in the comparisons also.

Parallel research on semantic mapping has demonstrated values similar to those derived from structured overviews in the use of word clusters for teaching concepts (Johnson and Pearson 1978; Heimlich and Pittelman 1986). As with graphic organizers, semantic maps are used to portray links among words that comprise a concept cluster. Words are arrayed to display their superordinate and subordinate relationships (see Example 7-3).

Refining Vocabulary

You expand students' vocabularies by selecting, presenting, and teaching words. Through these activities students become acquainted with the definitions and meanings of the technical vocabulary of your subject. While vocabulary-expansion activities are *necessary* for helping students to gain control over the technical vocabulary of your subject, they are *not sufficient* for assuring that level of competence. Vocabulary-refinement activities must be added.

Your own experience in learning the technical language of your subject illustrates the difference between vocabulary expansion and vocabulary refinement. When you began studying your subject, you added many new words to your vocabulary. Early on, newly acquired words were not sufficiently familiar to you for easy recall and use. Sometimes, when you did recall words, you were not always confident that you were using them appropriately. Your confidence increased, however, as you had the opportunity to use the words in discussions with your instructor and fellow students as well as in your writing.

Using new words in a variety of contexts, with confirming responses from colleagues, enabled you to *refine* your understandings of the words, to capture their nuance, and to include them in communication as a natural part of your language. Refining your understandings of words in your technical vocabulary gave you what Nagy (1988) calls an "encyclopedic knowledge" of the words. Activities that refine vocabulary help your students develop an encyclopedic knowledge of the words you present and teach to them.

Activities for refining vocabulary fall into two broad categories:

1. Those that reinforce knowledge of definitions of words
2. Those that reinforce understanding of the meanings of words

Earlier in this chapter we drew distinctions between definitions and meanings of words. Definitions provide information about the word; meanings reflect ideas represented by the word.

Refining Definitions

Activities that refine definitions provide students with repeated experience in discerning appropriate definitions for selected words and in using the definitions in their discussion and writing. A simple matching of words with their definitions is a traditional reinforcer (see Example 7-13).

This activity assumes some prior exposure to the words (usually through the teacher's presentation and teaching of words drawn from a cluster). The activity also assumes that students work on the materials together in small groups. Students consider the definition of each word several times as they make the appropriate match, present the results of the matching to peers, and resolve differences among group members through small-group discussion. This raises the probability of definitions being fixed in students' minds and the words being more readily available for use in their speaking, writing, and reading.

Many different kinds of materials can be designed to provide this refining experience with definitions of words. Examples 7-14 and 7-15 present two more types (see pages 186 and 187).

You can vary the sophistication and difficulty of these materials by adjusting the level of independence at which students must function in order to complete the tasks. Such variations allow you to make some accommodation to the range of abilities you have in your class. They also allow you to move your entire class along in the levels of sophistication at which they can function. For example, in a matching activity, you can withhold some of the definitions so students have to recall them and then check with the dictionary to confirm their recollection.

Now it will be helpful for you to practice on the design of materials to refine definitions. A set of words for a seventh-grade science unit on food

EXAMPLE 7-13

Word Matching

(From introductory-calculus materials on vocabulary development. The organizing idea is "A picture is worth a thousand words.")

Directions: Under the column labeled "words" are ten terms. Under the column labeled "definitions" are possible definitions for the terms. Match each term with its most appropriate definition. Do so by writing the letter of the definition on the numbered line of the term. Be ready to discuss evidence you draw upon to support your decisions. Throughout this work, let f(x) be a function.

Words

_____ 1. asymptote

_____ 2. inflection point

_____ 3. x-intercept

_____ 4. y-intercept

_____ 5. relative maximum point

_____ 6. relative minimum point

_____ 7. absolute maximum point

_____ 8. absolute minimum point

_____ 9. undefined point

_____ 10. endpoint

Definitions

a. The largest function value on the domain of f(x)

b. The point where the graph of f(x) intersects the y-axis

c. The point on the graph of f(x) where the graph changes concavity

d. An imaginary line that the graph tends toward

e. A point on the graph of f(x) where the x value is from the extreme left or right of the domain

f. An x value for which there is no function value

g. The smallest function value on the domain of f(x)

h. A point on the graph of f(x) that is higher than the other points near it

i. A point where the graph of f(x) intersects the x-axis

j. A point on the graph of f(x) that is lower than the other points near it

and nutrition is presented in Practice 7-1. The organizing idea for the unit is "As supply increases, demand decreases; as demand increases, supply decreases." Design one or more sets of materials to help students refine their knowledge of the definitions of these words. In Appendix A there are mate-

EXAMPLE 7-14

Definitions of Words

(From tenth-grade American history materials on vocabulary development. The organizing idea is "For every action there is an equal and opposite reaction.")

Directions: At the bottom of the page are eleven definitions of words used in our study of immigration. At the top of the page are eleven numbered sets of dashes. For each definition, write the word being defined on the correspondingly numbered set of dashes. Only one letter is written on each dash. The same letter should appear in the word being defined where it appears on one of the dashes. When you fill in all of the dashes correctly, another word will appear when you read down the letters in parentheses. That word is defined as "movement into another country to take up residence in that country."

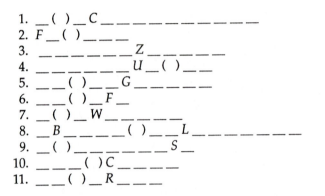

1. _ ( ) _ C _ _ _ _ _ _ _ _ _ _
2. F _ ( ) _ _ _ _
3. _ _ _ _ _ _ Z _ _ _ _ _ _
4. _ _ _ _ _ _ _ U _ ( ) _ _ _
5. _ _ ( ) _ _ G _ _ _ _ _ _
6. _ _ ( ) _ F _
7. _ ( ) _ W _ _ _ _ _ _
8. _ B _ _ _ _ _ ( ) _ _ _ L _ _ _ _ _ _ _ _
9. _ ( ) _ _ _ _ _ _ _ _ S _
10. _ _ _ _ ( ) C _ _ _ _ _
11. _ _ ( ) _ R _ _ _ _

1. Positive or negative distinction between individuals or groups based on something other than merit
2. Extreme and general scarcity of food
3. Replacement of manual labor with machines
4. A situation favorable for attainment of a goal
5. Forced or voluntary separation of a race, class, or ethnic group from the rest of society
6. A tax levied on imported goods
7. Theory that the origin of species is derived as the species is constantly changing through the natural selection of those best adapted to survive
8. Person who lives somewhere other than in the rental property and hires another to manage it
9. Belief in the freedom of the individual and government's guarantee of those rights and liberties
10. Government which has unlimited control through an absolute ruler
11. Group differing in race, religion, or ethnic background from the majority of population

EXAMPLE 7-15

Definitions of Words—Multiple Choice

(From a sixth-grade social studies unit on ancient Rome. The organizing idea for the unit is "All roads lead to Rome!")

Directions: Read each sentence. Using your knowledge about Ancient Rome, decide which word below the sentence belongs in the sentence. Then write the word on the blank line. Be ready to discuss the reasons for your choices.

1. A building of ancient Rome used for sports and spectacles was a(n) _____.

    forum   arena   amphitheater

2. A kind of boat is a(n) _____.

    gondola   arena   breakwater

3. A Roman noble was a _____.

    plebeian   patrician   gladiator

4. A large division of Roman troops was a _____.

    Fascist   tribune   legion

5. In ancient Rome an armed man who fought to amuse people was a _____.

    gladiator   tribune   barbarian

6. In ancient Rome a leader given absolute power in time of war was a _____.

    republic   dictator   forum

7. By shouting "Veto!" the _____ could prevent decisions which they thought were unjust.

    patricians   tribunes   gladiators

8. The _____ in a Roman city was the open space where markets and public festivals were held.

    breakwater   arena   forum

9. The Roman amphitheater was called the _____ because of its great, or colossal, size.

    tribune   forum   colosseum

PRACTICE 7-1

Categorizing Words—2

carbohydrates, balanced diet, carbon, hydrogen, oxygen, energy, sugar, simple sugars, complex sugars, normal diet, cereal grains, nitrogen, sulfur, phosphorus, molecule, anemia, lean meat, regulators, concentrated, ultraviolet light, nutrients, protein, fats, minerals, vitamin, undernourished, starch, glucose, sucrose, hemoglobin, amino acids, protoplasm, excretion, albumin, legumes, gluten, casein, saturated fats, unsaturated fats, oleomargarine, calcium, chlorides, cobalt, copper, iodine, iron, magnesium, potassium, sodium, zinc, deficiency diseases, night blindness, beriberi, scurvy, digestion, secretions, glands rials that another teacher designed for these words. You may want to compare your work with his/hers when you finish.

Refining Meanings

Repeated opportunities to apply multiple meanings of words in a variety of contexts help refine students' understanding of those meanings. Activities that refine meanings provide students with repeated experience in applying appropriate meanings for selected words during their oral discussions and writing.

The activity shown in Example 7-16 assumes some prior exposure to the words (usually through the teacher's presentation and teaching of words drawn from a cluster as well as through activities for refining definitions). The activity also assumes that students work on the materials together in small groups. By creating the categories, by placing each word under its relevant category, by presenting the results of the categorizing to peers, and by resolving differences among group members through small-group discussion, students consider the meanings of each word several times. This raises the probability of the meanings being fixed in the students' minds and the words being more readily available for use in their speaking, writing, and reading.

EXAMPLE 7-16 ━━

Categorizing Words—1

(From a resource unit on the Greek and Roman civilizations. The organizing idea for the unit is "The roots of Western culture can be found in the Greek and Roman civilizations.")

Directions: Work together in groups on this activity. Listed below are words from the unit we have been studying. The words can be divided into three broad categories. Look for the relationships among the words, and identify the three areas by filling in the three blank lines. Place words from the list under the categories to which they belong. You may wish to use some words more than once. Be ready to discuss the reasons for your decisions.

assembly	Delian League	helots
social class	republic	Justinian Code
Punic Wars	senate	military
city-state	isolated	patricians
Spartan	tribune	slaves
consuls	direct democracy	disciplined
Persian Wars	plebeian	council

_____	_____	_____

Many kinds of materials can be designed to provide this refining experience with word meanings. Example 7-17 provides a second variation on categorizing.

A third kind of categorizing is presented in Example 7-18 (see page 190).

In addition to categorizing, making analogies is also useful for vocabulary refinement. Analogies support students' developing understanding of the conceptual connections that comprise curricula in most content areas. More than a dozen different types of analogies can be drawn upon when constructing student support materials.

1. *Characteristics:* rain *is to* wet *as* sun *is to* dry.
2. *Part/whole:* leaf *is to* tree *as* feather *is to* bird.
3. *Whole/part:* cup *is to* handle *as* clock *is to* hands.
4. *Location:* teacher *is to* classroom *as* sailor *is to* ship.
5. *Action/Object:* run *is to* track *as* swim *is to* pool.
6. *Agent-action or object:* teacher *is to* students *as* doctor *is to* patients.
7. *Class or synonym:* smell *is to* sniff *as* see *is to* look.
8. *Familial:* Uncle *is to* nephew *as* aunt *is to* niece.
9. *Grammatical:* hear *is to* heard *as* look *is to* looked.
10. *Temporal or sequential:* fifth *is to* first *as* twenty-fifth *is to* fifth.

EXAMPLE 7-17

Categorizing Words—2

(From an art appreciation class. The organizing idea is "Art is a lie that makes us realize the truth.")

Directions: Given below are four sets of words. In your group, discuss what is common among the words in each set. For each set, chose from the following labels the one that best fits that set. Label each set and be ready to discuss the reasons for your choices.

periods	influences	shapes	mediums

Cezanne	collage
Impressionists	pottery
Egyptian art	print making
Totem poles	lithograph

Cone	Blue
Cube	Rose
Cylinder	cubism
Prism	

EXAMPLE 7-18 ━━━━━━━━━━━━━━━━━━━━━━━━━━━━━

Categorizing Words—3

(From a twelfth-grade English unit on the human condition in society. The organizing idea is "Irreconcilable alienation leads to inevitable separation.")

Directions: Place an *x* on the blank line to the left of each word in the third column that creates a sensible relationship when combined with other words in the set. Think of a word or phrase that describes the relationship that you see among the words in the set. Write out your ideas on the blank line that follows the set.

1. sallow	pallid	___ usurp
		___ hue
		___ vile
		___ torrent
2. insolent	choleric	___ prudence
		___ efficacy
		___ obstreperous
		___ pensive
3. forlorn	melancholy	___ despondent
		___ alacrity
		___ temperate
		___ procure
4. temperate	mollified	___ choleric
		___ sagacious
		___ remunerative
		___ acquiescent
5. condolence	melancholy	___ purveyor
		___ eccentric
		___ perplexity
		___ misery
6. scrivener	avocation	___ vagrant
		___ libertine
		___ cistern
		___ abode

11. *Synonyms:* smile *is to* happy *as* frown *is to* sad.
12. *Object-function:* wine *is to* bottle *as* crackers *are to* box.
13. *Opposite sensations:* ice cream *is to* pickle *as sweet is to* sour.
    (Johnson and Pearson 1978, 47.)

Example 7-19 presents an example of analogy support materials that refine students' vocabulary.

A third way to refine students' understanding of words is with the use of context. You can construct support materials of the sort shown in Example 7-20 (see page 192).

EXAMPLE 7-19

Analogies

(From the study of poetry in a literature class—Carl Sandburg's "Limited" and Robert Frost's "The Road Not Taken." The organizing idea is "Man seeks a perspective on fate, sometimes through reality, sometimes through imagination.")

Directions: On each of the numbered lines are two words separated by the sign :, followed by the sign ::, followed by one word and the sign :, and followed by a blank space. The sign : stands for the words *is to*. The sign :: stands for *as.* Thus, you read line 1 as follows: "Boy is to man is girl is to blank." Your job is to think of a word to fill in the blank to complete the comparison. Who or what is related to girl in the same way that man is related to boy? Probably you guessed *woman,* and you would be right.

Now, work with your group to complete each of the remaining comparisons, lines 2 through 9. You may use the list of words at the bottom of this page, or from other sources, if you need some ideas to consider.

Be ready to give reasons for the choices you make to fill the blanks.

1. boy	:	man	::	girl	:	
2. car	:	home	::	vehicle	:	
3. questions	:	answers	::	problems	:	
4. slow	:	plod	::	fast	:	
5. death	:	life	::	mortal	:	
6. gather	:	disperse	::	integrate	:	
7. perspective	:	perception	::	insight	:	
8. decisions	:	choices	::	answers	:	
9. motion	:	progress	::	activity	:	

questions	woman	disintegrate
understanding	action	solutions
hurtle	immortal	destinations

EXAMPLE 7-20 ─────────────────────────────────────

Words in Context

(From an introductory course on computing. The organizing idea is "The whole is greater than the sum of its parts.")

Directions: Listed below are nine statements, each containing an underlined word and each followed by a set of three words. Read each statement and then circle one of the three words in its set that explains or means approximately the same as the underlined word in the statement. Be prepared to discuss the reasons for your choices.

1. Separating each page of continuous forms is called *bursting* the report.

    a. exploding   b. breaking apart   c. distributing

2. The users of computer systems are the reason for the *existence* of computers.

    a. life   b. growth   c. creation

3. The central processing unit (CPU) contains electronic, *circuitry* which actually causes processing to occur on the computer system.

    a. power   b. connections   c. input

4. Main computer storage consists of *components* that can electronically store letters of the alphabet, numbers, and special characters.

    a. parts   b. memory   c. output

5. A computer operator communicates with the processor unit through the *console* terminal.

    a. processing   b. work station   c. printer

6. Programmers design, write, test and *implement* the programs that process data on the computer system.

    a. print   b. use   c. update

7. Large computers are called dinosaurs by some people because the computers are large and these people think they will soon be *extinct*.

    a. dead   b. useless   c. too large

8. Is the so-called computer-revolution really a revolution, or is it more the steady growth of a new industry?

    a. rebellion   b. change   c. rotation

9. Two departments found that their efforts to produce the same data were unnecessarily *redundant*.

    a. restrictive   b. competitive   c. repetitious

PRACTICE 7-2 _____

wastewater treatment plants, smog, sewage, sludge, recycle, aerosols, deci-bels, technology, thermal inversion, PSI, primary sewage treatment, open dumps, psychological, analogy, radioactive, propellant, pollution, toxic sub-stances, ozone layer, acid rain, sanitary landfill, hazardous wastes, organic wastes, stationary, sedimentation, pesticides, nuclear waste

_____

Appendix B contains additional examples of material used to support students' refinement of vocabulary. Chapter 11 also includes similar materi-als within the lessons and units that are presented there.

Now it will be helpful for you to have some practice on the design of materials to refine word meanings. Practice 7-2 contains a set of words from a health unit on pollution. The organizing idea for the unit is "Each person is responsible for his or her actions." Design one or more sets of materials to support students as they refine their understandings of the meanings of these words, adding or deleting words as appropriate for what you design. In Appendix A there are materials that another teacher designed for these words. You may want to compare your work with those materials when you finish.

Vocabulary and the Instructional Framework

The Instructional Framework is a structure for teaching so that the substance of what is being studied can be taught simultaneously with the means by which that substance is learned. The lesson structure is a vehicle for prepar-ing students to study the organizing idea of a lesson, for guiding students in their study of that organizing idea, and for developing students' inde-pendence as they apply what they have learned about that organizing idea. Simultaneously the lesson structure is a vehicle for preparing, guiding, and developing students' independence in the use of appropriate learning pro-cesses.

Vocabulary acquisition is one of the learning processes that interfaces instructionally with the content of your course. It is one of the processes that your students can develop and refine through your use of this lesson struc-ture. Thus, you can use vocabulary development to support students' con-tent learning.

Vocabulary and Preparation

Vocabulary development is associated principally with the preparation phase of the lesson structure. Presentation and teaching of selected words helps prepare students for the reading and writing they will do in the lesson. Use of definition-reinforcing materials also prepares students for reading and writing.

Instructional activities such as structured overviews and semantic maps help prepare students conceptually for the ideas to be studied. Using word-association activities helps establish experiential contexts for concepts to be studied, an important aspect of preparation.

Vocabulary and Guidance

The guidance phase of the lesson to show students how to acquire and apply concepts and relevant learning processes. Guidance of students' reading, writing, and reasoning necessarily includes guidance of vocabulary expansion and enrichment.

Application of vocabulary knowledge and understanding is expressed through reading, writing, and reasoning. Emphasis on word meanings has an interactive relationship with the guidance phase of the lesson. Word meanings enrich reading and writing; reading and writing enrich word meanings.

Vocabulary and Independence

The independence phase of the lesson enables students to use what they learned through preparation and guidance. Technical vocabulary is part of what students apply.

Students refine, extend, and share the vocabulary that they acquired during the lesson. Use of meaning-reinforcing materials facilitate this refinement. Use of cooperative grouping facilitates the sharing. Instructional activities such as the graphic organizer provide for review of both the content and process developed during the preparation and guidance phases of the lesson.

Summary

One person's jargon is another person's technical vocabulary! The difference comes from belonging to the speech community that uses the language.

Vocabulary development is appropriate in content-area curricula to initiate students into the speech community and to saturate them with the language. Given the extensiveness of the technical language in most subjects, the task content teachers face can be rather daunting. However, application of disciplined and organized procedures enables content teachers to meet the challenge:

1. Having clear criteria by which to select vocabulary for emphasis
2. Distinguishing between the presentation and the teaching of words
3. Distinguishing between the definitions of words and the meanings of words
4. Distinguishing between strategies involved in word recognition and word acquisition
5. Providing opportunities for students to reinforce, refine and extend their understandings of both definitions and meanings of words
6. Providing an instructional context in which students have frequent and enjoyable opportunities to use their developing technical languages in ways that enable them to understand the concepts represented by the words

---

REACTIONS

Journal Entries and Discussion

Study the diagram, the graphic organizer, that you developed for the first item under "Reflections" at the beginning of this chapter. Revise or refine it according to your current understanding of developing vocabulary. List issues or factors that were added to or clarified in your knowledge by this experience with the topic of vocabulary development.

Create a semantic-feature analysis of the topic of vocabulary development. Compare this display with the graphic organizer you just revised. What generalizations can you draw about differences in purpose, function, and results between the two devices?

Analysis and Discussion

Now that you have completed this chapter, consider the statements shown below. Check the numbered lines for statements with which you agree. Circle the numbers of statements you believe reflect the point of view of the authors. In writing, explore reasons for differences on any statements between your point of view and what you perceive to be the point of view of the auathors. Please share and discuss your writing with colleagues who also are reading this book.

_____ 1. Mere usage of words is not sufficient to enhance learning; the nature and quality of that usage are the determinants of learning.

_____ 2. Methods and materials for vocabulary development are constant, even though applied to different subjects and grade levels.

_____ 3. Selecting is not presenting; presenting is not teaching; teaching is not reinforcing.

_____ 4. It is better to help students relate their experience to what you are teaching than to ignore their experience and keep them on the edge of ignorance.

_____ 5. One can define a word and not know its meaning, but not the reverse.

_____ 6. Students can understand a concept or apply a process even though they do not know the technical name for either one.

_____ 7. Teaching inductively requires great flexibility because you cannot always be certain where you will wind up, even though you feel certain where you are going.

_____ 8. It is difficult to teach someone an idea that is not already dawning in his or her consciousness.

8

Using Reading to Support Content Learning

Organizing idea: Comprehension is connecting the known with the new.

Reflections

Before reading this chapter, please record in your journal your responses to the following task and questions. If possible, share your writing with other individuals who are also reading this book.

1. Someone said, "Travel without reading is just a change of sky." Try your hand at a creative essay, applying this image to students and schooling. Do you find implications in this image for your own teaching?

2. Is the comprehension process the same for all subject areas, or does each subject have its own unique set of comprehension skills?

3. What is the more appropriate vehicle for teaching the comprehension process in content areas: (a) resource materials that constitute the required reading in those subjects; (b) materials especially designed to teach comprehension?

HOW MUCH—AND HOW OFTEN—do you have your students read for the courses you teach? Probably it depends on your perception of how well your students read. The more teachers doubt their students' ability to read, the less they assign readings from the texts in their courses (MacGinitie and MacGinitie 1986). With limited opportunities to read and with little instruction in how to read what they are assigned, such students learn little about how to read subject-related materials. They come to rely principally on the teacher as an information source, depending on lectures, demonstrations, and the like. They become captive of catch-22. Lacking proficiency in reading, they are not given reading assignments. Lacking impetus for reading, they do not develop reading proficiency. Lacking proficiency in reading, they are not given reading assignments. Lacking . . . (and on and on). So it is that poor readers remain poor readers.

More able readers do not necessarily fare better. Some teachers often find it "more efficient" to provide information themselves rather than to depend on students to acquire that information through their reading. Because these teachers tend to "go over" material contained in the text, the value of having students read the text is questioned—by students, even if not by their teacher. Who hasn't skipped reading the text for a given class because "the teacher covers it all in class anyway"? In such circumstances, even students with reasonable proficiency in reading may have limited opportunities to refine or extend the reading skills they possess.

This chapter presents a different perspective on the place and value of reading to support content learning. The chapter also shows how the contributions of reading to content learning are strengthened by infusions of writing and reasoning.

We discuss strategies for using reading to support content learning in the context of the Instructional Framework. We want to reinforce in as many ways as possible the belief that reading instruction should not occur apart from content instruction. Thus, we review elements of the preparation and independence phases of the framework that were discussed in more detail in Chapter 5. We discuss particular instructional strategies for developing students' reading proficiency in the context of the guidance phase of the framework.

Reading and the Instructional Framework

You'll recall that the Instructional Framework is a structure for teaching. It is through this lesson structure that you can emphasize both the content (the substance of what is being studied) and the process (the means by which that substance is acquired) of your curriculum. The lesson structure is a vehicle for preparing students to study the organizing idea of a lesson, for guiding students in their study of that organizing idea, and for developing students' independence as they apply what they have learned about that organizing idea. Simultaneously, the lesson structure is a vehicle for supporting students' appropriate use of reading, writing, and reasoning as they are prepared to study the organizing idea, as they are guided in that study, and as they apply what they have learned through that study. These three learning processes are applied interactively as students study the content of the lesson. As the lesson structure creates an interface between these learning processes and the content of the lesson, students simultaneously learn both content and process.

Reading is one of the learning processes that instructionally interfaces with the content of your course. It is one of the processes your students can develop and refine through your use of this lesson structure. While preparing students to study an assigned topic, while guiding them as they study, and while developing their independence in the application of what they have learned from their study, you are also developing their proficiency in reading. Thus, you show students how to use reading to support their content learning.

Preparation for Reading

In many respects, students' success in completing a reading assignment depends on how well they are prepared for it. The preparation phase of the Instructional Framework is designed to provide this readiness.

Chapter 5 presents the rationale and instructional strategies for the preparation phase of the Instructional Framework. A few of the strategies are reviewed in this section. You may wish to refer to Chapter 5 for more detail.

Organizing Idea

Preparing students for reading they must do in a lesson starts with your own preparation for the lesson. Central to that preparation is identifying the organizing idea of the lesson. Everything you do flows from that idea: the information you stress, the resources you select, the activities you plan, and the support materials you create. You'll recall that the organizing idea is sufficiently specific to be obviously related to your subject area, but it is also sufficiently general to be illustrated by information and ideas drawn from a variety of background experiences. Illustrative organizing ideas, drawn from lessons in different subject areas, are listed in Chapter 2.

Tapping Prior Knowledge

The influence of students' relevant prior knowledge of the organizing idea on their success in studying that idea is discussed in Chapter 2. Research over many years attests to the strong influence prior knowledge has on readers' comprehension (Chall 1947; Ausubel 1968; Smith 1971; Rumelhart 1980; Anderson and Pearson 1984; Anderson 1985). Helping students activate, organize, and use relevant prior knowledge is an essential part of preparing them to read (Earle and Barron 1973; Pearson and Spiro 1982;

Chall 1983; Phelps 1984; Valeri-Gold 1987). Among a variety of ways to provide this help, the following two are particularly useful.

Word Association

Word association is a powerful strategy for stimulating recall and for motivating critical and creative reasoning applied to the product of the recall. The strategy is applied in the following manner:

1. You select a stimulus word that reflects the conceptual focus of the organizing idea of the lesson. The stimulus word is the one around which students generate a list of associated words. Sometimes the stimulus word is contained in the organizing idea itself. Sometimes the stimulus word reflects the organizing idea but is not expressed in the idea. Example 8-1 lists some organizing ideas and their stimulus words.
2. You give students the stimulus word and ask them to list words or phrases that they connect in some way with the stimulus word.
3. You give students a brief time to write their associations, somewhere between ninety seconds and two minutes. Students work together in small groups, with one student serving as recorder and all students contributing to the list.
4. After the listings are completed, you have the groups read their lists. You lead the class in making comparisons across groups, with similarities and differences noted and discussed. You encourage students to explain "outliers," associations that seem unusual or unrelated. Often what appears to be unusual or unrelated is not so when the reasons are given. These outliers may reveal an unusual background, a lively imagination, or strongly divergent thinking —if you give students an opportunity to talk about their associations.
5. You lead students in an examination of the lists to infer categories of information and ideas that seem to have stimulated the associations. You (with your students) list these categories and discuss conceptual connections that are apparent among the categories. You emphasize categories and associations that support the organizing idea of the lesson, along with the reasons for their relevance.

An important outcome of the word-association activity is the demonstration that students, collectively, already have a substantial understanding of the organizing idea of the lesson. Categories and associations not directly supportive of the organizing idea also are noted, even though they are set aside. In this manner you acknowledge the breadth and diversity of the students' knowledge and the concepts and principles with which students are familiar.

Example 7-5 in Chapter 7 shows how a science teacher used the word-association activity with her eleventh-grade chemistry students studying

EXAMPLE 8-1 _____

Some Organizing Ideas and Their Stimulus Words

1. While change is inevitable, it has both a positive and a negative impact on society. (Stimulus word: change)
2. It is possible to attain one's objective by making that which is not seen like that which should be. (Stimulus word: illusion)
3. The development of new systems impacts negatively and positively on societal and environmental issues. (Stimulus word: change)
4. Differences among people cause conflicts among nations. (Stimulus words: difference and conflict)
5. A picture is worth a thousand words. (Stimulus word: portrayal)
6. People without internal control are subject to external control. (Stimulus word: control)
7. The individual is an instrument of creativity. (Stimulus word: creativity)
8. Loss of our treasures often leads to discoveries of even greater worth. (Stimulus word: value)

nuclear power. As the recorders reported their lists, she wrote the words on the board in sets, or groups. When the lists were completely reported, she then asked the students to label the groups. Example 7-6 is the product of this listing and labeling.

Structured Overview

The process of review is connected strongly to the activation of students' prior knowledge (Langer and Nicolich 1981; Richardson and Morgan 1990; Manzo and Manzo 1990). Consequently, review serves an important function in preparing students to study the organizing idea of a lesson. It also serves to prepare them for the reading that is to be done.

The process of review can be facilitated by the use of a structured overview (Barron 1969; Earle and Barron 1973; Alvermann and Boothby 1983). You prepare the review by identifying previously studied concepts that have relevance to the organizing idea of the lesson in progress. You direct the review by raising questions about these relevant concepts. As you listen to students' responses to your questions, you infer key words that stand for pivotal information and ideas in their answers. You test your inferences by asking students if the key words appropriately represent what they were presenting in their responses. You encourage them to offer alternatives that might better represent their ideas.

As you identify the key words during this interaction with your students, you arrange the words in some visual display. The display can be written on a transparency, a chalkboard, oak tag, or a computer screen. You create the display so interrelationships among the key words can be visualized. The display—a structured overview—represents the background knowledge your students have, collectively, for the upcoming lesson.

This structured overview serves as a stimulus to the study of the organizing idea of the upcoming lesson. It also serves as a context for studying the new organizing idea. Indeed, the visual display can show how ideas drawn from the review relate to the organizing idea for the upcoming lesson.

Example 8-2 shows a structured overview developed in this manner by an eighth-grade history teacher.

EXAMPLE 8-2 ————————————————————————————————

Structured Overview

In a unit on the Constitution, the teacher was starting the study of separation of powers and division of powers. He reviewed concepts students already had studied, using the upper part of the structured overview to do so. Students discussed different kinds of power, eventually focusing on political power as the focus for the lesson. The teacher taught the word *balance* (comes from *bi-lanx* which means "two plates") and related it generally to political power. He drew from students' knowledge about levels of government as well as about branches of government. He elicited from them the labels *state* and *federal* for levels of government and the labels *legislative*, *executive*, and *judicial* for branches of government. He then presented the term *division of powers* and connected it with levels of government and the term *checks and balances* and connected it with branches of government.

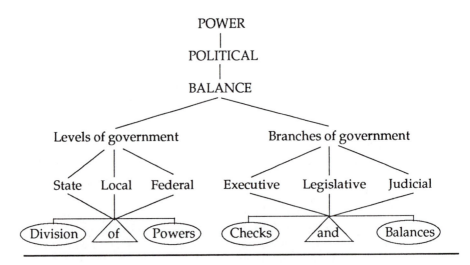

Vocabulary Development

Acquainting students with relevant technical vocabulary is an essential part of preparing students to read a text or other resource material. Chapter 7 presents ways to expand and refine students' technical vocabularies. These vocabulary expansion and refinement activities are appropriate to the preparation phase of the Instructional Framework.

You'll recall that the words to be emphasized in a lesson are identified according to their relevance to key concepts associated with the organizing idea of the lesson. Words that cluster around these key concepts are taught and/or presented (See Chapter 7 to refresh your understanding of the distinctions between teaching and presenting vocabulary.) The structured overview is an excellent vehicle for presenting and teaching vocabulary.

Chapter 7 also discusses ways to refine students' technical vocabularies as part of the preparation phase of the Instructional Framework. Activities such as matching, sentence completion, categorizing, and analogies refine students' understandings of definitions and meanings of words that have been presented and taught. Such activities increase the likelihood that students' will subsequently read the text or other resources with greater understanding because of this study of relevant vocabulary.

Anticipation and Prediction

Consider how much of what you do is conditioned by what you already have done, or how much of what you think is conditioned by what you already have thought, or how much of what you expect is conditioned by what you already have experienced. Most people tend to be predisposed toward certain actions or conditions or ideas because those actions or conditions or ideas are familiar and comfortable. This familiarity and comfort tends to govern expectations.

When you experience something contrary to what you expect, you are surprised. If the surprise involves something that you believe to be important, you think about reasons for the difference between the experience and the expectation. You store that difference in your memory and, thus, add to your bases for future expectations.

Think about what happens to readers when there is a difference between what is expected and what is experienced. Good readers expect what they are reading to make sense. If, while reading, they misread a word so the message does not make sense, they stop, reread, and figure out what the problem is. Many poor readers, remarkably enough, do not seem to expect what they are reading to make sense (Goodman 1970). When they misread a word so the message is garbled, it does not matter because they did not expect to receive an understandable message in the first place. Unfortunately, such readers are often diagnosed as being deficient in basic skills and are recycled through instruction in word-recognition skills. What they really need to learn is that reading is supposed to make sense. They should also learn that making sense involves developing a sense of expectation for meaning.

Research over the past fifteen years has clearly established the influence of prior knowledge on reading comprehension (Rumelhart 1980; Anderson and Pearson 1984; Anderson 1985). Comprehension involves the active construction of meaning by readers which, in turn, involves the readers in making connections between what is known and what is new. Anticipation and prediction serve to facilitate that connection.

Both anticipation and prediction promote active, constructive reading. Anticipation draws on prior knowledge in a broader, more general fashion than prediction. Anticipation is a form of expectation—a form of looking ahead—and it serves an important function in reading and writing. Anticipations are set around general ideas, actions, or conditions related to the concept under consideration. Discussions of what is anticipated usually are grounded in general knowledge, not in specific knowledge related to the material to be studied, as you will see in Dialogue 8-1. Here is how a reading teacher helped his students develop a sense of anticipation for what they were about to read.

After discussing their anticipations, students confirm or disconfirm them against the actuality of what is presented in the lesson materials. The level of analysis of materials to confirm anticipations is less specific and detailed than analysis of materials to confirm predictions (as is the case for the predictions shown in Dialogue 8-2).

Prediction is the other dimension of expectation. While anticipation and prediction seem similar in nature, there are important differences to consider. Prediction requires an investment on the part of readers that is more specific than that required by anticipation. Prediction draws on prior knowledge in a narrower, more specific fashion. As seen in Dialogue 8-2, predictions are set around specific ideas, actions, or conditions related to the concept under consideration.

DIALOGUE 8-1

The teacher guided his students through a discussion of the organizing idea for a lesson on blindness, "For blind people especially, necessity is the mother of invention." The teacher first developed students' understanding of the metaphor, asking them for examples from their own experience. He then asked them to write a brief statement about how this metaphor is especially applicable to blind people. Students shared their written statements within their small groups. The teacher used their statements and ensuing discussion as a means for building their sense of anticipation for the study of blindness as a handicapping condition.

DIALOGUE 8-2

The music class had studied various instruments in the orchestra and the contribution each makes to the total orchestration. Taking this knowledge into account, she hypothesized a situation in which instruments were placed in a random fashion without regard for regard for the quality and level of sound they produced. In this hypothesized situation, the orchestra players are puzzled and troubled by the sound they produce, noting that some instruments seem too loud and others cannot be heard at all. These hypothetical players discuss the problem and decide to reorganize themselves, which they did. The reorganized orchestra now produce quality sound that is well balanced for both players and listeners.

The teacher displayed a chart to show how the orchestra was reorganized. She then asked the class to hypothesize (predict) rules the orchestra players may have followed to reorganize themselves this way, and she noted the students' suggestions. She then gave students the following list of rules drawn from music texts and asked them to determine how closely their hypotheses fit the rules.

1. Keep the same instruments sitting together in a group.
2. Balance the seating of different sections of the same family.
3. Lower and/*or* louder instruments are usually toward the back.
4. Higher and/*or* softer instruments are toward the front.
5. The conductor decides where certain instruments will be heard or seen best.

Here is how a music teacher helped her students develop a sense of prediction for what they were about to read.

After discussing their predictions, students confirm or disconfirm them against the actuality of what is presented in the rules. The level of analysis of materials to confirm predictions is more specific and detailed than analysis of materials to confirm anticipations (as is the case for the anticipations shown in Dialogue 8-1).

The beneficial effects of prediction on reading comprehension seem clear. Students analyze their knowledge and make logical projections of how that knowledge will work in situations not fully known. They then analyze the situations and confirm or disconfirm their predictions. They elaborate or modify their prior knowledge according to what they find. Thus, prediction involves students in the active construction of meaning that is characteristic of good comprehension.

Anticipation and prediction have a positive impact on students' reading performance. When students look for something as they read, they generally find it. When they look for nothing, they find it, too. The instructional task is to provide students with sufficient models and guidance that anticipation of and prediction for meaning become a natural process for them as they read.

Cooperative learning, in turn, has a positive impact on anticipation and prediction. As students exchange and discuss ideas, a productive interaction occurs among the concepts being studied, the materials used to facilitate students' response to those concepts, and the discussions students have as they respond to the concepts and materials. Students probe their backgrounds of knowledge and experience while establishing expectations for what they will encounter during the reading of a selection from their text. In doing so, they enrich one another's experience and learn to calibrate reasonableness of expectation. As they project their knowledge into concepts they are just beginning to understand, they test their predictions on one another. Subsequently they discuss the validity of confirming or disconfirming evidence. Particularly for students who have difficulty speaking out in front of a full class, the small groups provide an opportunity for participation in clarifying discussion, for testing out ideas, for immediate feedback on questions, and for enrichment of information and ideas.

Guiding the Reading

This chapter deals with ways that reading can support content learning. Successful reading of resource materials enables students to acquire essential information related to the content being studied, to develop an understanding of ideas embedded in the information, and to apply the ideas in some expanded or extended form. The guidance part of the Instructional Framework involves showing students how to do this kind of reading.

Making Reading Instruction Manageable

When content-area teachers think seriously about integrating instruction in reading with instruction in course content, they raise two important questions: What skills do I teach? How do I teach them?

The answer to the first question is simplify. The answer to the second is simulate.

Simplify the Process

In Chapter 1 we state that "this entire book, both directly and indirectly, is based on the holistic perspective of reading and writing processes and on the belief that these processes can be taught simultaneously with the course content in any subject area."

Some people believe that the reading process is made up of discrete, identifiable skills and that these skills can and should be taught as separate entities. It is difficult, if not impossible, to integrate instruction in course content with instruction in these separate, discrete skills. Resource materials used in content areas are not designed to support such instruction. Attempting to teach discrete reading skills that do not necessarily support students' reading in required resource materials establishes a dichotomy between instruction in reading and instruction in course content. Such a dichotomy unnecessarily complicates the management of reading instruction in content areas.

Reading instruction can be simplified and made much more manageable for content-area teachers when reading is viewed as a holistic process. Reading can be operationally defined as processes of vocabulary acquisition, comprehension, and reasoning applied to resource materials. Consequently, reading is viewed as a meaning-acquisition, natural-language process. Meaning resides in readers so what readers bring to the text determines what they take from the text. Instruction in this meaning-acquisition process does not require that language be broken down into discrete parts to assure understanding of the whole. Rather, instruction requires sufficient prereading preparation of readers so they can make connections between what they already know and what is being presented in the language of the text. The reading instruction provides sufficient support of readers so they will make connections with, attribute meanings to, and develop understandings from what they read.

While profound in its importance, the reading process we recommend you teach is also elegant in its simplicity. The reading process is manageable by most content-area teachers because it fits naturally with the resource materials used in most content areas.

Simulate the Process

In Chapter 6 we define simulation as "an artificial representation of a real experience; a contrived series of activities which, when taken together, approximate the experience or the process that ultimately is to be applied independently."

You can show students how to read effectively in your content area by creating materials that support students' comprehension of the resources you assign. The materials raise students' consciousness about how comprehension works. The materials also focus students' attention on the concepts you want them to learn. In this fashion you can simulate the comprehension process for your students as they read the materials you require.

The balance of this chapter focuses on two instructional strategies that support the development of students' comprehension. The first is called levels of comprehension. The second is called organizational patterns.

Levels of Comprehension Strategies

We want you to experience what it is like to use the instructional materials for levels of comprehension before we discuss the design and use of the materials in detail. Before you read the materials in Practice 8-1, you should engage in a word-association activity with a group of colleagues who are also reading this book. Do the following:

1. Give yourselves about three minutes to write out words or phrases that you associate in some way with the word *problem.*
2. After you complete your listing, compare your results with those of other groups (if you are in a class).
3. Give yourself another three minutes to write words or phrases that you associate in some way with the word *solution.*
4. Compare your listing for *solution* as you did for *problem.*
5. In your group create logical pairs of words by drawing one word for a pair from the list of problems and the other word from the list of solutions. Make as many pairs as you can in five or ten minutes.
6. In your group discuss how pairs you created relate to the statement, "Universal problems yield to interactive solutions."
7. After you complete this discussion, please read the materials and follow the directions in Practice 8-1 in the order in which they are given.

Now that you have experienced this instructional strategy for supporting comprehension, let's consider what it is and how it works.

Background

Integrating reading instruction with content-area instruction has been a long-term objective of school-based research and practice (Moore, Readence, and Rickelman 1983). Central to that objective has been a search for practical ways to help content-area teachers improve their students' reading comprehension. Practicality suggests manageability; so the need has been to find a simple way to manage a complex process. Part of the response to the need can be found in the operational definition given to the process of comprehension. Another part of the response to the need can be found in the instructional strategies that flow from the operational definition.

Definitions
William S. Gray, an early researcher and practitioner in the field of reading, providedan operational definition of comprehension that is simple yet comprehensive. He said that comprehension involves

- Reading the lines
- Reading between the lines
- Reading beyond the lines (Gray 1960)

Gray's descriptors indicate how readers comprehend by interacting both with the text (reading the lines and reading between the lines) and with

PRACTICE 8-1

Now There's a Kinder, Gentler Argument in Favor of a Free Press

Level One

Directions: Listed below are ten statements. As you read, place a check on the numbered line of each statement that presents information found in the article on the free press. Be ready to provide evidence from the text to support your decisions. Discuss your decisions and supporting evidence with other members of your group.

_____ 1. A free press promotes peace and democracy and is the bridge between the two.

_____ 2. Except in a time of war, censorship and democracy are incompatible.

_____ 3. The most democratic countries have the freest media, and the least democratic have the most restricted media.

_____ 4. Democracies do not make war on each other; most war occurs between the least free countries.

_____ 5. Democracies tend to have the least internal violence; those countries with the least freedom tend to have the most.

_____ 6. Democratic governments simply do not kill their own citizens for any but the most reprehensible acts; the least free governments tend to kill their citizens by the millions for political, religious, or racial reasons.

_____ 7. The twentieth century's blood bath includes more than 100 million people, but not one was killed in war between democracies.

_____ 8. Democracies are a way to nonviolence; promoting democracy is promoting world peace.

_____ 9. Since advancing freedom of the press furthers democracy, spreading freedom of the press promotes world peace.

_____ 10. To foster peace, foster freedom of the press.

Newspaper editors hardly have to be told about the importance of press freedom. Nor do they need to be lectured on the virtues of peace. But surprisingly few editors seem to be aware of or articulate the strong connection between the two. Leaving aside newspapers' need for a free press, and citizens' need for free expression, my research has proved that a free press promotes peace. The bridge between the two is democracy.

To most people, democracy is easily defined by certain rights: that of voting and the secret ballot, of being able to run for any political office, including the highest, and of freedom of speech. And the latter, of course,

(continued)

PRACTICE 8-1 Continued

means not only the freedom to publish criticism of the government, but even to advocate revolution. Except in a time of war, censorship and democracy are not only seen as incompatible—they are incompatible.

The annual Freedom House survey of freedom, "Freedom at Issue, January/February," shows that the most democratic countries have the freest media, and the least democratic have the most restricted media.

Now, research on war and peace has shown the following: First, democracies do not make war on each other. There has been no war and virtually no threat of violence between two countries that are democratic. The most war occurs between the least free countries. Note that there are 167 sovereign nations in the world today, 60 of them democracies. There has been no war between them. There is now no war between them. There is not even a threat of war; none of these democracies arm against each other. After its long, bloody history, for example, Western Europe is finally at peace. There is no expectation of war among the countries there. And, it is no accident that Western Europe is also totally democratic.

Second, democracies tend to have the least internal violence (riots, revolutions, guerrilla warfare, civil war); those countries with the least freedom tend to have the most.

Finally, democratic governments simply do not kill their own citizens for any but the most reprehensible criminal acts, such as murder; the least free tend to kill their citizens by the millions for political, religious, or racial reasons. In much of the world, genocide and totalitarianism are almost synonymous.

Consider that in this century alone, aside from foreign or domestic wars, totalitarian governments have killed in cold blood more than 115 million people, over three times the number killed in battle in all wars in this century, including the two world wars.

The major perpetrators are well known; disagreement exists only about the numbers: Hitler may have slaughtered as many as 14 million people, including nearly 5 million Jews; Stalin surely outdid him by murdering well over 20 million; Mao Tse-tung possibly liquidated even more; Pol Pot in Cambodia exterminated around 2 million Cambodians; the Young Turks killed more than 1 million Armenians during World War I. And then there were the assorted butcheries in Ethiopia, Vietnam, Syria, Uganda, Rwanda, Burundi, Indonesia, East Pakistan, and elsewhere.

The twentieth century's global blood bath of political violence covers more than 100 million, and more than 140 million people when battle deaths in foreign and domestic wars are included. But not one of these millions were killed in war or violence between democracies; few, if any, citizens of a democracy have been killed by their own government for other than crimes like murder (the number of criminals executed in the whole history of the United States by federal and local authorities up to 1982 is 13,630).

(continued)

PRACTICE 8-1 Continued ━━━━━━━━━━━━━━━━━━━━━━━━━━

It should be clear that democracies are a way to nonviolence. In fact, promoting democracy is promoting world peace. For were democracy universalized, the lesson of history and contemporary events is that international war would be eliminated, domestic violence minimized, and genocide and governmental mass murder of its citizens ended.

Since advancing freedom of the press furthers democracy, spreading freedom of the press promotes world peace. And the reverse logic is also true. Without democracies, there will be war; without freedom of the press, democracies cannot exist. Newsmen everywhere should remember this simple equation. To foster peace, foster freedom of the press.

Source: R. J. Rummel, "Now There's a Kinder, Gentler Argument in Favor of a Free Press," *The Bulletin of the American Society of Newspaper Editors*, February 1989, #711, p.27.)

Level Two

Directions: Listed below are eight statements. Place a check on the numbered line for each statement that can be supported by combinations of information found in the article on the free press. Be ready to cite evidence from the article to support your decisions. Discuss your decisions and supporting evidence with other members of your group.

_____ 1. Peace and a free press are inextricably intertwined.

_____ 2. Democracy is the vehicle by which a free press promotes peace.

_____ 3. If two countries have not had war between them, the probability is high that both are democracies.

_____ 4. Countries that provoke war most support freedom least.

_____ 5. Citizens of democracies have less reason to fear for their safety than citizens of totalitarian governments.

_____ 6. Of the more than 100 million casualties of political violence in the twentieth century, none have been caused by wars between democracies and few, if any, by democratic governments acting against their citizens.

_____ 7. To assure world peace, assure world democracy.

_____ 8. Peace is the result of a free press and both are the result of democracy.

Level Three

Directions: Listed below are six statements. Place a check on the numbered line for each statement that you can support with ideas derived from the article on the free press *and* from your own knowledge and experience. Be ready to provide evidence from *both* sources to support your decisions.

(continued)

PRACTICE 8-1 Continued ━━━━━━━━━━━━━━━━━━━━━━━━━━━━━
Discuss your decisions and supporting evidence with other members of your group.

_____ 1. Freedom is an outcome, not an imposition.

_____ 2. Where there is no respect for freedom, there is no respect for life.

_____ 3. The freedoms of press and society are reciprocal and interactive.

_____ 4. Fame can come from evil as well as from good.

_____ 5. Altruistic societies have little to fear from one another; despotic societies have everything to fear.

_____ 6. Profound problems can be resolved with simple solutions.

factors outside the text (reading between the lines and reading beyond the lines).

We agree with Gray's parsing of comprehension into the three phases, but we use descriptors to identify a kind of comprehension that is occurring in each phase. We use *literal* to describe reading the lines, *interpretive* to describe reading between the lines, and *applied* to describe reading beyond the lines (Herber 1970, 1978, 1985).

Literal comprehension involves the process of acquiring basic information from text or the process of determining what the authors are saying. Literal comprehension is necessary but not sufficient for developing an understanding of concepts imbedded in the text or for making use of those concepts once they have been understood. Literal comprehension provides information out of which concepts are constructed. Literal comprehension also provides information that serves as evidence to support concepts brought to the text from prior knowledge and experience. Acquiring the information is not acquiring the idea; literal comprehension is just reading the lines.

Interpretive comprehension involves the process of deducing, or inferring, ideas from information presented in text or the process of determining what authors mean by what they say. Skilled readers analyze information acquired at the literal level of comprehension, looking for ways information fits together. As readers perceive connections, concepts begin to take shape that give meaning to what the authors are presenting. Skilled readers also perceive connections that support previously acquired concepts that have bearing on and give meaning to what the authors are presenting. Inferring the ideas requires analysis of the information; interpretive comprehension is reading between the lines.

Applied comprehension involves the process of synthesizing ideas from multiple sources or the process of making use of ideas found in text. By this synthesis, skilled readers connect ideas already in their schemata with ideas presented by authors of the text being read. Products of this synthesis are broad generalizations that embrace the ideas from both sources. Conceptualizing broad generalizations requires synthesis of ideas from multiple sources; applied comprehension is reading beyond the lines.

Research on comprehension and schema theory confirms the appropriateness of these descriptors of comprehension and the practicality of the instructional strategy they form. Drawing on this research, Pearson and Johnson (1978) created a taxonomy of comprehension questions and answers that is similar in purpose and function to the levels of comprehension already described (see Figure 8-1).

Pearson and Johnson use the term *textually explicit* to describe comprehension that involves readers in identifying explicit information in text. They use the term *textually implicit* to describe comprehension that involves readers in identifying ideas that can be inferred from text. They use the term *scriptally implicit* to describe comprehension that involves readers in relating ideas from prior knowledge to ideas drawn from the text. Chapter 12 contains a discussion of how Pearson and Johnson's taxonomy was used by Raphael (1984, 1986) to design a system for creating questions to guide students' reading comprehension. The levels-of-comprehension construct has been widely used in school programs and widely promulgated in professional texts (Vacca and Vacca 1989; Manzo and Manzo 1990; Richardson and Morgan 1990; Irwin and Baker 1989; Estes and Vaughan 1978).

Analysis of Levels of Comprehension

It is important now to analyze each of the levels in more detail. Please recall your experience in using the levels as you responded to the material in Practice 8-1. You will find it useful to reflect on this experience as you read through the analysis of each of the levels.

Literal Comprehension

Literal comprehension is, as Gray (1960) says, reading the lines. The purpose of literal comprehension is to identify specific information presented by the authors of the text. Because texts are filled with specific information, readers need criteria to determine what information to identify and subsequently to remember.

FIGURE 8-1   Taxonomies of Comprehension

Gray	*Herber*	*Pearson and Johnson*
Reading the lines	Literal	Textually explicit
Reading between the lines	Interpretive	Textually implicit
Reading beyond the lines	Applied	Scriptally implicit

Independent readers set their own purposes for reading and thereby establish criteria for targeting specific information. In instructional settings, teachers use an organizing idea to help students establish purposes for reading. Information that contributes to an understanding of the organizing idea is the target of the literal comprehension.

To guide students' literal comprehension, you provide declarative statements that duplicate information found in the text, often word-for-word. You include information you believe supports an understanding of the organizing idea of the lesson. The students' task is to determine whether the information included in the statements is present in the text. Students do this work in small groups, sharing with one another the specific location in the text where they find the target information.

When you responded to the statements in Level One of Practice 8-1, you read at the literal level of comprehension if you followed the directions carefully. You first read a statement and then looked in the text to determine if the information included in the statement was present in the text. You applied this same procedure to each of the statements, and you discussed your decisions with others who were doing the same activity. In so doing, you concentrated on information from the text that contributes to the organizing idea for that particular lesson, "Universal problems yield to interactive solutions".

Interpretive Comprehension

Interpretive comprehension is, as Gray (1960) says, reading between the lines. The purpose of interpretive comprehension is to infer ideas that can be logically drawn from information presented in the text. In literal comprehension, readers establish what they think authors say. In interpretive comprehension, readers establish what authors mean by what they say. In literal comprehension, readers identify information that the authors present. In interpretive comprehension readers conceptualize ideas that the authors imply. Independent readers are able to look across the information presented in text and perceive implicit conceptual relationships. Relationships they perceive are influenced by purposes they have for reading and by what they already know about the concepts about which they are reading. They are able to express in oral or written form the inferences, deductions, or conclusions that they draw from the information presented in the text.

In instructional settings, teachers support students' interpretive comprehension by reviewing what they already know about the topic, by helping them establish purposes for reading, and by guiding their interpretation of the text. Concepts that contribute to an understanding of the organizing idea are the target of interpretive comprehension.

To guide students' interpretive comprehension, you provide declarative statements that reflect ideas that are implied by information contained in the text. You include as declarative statements ideas that are supported by the text and contribute to an understanding of the organizing idea of the lesson. You can include distractors among the statements, if you wish. These are expressions of ideas that are not supported by information in the text being read.

The students' task is to determine whether the ideas expressed by the statements are supported by information from the text. Students do this work in small groups, sharing with one another information from the text that supports or rejects ideas expressed by the statements. As they connect information to support or reject the statements, they are engaging in the same processes of drawing inferences, deductions, or conclusions by which you created the statements in the first place. As students discuss their responses, their use of inference, deduction, and drawing conclusions is reinforced.

When you responded to the statements in Level Two of Practice 8-1, you were reading at the interpretive level of comprehension if you followed the directions carefully. You first read a statement and then looked to see if it could be supported or rejected by information included in the text. You applied this same procedure to each of the statements, sharing with colleagues the evidence you used to support your decisions. In so doing, you concentrated on ideas from the text that contribute to the organizing idea for that particular lesson, "Universal problems yield to interactive solutions."

Applied Comprehension

Applied comprehension is, as Gray (1960) says, reading beyond the lines. The purpose of applied comprehension is to connect prior knowledge and experience with ideas that are inferred or deduced from the text. In literal comprehension, readers identify information that authors present. In interpretive comprehension readers conceptualize ideas that authors imply. In applied comprehension readers synthesize generalizations out of a connection between their own ideas and the authors'.

Independent readers are able to synthesize ideas drawn from a variety of sources, ideas found in resources they read and ideas grounded in their previous experiences. In addition, independent readers are able to express in oral or written form the products of this synthesis in terms of generalizations or statements of principle.

In instructional settings, teachers support students' applied comprehension by helping them establish purposes for reading, by reviewing what they already know about the topic, and by guiding their literal and interpretive comprehension of the text. General principles that refine and expand students' understanding of the organizing idea become the target of applied comprehension.

You guide students' applied comprehension with general principles related to the organizing idea of the lesson. These general principles are expressed as declarative statements that can be supported (or rejected) by ideas drawn *both* from the text *and* from the students' prior knowledge and experience. You may wish to include the organizing idea of the lesson among the statements. You may wish to include similes or metaphors that illustrate the organizing idea. You may wish to include distractors among the statements, general principles that are unlikely to be supported by ideas from the text or ideas from students' prior experiences. We say "unlikely" because sometimes students will think of supporting ideas or experiences you did not have in mind when you created a distractor in the first place.

The students' task is to determine whether the general principles expressed by statements can be supported *both* by ideas from the text *and* by ideas from their prior knowledge and experience. Students do this work in small groups, sharing with one another the reasons for their support or rejection of the statements. As they connect the ideas from the text with ideas from their prior knowledge and experience, they apply the same processes of synthesizing and generalizing by which the statements were created in the first place. As they discuss their responses, their applications of these processes are reinforced.

When you responded to the statements in Level Three of Practice 8-1, you were reading at the applied level of comprehension if you followed the directions carefully. You first read a statement and then considered whether it could be supported or rejected by your own knowledge and experience *and* by ideas drawn from the text. You applied this same procedure to each of the statements and you discussed your decisions with others who were doing the same activity. In so doing, you concentrated on ideas that refine and expand the organizing idea for that particular lesson,

Universal problems yield to interactive solutions.

Design of Levels Guides

You have experienced the use of a levels guide. You have studied the definitions of literal, interpretive, and applied comprehension and have practiced discerning declarative statements that reflect the three levels of comprehension. Now you need to consider how to design levels guides.

Your objective in designing a levels guide is to support students' comprehension of the assigned text. In many respects, levels guides you prepare reflect your own comprehension of the text. In that you are a skilled reader and an expert in the content being covered, the guide you design will serve as a model of how to comprehend resource materials in your subject.

Recall what constitutes the three levels. Literal comprehension involves readers in identifying basic information in the text. Interpretive comprehension involves readers in conceptualizing ideas the authors are presenting. Applied comprehension involves readers in synthesizing the authors' ideas with their own ideas and in applying both to a set of general principles. Your task is to create declarative statements that will guide and support students' comprehension at each of these levels.

In designing the guide, you first establish the organizing idea for the lesson. Next you examine the section in the text that you will be assigning to determine how it should be read. Emphasis on levels of comprehension is appropriate for most expository text. Having determined that you will use the levels-of-comprehension strategy, you create the guide level by level, using declarative statements.

For the literal level, you identify significant information that supports the organizing idea. You place this information in the literal-level guide as a series of declarative statements. You write directions that describe the task and reinforce the process being applied. Example 8-3 illustrates sample directions for a literal-level guide.

For the interpretive level, you identify relationships among all the pieces of information that seem reasonable in light of the organizing idea for the lesson. You create statements that reflect possible interpretations of those relationships: inferences, deductions, and conclusions. You write out these possibilities and place them in the guide as declarative statements. You write directions that describe the task and reinforce the process being applied. Example 8-4 (see page 218) illustrates sample directions for an interpretive-level guide.

For the applied level, you identify universal ideas or general principles that relate in some fashion to the organizing idea. These are ideas or principles that can be illustrated by concepts drawn from the text as well as from students' own knowledge and experience. You list these universal ideas and general principles in the guide as a set of declarative statements. You write directions that describe the task and reinforce the process being applied. Example 8-5 (see page 218) illustrates sample directions for an applied-level guide.

Declarative Statements (Revisited)

In Chapter 6 we discuss the use of declarative statements in the design of materials that show students how to comprehend text. As noted in the explanation of how to design levels guides, declarative statements are used at each level.

The declarative statements used in the levels guides are the product of your own comprehension process as you ask yourself questions about the text and the organizing idea of the lesson: What is the essential information?

EXAMPLE 8-3 —————————————————————————————

Sample Directions For Literal-Level Guide

Directions: Listed below are xx statements. Place a check on the numbered line of each statement that presents information found in the article on the free press. Be ready to provide evidence from the text to support your decisions. Discuss your decisions and supporting evidence with other members of your group.

EXAMPLE 8-4 ▬▬▬▬▬▬▬▬▬▬▬▬▬▬▬▬

Sample Directions For Interpretive-Level Guide

Directions: Listed below are xx statements. Place a check on the numbered line for each statement that can be supported by combinations of information found in the article on the free press. Be ready to cite evidence from the article to support your decisions. Discuss your decisions and supporting evidence with other members of your group.

What ideas are being presented? What generalizations can we draw from this material as it relates to what I already know? You write out answers to these questions and give them to your students, organized into the levels-of-comprehension format.

Students take this product of your comprehension and decide whether its parts are consistent with the text and the organizing idea of the lesson. By citing evidence to support or reject your declarative statements, students develop an awareness of how such statements are derived. This gives them a feel for how the comprehension process works within and across the three levels. They are able to talk about the process with their teachers and peers. They also are able to talk about the ideas derived through their application of the comprehension process. Thus, reading supports content-area learning.

Order Among Levels

Because we use the term *levels* in this instructional strategy, you can easily infer that we believe in some hierarchical or linear relationship among these levels. In actual fact, we think of the relationship among the levels as taxonomic in nature. That is, definite relationships exist among the levels, but the relationships are interactive, not necessarily linear. Order of use among the levels depends on the purposes for reading, familiarity with content, the performance levels of readers, and the anticipated outcomes from the reading.

EXAMPLE 8-5 ▬▬▬▬▬▬▬▬▬▬▬▬▬▬▬▬

Sample Directions For Applied-Level Guide

Directions: Listed below are xx statements. Place a check on the numbered line for each statement that you can support with ideas derived from the article on the free press *and* from your own knowledge and experience. Be ready to provide evidence from *both* sources to support your decisions. Discuss your decisions and supporting evidence with other members of your group.

Students move back and forth between and among the levels as they read the text and discuss what they have read. When reading at the literal level, they already are developing a sense of relationships among the details. When reading at the interpretive level, the ideas they develop trigger new insights about the details and, in turn, modify the ideas they are inferring. When reading at the applied level, the ideas they encounter give new insights into the text and their own experience as well as into the broader world of universal ideas. Thus *interactive* is an appropriate descriptor for the levels.

Teachers who use the levels-of-comprehension construct in their teaching tend to apply the strategy mainly in the literal-interpretive-applied order. However, teachers also find it useful to apply the strategy in the applied-literal-interpretive-applied (revisited) order. When used in this latter order, students react first to the broad principles presented in the applied-level guide. They draw principally on their own knowledge and experience for evidence to support or reject the statements. They then read the text, guided by the literal and interpretive-level guides. They then return to the applied level and decide whether they would change any of their responses given their now-expanded knowledge. They draw evidence from the text as well as from their prior knowledge during this second use of the applied-level guide.

An Instructional Strategy

The levels-of-comprehension construct becomes an instructional strategy when the levels are represented in instructional materials called levels guides. Levels-guide materials are designed to support students as they read and respond to text at each level of comprehension. They provide the scaffolding discussed in Chapter 6.

These guides are used to support students not only as they read text but also as they discuss what they have read with other students and with their teacher. In providing this supporting function, guides serve as mediators (Shoemaker 1977), a particularly apt simile. That is, the levels guides provide a link between readers and text in a way that promotes understanding of text and facilitates communication among the readers. Guides for literal and interpretive levels of comprehension mediate between students and text, facilitating students' acquisition of essential information and their analysis of implicit ideas. Guides for the applied level of comprehension mediate between students' prior knowledge and the ideas implicit in text, enabling them to develop new or expanded concepts.

Levels guides mediate discussions among students as they draw information, ideas, and generalizations from the text and from their prior knowledge. Mediation of students' interaction is particularly important because students often work in small groups as they respond to the guides. The guides give focus and purpose to students' interactions and increase the efficiency and productivity of their work. The guides, used in small groups, increase opportunities for individual students to develop and refine their proficiency with the comprehension process.

The guides also mediate the communication between the students and teacher, giving focus to that communication. The structure of the guides enables teachers to identify more easily needs of students relative to comprehension and to provide more easily the needed instruction (see discussion of functional assessment in Chapter 12).

Sample Guides

In Appendix B we have included a set of levels guides drawn from the work of teachers in different subject areas. We present them as examples of what teachers have created for their own students. We include the organizing ideas of the lessons for which these guides were created. You will find it useful to look over these examples at this time.

Practice

Distinguishing among Levels

Before you practice designing a three-level guide, you should calibrate your sense of the conceptual and operational differences among the three levels. You can develop this calibration by completing Practices 8-2 and 8-3 (see pages 221–224). It is important for you to do both of them. In each case, read the article first, and then do the tasks described in the directions that follow.

This analysis of statements is *not* something we recommend you do with your students. The purpose of the exercise is to give you practice in discriminating among statements to identify the levels of comprehension they represent. This experience is part of helping you learn about the levels of comprehension before you create levels guides of your own.

Your purpose in using levels guides is to teach students about *how to* comprehend, not to teach them *about* comprehension. Thus, there is no reason to have students go through this activity and discriminate among statements on the basis of the levels of comprehension they reflect.

Internal Consistency

If you are like most readers of this text, you undoubtedly differed with some of our decisions as to what levels of comprehension were represented by some of the statements included in Practices 8-2 and 8-3. Most of the differ-

PRACTICE 8-2

Verbal Jabs Don't Have Equal Punch

The teasing and ridicule adolescents engage in are distinct behaviors and have very different relationships with self-esteem. This finding, from a study by Andrew J. Fuligni, a psychology graduate student at the University of Michigan, and Ritch C. Savin-Williams, associate professor of human development and family studies in the College of Human Ecology, goes against the conventional assumption that teasing and ridicule are the same behavior. (The data were gathered while Fuligni was a senior honors student in Human Ecology.)

Study participants were 384 high school students enrolled in a pre-college summer program at Cornell. They were given various questionnaires that probed for level of self-esteem, extroversion and introversion, social anxiety, and the frequency with which they were teased and ridiculed or teased and ridiculed others.

As correctly defined, the researchers say, teasing is playful and generally used to express positive feelings about a person, albeit sometimes in caricature form. It can indirectly convey social concerns and norms, as well as underlying feelings of embarrassment or tension. Ridicule, in contrast, is used to communicate such feelings as anger, dislike, or disrespect, and aims to hurt the recipient.

Teasing was reported to occur much more often than ridicule. The results also show that those who perceive that they are frequently teased have high self-esteem. The researchers note that youths' existing self-esteem may affect how they interpret others' remarks, and the interpretations sustain that level of self-esteem. Youths with high self-worth may interpret a verbal ribbing as fun, which results in further positive feelings. Those with low self-worth may regard the same comments as a verbal assault, which perpetuates a poor self-image. On the other hand, youths may correctly interpret a remark as ridicule—for example, if it is cruel or if the source is someone they are not friendly with—and be affected accordingly.

An adolescent's self-regard may elicit certain verbal behavior, the researchers point out. Youths who have a high self-concept may attract the positive attention of peers, who use teasing to establish rapport with them. Likewise, youths with a negative self-concept may turn off their peers, who use ridicule as a way to distance themselves.

Adolescents who tease others but are not teased themselves have significantly lower self-esteem than those who both tease and are teased. They may keep attempting to tease with the hope they'll be teased in return, said Savin-Williams, "but their low self-esteem may be causing a negative reaction, or their timing or delivery could be off, and they're unable to gain credibility with this behavior."

(continued)

PRACTICE 8-2 Continued ━━━━━━━━━━━━━━

The prevalent view among researchers that teasing and ridicule are identical has resulted in a misunderstanding of a major aspect of adolescent development, he said. "There is a negative notion of teasing, but teasing is actually desirable. Kids like it because it shows they're connected to others and are accepted. If they aren't teased they feel isolated. Mutual teasing plays an important part in the development of high self-esteem and positive interactions with others.

Source: Zorika Petic Hinderson, "Verbal Jabs Don't Have Equal Punch," *Human Ecology Forum*, Winter 1989, vol. 17; no. 2, p. 28. Vol. 17: No. 2, p. 28)

Directions: Now that you have read the article, read the following twelve statements. Decide the level of comprehension represented by each statement. On the numbered line write "1," "2," or "3" (for literal, interpretive, or applied, respectively) to indicate your decision. Do this individually, and then discuss your responses with others in your group. Our decisions are found in Appendix A. The organizing idea used in creating these statements is "No pain, no gain."

_____ 1. The teasing and ridicule adolescents engage in are distinct behaviors and have very different relationships with self-esteem.

_____ 2. The results show that those who perceive that they are frequently teased have high self-esteem.

_____ 3. A single comment can be interpreted as teasing by persons of high self-worth and as ridicule by persons of low self-worth.

_____ 4. Teasing was reported to occur much more often than ridicule.

_____ 5. A research study revealed that teasing and ridicule are not the same behavior.

_____ 6. Adversity may be essential to progress.

_____ 7. Teasing that is forced or unnatural may be misinterpreted by the recipients.

_____ 8. People not skilled in receiving usually are not skilled in giving.

_____ 9. Kids like teasing because it shows they're connected to others and are accepted. If they aren't teased they feel isolated.

_____ 10. How people feel about themselves may influence their beliefs about how others feel about them.

_____ 11. Teasing is used to express positive feelings or to educate, while ridicule is used to express anger or to hurt.

_____ 12. Commonly held beliefs, even by experts, can be proven wrong through research.

PRACTICE 8-3

Never Mind Your Number—They've Got Your Name

Trapped—that's what most Americans are when it comes to ending up in credit reports. There are avoidance schemes, such as guarding your social security number. But only one strategy really works: Pay cash. Avoid credit. Don't sign up for government programs. Walk, don't drive. Live under a rock. In short, for most ordinary people, there is no way out.

Early on, the social security number was the culprit—the tag for information on individuals. Originally, citizens had to disclose their number only when dealing with the Social Security Administration. But by the early 1960s, the Internal Revenue Service and other government agencies could demand the number for use in their identification systems. By the mid-1970s, states could ask for it on driver's license applications. Soon, universities, banks, and employers used it for identification, too. About then, the credit bureaus were converting to computers. And the social security number was a handy way to index their files.

The bureaus still use it a lot. Consumers usually can't borrow wads of money without providing the number and having their spending habits checked. But increasingly, the social security number is just a convenient aid. Americans apply for credit so often, and use their credit so much, that credit reports are updated monthly. The news that you paid on time pops up with our name and address attached. And the frequency of this makes the reports as good a tool as any number for keeping track of you.

Consumers will feel the effect as the credit bureaus develop new products. As they try to grow, one of their goals is to sell more data on life-styles in addition to credit reports. They buy subscription lists, census records, real estate and insurance information, and marketing surveys. Mail-order pharmacies provide lists of their regular customers and the vitamins and drugs they use. Even charities sometimes give out lists of their best contributors. None of these records has a social security number attached. But every one has a name and address. Provide someone's name, and the credit bureau will come up with the Social Security number that goes with it.

The ease of tracking people by name may help the concept of targeted marketing, new in the past few years, to blossom in the future. Already, it's possible to produce crude profiles predicting what goods individuals may buy and where—at the mall or at local shops. The next step, as the technique is refined, is to anticipate what products a family will be ready for next—from shoes to vacations or minivans—and try to influence even earlier the way decisions are made. In *1984*, the George Orwell classic, Big Brother was a political dictator. In twenty-first century America, he may be a marketing whiz.

Source: Stephen Phillips, "Never Mind Your Number—They've Got Your Name," *Business Week*, September 4, 1989, p. 81.

(continued)

PRACTICE 8-3 Continued

Directions: Now that you have read the article, read the following twelve statements. Decide the level of comprehension represented by each statement. On the numbered line write "1," "2," or "3" (for literal, interpretive, or applied, respectively) to indicate your decision. Do this individually, and then discuss your responses with others in your group. Our decisions are found in Appendix A. The organizing idea used in creating these statements is "Personal rights once lost are rarely regained."

_____ 1. Social security numbers are available to government agencies, educational and financial institutions, and credit bureaus.

_____ 2. Beware the camel getting his nose in your tent!

_____ 3. Appearance on one consumer list increases the probability of appearance on multiple lists.

_____ 4. You can run but you cannot hide.

_____ 5. There is no way to avoid being listed in credit reports and other data bases.

_____ 6. Credit bureaus eventually may be able to anticipate purchases and influence how decisions are made.

_____ 7. The utility of a unique number for each person in the country made inevitable the use of social security numbers by governmental, social, and business institutions and agencies.

_____ 8. Once credit bureaus needed a social security number to find a name; now they can use a name to find the number.

_____ 9. Patterns of past behavior validate future behavior.

_____ 10. Living a normal life requires some compromise on a desire for privacy.

_____ 11. Personal rights once lost are rarely regained.

_____ 12. Targeted marketing owes its existence to ease in tracking people by name.

ences have to do with the issue of internal consistency in the construction of levels guides.

Internal consistency has to do with the degrees of abstraction found among the three levels within a given guide. If your level-one statements are "literally literal" (exact, word-for-word duplications of information found in the text), then your level-two and level-three statements will involve less abstract and complicated inferencing. If, on the other hand, your level-one statements are paraphrasing (not exact, word-for-word duplications of text) that reflect information without interpretation, then your level-two and level-three statements will involve more abstract and sophisticated inferencing.

The level-one statements for the guide in Practice 8-2 are mainly "literally literal." In contrast, the level-one statements for the guide in Practice 8-3 are mainly paraphrasings of information. In each case, statements for levels two and three are consistent in abstraction and sophistication with their respective level-one statements.

Probably you assigned level one to some of the level-two statements for the guide in Practice 8-2. This is because they are less sophisticated interpretations, much like the paraphrasing used for level one in Practice 8-3. Because level-one statements in Practice 8-2 are "literally literal," their related level-two statements take the form of paraphrasing to be consistent in abstraction and sophistication. Likewise, because level-one statements in Practice 8-3 are paraphrasing, their related level-two statements are more like level-three statements in Practice 8-2 in terms of abstraction and sophistication. The level-three statements in Practice 8-3 are quite abstract and sophisticated, much more than the level-three statements in Practice 8-2.

Thus, in the construction of three-level guides, don't be as concerned about comparability among guides as you are about consistency across levels within guides. This flexibility in the design of guides enhances their ease of construction and ease of use. This flexibility also allows you to tailor the sophistication of the guides you design to the specific needs of your own classes.

Designing a Guide

Practice 8-4 (see page 226) presents a brief reading selection for you to use in practicing the design of a three-level guide. Decide on an organizing idea for a lesson in which you would use the selection. Then create a three-level guide. You can compare your response with ours, if you wish, by looking at our product in Appendix A.

Organizational Patterns

Before we discuss how organizational patterns can be used instructionally, we want you to experience what it is like to use instructional materials for one of the more common patterns. Before you read the materials in Practice 8-5, you should engage in a word-association exercise with colleagues who are also reading this book.

1. Give yourselves about three minutes to write out words or phrases that you associate in some way with the word *appearance*.
2. After you complete your list, look for ways to group the words into a variety of categories.
3. With your colleagues, label the categories with words or phrases.

PRACTICE 8-4 _____

The Future of Pennies

The proposal that the United States get rid of pennies is, like many proposals that smack of cool-headed, cold-blooded pragmatism, one that should be implemented on another planet. It is the kind of apparently sensible yet hugely disruptive reform that a wise society will treat with the same disdain that America has already shown for the metric system and phonetic spelling.

Should we stop making cents? The penny we now have was issued in 1909 to celebrate the centennial of our sixteenth President's birth, and its name and ancestry go back to the eighth century. From the start the penny's biggest foe has been inflation, which has for centuries threatened to render the coin valueless. And yet, monarch and prime ministers have deemed this insufficient cause to rid themselves of it, preferring to let the penny be and to invent higher denominations of currency—as when Edward II established the groat. Indeed, by its continued existence the penny has served notice that the value of money cannot be infinitely debased, that the monetary systems of the English-speaking world have an anchor, albeit a shifting one. As long as the penny exists, there will be things you can buy with one or two or three or four of them. Get rid of it and nothing will cost less than a nickel.

That is the economic defense of the penny. Pennies also serve important social functions. They inform millions of children who may have been exposed to nothing but textbooks that there once was a man named Lincoln who occupied a position of some importance. They are responsible for initiating millions of conversations in stores every day between people who otherwise would complete their transactions in anomic silence. From time to time these transactions are punctuated by mild bleats of satisfaction—"Wait, I have a penny!" Such moments, occurring all across the nation and around the clock, contribute modestly but directly to social comity.

Pennies, moreover, are so deeply embedded in our culture that extracting them would leave small emptiness in the very substance of life. Pennies help to mark the stages of man. They're the first allowance we receive. Later we put them on railroad tracks, and later still in loafers, and later still in fuse boxes. Inevitably the day comes when a penny falls from the hand and one decides not to pick it up. In the mature adult this prompts a fleeting sense of contentment, for he has acknowledged the fact of his own security. We wish on pennies at fountains and wells, knowing that dimes and nickels won't work. In a pocketful of change pennies serve as an essential garnish, relieving an otherwise drab monochrome like radishes in a salad. And in our language they are called upon liberally when precepts of formidable consequence must be conveyed. "Look after the pennies and the pounds will take care of themselves." "A penny saved is a penny earned." Thanks to exhortations like these, it may very well be that if all the pennies hoarded in bowls

(continued)

PRACTICE 8-4 Continued ━━━━━━━━━━━━━━━━━━━━━━━━━━━
and jars were taken into account, the often maligned savings rate would approach that of Japan.

The elimination of the penny might afford some slight physical convenience, but the total social costs exceed what a liberal democracy ought to countenance. It would be nothing less, one might say, than penny-wise and pound-foolish.

Cullen Murphy, "The Future of Pennies," *The Atlantic Monthly*, December 1989, vol. 246; no. 6, 22.

━━━

4. Discuss how the words and categories you produced relate to the statement: *Appearances can be deceiving.*
5. After you complete this discussion, please read the materials and follow the directions in Practice 8-5 in the order in which they are given.

You will recognize this article as one you read in Chapter 2 while practicing the creation of organizing ideas. Now you can see how a patterns guide supports comprehension of this material.

Now that you have experienced this instructional strategy for using an organizational pattern to support comprehension, let's consider what the strategy is and how it works.

Background

In Chapter 3 we discuss the nature of expository material in detail. Included in that discussion are identifications of the four different organizational patterns that are found in expository material as well as presentations of expository material that reflect the different patterns. What follows in this chapter is a brief review of that material.

Textbooks used in most content areas include some form of expository material. *Exposition* is defined as "discourse or an example of it designed to convey information or explain what is difficult to understand" (*Webster's Ninth New Collegiate Dictionary*, 1988). *Discourse* is defined as "formal and orderly and usually extended expression of thought on a subject" (*Webster's Ninth New Collegiate Dictionary*, 1988).

A good synonym for the word *exposition* is "explanation." The purpose of most content-area texts is to explain principles or procedures, actions or conditions, information or ideas. Expository writing, or exposition, contrasts with narrative writing, or narration. Essentially, narrative writing is used to tell a story or to relate an incident.

Comprehending explanations in expository material requires a different way of reading than does comprehending stories in narrative material. Comprehension of both exposition and narration requires some awareness

PRACTICE 8-5

Turbocharging

Part One

Directions: On each of the following numbered lines there is a pair of words or phrases separated by a slanted line. As you read the article on *Turbocharging,* decide whether what the first word or phrase stands for is the cause of what the second word or phrase stands for in a pair, according to the text. If you believe it does, place a check on the numbered line. Follow this procedure with each of the pairs. Be ready to support your decisions with information and ideas from the text.

_____ 1. High power/ high gas consumption
_____ 2. Preconceptions/ misconceptions
_____ 3. Increased compression/ increased power
_____ 4. Spinning fan/ air compression
_____ 5. Extra fuel/ extra power
_____ 6. Increased size/ increased power
_____ 7. Spinning shaft/ rising heat
_____ 8. Oil and coolant/ heat reduction and dissipation
_____ 9. Careful maintenance/ long-lasting performance
_____ 10. Direct experience/ assured satisfaction

When you think of a turbocharged engine, do you picture a high-powered "muscle car"? Lots of folks do. Many people also imagine that a turbocharger makes incredible demands on an engine and uses great quantities of gasoline.

These preconceptions are often misconceptions. A turbocharger does boost available power. But it does so efficiently and economically.

The power you get when you step on an accelerator comes from the ignition of air that is pumped into engine cylinders. The more air that can be forced into the cylinders, the greater the power you can generate. That is where a turbocharger comes in.

A turbocharger is actually a marvel of efficiency. It is basically a fan driven by exhaust gases that would otherwise be wasted, monitored by an electronically controlled computer system. When you call for power, the turbocharger fan (impeller) spins, compresses the air, and feeds it to the cylinder. But overstuffing the cylinder is only half of the formula; the computer then takes over and provides the extra fuel. You get the power you need, when you need it.

Before turbo technology, the traditional way to increase power was to increase engine size. This meant greater weight, higher fuel consumption, and less efficiency. That big engine had to be fed, even when it was "loafing." With a turbo you get increased power without increased engine size.

(continued)

PRACTICE 8-5 Continued ━━━━━━━━━━━━━━━━━━━━━━━━━━━━

What about durability and reliability? A turbocharger's shaft can spin at incredible speeds—up to 130,000 RPM! That can generate lots of heat, but turbocharging systems now use the twin weapons of engine oil and coolant to fight friction and dissipate heat. The result is rugged, long-lasting performance.

Some people think turbocharged engines need special care and feeding. They do not. In fact, it is no harder to maintain a turbo engine than a normally-aspirated one. Just make sure to **check your oil and coolant regularly.** Replace them in accordance with a maintenance schedule.

Part Two

Directions: Listed below are five statements. Place a check on the numbered line for each statement that expresses an idea that can be supported by the text *and* by your knowledge and experience. Be ready to share the reasons for your decisions.

_____ 1. Appearances can be deceiving.
_____ 2. There are more attributes to power than size.
_____ 3. That which is serviced carefully serves faithfully.
_____ 4. For every action there is an equal and opposite reaction.
_____ 5. High compression and rapid expansion, when controlled, can
　　　　　　　produce significant power.

───────────────────────────────────────

of and dependence on how the two kinds of materials are organized. Narrative material is organized essentially around some form of story line. Information in expository material is organized essentially around some pattern of relationships. The purpose of this section is to identify these patterns:

- Cause/effect
- Comparison/contrast
- Time order
- Simple listing (Niles 1965).

Efficient readers can use these four patterns to enhance their comprehension of expository text. They use word clues to determine the predominant pattern being use in the selection they are reading. For example, you undoubtedly noted the following words in the article on turbochargers and recognized the cause/effect pattern: does so; comes from; the more . . . the greater . . . ; the way to . . . was to . . . ; the result is . . . .

Efficient readers recognize that patterns can become intermixed, that comparison/contrast can exist within cause/effect or vice versa. However, they recognize that one pattern usually dominates in a given passage, even when they are mixed.

Efficient readers also recognize that relationships within these patterns can be either explicit or implicit or both. That is, they can identify information that is either explicitly or implicitly related to other information in the pattern. Reading to perceive explicit and implicit relationships in these patterns is equivalent to reading at the literal and interpretive levels of comprehension. For example, pairs 2, 4, 6, 7, and 8 in Part One of Practice 8-5 reflect explicit cause/effect patterns and pairs 1, 3, 5, 9, and 10 reflect implicit cause/effect patterns. Thus, Part One of a patterns guide supports students' literal and interpretive comprehension.

Taking the products of the explicit and implicit relationships and relating them to relevant prior knowledge and experience is equivalent to reading at the applied level of comprehension. For example, statements 1 through 4 in Part Two are like the applied level. Statement five in Part Two requires readers to use prior knowledge to perceive relationships across information and to draw abstract conclusions. This involves high-level interpretation. Thus, Part Two of a patterns guide supports students' interpretive and applied comprehension.

You can help your students increase their comprehension efficiency by showing them how to use the organizational patterns as they read. The showing how involves the design and use of patterns guides.

Design of Patterns Guides

As you observed in your guided response to the article on turbochargers, a patterns guide is organized into two parts.

Part One

Patterns guides are constructed on the same principle of showing how as are guides for levels of comprehension. Declarative statements are used to simulate the application of a pattern and to raise students' consciousness about how the pattern contributes to their comprehension.

1. You establish the organizing idea for the lesson and decide on some means of helping students make a conceptual connection between that idea and their own prior knowledge and experience.
2. You examine the reading selection and determine that it is organized around a particular pattern of relationships.
3. You identify which organizational pattern fits the relationships.
4. You create a patterns guide to facilitate students' reading about the organizing idea of the lesson.

Assume for illustrative purposes that your students need to use the cause/effect pattern as they read the assignment in their text. In creating a guide for this pattern, you identify cause-and-effect relationships that are critical to an understanding of the organizing idea of the lesson. Then you display these relationships in a guide as was done for the article on turbochargers in Practice 8-5. In this particular format, two words or phrases are placed on a line with the first being separated from the second by a slanted line. The directions note that the first word or phrase represents actions or conditions that possibly caused actions or conditions represented by the second word or phrase. The directions ask students to determine if these cause-and-effect relationships are present in the text. The directions further ask students to be ready to offer proof for their decisions. Often this evidence is developed in written form before it is presented in oral form. Students work together in groups to facilitate their work and to derive the benefits from cooperative learning.

As students develop sophistication in their use of a pattern, you will want to raise the challenge level of your guides accordingly. You can do so by setting up a matching format, with causes listed on the left and effects on the right. Directions for the guide ask students to show the cause-and-effect relationships found in the text by matching causes with effects.

Some of the cause-and-effect relationships represented in the part one of the guides may be explicitly stated by the authors. Others may only be implied. Thus, by using these guides to respond to the text, students read at both the literal and interpretive levels of comprehension. Both levels contribute to readers' understanding of authors' ideas.

What is applicable in the design of guides for the cause/effect pattern is applicable to the other patterns as well. Appendix B contains guides for the different organizational patterns in a variety of content areas.

Part Two

You have seen how part one of a patterns guide supports students' application of a particular organizational pattern at both the literal and interpretive levels of comprehension. Part two of a patterns guide is similar in function to the applied-level guide. That is, declarative statements are used to represent general principles that have possible bearing on the organizing idea of the lesson. Students draw on their own knowledge and experience as well as on ideas from the text to support or reject the statements. They are asked to provide evidence to support their decisions, and this evidence usually is developed in written form. Students work together in groups as they make their decisions, formulate the reasons for their decisions and report their results to the rest of the class.

Notice that we said that part two of a patterns guide is similar to—not the same as—the applied level of a levels guide. Recall that part one of a patterns guide reflects information and ideas that are explicitly or implicitly presented in the text. This means that the statements in part one can be both literal and interpretive in nature. Part two also contains a spread. Many statements are at the applied level, but some may also be at the interpretive level. This flexibility allows an accommodation to the complexity of the text and the level of sophistication of the students' academic performance. For example, if the text is explicit in its presentation of cause-and-effect relationships, most of the statements in part one will be literal in nature. In that case, most of the statements in part two probably will be interpretive in nature. If students are having difficulty just acquiring basic information from the text, you may focus more on explicitly expressed relationships in part one and use more interpretive statements in part two to help them deal with the development of implicit relationships.

On the other hand, if the text is more implicit in its presentation of cause-and-effect relationships, most of the statements in part one will be interpretive in nature. In that case, most of the statements in part two probably will be applied in nature. If students are more sophisticated in their reading performance, you may focus more on implicitly expressed relationships in part one and use more applied statements in part two to help them deal with relevant generalizations.

Use of Patterns Guide

Patterns guides are used to facilitate the integration of content and process in teachers' teaching and students' learning. Thus, the use of patterns guides is a natural part of the Instructional Framework.

Place in the Instructional Framework

Patterns guides are used during the guidance part of the Instructional Framework. The purpose of their design is to support students' reading of the resource materials and to mediate students' interaction with peers and the teacher. Use of the guide assumes that appropriate activities have occurred in the preparation part of the Instructional Framework: setting a purpose for reading, anticipating the use of an organizational pattern, exploring concepts relevant to the organizing idea of the lesson, and establishing what students already know about the organizing idea.

Relationship with Levels Guides

There seems to be a logical order in the instructional use of levels guides and patterns guides. Because part one of a patterns guide usually contains a mix of explicit and implicit relationships, it is useful for students to have had some experience with literal and interpretive levels of comprehension before they start using patterns guides. Also, because part two of a patterns guide usually contains a mix of implicit relationships and broad generalizations, it is useful for students to have had some experience with interpretive and applied levels of comprehension before they start using patterns guides.

It seems logical, therefore, to use levels guides first with a given set of students to acquaint them with literal, interpretive, and applied comprehension. Subsequently, you can use their experience with levels guides to explain how literal and interpretive comprehension works in part one of a patterns guide and how interpretive and applied comprehension works in part two. Although we know of no research data that supports the logic of this order, it seems sound, and you may wish to follow it in your own use of these two types of instructional materials. Teachers who follow this order confirm its logic and its value.

Materials Constructed from Answers

Statements used in patterns guides are really answers rather than questions. The statements are products of your own comprehension process as you ask yourself these questions: How have the authors organized their material? What patterns have they used? What is the predominant pattern, given the thrust of the organizing idea of the lesson? What explicit information has a bearing on the organizing idea? What implicit ideas have a bearing on the organizing idea? What general principles, related to the organizing idea, can be drawn from the material?

In responding to the statements in a patterns guides, students *confirm the product* of comprehension; they do not actually create the product. Because you give them the products of your comprehension, they have only to judge whether or not the products are appropriate and supportable. By citing evidence to support or reject the statements, however, students develop an awareness of how such statements can be formulated. They see how they can fully comprehend the content of the text by synthesizing information and ideas drawn from the text with ideas drawn from their own experience. In this manner students expand their understanding about the comprehension process. They are able to talk about the process with their teachers and peers. They also are able to talk about the ideas derived through their application of this comprehension process. In this manner, then, reading supports content-area learning.

An Instructional Strategy

The organizational-patterns construct becomes an instructional strategy when patterns are represented in instructional materials called patterns guides. Patterns guides are designed to support students as they read and respond to text organized in a particular pattern. These guides are used to support students not only as they read text but also as they discuss what they have read with other students and with their teacher. In performing this supporting function, guides serve as mediators (Shoemaker 1977). That is, the patterns guides mediate between readers and text to promote understanding of text and to facilitate communication among readers.

Part one of the patterns guide mediates between students and text, facilitating students' acquisition of essential information and their analysis of implicit ideas. Part two of the patterns guide facilitates students' analysis of implicit ideas and mediates between students' prior knowledge and ideas implicit in text, enabling them to develop new or expanded concepts.

Patterns guides mediate discussions among students as they draw information, ideas, and generalizations from the text and their prior knowledge. Mediation of students' interaction is particularly important because students often work in small groups as they respond to the guides. The guides give focus and purpose to students' interactions and increase the efficiency and productivity of their work. The guides, used in small groups, increase opportunities for individual students to develop and refine their proficiency with the comprehension process. The guides also mediate the communication between the students and teacher, giving focus to that communication. The structure of the guides enables teachers to more easily identify needs of students relative to comprehension and to more easily provide the needed instruction (see discussion of functional assessment in Chapter 12).

Sample Guides

In Appendix B we have included a set of patterns guides drawn from the work of teachers in different subject areas. We present them as examples of what teachers have created for their own students. We include the organizing ideas of the lessons for which these guides were created. You will find it useful to look over these examples at this time.

Practice

Practice 8-6 presents a reading selection for you to use in practicing the design of a patterns guide. Please do the following:

1. Establish an organizing idea for a lesson in which the selection could be used.
2. Identify what you believe to be the predominant organizational pattern in the material.
3. Create a patterns guide, including both part one and part two.
4. Compare your response with ours by looking at our product in Appendix A.

PRACTICE 8-6 ━━━

Women in Architecture

Ada Louise Hustable has called architecture "the last profession to be liberated by women." Last December, the Boston Society of Architects commemorated the 100th anniversary of one of the first steps in this liberation: the 1888 election of the first woman architect to the American Institute of Architects.

The BSA's program of exhibits and lectures evoked articulate responses from many women architects. These responses varied by generation, revealing the changes in the professional environment during the last twenty years. The small number of women principals in Boston's architecture firms today—those who established their own firms, often with their husbands, and those who fought their way up in the ranks of old, established firms—pioneered the paths that are now traveled by increasing numbers of women with greater ease.

In the late 1960s, when Andrea Leers of Leers, Weinzapfel Associates, and Dell Mitchell, a partner at Perry, Dean, Rogers and Partners, attended architecture schools, they each had only one or two female classmates. When they graduated, both were denied jobs because of their sex, and both spoke of having to overcome what Leers calls "a hurdle of doubt" about women's abilities. Once she landed a job, Mitchell met clients who would not trust a woman to execute a large building design.

Both Mitchell and Leers believe that women have had to work harder than men to excel. "When I began teaching in the mid-1970s," recalls Leers, "I saw only exceptional women in schools, compared with a more-average range of talents among men. Although that's normalizing a little now," she says, "it still takes a certain excess of ambition, energy, and talent for women."

Leers and Joan Goody, of Goody, Clancy, and Associates, stress that they love what they do despite the hurdles. Goody, whose many and varied projects are highly visible throughout Boston, describes architecture as a wonderful field for women. "I find nothing to discourage women," she says, "and a great deal that is suited to them in as far as this field requires an artist who is also sensitive to a client's needs. Women are good team players on large projects that require a team effort."

As one of only a few women at the Graduate School of Design in the 1950s, Goody admits that "there may have been more slights than I noticed in that era before consciousness-raising. I did well, and I was thick-skinned, and it never occurred to me to look for them." Oddly enough, bias in schools seems more painful to recent graduates for whom women such as Goody, Leers, and Mitchell have paved the way. As women's enrollment rose from 2 percent in the late 1960s to the current averages of 25 to 50 percent, women's expectations also rose and further exposed prejudice.

(continued)

PRACTICE 8-6 Continued ———————————————————————

In fact, the changing educational philosophy has made schools more competitive for men and women. "The 1960s' attitudes toward teaching and learning as participatory processes really ended with the 1970s," Leers observes. "The 1980s have brought a conservative focus on career making and the dogma attendant on it."

Younger women architects in Boston agree. Brigid Williams, who graduated from Yale's School of Architecture in 1978 and is a principal in the young firm of Hickox-Williams, recalls, "I was in school at kind of a golden moment when there were fewer prescriptions of style. You could do whatever you could defend in an articulate way. By the time I left, though, that was beginning to change." Of the dearth of women teachers, she remembered, "We were always thrilled when we had a woman studio head. I think there is a truth to the idea that you need to be able to visualize yourself in a role to attain it."

Women who now have the benefit of female role models also have the luxury of not feeling confined to make prescriptions for their design process. "I think each individual designs differently," says Ray Kinoshita, "and some of the differences run along sex lines." She and her partner, Ann Marshall, won a competition to design the Women's Rights National Historical Park in Seneca Falls, New York, during their last year at the Graduate School of Design in 1987. As they design the memorial, they now allow themselves a subtler, more complex, and intuitive design process than they could have defended in school, where the required approach called for "a single strong idea."

Brigid Williams welcomes the notion of different approaches to design among men and women. She sees "no limit for women in architecture right now." As a member of a husband-wife design partnership, she observes that the difference in approach "should be made a virtue rather than a hindrance." Williams says her own approach to design projects originates from more tangible and functional considerations, and that her husband's approach tends to be more from the abstract. "We work well together because of these complementary approaches," she adds.

"Some of the literature from the 1970s seems to say there *must not* be a difference—because no right-thinking person wants a difference," says Williams, summarizing an era in which the difference between men and women was often interpreted as the inferiority of women. Williams and her peers, following the trails blazed by Goody, Leers, and Mitchell, bring with them a growing confidence in their contributions. And like their predecessors, they bring a passion for what they do. "Architecture isn't a profession," says Ann Marshall, "it's what I am."

Source: Ann Mackin and Ingrid Strong, "Women in Architecture," *Art New England*, March 1989, p. 14.

Summary

Reading can support content learning when instruction in reading is integrated with instruction in content. Treating reading as a holistic process rather than as a set of specific skills makes this integration manageable for most content-area teachers.

The constructs of levels of comprehension and organizational patterns provide two instructional strategies for supporting students' reading of content-area resources. The support is provided through materials that guide students' reading of resources at higher levels of sophistication and abstraction than they could without that support. The confidence and insight students gain from this nurturing instruction ultimately lead to students being able to manage their own learning. Over time, then, students learn to read to learn and, in so doing, learn the content they are supposed to learn.

REACTIONS

Journal Entries and Discussion

Using a semantic feature analysis, analyze the similarities and differences in comprehension taxonomies developed by Gray, Herber, Pearson and Johnson. With what other instructional approaches to comprehension do these taxonomies contrast? What factors comprise the difference?

Reflect on the relative function, purpose, and value of both questions and declarative statements as vehicles for supporting the development of students' comprehension.

Analysis and Discussion

Now that you have completed this chapter, consider the statements shown below. Check the numbered lines for statements with which you agree. Circle the numbers of statements you believe reflect the point of view of the authors. In writing, explore reasons for differences on any statements between your point of view and what you perceive to be the point of view of the authors. Please share and discuss your writing with colleagues who also are reading this book.

_____ 1. Differences in the comprehension process applied to various content areas have more to do with the nature of the content than with the function of the process.

_____ 2. In the simplification of a process, what you lose in sophistication you gain in utility.

_____ 3. The use of levels of comprehension can facilitate the accommodation of instruction to the range of students' achievement found in most content-area classes.

_____ 4. It requires more objectivity by the reader to determine what an author means than to determine what an author says.

_____ 5. The function of the applied level of comprehension is to allow subjectivity in reading to make use of prior knowledge and experience.

_____ 6. While assumptions are implicit in the use of both declarative statements and questions to guide students reading, the nature and substance of the assumptions are quite different for the two.

_____ 7. Because independence is a relative state, the cycle of support must be repeated as needed at each new level of sophistication.

_____ 8. The levels guide is only a guide, for only with thoughtful discussion of the information and ideas which the guide draws from the text and the readers, will the students develop a simultaneous understanding of content and process.

9

Using Writing To Support Content Learning

Organizing idea: "Writing is a record of the mind in the act of knowing" (Gray 1988, p 729).

Reflections

Before reading this chapter, please record in your journal your responses to the following questions. If possible, share your writing with other individuals who are also reading this book.

1. How much writing is involved in the study of your subject? In what ways do you promote, support, and provide feedback on this writing?

2. What considerations do you give to preparing students for the writing that you require of them? What strategies do you use in providing this preparation?

3. What are the beneficial effects to be derived from having students work together while writing?

WHEN ASKED WHAT she thought about a particular issue, a colleague replied, "I don't know. I'll have to wait until I see what comes out of my typewriter." Her answer was consistent with the organizing idea of this chapter, that writing is a record of the mind in the act of knowing. She came to know what she thought about the issue by writing about it. She developed her understanding of the issue by organizing her ideas on paper. It was literally true that until she wrote about the issue, she really was not certain what position she should take on it.

This is the power of writing. It helps to develop, crystalize, and synthesize knowledge and understanding, and to communicate to others what is known and understood (Squire 1984). This power is available to students when they learn how to use writing to develop their own understandings of a concept being studied in a given lesson. In this manner the writing process can be used to support content learning.

Unfortunately, using writing to *support* content learning is not the norm in most schools (Applebee 1986). Writing is used principally to *evaluate* content learning, that is, to determine what information and ideas students already have learned. Writing is not often used to help students acquire information and develop ideas in a content area. As Applebee reports,

> In most classrooms, writing requires recitation of what the student has learned whether from a textbook or from the teacher's lectures. The accuracy of that recitation is what matters ... Across subjects and grades, the typical writing assignment in American schools is a page or less, first-and-final draft, completed within a day (either in class, or taken home to finish up), and serving an examining function (Applebee 1986, 99).

When teachers use writing principally as a means for assessing acquired knowledge, students do not learn how to use writing as a means for acquiring knowledge. In such settings, students do not experience or understand the power of writing.

Product-Oriented Writing

Traditions of writing instruction mitigate against content-area teachers becoming involved in the use of writing for much other than evaluative purposes. Historically, writing instruction has focused on the creation of a product, not on the development of a process. As reported by Applebee,

> The traditional approach to writing instruction in American schools has been prescriptive and product centered. At the sentence level, instruction has emphasized correct usage and mechanics; at the text level, it has emphasized the traditional modes of discourse (narration, description, exposition, persuasion, and sometimes poetry) (Applebee 1986, 95).

Much of a teacher's time is spent in correcting usage and mechanics and in judging whether students have met the criteria for the mode of discourse they are producing.

Most teachers identify with this prescriptive and product-centered approach to writing because it is the kind of instruction they themselves received. In addition, it often is the kind of writing instruction that occurs in their own schools. Based on their experience and observation, they disregard suggestions to include some form of writing instruction in their curriculum. Even without the inclusion of writing instruction in their teaching, they have limited time to teach the content of their courses. They do not want to use the time they do have correcting countless papers.

Decisions to leave writing out of content-area curricula are unfortunate for several reasons:

1. The thinking that goes into careful writing can be used to develop, clarify, and refine students' understandings of concepts being studied. Thus, keeping writing instruction out of a subject area precludes the availability of a powerful tool for learning.
2. Writing is an excellent means for strengthening students' use of language. Keeping writing instruction out of a subject area precludes opportunities to refine students' understanding of the technical language of the discipline.
3. Writing is central to effective communication in a variety of contexts. Disconnecting writing instruction from the study of various subjects precludes opportunities for students to learn to write for a variety of purposes and audiences.

Given the limited use of writing to support content learning, reasons for keeping writing instruction out of content-area curricula seem operationally more compelling than reasons for including it. What is needed, then, is an instructional approach to writing that mitigates reasons for keeping it out and magnifies reasons for keeping it in. Such an approach is one that you have been experiencing as you read this book (if you have been fully doing the suggested activities throughout the chapters). It is an instructional approach that makes writing a natural part of content learning.

Process-Oriented Writing

Think about the writing-related activities you have engaged in as you have read this book. You have engaged in brainstorming tasks, writing lists of words, organizing those lists, and writing reactions to the lists to identify or clarify the ideas that prompted the lists. You have written out your feelings or beliefs on issues before you have studied them. You have hypothesized in writing about possible directions that certain concepts might develop. You have been asked to share your writings with other readers of this book and to incorporate their responses into new drafts of your writings.

You have written in response to ideas that you have explored through carefully structured activities. You have been asked to share your writings and to consider the responses as you compose new drafts. In this manner you have been supported as you develop and refine your understanding of concepts related to the content of this book.

You have written brief essays that synthesize the ideas you have acquired by reading a section or chapter in the book. You have been asked to share that writing and to consider the responses as you compose a new, and eventually final, draft. In developing the final draft, you have been asked to attend to details of mechanics and usage—to make it of publishable quality (were you actually in our class, you would submit that paper for evaluation). In this manner you have developed some independence in your analysis, synthesis and application of concepts related to this course.

In your own experience with this book, then, writing has been an integral part of your learning what the book has to offer. Thus, while learning the concepts, you also have had an opportunity to refine your writing proficiency. The point of this chapter is that even as you have experienced the integration of instruction in writing with instruction in course content, so can your students. They can, that is, when you use writing to support content learning in your classes.

Integration of writing with course content can be characterized as a process approach to writing instruction. Emphasis is on the total writing process: prewriting activities that stimulate thinking and organize information and ideas; writing activities that create drafts of products and subsequent revisions according to readers' responses; refining products so they can "go public."

The writing process is not applied in a vacuum. The content of the writing is not randomly determined. Rather, writing tasks address concepts related to the organizing idea of the lesson or unit and support students' study of those concepts. As you progress through this chapter you will see how the *process approach* to writing instruction conceptually parallels the *functional approach* to reading instruction. Both approaches adhere to the principle that "content determines process" (Parker and Rubin 1966). Both the reading and the writing that are done during a lesson or unit are natural to and conditioned by the substance of the concepts being studied. In Chapter 8 you saw how the functional approach to reading supports content learning. In the balance of this chapter, you will see how the process approach to writing supports content learning.

Writing and the Instructional Framework

As noted in Chapter 5, the Instructional Framework is a structure for teaching. You'll recall that through this lesson structure you can emphasize both the content (the substance of what is being studied) and the process (the means by which that substance is acquired) of your curriculum. The lesson structure is a vehicle for preparing students to study the organizing idea of a lesson, for guiding students in their study of that organizing idea, and for developing students' independence as they apply what they have learned about that organizing idea. Simultaneously, the lesson structure is a vehicle for supporting students' appropriate use of reading, writing, and reasoning as they are prepared to study the organizing idea, as they are guided in that study, and as they apply what they have learned through that study. These three learning processes are applied interactively as students study the content of the lesson. This is true both within each part of the Instructional Framework and across the whole framework. As the lesson structure creates an interface between these learning processes and the content of the lesson, students simultaneously learn both content and process.

You have already studied ways that reading supports content learning. Writing is another of the learning processes that instructionally interfaces with the content of your course. Because of the interactive relationships between writing and reading, many of the activities that prepare and guide students' reading also prepare and guide their writing. Thus, while preparing students to study an assigned topic, while guiding them as they study, and while developing their independence in the application of what they have learned from their study, you are also developing their proficiency in reading *and* writing.

Preparation for Writing

The preparation phase of the Instructional Framework deals with both content and process. That is, students are prepared to deal with the concepts that comprise the organizing idea of the lesson. The also are prepared to do the reading, writing, and reasoning by which they will acquire and apply those concepts.

Preparation for Content Development

One major purpose of the preparation phase of a lesson is to help students prepare their minds for studying the organizing idea of the lesson. Developing conceptual and experiential contexts is an important part of this preparation.

Reviewing concepts previously studied and relevant to the current organizing idea establishes a familiar context within which the new concepts are studied. Use of the structured overview or other graphic organizers facilitates such review and helps establish the conceptual contexts. Students write and share summaries or analyses of the conceptual contexts and, in so doing, more firmly establish known information, which they eventually will connect with new information.

Probing students' experiences for events, or actions, or conditions establishes a context of familiar experiences within which new concepts are studied. Use of anticipation and prediction activities or word-association activities facilitates such probing and helps establish the experiential context. Students write and share summaries or analyses of the experiential contexts and, in so doing, more firmly establish known information, which they eventually will connect with new information.

Blending the conceptual and experiential contexts provides students with a comprehensive sense of what they already know about what they are going to study. The dual contexts provide the basis for students' eventual synthesis of known information with new information. Helping students understand that they already possess important knowledge about the new organizing idea motivates their interest in the upcoming lesson. Knowing what you know helps establish what you need to know. Hence, developing these two contexts contributes to students' purposes for studying the organizing idea for the new lesson.

Preparation for Process Development

A second major purpose of the preparation phase of a lesson is to help students prepare for the application of learning processes as they study the organizing idea of the lesson. These learning processes involve reading, writing, and reasoning.

In the same sense that you prepare students for the reading they are to do and then guide them as they read, you can prepare students for the writing they are to do and guide them as they write. Indeed, many of the activities used to prepare students for reading simultaneously prepare them for writing. For example, the technical vocabulary that you teach and present prepares students to write as well as to read. Word-association and similar activities that activate prior knowledge contributes to writing as well as to reading. Activities that emphasize anticipation and prediction enrich both the reading and the writing that students do.

Writing to Write

Writing is part of the preparation phase of the Instructional Framework when it prepares students to write. An important part of the writing process is stimulating the act of writing. This involves preliminary writing that is done before the substance and form of the final product is created. For example, we have demonstrated the value of brainstorming to help students discover what they already know about the organizing idea to be studied. This knowledge, when identified, becomes part of the substance of what is being studied. After students generate lists of facts and ideas about a topic, they work in groups to organize the information into logical categories. Then, in groups, they frame paragraphs from the information contained in combinations of these categories. They organize paragraphs into a logical order and draft introductions and conclusions. The products of their writing can be used as tentative contexts for analyzing the resources used to present information about the organizing idea. As resources are interpreted, this collaborative document can be revised, refined, and turned into a cohesive report of what has been learned. It all starts with preparation, having students discuss what they know about the topic and having them write out and organize what they discuss. It can be said, then, that *writing prepares students for writing*.

Journals contribute in an important way to students' writing. Kirby and Liner (1988) emphasize the flexibility and versatility of journals by identifying four types, each having a different purpose: writer's notebook, class journal, project journal, and diary.

Keeping a writer's notebook type of journal is a way that writing prepares students for writing.

> *The notebook becomes the writer's workbench. The writer returns to the notebook periodically, reviews what's there, selects a project or two, and then works and reworks it. The notebook is a place to save things: a word, a phrase, an unrefined thought, the title of a poem or song . . . The writer's notebook is a miniature greenhouse. If you keep planting seeds and nurturing the ideas stored there, good things happen and the results are sometimes surprising (Kirby and Liner 1983, 48).*

As a sourcebook of ideas, the writer's notebook has the added benefit of building students' confidence in their own thinking and respect for their own ideas. Seed thoughts not developed fully enough to share can be stored in the notebook for further reflection. As those thoughts are cultivated, they mature into ideas that can be shared. In that sharing, students perceive how the product of their thinking is valued. The receptivity to their work reinforces the confidence they have in their own thinking.

Keeping a writer's notebook increases the likelihood that students will become more immersed in the substance of your discipline. The notebook encourages reflection on what has been—or is being—studied. The content of the course is not kept at arm's length, as something to be memorized but not absorbed. Rather, the content is embraced, thought about, and reflected upon. In some respects, encouraging the use of the writer's notebook enlarges Schön's (1983) notion of "reflective practitioner" to include students as well as teachers.

Writing to Read

Writing is part of the preparation phase of the Instructional Framework when it prepares students to read. For example, during a unit of study on the Civil War, an eighth-grade history teacher showed his class a picture of carpetbaggers disembarking from a train. He was using the picture as the basis for reviewing some concepts already covered in the unit as well as for leading into new material on the Southern reconstruction period. The organizing idea for the lesson was

"A 'new South' evolved as Southern whites reacted to reconstruction."

The picture had no names or titles or other graphic identification. The teacher gave students five minutes to write about the picture in their journals. He asked them to speculate on the following information as they wrote: what the picture presented (people and location); who the people were; where the people came from; where the people men were going; (possibly) what the people were going to do when they got where they were going.

When students finished writing, the teacher asked some of them to share with the full class what they had entered in their journals. He asked students to comment on or raise questions about the journal entries that were read. He drew from their contributions to develop the organizing idea for the lesson and to establish the purpose for a reading assignment from the class text. In this manner the teacher used *writing to prepare students for reading*.

The history teacher was using the type of journal that Kirby and Liner (1983) call the class journal. They suggest that the class journal be used as a means for students to respond to classroom activities. They also suggest that the writing be done during the regular class period. The writing can be in response to something that has been studied or in anticipation of something about to be studied. Kirby and Liner observe that "the CJ (class journal) is particularly effective for getting students comfortable with writing as a way of responding. Students frequently like to share excerpts from their CJs, so writing facilitates talk and vice versa" (Kirby and Liner 1983).

As noted, writing also can facilitate reading which, in turn, can facilitate writing.

Reading to Write

Clearly, writing is an important part of the preparation for reading. It is also true that reading is an important part of the preparation for writing. For example, an English teacher had her students read the story *A Man of Peace*. She used this reading as preparation for two writing activities.

The first writing activity was for students to write about the ideas and feelings the story created in them. She asked them also to include how they felt toward the characters in the story. They shared their writing in small groups and, selectively, by groups to the whole class.

Following the sharing of their responses to the story, the teacher set the parameters for the second writing task (see Dialogue 9-1).

The students shared ideas for their prospectus; decided what focus to give it; and described the characters, contexts, and actions. In this manner they used *reading as preparation for writing* what, ultimately, was a group composition.

The group composition of a prospectus is a good example of how the composing process is shaped by two influences: by what is in the writer's mind and by the context in which that mind is working.

DIALOGUE 9-1

What I would like you to do is think about a new version of this story. I'm going to ask you, in groups, to create a new version of the story; in other words, to rewrite the story, in a sense.

Suppose that the story was taking place here in your own city on this very date. What do you think the story might be like? You don't have to answer this question now, but it's the question I want you to have in the back of your minds. So that's the first thing you should consider.

Now some of you wrote some things yesterday in class that indicated that you have some ideas about the story—because you identified with some of the characters in the story or you know people who might be like the characters. A couple of you mentioned incidents in tennis or wrestling . . . some things that have happened in your lives that sort of sounded like the situation that occurred in the story.

The second thing I want you to think about is this. You probably have seen some movies that were actually derived from novels. When you want to make a story into a movie, you have to go to someone and get some money to support the project. So you go to Steven Speilberg, or someone like that, who has lots of money and produces movies.

What would you have to tell Steven Speilberg in order to convince him that you had a movie worth making? I'm going to ask you to talk in your groups about your updated version of the story and to create a prospectus that you would present to a producer to convince him or her to produce your movie. You have different ideas, I'm sure, about what the story should be, but I want you to come to agreement in your groups and create one prospectus per group. When you finish, we'll come back together as a full class and share the work you have done.

The prospectus is not the story itself. Rather, it tells enough about the story so that the producer can make a decision as to whether he or she wants to support it. So, you are not writing the whole story, just a prospectus on the story.

Influence of Schemata

Students draw on their schemata to construct meaning as they read (Anderson 1985). They do the same thing to construct meaning as they write (Hennings 1984). Preparation that activates students' schemata has the potential for enriching what they eventually write. As was done in Dialogue 9–1, students can create descriptions of situations analogous to ones about which they have read. The substance of their analogies comes principally from their own knowledge and experience. Discussions among students in groups are mutually enlightening as they gain insights from one another. As they share their thoughts, they shape their analogies. As they shape their analogies, they modify their thoughts, and new memories of related experiences are prompted.

What students experience collectively can be experienced individually when students are given the time to let their schemata shape their writing and their writing shape their schemata. The reciprocal influence between schemata and written products is such that among experienced writers the composition seems to have a life of its own—to such an extent that sometimes writers are surprised and enlightened by what they finally produce. (We already have mentioned the colleague who deferred stating her position on one issue until she had an opportunity to write about the matter and discover what she thought about it.)

Given this reciprocal relationship between the writer's schemata (stimulated by reading and other activities) and the writer's product, writing is itself a preparation for writing in a variety of ways.

Guidance of Writing

The purpose of the guidance phase of the instructional framework is to show students how to move their thoughts from their minds to their papers. This is no easy task if you subscribe to the more traditional view of writing instruction with its focus on the written product. It is a less daunting task if you subscribe to the process approach to writing instruction.

Background

Applebee provides a sense of what the process approach involves.

> *Process approaches . . . are marked by instructional activities designed to help students think through and organize their ideas before writing and to rethink and revise their initial drafts. Instructional activities typically associated with process approaches include brainstorming, journal writing, focus on the students' ideas and experiences, small-group activities, teacher/student conferences, the provision of audiences other than the teacher, emphasis on multiple drafts, postponement of attention to editing skills until the final draft, and elimination or deferment of grading (Applebee 1986, 95–96).*

This approach to writing instruction treats writing as a whole rather than as a composite of language parts. In this respect, writing instruction parallels reading instruction. Neither is treated as a set of separable skills, though some instructional approaches to reading and writing do exactly that. Some approaches to writing instruction, principally those that focus on product rather than on process, move in their concentration from part to whole rather than from whole to part. That is, the instructional emphasis shifts from word to sentence to paragraph to multi-paragraph piece. Squire, among others, believes that while such order of emphasis "may seem right,

. . . it is psychologically wrong." Rather, ". . . in learning to write, young people must understand the whole in order to cope with the parts" (Squire 1984, 27).

In the process approach to writing, emphasis is given to writing as a means of communicating information and ideas.

> *Findings [from research on the process approach have] provided a new way to think about writing in terms of what the writer does (planning, revising, and the like) instead of in terms of what the final product looks like (patterns of organization, spelling, grammar) (Applebee 1986, 96).*

Although the writing process has identifiable activities that are interactive in nature, this is not the same as breaking writing down into words, sentences, paragraphs, and so forth. Rather, as Applebee suggests, "process activities are often partitioned into stages such as prewriting, drafting, revising, and editing, usually with the caveat that the processes are recursive rather than linear, complex rather than simple" (Applebee 1986, 96).

Being recursive, the stages appear and reappear as writing related to an organizing idea extends from the preparation to the guidance to the independence phase of the Instructional Framework. Prewriting, drafting, and revising activities may occur in the preparation phase. The guidance phase may require redrafting and additional revising. The independence phase may require editing, which may lead to redrafting, revising, and reediting. Such a recursive process supports the exploration and analysis of ideas in a content area. The focus is on acquisition, development, and refinement of ideas contained in the curriculum. These recursive stages of the writing process are consistent with a curriculum that is conceptually based. Application of the stages makes it possible for writing to support content learning.

Facilitating Factors

Students need support when they learn to write to learn. In Chapter 6 we discuss this need and how it can be served by the kind of instruction provided. The guidance phase of the Instructional Framework is particularly critical in providing this support. Several factors facilitate the essential guidance.

Supporting Structures

Guidance that shows students how to learn to write has two characteristics. First, it provides sufficient support to enable students to perform required tasks. Second, the tasks are pitched at levels of sophistication and abstraction that are higher than students could perform without the support that is provided. The support takes several forms: materials; organization; environment.

Supporting Materials You have experienced and studied how students' use of levels and patterns guides, as well as vocabulary-development materials, support their content learning (see Chapters 7 and 8). In the next chapter you will be introduced to materials called reasoning guides. All of these materials support students' acquisition and exploration of information and ideas. These materials invite students to use writing as a means of formulating, clarifying, and refining concepts as they study the organizing ideas of lessons and units. Writing that is done in the preparation phase of the lesson is carried over into the guidance phase. As students respond in writing to statements in the levels guides, their ideas begin to take shape. As they share their writing with their peers and with you, they refine their thinking and, consequently, their writing.

Supporting Organization You also have experienced and studied how students' participation in cooperative grouping supports their learning of course content (see Chapters 4, 6, 7 and 8). Documentation is ample to show how students' learning is enhanced when they have opportunity to interact with one another in small groups as they acquire information and develop, refine, and apply ideas (Johnson and Johnson 1987).

Guide materials provide the structure within which students' interactions occur. The content of resources being used provides the substance around which the interactions take place. Interactions among students occur in both oral and written form. As students speak and write, they give shape to their ideas. They refine their thinking as they receive oral and written feedback on ideas they have expressed in oral and written form. For example, directions for levels-of-comprehension materials ask students to cite evidence to support their decisions to accept or reject specific statements in the guide. Sometimes they present their evidence in oral form, sometimes in written form.

Supporting Environments When you use the guide materials and provide opportunity for students to work together in groups, you thereby create a classroom environment that is positive, supporting, and nurturing. It is an environment that supports both convergent and divergent thinking as it is reflected in students' written and oral communication. It is an environment that invites students to share their thinking in both oral and written form, an environment in which the sharing is positive and beneficial rather than negative and humiliating. Teachers' responses to oral and written communication should be for purposes of clarifying, refining, and confirming the thinking that has occurred. In particular, teachers' responses to oral and written communication encourage the continuation of shared thinking that is occurring among students in the classroom.

For example, the eighth-grade history teacher who had his students write about a picture in their journals, subsequently guided their reading of the text with a patterns guide. As he circulated among the groups and observed their work on part two of the guide, he had this to say to the class: "I've heard more good thinking on these three ideas than has come out of here in a long time." The teacher then called on groups to share with one another the results of this thinking as they explored the organizing idea of the lesson.

Consistent with the notion of scaffolding (Applebee 1986), support materials allow students to perform reading and writing tasks at higher levels of sophistication and abstraction than they would be able to without that support. As discussed in Chapter 6, this provision of scaffolding is one of the major benefits of using declarative statements to guide students' response to resources. When students have to originate ideas they write or talk about, the ideas can be no more sophisticated or abstract than the performance level the students already have attained. However, when more sophisticated and abstract ideas are presented to students for confirmation, rejection, and elaboration (always with reasons and evidence), they actually experience what it is like to create ideas at these more advanced levels. The experience builds their confidence and increases the likelihood that ultimately they will be able to function with some independence at these more advanced levels.

Audience

A major purpose for having students write in content areas is that the process of writing helps them to formulate and refine their understandings of ideas under consideration. Sometimes writers themselves are the only audience for their writing, and appropriately so. At some stages in the development of ideas, it seems too early to share what has been written because one's thoughts are still being formulated. Sometimes one does not wish to share because what has been written is too private for others to read. But there are times when the audience should be extended to include other people. In content-area classes, fellow students and teachers constitute logical audiences. Both are important; both have unique contributions to make.

When you have your students working together in groups, it is natural for them to serve as an audience for one another. You have already noted the value and importance of group compositions (see Dialogue 9–1) and how students can work together to formulate a plan and then produce a draft for sharing. During the collaborative process of creating a draft, students within a group serve as an audience to one another as they try out words or phrasings on one another. When drafts are ready for more public sharing, each group presents its work to the other groups. This can be done by reading drafts to the groups or by having groups read the drafts themselves. In either case, a group that is sharing will benefit from a response to its work in progress. How the responses can be both supportive and informative is discussed in the next section.

Having peers serve as audience is not limited to students working on a group composition. As students react individually in writing to statements presented in the guides and to ideas developed in resource materials, they can share drafts of their responses with other members of their group. This sharing also can be accomplished by having writers read their drafts to individuals or by having individuals read the drafts of other writers and then respond to the writers. In either case, writers that are sharing their drafts will benefit from responses to their work in progress.

Teachers usually are the assumed audience for students' writing, and the writing for which teachers serve as the audience is typically students' final product. Applebee (1986) found that this final product usually is also the students' first and only draft (frequently passed in without being read). When the teachers respond to the product by correcting and grading it, students rarely look at it again. Consequently, teachers often are the only ones who ever really read the papers! Students learn little of value from having written the paper or from having had their teacher as an audience. You can be most helpful as an audience for your students' writing by responding to drafts of their writing while it is in progress.

Responding to Writing in Progress

In a variety of ways, responding to students' writing in progress is different from correcting it. The main difference is that responding focuses on the writing *process* and correcting focuses on the writing *product*. Both the process and the product are important. However, if the process is emphasized, the product will develop. If the product is emphasized, the process may never be perceived.

For responses to writing in progress to be effective, the responding audience must be aware of the writer's purpose, the substantive focus of the writing, and the kind of feedback the writer needs. Maimon (1988) suggests that writers who desire a response to their writing provide their audience with answers to the following questions:

1. How close to being finished is this project?
2. What steps do you plan to take to complete the project?
3. What is the major idea that you are working to express? (What are you driving at?)
4. How can readers most effectively help you at this stage?

Maimon explains.

When writers answer those questions in advance, the conference with the instructor, the instructor's written comments, and conversations with peers are placed in a more constructive context. The writer is asking for help rather than waiting for the instructor and classmates to find problems that the writer missed (Maimon 1988, 736).

This procedure assures an informed audience and a response that is useful to the writer. With feedback from their audience, writers can proceed with redrafting, revising, or editing until they feel the need for another response. How many responses are necessary or useful depends on the writer as well as on the complexity and substantive focus of the writing. Writers should be encouraged to revise and refine if the writing is unclear to the audience. Responding with an understanding of the writers' intentions enables you to be positive and informative in your feedback. Your responses can be framed as *invitations* to revise and refine what has been written.

When criteria have been established to guide the responses to the writing, serving as a supportive and responsive audience to work in progress need not be prohibitively time-consuming. Having clear purposes to guide your responses increases the efficiency of your work. Your response is clearly focused. Students accept your response and incorporate your suggestions more when they have helped set the criteria used in the response to their work.

Efficiency in response to writing in progress increases as students learn to respond to one another's drafts and, thus, share the load. By your own responses you model appropriate and helpful ways to respond to drafts in progress. When students themselves serve as an audience to their peers' writing in progress, their responses reflect what you have modeled in your responses. As a consequence, their responses also are appropriate and helpful.

Having students serve as an audience for their writing is good for them and also good for you. It is a wonderful time-saver in that you do not have to respond to all of the writing that you are stimulating in your classes. Your students can help. By monitoring their responses while they serve as an audience, you can be assured that appropriate and constructive feedback is occurring even though you are not providing it directly yourself (Maimon 1988).

Another side benefit is derived from having students serve as an audience. As they respond to their peers' writing, they learn to read like a writer (Smith 1984)—attending to the ideas being presented as well as to the manner of presentation. Reading like a writer gives students new insights into the writing process that carry over into their own writing.

Structuring the Writing

General Structure

The principle *content determines process* (Parker and Rubin 1966) is applicable when considering how to structure students' writing. Writing reflects tasks to be performed, messages to be delivered, requirements to be completed, and the like. Some writing is formal; some, informal. Some writing is cognitively oriented; some, affectively. When integrated with the study of course content, writing is taught functionally. The form and content of the writing is dictated by the conceptual focus of the lesson and by the relevant tasks that require written responses. Because content areas differ in their concepts and objectives, writing tasks and writing products vary across content areas.

In terms of the writing process, however, commonalities do occur across content areas. Applebee, for example, speaks of "planning, monitoring, drafting, revising, and editing" (Applebee 1986) as generally applicable subprocesses in writing. Maimon (1988) identifies six stages of the writing process: prewriting, drafting, sharing, revising, editing, and publishing.

Applebee (1986) underscores the recursive nature of the subprocesses, noting that they are usually applied in a cyclical rather than in a linear fashion as writers move toward a final product. Similarly, one can see the recursive nature of Maimon's six stages. For example, in drafting a piece, writers may perceive the need for additional information and cycle back to the prewriting stage to collect what is needed for inclusion in a new draft. Writers may gain insights through sharing drafts of their work, and the sharing may lead to revising; however, the writers may cycle back to sharing again before moving on to editing their drafts.

Given the nature of these subprocesses, or stages, it is reasonable to think of them as applicable in any content area in which emphasis on the writing process is part of the curriculum.

1. Regardless of the subject area, effective writers engage in some planning and prewriting activities.
2. Regardless of subject area, effective writers construct drafts of their work and obtain some form of response to the ideas they contain and feedback on the extent to which the intended message is communicated.
3. Regardless of subject area, effective writers revise their work when warranted by responses they receive from sharing it, and they often share additional drafts after revisions have been made.
4. Regardless of subject area, effective writers eventually edit their work so they can "go public" with it when they are certain that it is consistent with the accepted conventions of written communication.

Specific Structures

When you guide students' writing, you need to provide a structure that supports their work but does not stifle their thinking. The structure should support their applications of the writing subprocesses described earlier. The structure should simultaneously encourage students to communicate how *they* have come to understand information and ideas they are studying in your class.

Use of Guides   Specific structures can be provided in a variety of ways. For example, materials you design to guide students' vocabulary acquisition (see Chapter 7), reading comprehension (see Chapter 8), and reasoning (see Chapter 10) can be used to stimulate and to guide their writing as well. Students' written responses to vocabulary-acquisition materials can range in complexity from the creation of labels for categories of words that have been grouped together, to the formulation of single sentences to present ideas prompted by collections and arrangements of interrelated words.

Students' written responses to literal or interpretive statements in levels-of-comprehension guides can range from single sentences to full paragraphs. In their writing they identify evidence from the text that they used to support or reject the statements. Similarly, they develop paragraphs to explain how they have synthesized ideas across information sources to support or reject applied-level statements. Reasoning guides and part two of patterns guides can be used to stimulate the writing of similar explanatory paragraphs. The reciprocity between sharing writing and responding to writing is accomplished through small-group discussions of what students have written for these guide materials.

Another way to use reading guides to structure students' writing was developed by Don Miceli (1980), a social studies teacher in District 11 in the Bronx in New York City. After students finished reading the text and completed their discussion of the related three-level guide, Miceli showed them how use the guide to construct an outline for writing a report on what they had been studying. They selected a statement from the applied-level guide to serve as the theme, or topic, for the report. They selected statements from the interpretive-level guide to serve as main headings in the outline and topic sentences in the report. They selected statements from the literal-level guide to serve as subheadings in the outline and details in the report. Early on the students worked in groups to construct the outline and write the report. Later, students developed their own outlines from the guides and wrote their own reports. Thus, the levels guide provided a means for creating a structure to stimulate and support students' writing. Miceli said his junior high students produced more and better writing than they had previously and that this outcome was true for his low-achieving students as well as for his more able students.

Use of Think Sheets   Raphael, Kirschner, and Englert (1988) suggest the use of "think sheets" as a way to structure students' expository writing. They developed these materials as part of their expository writing program (EWP). These think sheets are separate pieces of paper, each with a set of questions at the top appropriate to the focus and purpose of the particular think sheet. Think sheets are

> *designed to stimulate strategy use for planning and gathering of information as well as drafting, editing, and revising. Each think sheet helps address specific problems that both normally achieving and disabled learners display (Raphael, Kirschner, and Englert 1988, 791).*

The authors designed six kinds of think sheets:

1. Prewriting think sheet
2. Organizing think sheet
3. First-draft think sheet
4. Edit think sheet
5. Peer-Editor think sheet
6. Revision think sheet

1. The prewriting think sheet is designed to structure prewriting activities. The authors point out that good writers gather information and ideas before they write. Good writers consider what the conceptual focus of the writing will be, how the writing will be organized and who will read it. This constitutes prewriting planning. The prewriting think sheet

> *focuses students' attention on questions relevant to planning, including: My topic is. . . . Some things I already know that I can include in my paper are . . . Some ideas that I would like to put into my paper to make it interesting to my reader are . . . Who will read my paper? My audience will be interested in reading about this topic because. . . . I will put my ideas into this order. . . . (Raphael, Kirschner, and Englert 1988, 791)*

2. The organizing think sheet is designed to help students organize their ideas. This sheet

> *prompts students to think about information to include in their papers by focusing their attention on the different types of writing that answer different sets of questions. It also serves a monitoring function, reminding students to self check to ensure that all relevant information has been included (Raphael, Kirschner, and Englert 1988, 791).*

The organizing think sheet has different sets of questions according to the kind of expository writing that each is supporting. In Chapter 4 we discuss cause/effect, comparison/contrast, time order, and simple listing (or enumerative order) as four patterns of organization used in expository writing. An organizing think sheet can be designed for each pattern, with questions appropriate to the pattern listed on each sheet. For example,

> *The Comparison/Contrast Organizing think sheet includes: What are two things that I am going to compare and contrast? On what will I compare and contrast these ideas? What ways are my two people, places, or things alike? Different? What key words would be helpful for signaling my reader about the kind of paper I am writing? Where can I use these words (Raphael, Kirschner, and Englert 1988, 791–792)?*

A similar set of questions can be constructed for the organizing think sheet for each of the other patterns. Students use the questions as prompts as they think about what they are going to write. Subsequently, they use the questions as reminders as they write.

3. The first-draft think sheet is merely colored lined paper on which students write their first draft. The authors suggest colored paper because "white paper seems to invite the author to believe that a single draft may be sufficient" (Raphael, Kirschner, and Englert 1988, 792). Students are encouraged to refer to their prewriting and organizing think sheets as they develop their first drafts.

4. The purpose of the edit think sheet is to structure the writer's self-editing. Its purpose is to encourage students to move beyond a concern for grammar and mechanics of writing to a focus on ways to make ideas developed in the paper more easily understood as well as more interesting. The edit think sheet has three sections:

> *First, the author . . . focuses on the content of the paper, considering parts that are especially interesting and clear, and parts that may need changing . . .*
>
> *The second section focuses students' attention on the paper's organization, asking students to check to see that they have included relevant information to answer the text structure questions . . . and whether key words and phrases are strategically used . . .*
>
> *The third section focuses on planning for the next step in writing, either for a peer editing session (help I would like from my editor . . .) or for revisions (parts I plan to change are . . .) (Raphael, Kirschner, and Englert 1988, 792).*

5. The peer-editor think sheet is similar to the edit think sheet, with changes in wording to reflect the peer-editing functions rather than the self-editing ones.

6. The revision think sheet structures writers' utilization of suggestions made by those who have responded to the writing as well as by the self-editing process.

> *The revision think sheet . . . encourages students to not only acknowledge the feedback they have received but to take ownership of the revision plan by considering such questions as: What are the specific suggestions my editor and others have given me to improve my paper? What do I plan to do to make my paper more interesting? Easier to follow? What information will I add? What information will I take out (Raphael, Kirschner, and Englert 1988, 792)?*

It is important that students make appropriate changes on their first draft before they complete their final draft. This reinforces the importance of refining written products to make them as clear as possible.

The use of these think sheets is beneficial to students' reading as well as to their writing. Where students perceive related purposes among the six think sheets, their writing and reading improved.

> *EWP is effective because students learn the strategies used by authors of informational text, apply the strategies in their own writing, and through participation in the writing process learn to read critically and monitor the clarity of the text they are reading whether or not they themselves are the authors (Raphael, Kirschner, and Englert 1988, 795).*

Tried and True   You undoubtedly have writing tasks that have been instrumental in improving your students' writing abilities and have provided the means for them to reflect what they have learned. Obviously, you should continue using these tasks. You may want to review these tasks to determine the extent to which you include opportunity for students to receive responses to their writing while it is in progress. Both your responses and students' peer responses contribute to the improvement of students' writing in important ways. Cooperative grouping facilitates peer editing, supporting the openness and spirit of acceptance that is essential in providing responses to writing in progress.

Evaluating the Writing

When the written product eventually is to "go public," it is important for writers to do the final edit. In most classes, "going public" is submitting the paper to the teacher for final evaluation and grading. When students receive responses to their work while it is in progress, they become interested in and attuned to suggestions for editing that will improve their final product. If you have them use the revision think sheet, they will be reminded to attend to the issues of syntax, grammatical consistency, paragraph construction, parallel structure, logical progression, and the like, that were identified in the self-editing and peer-editing processes. In the context of the supportive classroom environment you create, including multiple audiences for obtaining responses to work in progress, students develop an interest in refining their products into (for them) the best possible form.

Maimon provides some helpful suggestions to consider with respect to evaluating students' writing.

> *Errors stem from different causes and require different remedies for different students. We must train ourselves to search for patterns. Sentence fragments and run-on sentences in a paper that also contains several instances of more conventional syntax may indicate fragmentary or associational thinking rather than the need for a grammar lesson.*
>
> *... the order of a well-crafted finished product rarely reflects the writer's schedule of composing the piece. Writers often need to write for themselves and to themselves—in effect, recording their own discoveries—before they can craft a text for an audience.*
>
> *... when teachers do not intervene in a student's work-in-progress, the paper ultimately submitted is usually a poor indication of the student*

writer's potential . . . I am suggesting that we design classroom practices so that we teach the concept of work-in-progress—and that we then read early drafts with an eye to responding to the seeds of thought that might be ready for cultivation.

> *Liberated from the demand for linguistic analysis, instructors of history, biology, mathematics, and art can intervene productively in their students' work-in-progress. If instructors across the curriculum would reallocate time from writing extensive comments on graded papers to writing brief comments and questions on work-in-progress, they might then channel much of the energy and concentration that students devote to writing into learning the subject matter of the course.*
>
> *Responding to student work-in-progress most effectively may require a redesign of classroom practices across the curriculum to allow for the integration of writing with learning. Students should be writing more, and teacher should be grading less (Maimon 1988, 734–745).*

Gray speaks to the importance of consistency between teachers' objectives and evaluation of learning outcomes, with particular emphasis on writing.

> *Let . . . teachers sort out the purposes of their teaching and connect writing to each of them. Then they will know what they want students to learn when they ask them to write. They will also know how to judge whether students have learned it (Gray 1988, 733).*

Focus on Content

While the orientation of this chapter is on the process approach to writing instruction, you should not infer a lack of value for the product. Without concern for the product of writing, the procedures that emphasize the writing process can become trivial and meaningless (Applebee 1986). The point is made repeatedly throughout this book that reading, writing, and reasoning support content learning and that instruction in these processes should be integrated with instruction in course content. Thus, the focus for most of the students' writing in content-area courses is on the concepts which comprise the curriculum. This focus not only provides substance for your students' writing, it also allows you to develop students' writing proficiency and still meet the content obligations of your curriculum.

Independence in Writing

A principal objective in guiding students' writing is for students to develop independence in their application of the writing process. As we point out in Chapters 5 and 12, independence is a relative state, conditioned by many variables. In instructional contexts, independence is conditioned by levels of sophistication of the curriculum, levels of abstraction at which learning processes are operationalized, and types of ability that students bring to the tasks. It is important to understand that students do not suddenly become independent in their acquisition and application of content and process. Guidance extends into the development of independence as well. However, this kind of guidance can require more independence from students in their application of the learning processes even while providing some structure to support the more independent functioning.

For example, during the guidance phase of the lesson, students can respond in writing to level-three statements related to one printed resource (a poem, a story, a chapter, a problem, a laboratory report, and so forth). During the independence phase of the lesson, students can apply these same level-three statements to supplementary and enrichment resources that deal with the same organizing idea. Use of the same set of statements from the guide provides a familiar structure for guiding students' response to the supplementary resources. The previous writing is expanded and refined to take into account variations in the structure and content of the supplementary resources. This constitutes a modest level of independence in the application of the writing process.

Independence in learning is not attained in a single step, as you well know. However, relative independence can be attained over time when instruction is designed to develop that independence in small increments (Bruner 1960). Chapter 12 presents a variety of suggestions for ways to develop students' independence in vocabulary acquisition, reading, writing, and reasoning.

Consequences of Emphasis on Writing

What are some changes that could be anticipated if content-area teachers were to give emphasis to a process approach to writing instruction? Applebee identifies several possibilities:

1. *Writing assignments would themselves be broadened to give scope for students' opinions and solutions rather than stressing material that has been presented and problems that have been solved in previous lessons.*
2. *Teachers' first and primary response to student writing would shift from evaluator of its quality or success to that of interested reader (and skillful editor), seeking to understand and clarify what the writer has to say.*
3. *. . . teachers' attention would shift from what students know about writing toward the strategies and procedures students need to learn in order to carry out more sophisticated writing tasks.*
4. *. . . the writing classroom would take on a shape and structure—a sense of purpose and direction—that process-oriented approaches have too often lacked.*

Taken together, . . . these changes require a fundamental shift in what counts as learning in American schools. It would no longer be sufficient, or even particularly necessary, for students to be adept at reciting of their teachers' points of view. Instead, what would count as important would be their ability to solve new problems, to make sense on their own terms of what they have learned, and to defend and elaborate upon their own ideas (Applebee 1986, 111).

Summary

Writing and reading are inextricably linked in their facilitation of content learning. Writing can be used to establish conceptual and experiential contexts for reading to be done. In this manner, writing can inform one's reading. Writing can be used to respond to and report on reading that has been done. In this manner, reading can inform one's writing.

Writing, of course, can be used apart from reading to support content learning—to explore ideas, to communicate ideas, and to record ideas. Content teachers need not be apprehensive about time requirements for including an emphasis on writing in their curricula. If teachers focus on developing students' understanding of the writing process rather than on their creating a written product, students can serve as audience to provide response and feedback for writing in progress. The amount of teachers' time dedicated to responding to students' writing, then, becomes manageable and reasonable.

Writing is a natural form of response to ideas. Writing is a natural means of exploring ideas. Thus, writing has a natural place in conceptually based curricula that are organized around the study of ideas.

REACTIONS

Journal Entries and Discussion

Write an analysis of the similarities between the functional approach to reading instruction and the process approach to writing instruction. What attributes of each approach contribute to the similarities?

Consider the procedures recommended for responding to students' writing in progress. What are the advantages you perceive? What are the disadvantages? Which of each are for teachers; which are for students?

Analysis and Discussion

Now that you have completed this chapter, consider the statements shown below. Check the numbered lines for statements with which you agree. Circle the numbers of statements you believe reflect the point of view of the authors. In writing, explore reasons for differences on any statements between your point of view and what you perceive to be the point of view of the authors. Please share and discuss your writing with colleagues who also are reading this book.

_____ 1. Similes and metaphors can be used to stimulate students' writing about what it is they will be reading or what they already have read.

_____ 2. Group interaction stimulates students' thinking about what ideas should go into their writing, and it gives shape to the final writing product itself.

_____ 3. Organizing ideas drive writing instruction as much as they do reading instruction.

_____ 4. Raising students' consciousness about the act of writing has an impact on their composing.

_____ 5. Even as one's experience can inform one's writing, one's writing can inform one's experience.

_____ 6. The clarifying effect of talking out an idea during small-group discussions has an interesting parallel with the clarifying effect of writing out an idea in a journal.

_____ 7. Thoughtful revision enhances the quality of a composition; thus, by encouraging self-initiated revision, word processing leads to a self-directed improvement of written products.

_____ 8. All writing has an audience, either private or public.

10

Using Reasoning To Support Content Learning

Organizing idea: Reasoning empowers learners and enables learning.

Reflections

Before reading this chapter, please record in your journal your responses to the following questions. If possible, share your writing with other individuals who are also reading this book.

1. Is reading, writing, or reasoning the most utilitarian in supporting students' learning in content areas? Given your answer, how can teachers assure that all students' derive value from this utility?

2. Will students be encouraged to reason if there is little or no acceptance of the product of their reasoning? What do teachers open themselves up to when they encourage students to develop their reasoning powers.

3. How much of the study of your subject involves the application of some form of expectation: hypothesizing, anticipating, predicting? In what ways do you apply these forms of expectation in your instruction?

THE TITLE OF this book is *Teaching in Content Areas with Reading, Writing, and Reasoning*. After having read the chapters on reading and writing, you may be wondering why it is necessary to have a separate chapter on reasoning. Certainly a lot of reasoning is involved in the processes of reading and writing. However, it is important to note that while reading and writing do require reasoning, reasoning does not require reading and writing. This is an important distinction for two reasons:

1. There are those who believe that students who have difficulty reading or writing are not able to benefit from instruction in reasoning.
2. There are those who believe that students who read and write well also reason well and do not need instruction in reasoning.

When these two beliefs are applied in classrooms, two significant groups of students are excluded from instruction in reasoning. The rationale for excluding the first group is found in the question: "Why try to teach these kids something they can't do?" The rationale for excluding the second group is found in the opposite question: "Why teach these kids something they already do well?"

This chapter is predicated on two opposite beliefs.

1. Students with deficiencies in reading and writing can benefit from instruction that focuses on reasoning about matters of substance, instruction that involves them in discussions about important concepts related to their course of study.
2. Students with proficiencies in reading and writing can benefit from instruction that focuses on reasoning about matters of substance, instruction that refines and extends their understanding about concepts they are studying.

When these two beliefs are applied in classrooms, both groups of students are included in reasoning instruction. In the first instance, students are included because participation in discussions about important concepts is not dependent upon an ability to read and write. Certainly, were they able to read and write well it would increase the likelihood that they would have something of substance to contribute to the discussions. Nevertheless, students can acquire information and ideas in ways other than reading and writing, making it is possible for them to contribute substantively to discussions from that acquired store of knowledge and experience.

In the second instance, students are included because instruction that refines and extends their understanding of concepts goes beyond the reasoning that is involved in reading and writing. Through application of their reading and writing abilities, these students acquire an deeper understanding of concepts under consideration. We know that their reasoning powers can be expanded as they refine and extend their understanding of the concepts they have acquired.

There is one further point to add to the rationale for this chapter: Successful experiences in reasoning seem to have a beneficial effect on students' reading and writing. Successful reasoning builds confidence among students whose reading and writing skills are limited, encouraging them to make better use of the skills they do have. Successful experiences in reasoning seem also to enrich the learning of students who already read and write well, encouraging them to read and write more critically and creatively. Thus, it is important to develop reasoning in, around, and beyond reading and writing.

Reasoning and the Instructional Framework

You'll recall that the Instructional Framework is a structure for teaching and that through this lesson structure you can emphasize both the content (the substance of what is being studied) and the process (the means by which that substance is acquired) of your curriculum. The lesson structure is a vehicle for preparing students to study the organizing idea of a lesson, for guiding students in their study of that organizing idea, and for developing students' independence as they apply what they have learned about that organizing idea. Simultaneously, the lesson structure is a vehicle for supporting students' appropriate use of reading, writing, and reasoning as they are prepared to study the organizing idea, as they are guided in that study, and as they apply what they have learned through that study. These three learning processes are applied interactively as students study the content of a lesson. As the lesson structure creates an interface between these learning processes and the content of the lesson, students simultaneously learn both content and process.

You have already studied ways that reading and writing support content learning. Reasoning is another of the learning processes that instructionally interfaces with the content of your course. Because of the interactive relationships among reading, writing and reasoning, many of the activities that prepare and guide students' reading and writing also prepare and guide their reasoning. Thus, while preparing students to study an assigned topic, while guiding them as they study, and while developing their independence in the application of what they have learned from their study, you are also developing their proficiency in reading, writing *and* reasoning.

Preparation by Reasoning

Chapters 7, 8, and 9 discuss how vocabulary, reading, and writing support content learning. Each chapter presents a variety of instructional procedures that fit into the preparation part of the Instructional Framework. Looking through the chapters at these suggestions for preparing students to study particular concepts, one can see the interactive nature among processes of vocabulary development, reading, and writing. Generally speaking, we have seen how reading prepares students for writing and how writing prepares them for reading. We have seen how vocabulary development prepares students for both writing and reading and how both reading and writing refine and expand vocabulary. We have seen how these combinations prepare students for the study of the organizing ideas of lessons.

As we have noted already, the process of reasoning interacts with the processes of vocabulary development, reading, and writing. Consequently, reasoning is embedded in all of the preparation activities related to vocabulary development, reading, and writing. Reasoning also stands by itself, functioning apart from vocabulary development, reading, and writing.

The process of reasoning is particularly important to the preparation part of the Instructional Framework. Much of what is done to prepare students for the study of a topic does not involve the formal teaching of vocabulary, even though words are being manipulated. Similarly, aspects of preparation involve neither the formal reading of resources nor the formal writing of analyses or impressions. However, any preparation activity that requires more than just a rote response involves reasoning. This is why we label this section "Preparation *by* Reasoning." Reasoning permeates the preparation part of the Instructional Framework.

Making Connections

The principal purpose for the preparation part of the Instructional Framework is to help students make connections. Comprehension (or understanding) is making connections between what you already know about an idea and the new information you are acquiring about that idea. The purpose of preparation is to set up pathways over which these connections can be made. If you have used a computer, you know that you can open files only when you have fully specified the paths by which the files can be accessed. Connections are not possible unless the paths are clear. While the analogy has limitations, you can help students define, develop, and/or discover paths that enable them to connect known information with new information as they study the organizing idea for a lesson.

The power to reason carries with it the potential for establishing the paths and for making the connections between known information and new information. Showing students how to use their reasoning powers facilitates their making connections. Thus, raising students' consciousness about how to maximize their reasoning powers is an important aspect of the preparation part of the Instructional Framework.

A variety of activities to promote students' reasoning can be incorporated into the preparation phase of the Instructional Framework. You have already considered such activities in the chapters on vocabulary development, reading, and writing. The purpose in presenting some of them again is to emphasize how they also can be used to show students how to reason and to increase their reasoning powers.

While considering the following activities, it is important to remember that their related purpose is to prepare students to study the organizing idea of the lesson. The purpose is not to teach reasoning for its own sake but, rather, to show students how their reasoning power can be used to develop and enhance their understandings of what it is they are studying.

Classification

The ability to classify and categorize is one that sets human beings apart from lower forms of life (Stauffer 1969a). Classification is the systematic arrangement in groups or categories according to specific criteria. Classifying involves the arrangement of entities into classes or the assignment of entities to categories. A category is a division within a system of classification. Categorizing involves the placement of entities into categories. Classifying and categorizing utilize the ability to draw inferences, to deduce, and to interpret. Classification can be applied in a variety of ways.

List, Group, Label Taba (1967) suggests utilizing categorizing in an activity she calls "list, group, and label." Students work together to create a list of words associated with an idea that is the subject of study. The list is then examined for the presence of sets of words that fit together in some way. Each set of related words is then examined to determine the nature of the relationship among the words and to conceptualize a label that describes that relationship. The label, then, becomes the name of the category with which the words in the set are associated. The labels can refer to actions, conditions, ideas, events, or individuals. Students' own experiences as well as the academic context dictated by the subject matter being studied helps to shape the kind of labels that students conceptualize.

Here is an example of a seventh-grade social studies class applying the list-group-label activity. The organizing idea for the lesson was "Independent nations are interdependent." With students placed in cooperative-learning groups, the teacher had them create lists of words associated with the key word *interdependence*. When students completed their group lists, she had them compare lists and create the composite shown in Example 10–1.

Next the teacher had students examine the composite list to identify sets of related words. She helped them establish criteria for their groupings ("What do these words have in common?" "What sets these words apart from others in the list?" "What objects, actions, or conditions do these words imply?") In this manner she helped identify and reinforce different kinds of

---

EXAMPLE 10-1 ────────────────────────────────

tariff, nuclear, organization, coffee, proportion, import, alliances, hunger, surplus, quota, bananas, fraternities, population, export, product, percentage, share, tea, cocoa, agencies, resources, unions, pollution, allotment, oil

EXAMPLE 10-2 _____

tariff	allotment	oil	organization	hunger
surplus	proportion	coffee	alliances	population
export	quota	bananas	unions	pollution
import	percentage	tea	agencies	resources
product	share	cocoa	fraternities	nuclear

reasoning that are part of this categorizing process. Example 10–2 shows the sets of words grouped together from the composite list.

When students placed words into groups, they did so in reference to some element the words had in common. In so doing, students anticipated what the descriptive labels for the groupings should be. This meant that part of the conceptualizing of labels for the categories was already done when the groups of words were formed. Nonetheless, the teacher worked with the students to confirm what they had anticipated and helped them to apply the labels formally. Example 10–3 shows the labels given to the sets of words.

One purpose served by the list-group-label activity is to help students discover what they already know about the organizing idea of the lesson. Being able to group and label the product of their word association helps them refine what they already know. Also, the activity helps them set the stage for connecting this knowledge with new information they are about to acquire.

A second purpose for the list-group-label activity is to help students develop their reasoning power. Students apply reasoning when they classify and categorize the words they have listed. Through the discussions of how they derived the labels for the groupings, they become more conscious of the kind of reasoning that is required in order to perform such tasks.

Developing students' awareness of how they are performing tasks increases the likelihood that they will be able to perform the tasks with greater understanding and independence. Probing students' responses helps them think through the reasoning processes they have applied to the list.

EXAMPLE 10-3 _____

Trade	_Distribution_	_Products_	_Interdependence_	_Danger_
tariff	allotment	oil	organization	hunger
surplus	proportion	coffee	alliances	population
export	quota	bananas	unions	pollution
import	percentage	tea	agencies	resources
product	share	cocoa	fraternities	nuclear

EXAMPLE 10-4 ━━━━━━━━━━━━━━━━━━━━━━━━━━━━━━━━━━━

nature, free, hiking, outdoors, camping, poems, boyfriend, bird, animals, happy, loose, carefree, exciting, anything, boring, a lot, no homework, living, solitude, teachers, family, no one, sky, airplane, smoking, sex, girlfriend, relationships, life, babies, waterfall, fish

---

Maintaining connections with the conceptual focus of the lesson sometimes can be difficult during this activity. It is important to be accepting of diversity if you want students to apply their reasoning power to the task at hand. Even so, students' responses sometimes can be surprising.

Example 10–4 shows a list of words created by one group of students in an American history course in response to a word-association task. The students were studying the Declaration of Independence. The key word for the word-association task was *freedom.* When you read the list, you will understand why the teacher was surprised.

Categorize   A variation on the list- group- label procedure is for you to give students a list of words and an accompanying set of labels (categories). You ask students to place each word on the list under the label or labels to which it belongs. Students do this work in groups, comparing their responses and reconciling or (retaining) their differences. Example 10-5 presents this kind of categorizing activity.

EXAMPLE 10-5 ━━━━━━━━━━━━━━━━━━━━━━━━━━━━━━━━━━━

(From eleventh- and twelfth-grade computer science elective. The organizing idea is "The whole is greater than the sum of its parts.")

Directions: Listed below are some of the words that have been covered in the introduction to the lesson on how a computer works. Following the word list are the names of four categories. Under each category, write the words from the list that can be associated with that category. Words may be placed in more than one category. Be ready to share your reasons for the placement of the words.

data	arithmetic operations	program	hard disk
CRT	input/output	printer	control unit
joystick	arithmetic/logic unit	files	diskette
tape	impact printer	keyboard	

| *Input Devices* | *Output Devices* | *CPU* | *Capabilities* |

Categorizing is useful for review as you prepare students for the study of a new concept. Relevant words from previous lessons can be included on the list. Concepts that bridge across lessons, including the upcoming lesson, can be used as labels for the categories. Each word on the list has to be interpreted in light of students' understanding of the categories. This process refines their understandings of both the words and the categories. The process establishes a strong context for the study of the new material.

As you can see, categorizing activities support content learning. You include words and labels according to the concepts you want to have your students review for the upcoming lesson. Students work out the categorization in groups, taking advantage of the value derived from giving reasons for one's intellectual decisions. You encourage students, during their discussions, to trace the reasoning that led them to the decisions they made. Raising their consciousness about the reasoning process also raises their consciousness about the information and ideas to which they were applying their reasoning. Thus, you are able to develop your students' reasoning simultaneously with their understanding of course content.

To give you a feel for how this categorizing activity works, we have included the words and categories in Practice 10–1. Read and follow the directions. If possible, do the work with someone else who is studying this book. You will notice that the words are drawn from previous chapters and the categories bridge from those chapters to this one. As you do the work, give some attention to how your mind is working. This is the kind of reasoning you can help your students develop.

Consider the kind of reasoning that you put into this categorizing activity. Explicit relationships between the words and the categories are minimal, if they exist at all. Most of the relationships are implicit. Thus, you have to give meaning to the labels and infer possible relationships that exist between the labels and the words. Because a given word might possibly fit with more than one label, you have to refine your inferencing by interpreting how the word could be connected with each of the categories. You are involved in both analytical and elaborative reasoning: analytical as you determine possible relationships and elaborative as you speculate on applications of words to multiple categories.

PRACTICE 10-1 ━━━━━━━━━━━━━━━━━━━━━━━━━━━━━━━━━━━━━━

rationale, showing how, support, comprehension, composition, acquisition, interaction, understanding, structure, contexts, resources, people, inform, refine, literal, creative, analytical, colleague, teach, learn, questions, answers, statements, ideas, information, thinking, cooperation, content, process

Connections   _Communication_   _Consequence_   _Consideration_

Analogies

Analogies facilitate students' understandings of conceptual connections. We discussed their purposes and forms in Chapter 7 where refining word meanings is discussed. A familiar form of analogy uses word pairs, with a complete relationship given in the first pair, an incomplete relationship given in the companion pair, and choices of words with which to complete the companion pair. A brief reminder of this type appears in Example 10–6.

Having completed the example, think about how you do analogies. The task is to supply the missing word so the relationship in the second pair parallels the relationship in the first. To begin, you have to identify the kind of relationship that is portrayed in the first pair. Is it quantitative or qualitative? Does it deal with individuals, objects, events, actions, or conditions? Given the first word of the second pair, you then have to add a second word so the pair will form a relationship that is the same or similar to the first pair.

The level of independence required in an analogy is controlled by whether you complete the analogy by producing the word independently or by selecting a word from a list of choices. The level of conceptual difficulty of an analogy is controlled by how technically specific or generally abstract the ideas are that the pairs represent. Example 10–6 is conceptually difficult for the uninitiated in science but does not require as high a level of independence in completing analogies as does Example 10–7. As you can see, Example 10–6 provides alternatives from which students can select their choices. The level of sophistication is controlled by how concrete or abstract the paired relationships are. Example 10–7, for example, is modestly abstract but requires a higher level of independence than Example 10–6 because Example 10–7 does *not* provide alternatives from which the answers can be selected.

Analogies fit well in the preparation part of the Instructional Framework, giving strong support to content learning. You can set up concrete pairs of words to review specific relationships that are critical to an under-

EXAMPLE 10-6 ───────────────────────────

Directions: Work with your group to choose the word that best completes each analogy.

1. green : chlorophyllous :: nongreen :

   a. phyla   b. achlorophyllous   c. mycology
2. green : nongreen :: algae :

   a. protist   b. mycologist   c. fungi
3. slime mold : mysomycophyta :: phycomycete :

   a. eumycophyta   b. vascular   c. fungi

EXAMPLE 10-7 ━━━━━━━━━━━━━━━━━━━━━━━━━━━━━━━━━━━

(From an ESL class at the university level. The organizing idea is "Writing reflects who you are and where you came from.")

Directions: This exercise is challenging. See if you can think of the words from your readings that can complete the following analogies:

1. God is to the white man as the _____ _____ is to the red man.
2. Talk is to speak as _____ is to think deeply or consider carefully.
3. As expressed by native Americans, mon is to day as winter is to _____ .
4. Circular is to round as _____ is to straight.
5. Accurate representation is to truth as _____ is to falsehood.

━━━

standing of the new concepts to be studied. You can set up more abstract or global relationships that represent the kind of connections to be studied in the upcoming lessons. Thus, you can facilitate students review of particular content that will contribute to their understanding of the new material. You can also make them aware of the kind of informational and conceptual relationships that they should be looking for in the upcoming lessons.

Simile and Metaphor

Simile and metaphor constitute another form of analogy. Each is a figure of speech used as a means of explaining. Each uses one factor or entity to explain another or to give meaning to another. Similes explain explicitly. They use the words *as* or *like* to make explicit connections between factors or entities. The assumption in a simile is that you will understand the unknown entity or factor because you understand the entity or factor to which it is being compared. Let's consider the simile

He is mad as a hatter.

This simile assumes you know that a century or more ago people involved in making hats frequently went insane. Eventually it was determined that the mercury used in the manufacture of hats was the cause of the problem. So, to be mad as a hatter is not to be angry but to be insane.

Metaphors are more subtle than similes. They explain implicitly rather than explicitly. Often they use some form of the verb *to be*. The assumption in this version of a metaphor is that your understanding of a target factor will expand as you attribute to it the qualities of the factor to which it is being connected. Let's consider the metaphor

He is truth personified.

This metaphor suggest the veracity of this person is such that he is the very embodiment of the ethical (perhaps religious) attribute called truth.

A more subtle version of metaphor uses one word or phrase, denoting a particular idea (or object or event), in place of another word or phrase in order to suggest a likeness or analogous connection between them. The assumption is that your understanding of the target idea (or object or event), and its related context, will expand as you apply to it the attributes of the substituted idea (or object or event). For example,

A slim willow, she stood by the river.

This metaphor depends on your knowledge of willows. There are reeds, slim and graceful, referred to as willows. There are both weeping and upright willow trees. Weeping willows are not slim but full and flowing. (Is this a sarcastic metaphor?) Upright willows are not slim either, in addition to which they are constantly shedding leaves and losing branches so that they are called a "dirty" tree. (Why is she standing by the river?)

Similes and metaphors establish analogous relationships that allow what Gordon (1961) calls "making the strange familiar." How often do you say, in your teaching or in every day conversation, "Well, it's like . . ."? Similes are used constantly to explain an unknown ("strange") object or idea or event. If you ask someone what cricket is, he or she will say, "Well, it's like baseball, with these exceptions. . . ." This, of course, assumes that you know what baseball is so that you can make the strange (cricket) familiar by comparing it with something you know (baseball). If you then asked whether cricket was an exciting game, your source might use a more qualitative simile. If your source does not think highly of cricket, he or she might say, "It's like watching grass grow." From this response you would conclude that cricket is a slow and boring activity.

In the preparation part of the lesson, you can use both metaphor and simile to explain new information and ideas. Such use of figurative language becomes as natural as breathing. Raising students' consciousness about the features and functions of similes and metaphors increases their understandings of both the concepts being explained and the reasoning processes being applied. As students perceive the conceptual connections between what they already have learned and what they are about to learn, they develop a more comprehensive understanding of your subject. The more they understand about the reasoning that similes and metaphors require, the more likely it is that they will be able to use them in their own speech and writing, as well as to recognize them through their listening and reading.

Similes and metaphors require both analytical and elaborative reasoning. The features and attributes of the known part of the simile or metaphor have to be analyzed. When an agreeable business partner is called a good team player, the reference is not to that person's having athletic ability but to his or her having attributes characteristic of groups joined in a cooperative endeavor. To understand the metaphor, you need to analyze the attributes of being a team player and then apply those that seem relevant to the context. You have to elaborate on the features to speculate on possible connections. You have to be creative in your speculations. You have to draw conclusions or draw inferences to confirm your speculations. Walking your students through this process is both instructive and beneficial.

Semantic Maps

Semantic mapping (Hanf 1971; Johnson and Pearson 1978; Heimlich and Pittelman 1986) provides another way to develop conceptual connections during the preparation part of the lesson. Originally conceived as a means of visualizing informational and conceptual relationships presented in the text, semantic maps also can be used independent of reading.

Semantic maps are constructed from words that represent ideas and contributing, relevant information. Circles and lines are drawn to portray relationships between and among the words. In this manner, relationships among the ideas and information are visualized. Example 7–3 in Chapter 7 presents a semantic map related to computers.

Semantic maps are used as review by teachers to direct the discussion. Through questioning they draw from students what they know about a topic and its relevant concepts. Teachers arrange words on the board to display conceptually the relationships designated by the students. In so doing, teachers model the construction of a semantic map. Subsequently, students working in groups can create semantic maps representing what they know about a topic. When the maps are completed by the groups, they can be compared and the differences discussed. If each group places the final version of its semantic map on a transparency, comparisons across groups are made more easily.

Semantic maps are maps of meaning. They show relationships among words that represent information and ideas. Creating and organizing the map involves inferencing and interpretation. As you encourage students to explain their contributions to the map and as you help them talk through the kind of reasoning that lead to their additions, you are supporting and strengthening their reasoning. In this manner, you are teaching reasoning processes and course content simultaneously.

The use of semantic maps as review supports content learning to the extent that the concepts being examined are relevant to the topic about to be studied. The maps provide a conceptual context for what is to be studied. They facilitate connections between what students bring to the study of a topic and what they gain from the study. The maps constructed during the preparation phase of the lesson can be carried on to the guidance phase.

New information and ideas can be added to the maps and the maps can be rearranged conceptually to reflect expanded understandings.

Et Cetera

You undoubtedly have other instructional strategies that involve students in reasoning processes as you prepare them to study specific topics in your content area. One of the difficulties in teaching the same subject over several years is that we become so familiar with the instructional activities we use with our students that we forget to let them in on the reasoning that the activities support and/or require. We forget that what we do each year, while familiar to ourselves, is new to our students. They need to know what we learned the first time we applied the teaching/learning strategy and discovered not only why it was valuable but how it worked. Making students aware of how processes work is vitally important to the instructional integration of content and process. You can accomplish this purpose by carefully explaining how a process works and how their minds are supposed to work while they are applying the process.

Take time to rethink the familiar instructional strategies you use to determine the kind of reasoning that they foster. Then take time to determine how you will explain this reasoning to your students so that they can fully benefit from your instruction.

Guidance of Reasoning

This chapter deals with ways that reasoning can support content learning. As noted earlier, reasoning occurs in, around, and beyond reading and writing. The study of the organizing idea for a lesson does not always involve reading or writing, but it always involves reasoning. Observing, listening, speaking, and taking some form of action all support content learning and all require reasoning. Add to this the reasoning that is involved in reading and writing, and reasoning becomes the all-pervasive and fundamentally important process to be integrated instructionally with course content.

We have already discussed the extent to which reasoning is involved in the preparation part of the Instructional Framework. Now we will examine how students' reasoning can be supported, enriched, and refined as part of the guidance part of the lesson structure. You'll recall that two main purposes drive the guidance: (1) to show students how to apply the relevant learning process (it being reasoning in this instance) and (2) to integrate instructionally the learning process and the content to be learned.

Before getting into the background information for guiding students' reasoning, we want you to experience some guided reasoning yourself. Before you read the article in Practice 10–2b, please join with other people reading this book and make a list of words that you associate with the word *compromise*. When you finish the listing, see what groupings of words you can formulate from the list. After you have identified word groups, please label them.

We want you to do one more thing before you read the article in Practice 10–2b. Please respond to the reasoning guide in Practice 10–2a, following the directions carefully.

Now, read the article in Practice 10–2b. As you do so, think about the six statements that you have just reacted to and discussed with your colleagues.

Now that you have finished reading the article in Practice 10–2b, follow the directions presented in Practice 10–2c (see page 278).

With this experience in mind, now consider the following background information about guiding reasoning.

Background

As a learning process, reasoning is a ubiquitous and pervasive presence in all content areas. But reasoning does not occur in a vacuum. Reasoning requires something upon which to act. Outside of school, the "something" is infinite in form, variety, and substance. Inside of school, the "something" is the information and ideas that comprise the curriculum in various content areas.

When you guide students' reasoning, you face a different issue than when you guide their reading and writing. Reasoning already is a natural and pervasive part of your students' functioning as human beings. Thus, when you guide their reasoning, you support and help refine what they are already capable of doing. In addition, you help them understand how the

---

PRACTICE 10-2A ──────────────────────────

Compromise

Directions: Read each of the following statements, and decide whether it seems reasonable to you. That is, does it fit well in your mind? Do you possess knowledge or have you had experiences that support the idea as it is expressed here? If so, place a check on the numbered line. If not, leave the numbered line blank. Be ready to discuss the reasons for your decisions.

_____ 1. Knowledge can exceed the capacity for its use.
_____ 2. Absolutes are rare; ambiguity is less so.
_____ 3. Compromise is essential when standards exceed control.
_____ 4. Uncertainty is the product of the mind, more imagined than real.

PRACTICE 10-2B

Leap Second to Put Clocks in Sync with Heavens

Washington—Poised on the brink of a new decade the world will pause tonight for just a second.

A "leap second" will occur at the very end of December 31, 1989, making it the longest day of the year.

The extra second is needed to keep the world's clocks in time with the rotation of the planet, according to government time-keeping officials.

The turning of the Earth has always been the time standard for humans, who marked the passage of days by the hours of light and darkness and years by the seasons as the planet moved around the sun.

But while early timekeeping sought to measure the planet's movement, today's clocks might be called more accurate than the Earth itself.

"Time measured by the rotation of the Earth is not uniform when compared to time kept by atomic clocks," reports the U.S. Naval Observatory, the government agency in charge of keeping track of what time it is.

As a result of this difference, atomic clocks can get out of sync with the Earth and have to be adjusted. Since it's the atomic clocks that are used to set all other clocks, a leap second has to be added or skipped from time to time to make up the difference.

Fifteen leap seconds have been added to human time since an international time agreement was signed in 1972, when a full 10 seconds had to be added to the atomic clocks to get them together with the Earth. This will be the first leap second in two years.

The leap second will occur officially at 23 hours, 59 minutes and 60 seconds, Coordinated Universal Time.

Source: *Syracuse Herald American*, December 31, 1989, B4.

---

reasoning power they already possess works for them in your academic setting.

The reasoning process is pervasive, in that thought processes occur whether you consider ideas specific to a particular subject or ideas that may relate to a broad spectrum of life. However, considerable debate has occurred regarding the question of whether cognitive processes are context bound or context free (Ennis 1989; Perkins and Salomon 1989). Do you reason with similar efficiency no matter the context in which the reasoning occurs? If so, that would suggest that cognitive processes are context free, that is, generally applicable across contexts. On the other hand, do you reason with differing efficiency depending on the context in which it occurs? If so, that would suggest that cognitive processes are context bound, that is, conditioned by the specific context in which they occur.

PRACTICE 10–2C

Compromise

Directions: Reread the statements in Practice 10–2a, and decide whether the author of the article would agree with your decision as to whether the statements are reasonable. Circle the number(s) of the statement(s) on which you and the author agree. Be ready to provide evidence from the article to support your decisions.

Imbedded in the general versus specific context questions is a question of the transferability of cognitive processes. If you learn a reasoning process in one context can you readily transfer it to another context and apply it equally well? If so, that would give added weight to the argument that cognitive skills are context free. On the other hand, does it seem that there is little transfer of what you learn in one context to its application in another, that you seem to have to learn different skills for each context in which you are doing the reasoning? If so, that would give added weight to the argument that cognitive skills are context bound.

Either/Or versus Both/And

The discussion of the influence of context on reasoning raises an essential question. Does context have an either/or influence on reasoning or a both/and influence. The either/or influence would be that reasoning is either context free or context bound. The both/and influence would be that reasoning is both context free and context bound.

We are persuaded by the arguments of those who subscribe to the both/and view. Ennis (1989) speaks of a mixed approach to the development of critical thinking. By *mixed* he means that reasoning is taught in contexts free of specific kinds of content as well as in contexts bound to specific subject matter. In his view, the context free environment may be a separate course, for example, where students study general principles of critical thinking. The context bound environment would be a specific subject-matter course and students would be "involved in subject-specific critical thinking instruction" in that course. Importantly, in this mixed approach, the same students would be involved in both the context free and the context bound study of reasoning. We will return to this point shortly.

Perkins and Salomon also support the both/and point of view, calling it a synthesis position. Their answer to the question of whether cognitive skills are context bound is, "yes and no," which is their version of "both/and." They say,

the approach that now seems warranted calls for the intimate intermingling of generality and context specificity in instruction . . . We believe that this direction in education is promising and provocative: it gets beyond educat-

ing memories to educating minds, which is what education should be about (Perkins and Salomon 1989, 24).

Ennis's explanation of the mixed approach seems to imply that general, context free instruction in reasoning should take place in separate courses while specific, context bound instruction in reasoning should take place in subject-specific courses. In this case, *mixed* would apply both to contexts for the instruction (context bound and context free) and to courses in which the instruction occurs (nonsubject specific or subject specific). Ennis, therefore, does not seem to advocate combining the general (context free) and specific (context bound) instruction in the same course. However, neither does he reject the idea.

If there are both general and specific dimensions to reasoning as they pertain to contexts and if reasoning instruction can be useful both when it is context free and when it is context bound, why is it not possible to provide both kinds of instruction in one course? The premise on which this book is built requires that the answer to this question be, "It *is* possible." This premise is confirmed by Perkins and Salomon when they refer to the importance of "bringing together context specific knowledge with general strategies knowledge" (Perkins and Salomon 1989, 23). What better place to accomplish this purpose than in content-area classrooms?

In this book we already have made the point of the importance of moving from the general to the specific in the teaching of concepts in order to connect information that is known with new information. We have made the same point in our discussions of guiding the application of learning processes. Now you see that moving from the general to the specific also is important when considering how to guide students' reasoning development as they study concepts that constitute the curricula in various content areas.

Think back, now, on your experience in responding to the statements in Practice 10–2a and Practice 10–2c along with your reading of the article in Practice 10–2b. Your first reaction to the statements involved reasoning in a broad, general manner. The key word in the word-association activity gave you some clues to the general focus of the upcoming article. However, you were not aware of the possible connections between the article and the statements. Thus, in many respects, your first response to the statements was context free.

Because the context was more general in your first response to the statements, your reasoning processes also were more general. You were free to let your reasoning roam to wherever it would take you, drawing on whatever prior knowledge and experience you deemed important and relevant to the ideas contained in the statements. By supporting your decisions on this first response to the statements, you actively engaged in this more contextually free reasoning. By this engagement you became more conscious of the reasoning processes you applied as you related your prior knowledge and experience to the ideas contained in the statements.

After completing the discussion of your general response to the statements, you read the article. You then responded to the same set of statements but, this time, with reference to the article. The article prescribed the statements and provided a specific context for your consideration of their relevance. Thus, in many respects, your second response to the statements was context bound.

Because the context was more specific for your second response to the statements, your reasoning processes also were more specific. You were constrained in your reasoning by the content of the article, referring back to it frequently to identify specific information or to draw relevant inferences to make your decisions. By making and subsequently supporting your decisions on this second response to the statements, you actively engaged in a more contextually bound reasoning. By this engagement you became more conscious of the reasoning processes you applied as you analyzed the text and related its information and implications to the ideas contained in the statements.

The general to specific cycle is clear in this example. The statements guide a response to the organizing idea of the lesson. First, the guidance is at a general level for both the content of the lesson and the reasoning process. The conceptual context for the lesson is free. The process context for the reasoning is also free. Second, the guidance is at a specific level for both the content and the reasoning process. The conceptual context for the lesson is bound by the text. The process context for the reasoning also is bound.

Types of Reasoning

What kinds of reasoning occur when it is contextually free and when it is contextually bound? An analysis of descriptors of reasoning found in the literature provides useful answers to that question (Herber 1978). When you sort through the descriptors, you find that they can be organized into pairs, as follows:

divergent—convergent
creative—critical
extensive—intensive
elaborative—analytical
subjective—objective
inductive—deductive
inferential—interpretive

The first reasoning process in each of the pairs can be thought of as more context free, as consistent with a broad and general consideration of concepts. Thus, you can be divergent, creative, extensive, and elaborative in your reasoning about an idea. You can be subjective in your reasoning as you inductively draw on your prior knowledge and experience and infer relevant generalizations.

The second reasoning process in each of the pairs can be thought of as more context bound, as consistent with a more focused and specific consideration of concepts. Thus, you can be convergent, critical, intensive, and analytical in your reasoning about an idea. You can be objective in your reasoning, deducing particular ideas as you interpret various information sources.

When guiding students' application of reasoning, none of these reasoning processes is taught directly. That is, you don't have specific lessons on the use of any of the reasoning processes, either singly or in pairs. Rather, you teach reasoning processes functionally, by guiding students in ways that require their application of different kinds of reasoning; by having them talk their way through decisions they have made, raising their consciousness about how their reasoning has worked for them; by clarifying and/or confirming the reasoning processes students used in making their decisions, based on their descriptions of the decisions.

Because the first response to the statements is more context free, the reasoning processes being applied also are more context free: divergent, elaborative, inferential, and so forth. As students draw generally on prior knowledge and experience to make and support their decisions, they become aware of how these processes work. As you confirm and/or clarify their reasoning, you reinforce their awareness and understanding of how these more context free reasoning processes work for them.

Because the second response to the statements is more context bound, the reasoning process being applied also are more context bound: convergent, analytical, interpretive, and so forth. As students draw specifically on information from the text to make and support their decisions, they become aware of how these processes work. As you confirm and/or clarify their reasoning, you reinforce their awareness and understanding of how these more context bound reasoning processes work for them.

Design of Reasoning Guides

You have now thought about context free and context bound reasoning. You also have experienced firsthand the use of what we call a reasoning guide. Now it is important to consider how to design reasoning guides.

In many respects, the reasoning guides that you prepare for your students reflect your own reasoning about the organizing idea of the lesson and the concepts supported by the various resources you draw upon for the lesson. Thus, the guide you design becomes for your students a model of how to reason about the concepts studied, as well as the resource materials you use, in your content area. Your task is to create declarative statements, or an adaptation of same, to guide students' reasoning. The guide you design becomes for your students a model of how to reason about concepts and resources in your subject area.

You'll recall the two dimensions of the reasoning process that we have focused on: context free and context bound. Context free reasoning is unconstrained by the particulars of specific concepts in specific subject areas, though it is prescribed by the comprehensiveness of one's prior knowledge and experience. Context bound reasoning is constrained by the particulars of specific concepts in specific subject areas as well as by the comprehensiveness of one's prior knowledge and experience. Both kinds of reasoning are appropriate for emphasis in content areas. The context free reasoning helps establish and confirm an experiential context for the concept to be studied. The context bound reasoning helps to link what is new with what is known and to refine an understanding of the connection.

To design a reasoning guide, you first establish the organizing idea for the lesson and decide on some means of helping students make conceptual connections between that idea and their own prior knowledge and experience For example, you might choose to use word-association tasks. You then create a reasoning guide to facilitate students' reasoning about this organizing idea. For the type of format you already have experienced, you create a set of declarative statements that are similar in nature to what you used at the applied level in your levels-of-comprehension guides. The directions ask students first to identify those statements that they can support out of their own knowledge and experience. Then students are asked to respond to some resource (text, visual, audio, manipulative, and so forth.) and decide if that resource would support the same statements that they originally supported. For both content free and content bound reasoning, students are asked to cite evidence to support their responses to the statements. Through this marshaling of supportive evidence, students become aware of the kind of reasoning that their responses require. By discussing the reasoning processes that students are applying, you develop and refine their understandings of how and when to use the reasoning processes. Variations in the design of reasoning guides are presented in Appendix B and in Chapter 11.

Use of Reasoning Guides

Flexibility of Use

Reasoning guides probably have more flexibility in their instructional application than any of the materials discussed in this book. Most teachers who use reasoning guides in their teaching tend to apply the instructional strategy in the context free then context bound order. However, they can be used before, during, or after the use of relevant resources during the conduct of a lesson or unit.

Before a resource is used, reasoning guides can be used to support students sorting through relevant prior knowledge and experience relative to the organizing idea of the lesson. Before a resource is used, a reasoning guide can be used to support students' hypothesizing about what it is they might encounter when they eventually respond to a resource.

The same reasoning guides mentioned above can then be used to support students while they are responding to the resources. In the first instance, they can determine whether information and ideas presented by the resources are supportive of the concepts presented in the guide. In the second instance, students can determine whether their predictions are accurate by citing evidence from the resources to support their judgment.

Reasoning guides also can be used after students have used a resource. The guide is used to help students refine their understanding of the information and ideas they derived more independently from the resource.

Materials Constructed from Answers

You will recall the point we made in our discussion of teaching as showing how in Chapter 6. In the context of discussing the use of guides to support students' reading, we said that declarative statements used in the guides are really answers rather than questions. They are the product of your own reasoning processes as you ask yourself the questions: What is the essential information? What ideas are being presented? What generalizations can we draw from this material as it relates to what I already know?

Thus, students do not actually create a product of their reasoning. Because you give them the product of your reasoning, they have only to judge whether or not your statements are appropriate and supportable. By citing evidence to support or reject the statements, however, students develop an awareness of how such statements can be formulated. In this manner students develop a consciousness about reasoning processes. They are able to talk about reasoning with their teachers and peers. Importantly, they also are able to talk about the ideas derived through their application of reasoning processes. Thus reasoning supports content-area learning.

An Instructional Strategy

The context free/context bound reasoning construct becomes an instructional strategy when the types of reasoning are represented in instructional materials called reasoning guides. These guides are used to support students within a broad framework of an organizing idea as well as within a more focused framework of particular representations or illustrations of the organizing idea within a specific content area. In providing this supporting function, guides serve as mediators (Shoemaker 1977). That is, reasoning guides provide a link between students and their own prior knowledge and experience, between students and varied resources, between students and teacher, and among the students themselves.

Reasoning guides mediate discussions among students both as they draw on their prior knowledge and as they analyze information and ideas from the resources in use. Mediation of students' interaction is particularly important because students often work in small groups as they respond to the guides. The guides give focus and purpose to students' interactions and increase the efficiency and productivity of their work. The guides, used in small groups, increase opportunities for individual students to develop and refine their proficiency with the reasoning process. The guides also mediate the communication between the students and the teacher, giving focus to that communication. The structure of the guides enables teachers to identify needs of students more easily relative to reasoning and to provide the needed instruction more easily.

Independence in Reasoning

One of the principal objectives in guiding students' reasoning is that they will develop independence in their application of reasoning processes. As we point out throughout this book, independence is a relative state, conditioned by many variables. For purposes of instruction, independence can be approximated for levels of sophistication of the curriculum, levels of abstraction at which learning processes are operationalized, and types of ability that students bring to the tasks. Through activities that reinforce, refine, and extend what has been taught, both content and process can be used by students with increasing levels of independence.

It is important to understand that students do not suddenly become independent in their acquisition and application of content and process. Guidance extends into the development of independence as well. However, this kind of guidance can require more independence by students in their application of learning processes even while providing some structure to support the more independent functioning.

For example, a reasoning guide is applied during the guidance phase of the lesson to one printed resource (a poem, a story, a chapter, a problem, laboratory report, and so forth.). This same reasoning guide can be applied subsequently, during the independence phase of the lesson, to supplementary and enrichment resources that deal with the same organizing idea. Use of the same set of statements provides a familiar structure within which students can respond to the supplementary resources. Variation in the structure and content of the supplementary resources requires adaptation, refinement, or extension of the reasoning processes students applied to the initial resource, a modest level of independent application of those processes.

Independence in learning is not attained in a single step, as you well know. However, relative independence can be attained over time when instruction is designed to develop that independence in small increments. Chapter 12 presents a variety of suggestions for ways to develop students' independence in vocabulary acquisition, reading, writing, and reasoning.

Sample Guides

In Appendix B we have included a set of reasoning guides drawn from the work of teachers in different subject areas. We present them as examples of what teachers have created for their own students. We include the organizing ideas of the lessons for which these guides were created. You will find it useful to look over these examples at this time.

Practice

Practice 10–3 (see page 286) presents a reading selection for you to use in practicing the design of a reasoning guide. Please do the following:

1. Establish an organizing idea for a lesson in which the selection could be used.
2. Create a reasoning guide, including both part one and part two.
3. Compare your response with ours by looking at our product in Appendix A.

Summary

Reasoning is pervasive, but its instruction is not. Learning in any content area requires some form of reasoning. Applying the processes of vocabulary acquisition, reading, and writing requires the application of different forms of reasoning. Some teachers tend to take for granted their students' reasoning proficiency if those students are successful in learning the course content. Some teachers tend to take for granted their students' inability to reason if they are not successful in learning the course content. Both cases are used as reasons not to teach reasoning.

Instruction in reasoning can be integrated with instruction in course content so an understanding of the two is developed simultaneously. Students' reasoning can be supported as they consider ideas that are relatively context free. Their reasoning can continue to be supported as they consider the same ideas placed in a specific context. The support takes the form of reasoning guides as well as other types of manipulatable material that are applied in a cooperative-learning environment. Thus, students learn how to reason to learn. They acquire an understanding of course content; they develop and refine their reasoning powers.

Practice 10–3

Law and Morality

Can a court force you to give up part of your body to a relative if you don't want to? That was the question recently brought before the court of common pleas in Allegheny County, Pennsylvania. The case involved a thirty-nine-year-old man who suffered from aplastic anemia, a rare disease of the bone marrow. The only chance the man had was to receive a bone marrow transplant from a compatible donor, and usually only close relatives can be compatible donors.

It turned out that the man had a cousin who could be a compatible donor. There was only one hitch: The cousin didn't want to give up any of his bone marrow—even though there was virtually no risk to him, and the chances of his cousin's recovering would be raised from near zero to 50 percent. The man with aplastic anemia pleaded with his cousin to let him have the transplant, but to no avail. As a last-ditch measure he went to court asking the court to grant a preliminary injunction ordering his cousin to give up twenty-one ounces of bone marrow.

The court began its opinion noting it could find no authority for such an order to be made. The plaintiff said there was a precedent in an ancient statue of King Edward I, a law that was more than seven hundred years old. That law said that an individual has a moral and legal obligation to secure the well-being of other members of society. But unfortunately for the plaintiff, since the thirteenth century not a single case could be found where such an obligation was enforced. In fact, to the contrary, the common law has consistently held that one human being is under no legal obligation to give aid or take action to save another human being or to rescue one.

The court said that such a rule, although revolting in a moral sense, is founded upon the very essence of a free society, and while other societies may view things differently, our society has as its first principle respect for the individual—and society and government exist to protect that individual from being invaded and hurt by another.

The court did say that the refusal of the defendant was morally indefensible, but a society that respects the right of one individual must not sink its teeth into the jugular vein or neck of another—that would be revolting to our concepts of jurisprudence.

The plaintiff is dead now, but the common law remains intact.

Source: Neil Chayet. (1986) Law and Morality. In D. Gavitch (Ed.) *Life Studies: A Thematic Reader*. (New York: St. Martin's Press).

REACTIONS

Journal Entries and Discussion

Go back to the analysis you wrote at the conclusion of Chapter 9 concerning the similarities between the functional approach to reading instruction and the process approach to writing instructions. Consider how the functional approach to reasoning fits with the other two approaches. What implications are there in your analysis for instructional interaction among the three processes and their instructional integration with course content?

Analysis and Discussion

Now that you have completed this chapter, consider the statements shown below. Check the numbered lines for statements with which you agree. Circle the numbers of statements you believe reflect the point of view of the authors. In writing, explore reasons for differences on any statements between your point of view and what you perceive to be the point of view of the authors. Please share and discuss your writing with colleagues who also are reading this book.

_____ 1. In connecting what is new with what is known, confirmation is as important as prediction.

_____ 2. Student interaction supports and facilitates the processes of anticipation and prediction.

_____ 3. Students will risk failure or being wrong in order to test out an idea if the teacher provides an instructional environment that is safe for such risks.

_____ 4. Guiding the development of students' reasoning is probably easier than guiding the development of their reading and writing.

_____ 5. Students themselves can serve as resources for information and ideas for nearly any principle we study in our content areas.

_____ 6. Reasoning guides and related activities not only develop students' facility with reasoning processes, they also help students develop a sense of the value of their own ideas and experiences, a sense that what they know and what they are learning can be fitted together into a structure that makes sense and has some use.

_____ 7. The various instructional options for improving students' reading and reasoning achievement need not be applied singly or in isolation; rather they can be applied in logical combinations.

_____ 8. Nothing prompts reading more than a need to read; and nothing develops a need to read more than a need to determine if one is right or wrong on an idea, issue, or action for which one has taken a stand.

SECTION IV
Applications and Outcomes

_11_

Pulling It All Together

Organizing idea: "The proof of a pudding is in the eating."
(Cervantes, *Don Quixote*)

Reflections

Before reading this chapter, please record in your journal your responses to the following tasks. If possible, share your writing with other individuals who are also reading this book.

1. In your journal, reflect on the difference between designing and using materials to support the application of a single instructional strategy and designing and using materials that support multiple instructional strategies applied in a full-lesson structure.

2. If you were to construct a lesson so another person could teach it, what format would you follow? What components would you include? In your journal, identify the format and list the components.

3. If you were to construct an instructional unit so another person could teach it, what format would you follow? What components would you include? In your journal, identify the format and list the components.

THE TEST OF INSTRUCTIONAL strategies is whether they work in the classroom to the benefit of students' learning. This chapter contains materials that were produced by educational practitioners for simultaneously teaching content and process in content classes. The materials can serve as models to follow in your own applications of what you have learned through this book.

The first section includes a suggested lesson format and a poetry lesson following that format. The materials develop students' understanding of the organizing idea that is articulated for the lesson. Simultaneously, they support students' application of learning processes presented in this book.

The suggested lesson format provides a general frame for organizing the materials for the lesson. One has to apply the format flexibly to fit the particulars of one's own subject, students, and purposes. One also has to be flexible in selecting from the instructional strategies that are available to support students' learning. Strategies actually selected will be dictated by the difficulty of the content and by the sophistication of students related to that content.

The second section includes a suggested unit format and unit materials that generally follow that format. The materials develop students' understanding of organizing ideas that are articulated for the unit and the constituent lessons. Simultaneously, the materials support students' application of learning processes presented in this book.

Three types of units are possible: (1) *multidisciplinary,* exploring an organizing idea from the perspective of more than one subject area; (2) *thematic,* drawing on multiple works to explore an organizing idea; (3) *single source,* drawing on one work or one text to explore an organizing idea. Such units are comprehensive in nature, developing learning processes that derive naturally from the resources used and the organizing idea(s) that drive the unit. Instructional materials within the unit support students' applications of learning processes and develop their understandings of relevant course content.

Space limitations precluded the inclusion a model for each type of unit. We decided to select a unit from Latin. Because it is a subject taught by relatively few teachers, we thought that the subject matter of the unit would be neutral for most teachers, enabling them to examine objectively the organization of the unit and its instructional materials. This Latin unit represents the single-source type of unit.

The suggested unit format provides a general frame for organizing the material for the unit. One has to apply the format flexibly to fit the particulars of one's own subject, students, and purposes. As is shown in both the illustrative lesson and illustrative unit, one draws selectively from available strategies and support materials to fit instructional purposes and organizing ideas being studied. The principle, *content determines process,* is consistently applied.

Lesson Materials

Lesson Format

A. Rationale

   1. How does the lesson relate to your definition of reading?
   2. Why do these students need this lesson?
   3. What previous learnings are you assuming?

    B. Organizing idea: What is the central concept that drives this lesson?

    C. Lesson plan

        1. Content objectives: What is it that you want students to know when the lesson is over?

        2. Process objective: What is it that you want students to be able to do when the lesson is over?

        3. Materials: What materials will you use to teach the lesson?

        4. Procedures

            a) Preparation: What strategies will you use to set the stage for learning?

            b) Guidance: What strategies will you use to support learning?

            c) Independence: How will you promote continued learning?

        5. Evaluation: How will you evaluate your students' accomplishment of the objectives?

Poetry Lesson

Lesson Plan for "Ozymandias"

A. Rationale

Poetry has both particulars and universals. The particulars are the facts and ideas in a poem that are bound to a given time, place, or situation. The universals are the ideas in a poem that go beyond the time, place, and situation to apply much more generally to the whole world of experience. Poets attempt to get maximum significance of meaning with a minimum of words within a poetic framework.

    Students often have difficulty comprehending poetry (1) because of the density of ideas presented in the compressed language of poetic form and/or (2) because of their inability to recognize from their own experience the universal ideas that the poet is expressing. Teachers can help students with these comprehension problems by helping them to anticipate the universal ideas at the level of their own experience and then to recognize those ideas in the poetry. Once they are able to recognize universal ideas imbedded in particular pieces of poetry, they will be better able to approach other poems in a search for meaning that lies beneath the surface.

    The following lesson, using "Ozymandias" by Percy B. Shelley and "Limited" by Carl Sandburg, is designed to help students anticipate the universal meanings in one poem and situation and then to discover many of the same universal ideas in another very different poem.

B. Organizing Idea
Things are not always what they seem to be.

C. Lesson Plan

1. *Content objective*: Students will understand that poets use the particulars of time, place, and situation to illustrate ideas that apply more generally.
2. *Process objective*: Students will be able to relate the particular ideas of each poem to the organizing idea and to the general statements of the anticipation guide.
3. *Materials*

   a. Copies of the two poems, "Ozymandias" by Percy B. Shelley and "Limited" by Carl Sandburg.
   b. Organizing idea, anticipation guide, and three-level guide.

4. *Procedures*

   a. *Preparation*

      (1) Use the organizing idea, "Things are not always what they seem to be," to explain to students that poets often use particular experiences to stand as examples of a more universal experience. Explain also that even though our experiences may be different from those of the poet, we can share his ideas by relating them to our own experiences.
      (2) Have students move into cooperative groups, and have each group select a recorder. Ask the groups to think of, and have each recorder write down, as many words as possible that relate to *both* the ideas of *time* and *desert*. (For example: The word *sand* relates *both* to time and the desert.) Give the groups three minutes to complete their lists. When the task is completed, ask the recorder of the group with the most words to read their list aloud while the others listen to see if they want to challenge any word for its relationship to the two ideas. Let other groups contribute other words that the first group did not have. As the words are discussed, be sure to point out to students that relationships can be metaphoric as well as concrete. (Shown below are examples of lists from a tenth-grade class in Boston, and a ninth-grade class in Phoenix. Can you label which is New England and which is Southwest? Experience shows, doesn't it?)

sand	heat	sand	changing
pyramids	wind	cactus	lizards
sphinx	ruins	sun	snakes
mummies	curse	moon	plants
ancient	tombs	heat	mirage
modern	archaeologists	seasons	ruins
sun	pueblos	erosion	nomads

Obviously the groups had differing schemata for the organizing ideas. The Southwest group was responding with words related to their experience with the living desert while the New England group was responding to their knowledge of the ancient desert. Both groups recognized relationships with time that were both literal and inferential. Differences in lists show up even among groups in the same classroom.

(3) Now that students have begun to think about time and the desert through their own words, use the anticipation guide in groups according to directions to help students think about and discuss some of the general ideas that they will later recognize when they read the poem "Ozymandias." When the groups finish the task, bring the groups together to share their ideas on the more difficult statements.

Think About It

Directions: Read each statement, and decide whether or not you really believe it is true, based on your own experience. When you discuss the statements in your group, try to think of exceptions that might support a different point of view as well as examples that support the idea. For example, in the first item, does time ever wait for anyone? What about time-out in a football game? Does time ever seem to slow down or speed up? Is time real, or have we created it? See if your group can come to an agreement on each statement.

_____ 1. Time waits for no one.
_____ 2. All people are mortal and someday will die.
_____ 3. Death is the great leveler.
_____ 4. An artist gets to know a lot about his or her subject.
_____ 5. Things are not always what they seem to be.
_____ 6. Pride goes before a fall.
_____ 7. All man-made things are temporal and someday will disintegrate.
_____ 8. A person's vision is temporal, even though his or her perspective is eternal.

(4) Before the students read the poem, the teacher may wish to use the vocabulary guide in groups according to directions to help students recognize some of the more difficult words of the poem.

Recognizing Related Meanings

Directions: For each set of words below, cross out the word that does not belong with the others. In the space provided, describe how the other three words are related or why they belong together. In your group, discuss the similarities and differences among the responses and why they occurred.

1. vast	limited	colossal	boundless _____
2. face	visage	front	rear _____
3. smile	sneer	laugh	frown _____
4. broken	whole	shattered	fragmented _____
5. column	mighty	pedestal	table _____
6. poet	artist	sculptor	scientist _____
7. emotions	passions	troubles	feelings _____
8. command	despair	abandon	hopeless _____

The exercise is designed to familiarize the students with the words that appear in the poem so they will recognize them when they read the poem. Working on the exercise as a group gives students the opportunity to hear the words pronounced, to see the words as they are being discussed, to recognize the relationships among the words, and to speak the words in the discussion. It should be noticed that several of the items are ambiguous in the sense that more than one answer is reasonable. Since this is a learning experience rather than a test, these kinds of items can be effective in focusing even more attention on the words and in requiring multiple recitation of the reasons for one grouping or another when students compare their responses. It should be pointed out to students, however, that on most well-designed multiple-choice tests there is only one best answer.

b. *Guidance*

(1) Read "Ozymandias" to the students.

Ozymandias   Percy B. Shelley

I met a traveler from an antique land,
Who said: Two vast and trunkless legs of stone
Stand in the desert. Near them, on the sand,
Half sunk, a shattered visage lies, whose frown,
And wrinkled lip, and sneer of cold command,
Tell that its sculptor well those passions read,
Which yet survive, stamped on these lifeless things,
The hand that mocked them and the heart that fed,

And on the pedestal these words appear:
"My name is Ozymandias, King of Kings.
Look on my works, ye mighty, and despair!"
Nothing beside remains. Round the decay
Of that colossal wreck, boundless and bare
The lone and level sands stretch far away.

(2) Use the following guide, as the first two levels of a three-level guide in groups according to directions. The guide should help students to reread and understand "Ozymandias" at the literal and interpretive levels.

Levels Guide for "Ozymandias"

Literal Level

Directions: The poem "Ozymandias" contains a description within a description. See if you can follow the action by deciding which statements listed below accurately describe what the poet says in the poem. Be ready to discuss the reasons for your decisions with other members of your group.

_____ 1. The poet met a traveler from a very old country.
_____ 2. The traveler told the poet about the remains of a large statue in the desert.
_____ 3. The legs of the statue remained standing, but the head was lying in the sand.
_____ 4. The details in the face of the fallen statue show that the sculptor knew his subject's feelings well.
_____ 5. The words written on the base of the statue told the name and occupation of the subject of the sculpture.

Interpretive Level

Directions: Poets usually write descriptions of incidents to communicate other ideas they want their readers to get from their poems. Decide which statements listed below present ideas that Shelley was trying to give you. Discuss with your group the reasons for your decisions.

_____ 1. Both the king and the sculptor are long dead.
_____ 2. Time destroyed both the statue and the power of the king.
_____ 3. There is a lesson to be learned from the statue.

(3) Reintroduce the anticipation guide (think about it) as the applied level of the three-level guide. Ask students in groups to discuss each of the statements to decide whether Shelley would agree with their responses to the statements. Ask them also to

provide evidence from "Ozymandias" in support of their decisions. The guide should help students reread and understand the poem at the applied level.

  c. *Independence*

    (1) Using the poem "Limited" as homework, ask students to review each statement on the same anticipation guide used earlier to decide whether Sandburg agrees with it and to garner evidence from "Limited" in support of their decisions.

Limited   Carl Sandburg

I am riding on a Limited Express,
one of the crack trains of the nation.
Hurtling across the prairie into blue haze and dark air
go fifteen all-steel coaches holding a thousand people.
(All the coaches shall be scrap and rust
and the men and women laughing in the diner and sleeper
shall pass to ashes.)
I ask a man in the smoker where he is going
and he answers: "Omaha."

    (2) As review (and to support the less able students), let the groups reassemble to discuss their homework and the bases for their decisions.

 5. *Evaluation*
Ask students to write on one or both of the following items:

  a) Discuss how the organizing idea of the lesson relates to the idea of poets' using particulars to communicate universal ideas. Use specific examples from the two poems "Ozymandias" and "Limited" in support of your discussion.

  b) Choose two of the statements from the anticipation guide and discuss how each poet supports the idea in his poetry. Use specific evidence from the poems in support of your discussion.

Unit Materials

Unit Format

Categories for Inclusion
  A. Cover page

    1. Title of unit
    2. Type of unit (multidisciplinary, thematic, single source)

   3. Grade level of unit
   4. Name of author
   5. Course name and number
   6. Semester and year

B. Introduction and descriptive information

   1. Brief rationale for unit
   2. Brief description of unit
   3. Organizing idea for unit (concept or theme statement)
   4. Content objectives for unit
   5. Process objectives for unit
   6. Resources for unit (list of materials to be used)

C. Unit focus (activities to introduce the unit)

   1. Organizing idea
   2. Experiential organizers
   3. General structured overview
   4. Anticipation/prediction guides
   5. Reasoning guides

D. Unit lessons (as many as needed for the content)

   1. Lesson objectives
   2. Preparation

      a) Organizing idea
      b) Anticipation/prediction guides
      c) Structured overview
      d) Vocabulary development
      e) Other

   3. Guidance

      a) Three-level guide
      b) Organizational pattern guide
      c) Reasoning guide

   4. Independence

      a) Concept review
      b) Vocabulary review
      c) Reasoning beyond
      d) Reading-study skills

E. Unit Review (putting it all together)

   1. Synthesizing activities

      a) Postreading organizers
      b) Graphic organizers

       c) Reasoning in, around, and beyond
       d) Oral/written composition

    2. Synthesizing processes

       a) Paired practice
       b) Triangular review
       c) Group composition
       d) Individual composition

F. Unit extension (going beyond)

    1. Extension bibliography
    2. Extension activities

G. Evaluation of lesson and unit objectives

    1. Group reviews (oral and written)
    2. Group tests
    3. Cloze tests
    4. Strategy tests
    5. Aided essay tests
    6. Independent essay tests
    7. Objective tests (with or without qualifications)

Single-source Unit

"Jason and the Argonauts"

A Content-Area Unit
Grades 10 and 11

by Diane Mannix

Unit Introduction

Rationale

This unit is from a second-year book. It is the first time students will read a Latin selection that is longer than one page. "Jason and the Argonauts" contains vocabulary and constructions that the students are familiar with, but they will be meeting most of them in context for the first time. This unit is a stepping-stone to the harder material they will encounter when they read Caesar.

I have chosen to focus on indirect statement because this story contains many examples of this construction. Students have trouble both recognizing indirect statement in context and translating it. They need practice with both skills.

No Latin unit would be complete without derivation, one of the great benefits to any student of the language. I have combined derivation and word building with the study of *ferre,* a common irregular verb that students are required to master. *Ferre* and its compounds occur many times in this unit and will also be found in any further reading the students do.

Description

This unit consists of seven Latin passages and several connecting summaries from "Jason and the Argonauts." This is the story of Jason, a Greek hero, and his quest to obtain the Golden Fleece in order to win his rightful kingdom. During this quest Jason meets Medea, a woman with magical powers and few scruples, and she becomes his wife. Their relationship has a tragic ending.

The chapters are:

1. A Careless Shoestring
2. The Journey Begins
3. Facing the Harpies and the Symplegades
4. Sowing the Dragon's Teeth
5. Medea's Choice (Escape from Colchis—A Summary)
6. The Death of Pelias
7. The Final Episode

Organizing idea: A hero's life is not easy.

Mythology is filled with the stories of heroes and their adventures. A hero's life is not easy. there is continual opposition from enemies. A hero's quest contains dangers that require either superhuman strength or supernatural powers, and sometimes a hero must even face family problems that threaten to be overwhelming.

Resources

Jenney, C. (1957). *Scudder's Second Year Latin.* (pp. 88–89, 98–114). New York: Allyn and Bacon.

The 10-year odyssey of Homer's wily hero. (1963). *Life Magazine, 54,* 62B–63.

Content Objectives for Unit

Pupils will:

1. Understand that a hero's life is not easy:

    a. He or she continually comes up against enemies and danger.
    b. He or she needs supernatural aid and/or superhuman strength to complete tasks.

c. He or she faces family problems that threaten to be overwhelming.

2. Understand that Ulysses is a Greek hero whose life illustrates Number 1.
3. Understand that Jason is a Greek hero whose life illustrates Number 1.
4. Understand Medea's character, actions, and her role in Jason's life.
5. Understand vocabulary necessary for reading the Latin passage.
6. Know the meaning of the parts of the word *Argonaut*.
7. Understand that other English words are formed the same way as *Argonaut*.
8. Know the principal parts and meanings of *ferre* and its compounds.
9. Know the meaning of Latin prefixes.
10. Know the meaning of English prefixes and suffixes.
11. Recognize English roots derived from *ferre*.
12. Recognize English words derived from *ferre*.
13. Compare two uses of the infinitive.
14. Recognize indirect statement in context.
15. Know the possible translations of indirect statement.
14. Recognize cases and meanings of nouns, and tenses, moods, voices, and meanings of verbs.

Process Objectives for Unit
Pupils will:

1. Tap their own experience with heroes.
2. Generate lists of words related to heroes.
3. Classify and develop category names for words related to heroes.
4. Classify their knowledge about Ulysses on a structured overview under specified categories.
5. Analyze pairs of words for similar and dissimilar meanings.
6. Identify the relationship among words in a set by deleting words that don't fit and describing the relationship among the others.
7. Match Latin words and their meanings.
8. Identify forms of words in context.
9. Determine the correct word to complete a sentence by examining the context of the sentence.
10. Use of a structured overview to review two uses of the infinitive.
11. Use a structured overview to analyze Latin construction before translation.
12. Use a structured overview to organize vocabulary in a selection.
13. Use a structured overview to determine relationships among characters.
14. Set purposes for reading.
15. Use their own experience and related knowledge as a context for reading new material.

16. Read at the literal level to identify factual information given in a selection.
17. Read at the literal level to recognize stated causes and effects.
18. Read at the literal level to recognize stated comparisons and contrasts.
19. Read a Latin sentence at the literal level to identify cases and meanings of nouns, and tenses, moods, voices, and meanings of verbs.
20. Read at the interpretive level to recognize ideas implied in a selection.
21. Read at the interpretive level to recognize implied causes and effects.
22. Read at the interpretive level to recognize implied comparisons and contracts.
23. Read a Latin sentence at the interpretive level to identify constructions, agreement, and relationships between words.
24. Read at the applied level to recognize, explain, and illustrate the application of ideas with respect to generalizations about the world of experience.
25. Read a Latin sentence at the applied level to recognize grammatical rules illustrated by the sentence.
26. Use the information from the selection, a map, and their own experience to draw conclusions about, and to predict, a character's actions.
27. Use their knowledge of unit content to arrive at conclusions about possible actions and statements of one character.
28. Apply knowledge gained from the text to generalizations about the world of experience.
29. Analyze derivatives, and explain the relationship of their meanings to the Latin words from which they are derived.
30. Explain the effect of a prefix on the meaning of a compound verb.
31. Build compound verbs by adding prefixes to a verb.
32. Apply knowledge of word parts to word building and creating definitions.
33. Use a dictionary to define words and verify answers.

Unit Focus

The students have previously studied the adventures of several Greek heroes during a unit on mythology. The Focus strategies will allow them to draw on this previous knowledge and their experience to introduce the concept of hero to be studied in this unit.

Mythology is filled with the stories of heroes and their adventures. A hero's life is not easy. There is continual opposition from enemies. A hero's quest contains dangers that require either superhuman strength or supernatural powers, and sometimes a hero must even face family problems that threaten to be overwhelming.

Hero:

1. A person of great courage
2. One admired for his or her exploits

What do *you* already know about heroes? With your group make a list of all the words you can think of that have to do with a hero. Here are some suggestions to get you started:

Courageous

Enemies

Ulysses

Next, categorize the words you have listed; that is, put the words into groups that have something in common. For example, you might use "names of heroes", "descriptions of heroes", "things heroes do," and so forth. The categories you use will be determined by the list of words you have made.

When you have developed your categories of hero words, read the statements below with your group. Place a check on the numbered line before each statement you agree with on the basis of your own experience and knowledge. Be ready to give reasons for your answers.

_____ 1. Heroes always defeat their enemies.
_____ 2. The gods are always on the hero's side.
_____ 3. The hero is always noble, good, and courageous.

Ulysses is a well-known Greek hero. We learned about him last year when we studied mythology. Look at the drawing that depicts his adventures after he left Troy. With your group classify these adventures under these headings:

1. Enemies and dangers
2. Supernatural aid and superhuman strength
3. Problems at home (family problems)

Use the structured overview for this activity.

Jason is another famous Greek hero. For the next few weeks we will be studying about his adventures. As we read, think about how he fits the description of a hero.

Organizing idea: A hero's life is not easy.

Structured Overview

Hero
|
— Ulysses —
|

Enemies and Dangers	Supernatural Aid and Superhuman Strength	Problems at Home
		(Family Problems)
1. Lotus Eaters	1. Aeolus	1. Penelope's suitors
2. Cyclops	2. Mercury	
3. Poseidon	3. magic herb	
4. his own crew	4. Tiresias' warning	
5. Giant Man-Eaters	5. Jupiter	
6. Circe	6. Minerva	
7. Underworld		
8. Sirens		
9. Scylla		
10. Jupiter		
11. shipwreck		
12. Charybdis		
13. Calypso		
14. suitors		

The Adventures of Ulysses

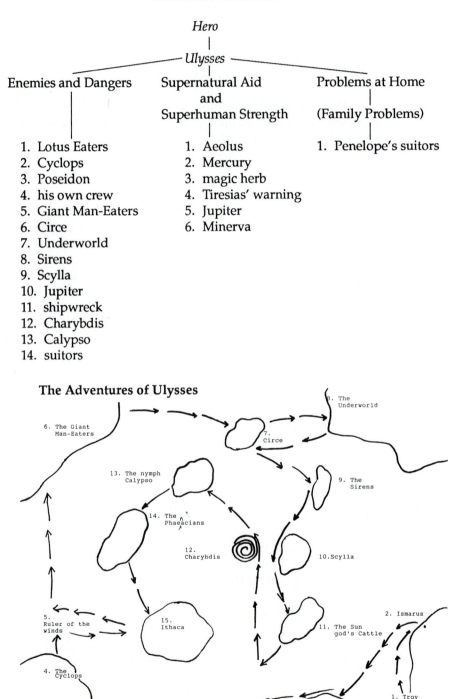

8. The Underworld
6. The Giant Man-Eaters
7. Circe
13. The nymph Calypso
9. The Sirens
14. The Phaeacians
12. Charybdis
10. Scylla
5. Ruler of the winds
15. Ithaca
2. Ismarus
11. The Sun god's Cattle
4. The Cyclops
1. Troy
3. The Lotus Eaters

Unit Lessons

CHAPTER ONE

Rationale
This is the first part of a seven-part story. It will be the first time the students are confronted with any Latin story that is over one page long. They need direction to work their way through his selection. Without it, they will translate words, try to work out the constructions, and end up with no meaning.

In this chapter, the vocabulary guide will present them with new and review vocabulary. By identifying the relationships among the words, they will develop an understanding of vocabulary they will be working with in this chapter. The organizing idea and three-level guide will help them obtain literal and implied meaning and relate it to their own experience. Levels two and three will involve them in reading at comprehension levels seldom, if ever reached while translating. The short reasoning/prediction exercise will allow them to draw conclusions from the information in this chapter, the map, and their own experience and will serve as an introduction to Chapter Two.

Content Objectives
Pupils will:

1. Understand the vocabulary necessary for reading this passage.
2. Understand that a hero's life is not easy.
    a. A hero faces enemies and danger.
    b. A hero needs supernatural aid.
    c. A hero faces family problems which threaten to be overwhelming.

Process Objectives
Pupils will:

1. Identify the relationship among words in a set by deleting words that don't fit and by describing the relationship among the others.
2. Read at the literal level to identify factual information given in a selection.
3. Read at the interpretive level to recognize ideas implied in a selection.
4. Read at the applied level to recognize, explain, and illustrate the application of ideas with respect to generalizations about the world of experience.
5. Use the information from the selection, a map, and their own experience to draw conclusions about, and to predict, a character's actions.

A Careless Shoestring

(Aeson was a king in Thessaly. His brother, Pelias, expelled him from his kingdom and even attempted to take the life of his son, Jason. However, Jason escaped, and he grew to manhood.)

Post breve tempus Pelias, veritus ne regnum suum tanta
vi et dolo occupatum amitteret, amicum quendam Delphos
misit, qui oraculum consuleret. Ille igitur quam celerrime
Delphos se contulit, et, quam ob causam venisset,
demonstravit. Respondit oraculum nullum esse in praesentia (5)
periculum; monuit tamen Peliam ut, si quis veniret calceum
unum gerens, eum caveret. Post paucos annos accidit ut
Pelias magnum sacrificium facturus esset; nuntios in omnes
partes dimiserat, et certam diem conveniendi dixerat. Die
constituta, magnus numerus hominum undique ex agris (10)
convenit; inter alios autem venit etiam Iason, qui a puero
apud <u>centaurum</u> quendam vixerat. Dum tamen iter facit,
calceum alterum in transeundo nescio quo flumine amisit.
Iason, igitur, cum calceum amissum nullo modo recipere
posset, uno pede nudo in regiam pervenit. Quem cum Pelias (15)
vidisset, subito timore affectus est; intellexit enim hunc
esse hominem, quem oraculum demonstravisset. Hoc igitur
iniit consilium. Rex erat quidam nomine Aeetes, qui regnum
<u>Colchidis</u> illo tempore obtinebat. Huic commissum erat
<u>vellus</u> illud aureum, quod Phrixus olim ibi reliquerat. (20)
Constituit igitur Pelias Iasoni negotium dare, ut hoc
vellere potiretur; cum enim res esset magni periculi,
sperabat eum in itinere periturum esse. Iasonem igitur ad
se arcessivit, et quid fieri vellet demonstravit. Iason,
autem, etsi bene intellegebat rem esse difficillimam, (25)
negotium libenter suscepit.

Line 12—**centaurus, -i,** m., centaur, a mythical creature, half-man and half-horse

Line 19—**Colchis, -idis,** f., Colchis, a province of Asia east of the Black Sea

Line 20—**vellus, velleris,** n., fleece

Note: Phrixus and Helle were the children of Athamas, king of Boeotia in Greece. Their stepmother planned to kill them, but through the aid of a god they escaped, riding through the air on a ram with golden fleece. Near the shore of Asia, Helle fell off and was drowned in the straits that still bear her name (Hellespont), but Phrixus reached Colchis in safety. Here he sacrificed the ram to Zeus and gave its fleece to Aeetes, who hung it up in the grove of Ares.

A Careless Shoestring (Translation for teachers)

(Aeson was a king in Thessaly. His brother, Pelias, expelled him from his kingdom and even attempted to take the life of this son, Jason. However, Jason escaped, and he grew to manhood.)

After a short time, Pelias, afraid that he would lose the kingdom he had seized by great force and treachery, sent a certain friend to Delphi to consult the oracle. Therefore, (his friend) proceeded as quickly as possible to Delphi and explained why he had come. The oracle responded that Pelias was in no danger at the present time; nevertheless, it warned Pelias to beware of anyone who came wearing one shoe. After a few years it so happened that Pelias was about to offer a great sacrifice; he had sent messengers into all parts, and he had appointed a certain day of assembling. On the appointed day, a great number of men assembled from all around the country; more-over, Jason, who had lived with a certain centaur from boyhood, also came along with the others. Nevertheless, while he was traveling, he lost his shoe while crossing some river or other.

Jason, therefore, since he was not able to recover his lost shoe, arrived at the palace with one bare foot. When Pelias had seen him, he was suddenly overcome with fear; for he knew that this was the man whom the oracle and foretold. Therefore, he formed this plan. There was a certain king named Aeetes who ruled at Colchis at that time. That golden fleece which Phrixus had left there had been entrusted to (Aeetes). Pelias, therefore, decided to give Jason the task of obtaining this fleece; for he hoped Jason would perish on the journey since this was a dangerous task. Therefore, he invited Jason to come to him, and showed him what he wanted. Jason, moreover, al-though he knew this was a very dangerous mission, willingly undertook the task.

Note: Phrixus and Helle were the children of Athamas, king of Boeotia in Greece. Their stepmother planned to kill them, but through the aid of a god they escaped, riding through the air on a ram with golden fleece. Near the shore of Asia, Helle fell off and was drowned in the straits that still bear her name (Hellespont), but Phrixus reached Colchis in safety. Here he sacrificed the ram to Zeus and gave its fleece to Aeetes, who hung it up in the grove of Ares.

Vocabulary Guide

A Careless Shoestring

Organizing idea: Evil men live in fear.

Directions: Work with your group. For each set of word or phrases below, cross out the word or phrase that does not belong with the others. In the space provided, describe how the three words or phrases you selected are related or why they belong together.

1. consilium	oraculum	timor	periculum
2. rex	regnum	regia	sacrificium
3. iter facere	se conferre	dimittere	pervenire
4. respondere	monere	demonstrare	consulere
5. vereri	cavere	timore affici	sperare
6. periculum intellegere	negotium suscipere	consilium inire	negotium dare
7. alterum calceum amitterre	uno pede nudo	unum calceum gerere	duobus pedibus nudis

1. _____

_____

2. _____

_____

3. _____

_____

4. _____

_____

5. _____

_____

6. _____

_____

7. _____

_____

Key for Vocabulary Guide

1. plan	oracle	fear	danger
2. king	kingdom	palace	sacrifice
3. to make a journey	to proceed	to send off	to arrive
4. to answer	to warn	to show	to consult
5. to fear	to beware	to be afflicted with fear	to hope
6. to understand the danger	to undertake the task	to form a plan	to give a task

7. to lose one	with one	to wear	with two
of two shoes	foot bare	one shoe	feet bare

A Careless Shoestring

Organizing idea: Evil men live in fear.

Part I (Levels of Comprehension)

Directions: Below you will find fifteen statements. With your group read each statement, and then look in the Latin passage to see whether it has the same information that is contained in the statement. Place a check on the numbered line if it does. The statement may be an exact translation, or it may use different words but say the same thing. Be ready to give reasons for your choices. The numbers in parentheses tell you at which line(s) in the passage you should look.

_____ 1. Pelias was afraid he would lose the kingdom he had seized by great force and treachery. (1–2)

_____ 2. Pelias sent a friend to Delphi. (2–3)

_____ 3. There was an oracle at Delphi. (2–3)

_____ 4. The friend was told that there was no danger at present. (5–6)

_____ 5. The warning stated that Pelias was to beware of anyone coming with one shoe. (6–7)

_____ 6. A few years passed; Pelias planned a great sacrifice; he invited men from everywhere. (7–11)

_____ 7. Jason, while traveling to the sacrifice, lost one shoe in some river. (11–13)

_____ 8. Jason arrived at the palace with one bare foot. (14–15)

_____ 9. When Pelias saw Jason, he was terrified. (15–16)

_____ 10. Pelias knew that Jason was the one about whom the oracle had warned. (16–17)

_____ 11. Pelias had a plan. (17–18)

_____ 12. Pelias wanted Jason to obtain the Golden Fleece from King Aeetes of Colchis. (18–22)

_____ 13. Pelias hoped Jason would die on the journey. (22–23)

_____ 14. Pelias summoned Jason to himself and asked him to undertake the mission. (23–24)

_____ 15. Jason refused this mission. (24–26)

Part II

Directions: Below you will find nine statements. With your group read each one, and think about how it relates to the information you discussed in Part I of this exercise. Place a check on the numbered line before each statement which expresses an idea you can find in the passage. Be ready to give reasons for your choices.

_____ 1. Pelias thought the Delphic oracle could give him some advice that would allow him to stay in power.

_____ 2. The Delphic oracle was known throughout Greece for its power to prophesy.

_____ 3. Since he was afraid, Pelias trusted no one.

_____ 4. The oracle was right that there was no present danger, and Pelias continued to carry out the day-to-day duties of a king.

_____ 5. Jason came wearing only one shoe because he knew the oracle's warning and he wanted to scare Pelias.

_____ 6. Pelias did not know that Jason was his nephew.

_____ 7. The king thought of a way to get rid of Jason before Jason could harm him.

_____ 8. Jason didn't suspect that Pelias had an ulterior motive for the quest he wanted Jason to undertake.

_____ 9. Jason was a brave man.

Part III

Directions: Below you will find four statements. With your group read each one. Place a check on the numbered line before each statement which you can support with ideas from the passage and with ideas from your own experience. Be ready to present evidence from both sources to support your decisions.

_____ 1. There is nothing to fear but fear itself.

_____ 2. Knowing what the future holds would make life a lot easier.

_____ 3. All is fair when you are trying to protect yourself.

_____ 4. A hero welcomes danger.

What Would You Do?

Now that you've read the first chapter of "Jason and the Argonauts," put yourself in his place and think about what you would do next. Make use of the attached map as you react to the following statements. Work with your group, and check each statement with which you agree. Be ready with reasons for your answers.

_____ 1. If I were Jason, I'd travel to Colchis by sea.

_____ 2. If I were Jason, I'd travel to Colchis by land.

_____ 3. If I were Jason, I'd go to Colchis alone.

_____ 4. If I were Jason, I'd find some companions to go with me.

_____ 5. If I were Jason, I'd want the bravest men in Greece to go to Colchis with me.

Now read the introduction to Chapter Two, and find out if Jason agreed with you!

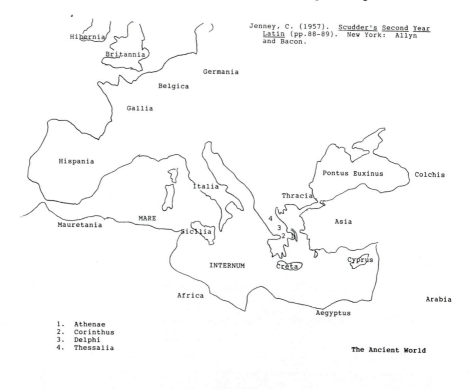

Jenney, C. (1957). <u>Scudder's Second Year Latin</u> (pp.88-89). New York: Allyn and Bacon.

1. Athenae
2. Corinthus
3. Delphi
4. Thessalia

The Ancient World

CHAPTER TWO

Rationale

This chapter is difficult because it contains two unrelated incidents in the Argonauts' journey. By analyzing pairs of words for similar or dissimilar meanings, students will be exposed to new and review words and/or phrases that are necessary to understand the text. The analysis will help the students remember the words when they encounter them in the text.

This passage contains many cause-and-effect relationships that will be best understood with the aid of an organizational patterns guide.

The word *nauta* is well-known to the students. Since *Argonauts* is used so frequently in this story and since it is so well analyzed right within the text, I have extended this analysis to other English words.

Content Objectives

Pupils will:

1. Understand that a hero's life is not easy.

    a. A hero continually comes up against enemies and dangers.

2. Know the meanings of the parts of the word *Argonaut*.

3. Understand that other English words are formed the same way as *Argonaut.*
4. Understand the vocabulary necessary to read the Latin passage.

Process Objectives
Pupils will:

1. Analyze pairs of words for similar or dissimilar meanings.
2. Read at the literal level to recognize stated causes and effects.
3. Read at the interpretive level to recognize implied causes and effects.
4. Read at the interpretive level to recognize ideas implied in a selection.
5. Read at the applied level to recognize, explain, and illustrate the application of ideas from the text to generalizations about the world of experience.
6. Analyze derivatives, and explain the relationship of their meanings to the Latin words from which they are derived.
7. Use a dictionary to define words and verify answers.

The Journey Begins

(Since Colchis was far away, Jason didn't want to travel alone, so he sent messengers to call heroes from all over Greece. Many came, and Jason chose fifty good men to accompany him. Among this number were Hercules, Orpheus, and Theseus. A ship was built and equipped by a skilled craftsman named Argus. When everything was completed, the ship was named the *Argo,* and it set sail.)

Haud multo post Argonautae (ita enim applellati sunt qui
in ista nave vehebantur) insulam quandam nomine Cyzicum
attigerunt, et e nave egressi, a rege illius regionis
hospitio excepti sunt. Paucas horas ibi commorati, ad solis
occasum rursus solverunt; at, postquam pauca milia passuum (5)
progresi sunt, tanta tempestas subito coorta est, ut cursum
tenere non possent, et in eandem partem insulae unde nuper
profecti erant, magno cum periculo deicerentur. Incolae
tamen, cum nox esset obscura, Argonautas non agnoscebant, et
navem inimicam venisse arbitrati, arma rapuerunt, et eos (10)
egredi prohibebant. Acriter in litore pugnatum est, et rex
ipse, qui cum aliis decucurrerat, ab Argonautis occisus est.
Mox, tamen, cum iam lux oriretur, senserunt incolae se
errare et arma abiecerunt; Argonautae autem, cum viderent
regem occisum esse, magnum dolorem perceperunt. (15)
    <u>Postridie eius diei</u> Iason, tempestatem satis idoneam
esse arbitratus (summa enim tranquillitas iam consecuta
erat), ancoras sustulit, et pauca milia passuum progressus,

ante noctem <u>Mysiam</u> attigit. Ibi paucas horas <u>in ancoris</u>
exspectavit; a nautis enim cognoverat aquae copiam, quam (20)
secum haberent, iam deficere; quam ob causam quidam ex
Argonautis, in terram egressi, aquam quaerebant. Horum in
numero erat Hylas quidam, puer forma praestantissima; qui
dum aquam aquaerit, a comitibus paulum secesserat. Nymphae
autem, quae rivum colebant, cum iuvenem vidissent, ei (25)
persuadere conatae sunt ut secum maneret; et <u>cum ille</u>
<u>negaret</u> se hoc facturum esse, puerum vi abstulerunt.
Comites eius postquam Hylam amissum esse senserunt,
magno dolore affecti, diu frustra quaerebant. Hercules
autem et <u>Polyphemus</u>, qui vestigia pueri longius secuti (30)
erant, ubi tandem ad litus redierunt, Iasonem solvisse
cognoverunt.

Line 16—**Postridie eius diei** = postero die

Line 19—**Mysiam**, Mysia, a country in northeastern Asia Minor

Line 19—**in ancoris**, at anchor

Line 26–27—**cum ille negaret**, when he said . . . not

Line 30—**Polyphemus**, one of the Argonauts

The Journey Begins (Translation for teachers)

(Since Colchis was far away, Jason didn't want to travel alone, so he sent messengers to call heroes from all over Greece. Many came, and Jason chose fifty good men to accompany him. Among this number were Hercules, Orpheus, and Theseus. A ship was built and equipped by a skilled craftsman named Argus. When everything was completed, the ship was named the *Argo*, and it set sail.)

Not much later, the Argonauts (for those who sailed in that ship were so called) reached a certain island named Cyzicus, and, having disembarked, they were received with hospitality by the king of that region. Having delayed there a few hours, they set sail again at sunset; but, after progressing a few miles, so great a storm suddenly arose that they were not able to hold their course, and they were forced back with great danger onto the same part of the island from which they had recently set out. The inhabitants, however, since it was a dark night, didn't recognize the Argonauts, and, thinking that an enemy ship had arrived, they seized their weapons and kept them from disembarking. A fierce battle was fought on shore, and the king himself, who had run out with the others, was killed by the Argonauts. Soon, nevertheless, since it was light, the inhabitants realized their error and threw down their weapons; the Argonauts, however, when they saw that the king had been killed, felt great grief.

The following day, Jason, thinking the weather was suitable enough (for a very great calm had already followed), raised anchor and, having progressed a few miles, reached Mysia before night. There he waited at anchor for a few hours, for he had learned from the sailors that the water supply which they had with them was already low; therefore, some of the Argonauts disembarked and sought water. There was in this number a certain Hylas, a very handsome lad; while he was seeking water, he had separated a little from his comrades. Moreover, when the river nymphs had seen the youth, they tried to persuade him to stay with them; and when he said he wouldn't do this, they took him by force.

After his comrades realized he had been lost, they were seized with great grief and they searched for a long time in vain. Moreover, when Hercules and Polyphemus, who had followed the boy's footprints for a long time, finally returned to the shore, they learned that Jason had set sail.

Vocabulary Guide

The Journey Begins

Organizing idea: The loss of a friend is always hard to bear.

Directions: Read each of the following pairs of words or phrases. Decide whether they have meanings that are similar or different. If they are similar, write "similar" in the blank; if they are different, write "different." Be ready to give reasons for your decisions. Use your Latin dictionary if necessary. Work with your group.

_____ 1. e nave egredi/navem solvere

_____ 2. hospitio excipere/prohibere

_____ 3. proficisci/deici

_____ 4. agnoscere/sentire

_____ 5. comes/inimicus

_____ 6. tranquillitas/tempestas

_____ 7. in ancoris exspectare/navem solvere

_____ 8. quaerere/sequi

_____ 9. abicere/rapere

_____ 10. commorari/progredi

Key for Vocabulary Guide

1. to disembark/to set sail
2. to welcome/to prohibit
3. to set out/to be thrown back
4. to recognize/to realize
5. comrade/enemy

6. calm/storm
7. to wait at anchor/to set sail
8. to look for/to follow
9. to throw down/to seize
10. to delay/to set out

Organizational Patterns Guide

The Journey Begins

Organizing idea: The loss of a friend is always hard to bear.

Part I

Directions: On each line below there are two words or phrases that are separated by a slanted line. Place a check on the line before each cause-and-effect relationship that you can support based on ideas from the story. Work with your group, and be sure everyone in your group is in agreement. The numbers in parentheses tell you at which line(s) in the story you should look for your answer.

_____ 1. sailing on the Argo/Argonauts (1–2)
_____ 2. hospitality/few hours delay (3–4)
_____ 3. storm/return (6–8)
_____ 4. night/misunderstanding (8–11)
_____ 5. hatred/war (8–11)
_____ 6. death/grief (12–15)
_____ 7. great calm/raised anchors (16–18)
_____ 8. need/search party (19–22)
_____ 9. attractiveness/attraction (22–26)
_____ 10. refusal/abduction (26–27)
_____ 11. missing friend/search (28–29)
_____ 12. prolonged search/abandonment (30–32)

Part II

Directions: Place a check in front of each statement below that you can support from the story and from your own ideas and experiences. Work with your group, and be ready to give the reasons for your choices.

_____ 1. In ancient times every stranger was an enemy.
_____ 2. A ship is at the mercy of the sea.
_____ 3. Things are not always what they seem to be.
_____ 4. When in doubt, shoot first and ask questions later.
_____ 5. A misunderstanding can lead to great grief.
_____ 6. As long as you are doing what you are supposed to be doing, you can't get into any trouble.
_____ 7. Physical attractiveness is always an asset.

_____ 8. A friend wants to help when you are in trouble.
_____ 9. You can lose sight of a goal during a crisis.
_____ 10. Life must go on.

The 3 "Nauts" (Word Derivations)

Directions: Work with your group to complete the following exercise.

We have seen in this chapter that Argonauts was the name given to Jason and his companions because they sailed on the Argo. *Argonaut* is derived from two Latin words:

1. *Argo,* name of the ship
2. nauta, sailor

In addition to Argonaut, there are two other "naut" words in English. For each of these, find the second Latin word from which it is derived and write that word in the blank below. (Be careful; number 2 is tricky!) Use your Latin dictionary if necessary.

1. aquanaut,_____+ *nauta*
2. astronaut,_____+ *nauta*

Now use an English dictionary to define each of these English words on the lines below. Be ready to explain how the Latin and English meanings are related.

1. aquanaut _____
_____
2. astronaut _____
_____

CHAPTER THREE

Rationale

The vocabulary guide will reinforce meanings of review vocabulary and present new vocabulary necessary to the passage. By finding the form of each word that occurs in the story, the students will be applying their knowledge of stems, cases, and forms, and they will already be starting to translate and read the passage.

An anticipation guide is used for this passage because it contains many ideas the students can relate to, both from their knowledge of Latin (gods, heroes) and from their own experience (rewards, procrastination, and so forth.).

A word-building vocabulary guide used *ferre*, a review verb with irregular principal parts and conjugation, and its compounds, many of which are found in this chapter. This guide will prepare students for translating *ferre*, its compounds, and other compounds that employ the same prefixes when they are used in future chapters.

CONTENT OBJECTIVES

Pupils will:

1. Understand the vocabulary necessary for reading the latin passage.
2. Understand that a hero's life is not easy.

   a. A hero continually comes up against enemies and dangers.
   b. A hero needs supernatural aid.

3. Know the principal parts of *ferre* and its compounds.
4. Know the meanings of *ferre* and its compounds.
5. Know the meanings of Latin prefixes.

Process Objectives

Pupils will:

1. Match Latin words and their meanings.
2. Identify forms of words in context.
3. Use a dictionary to verify answers.
4. Set purposes for reading.
5. Use their own experience and related knowledge as a context for reading new material.
6. Explain the effect of a prefix on the meaning of a compound verb.
7. Build compound verbs by adding prefixes to a verb.

Facing the Harpies and the Symplegades

(The Argonauts arrived at Thrace where they found that blind King Phineus had been punished by Jupiter for his cruelty toward his sons. Every time he reclined to eat, Harpies, monsters with the bodies of birds and the heads of women, stole his food. He was nearly dying of hunger.)

Res igitur in hoc loco erant, cum Argonautae navem
appulerunt. Phineus autem simul atque audivit eos in suos
fines egressos esse, magnopere gavisus est. Sciebat enim
quantam opinionem virtutis Argonautae haberent, nec
dubitabat quin sibi auxilium ferrent. Nuntium igitur ad (5)
navem misit, qui Iasonem sociosque ad regiam vocaret. Eo
cum venissent, Phineus demonstravit quanto in periculo suae
res essent, et promisit se magna praemia daturum esse, si

illi ei rei auxilium repperissent. Argonautae negotium
libenter susceperunt, et ubi hora venit, cum rege (10)
accubuerunt; at simul ac cena apposita est Harpyiae domum
intraverunt, et cibum auferre conabantur. Argonautae primum
gladiis volucres petierunt; cum tamen viderent hoc nihil
prodesse, <u>Zetes</u> et <u>Calais</u>, qui alis instructi sunt, in aera
se <u>sublevaverunt</u>, ut <u>desuper</u> impetum facerent. Quod cum (15)
sensissent Harpyiae, re novitate perterritae statim
aufugerunt, neque postea umquam redierunt.

    Hoc facto, Phineus, ut pro tanto beneficio meritam
<u>gratiam referret</u>, Iasoni demonstravit, qua ratione
Symplegades vitare posset. Symplegades autem duae erant (20)
<u>rupes</u> ingenti magnitudine, quae a Iove in mari positae erant
eo consilio, ne quis ad Colchida perveniret. Hae <u>parvo</u>
<u>intervallo</u> <u>natabant</u> et si quid in medium spatium venerat,
incredibili celeritate concurrebant. Postquam igitur a
Phineo doctus est, quid faciendum esset, Iason sublatis (25)
ancoris navem solvit, et <u>leni</u> vento provectus, mox ad
Symplegades appropinquavit. Tum in <u>prora</u> stans, <u>columbam,</u>
quam in manu tenebat, emisit. Illa <u>recta via</u> per medium
spatium volavit et, priusquam rupes conflixerunt, incolumis
evasit, <u>cauda</u> <u>tantum</u> amissa. Tum rupes utrimque (30)
discesserunt: antequam tamen rursus <u>concurrerent,</u>
Argonautae, bene intellegentes omnem spem salutis <u>in</u>
celeritate <u>positam esse,</u> summa vi remis contenderunt, et
navem incolumem perduxerunt. Hoc facto, dis <u>gratias</u>
libenter <u>egerunt</u>, quorum auxilio e tanto periculo erepti essent; bene
enim sciebant non sine deorum rem ita feliciter (35)
evenisse.

Line 1—**loco** – condition

Line 2—**simul atque** – as soon as

Line 3—**gaudeo, -ere, gavisus** – rejoice

Line 14—**Zetes** and **Calais** were winged youths, sons of the North
Wind, Boreas

Line 15—**sublevo, -are**, raise, lift

Line 15—**desuper** – down from above

Line 19—**gratiam referret** – show gratitude, make return

Line 21—**rupes, -is**, f., rock

Lines 22–23—**parvo intervallo** – a short distance apart

Line 23—**nato, -are**, swim, float

Line 26—**lenis, -e**, gentle, light

Line 27—**prora, -ae**, f., prow, bow

Line 27—**columba, -ae**, f., dove

Line 28—**recta via**, straight

Line 30—**cauda, -ae**, f., tail
Line 30—**tantum**, only
Line 31—**concurrerent**, they could rush together
Lines 32–33—**in . . . positam esse**, depended upon
Lines 34–35—**gratias . . . agere**, to give thanks

Facing the Harpie and the Symplegades (Translation for teachers)

(The Argonauts arrived at Thrace where they found that blind King Phineus had been punished by Jupiter for his cruelty toward his sons. Every time he reclined to eat, Harpies, monsters with the bodies of birds and the heads of women, stole his food. He was nearly dying of hunger.)

Such were the circumstances in this place when the Argonauts landed. Moreover, as soon as Phineus heard that they had come into his territory, he greatly rejoiced. For he knew how great a reputation the Argonauts had for courage, and he was sure that they could help him. Therefore, he sent a messenger to the ship to call Jason and his comrades to the palace. When they had arrived, Phineus showed the dangerous situation he was in, and he promised that he would give them great rewards if they would help him in this matter. The Argonauts willingly undertook the task, and when the time came, they reclined with the king; and as soon as the meal was served, the Harpies entered the house and began to steal the food. The Argonauts at first attacked the birds with swords; nevertheless, when they saw that this was to no avail, Zetes and Calais, who were equipped with wings, lifted themselves into the air, and made an attack from above. When the Harpies realized this, they immediately fled because they were terrified by the unusual attack. They never again returned.

After this was done, Phineus, in order to show his gratitude to Jason for such a great service, told Jason how he might be able to avoid the Symplegades. The Symplegades were two huge rocks which had been placed in the sea by Jupiter lest anyone reach Colchis. They floated a short distance apart, and if anything came between them, they rushed together with incredible speed. Therefore, after he had been told by Phineus what must be done, Jason raised anchor and set sail, and driven by a gentle wind, soon approached the Symplegades. Then, standing in the prow, he let go a dove which he held in this hand. The dove flew straight through the middle of the space, and before the rocks crashed together, escaped unharmed except for her tail. Then the rocks moved apart to their original positions; however, before they could again rush together, the Argonauts, knowing well that all hope of safety lay in speed, rowed with very great strength and brought the ship safely through. After this, they willingly gave thanks to the gods, whose aid had snatched them from such great danger; for they knew well that this had not happened without the gods' help.

Vocabulary Guide

Facing the Harpies and the Symplegades

Organizing idea: Danger takes many forms.

Directions: Choose the meaning of each of the following words from the list below, and write it on the line in Column I. Use your dictionary, if necessary. Then return to Chapter Three, "Facing the Harpies and the Symplegades," and find the form of the word that occurs in the story. Write this form on the line in Column II. Work with your group. Be ready to explain your answers.

	Column I	Column II
appellere	_____	_____
gaudere	_____	_____
praemium	_____	_____
ferre	_____	_____
suscipere	_____	_____
auferre	_____	_____
novitas	_____	_____
referre	_____	_____
ratio	_____	_____
tollere	_____	_____
provehere	_____	_____
stare	_____	_____
emittere	_____	_____
confligere	_____	_____
remus	_____	_____
eripere	_____	_____

reward	novelty, newness	oar
to dash together	to undertake	to bring, carry
to carry away	to send out	to carry forward
to rejoice		to bring back
to raise	to stand	to snatch, rescue
method	to land	

Key for Vocabulary Guide

Organizing idea: Danger takes many forms.

Directions: Choose the meaning of each of the following words from the list below, and write it on the line in Column I. Use your dictionary, if necessary. Then return to Chapter Three, "Facing the Harpies and the Symplegades," and find the form of the word that occurs in the story. Write this form on the line in Column II. Work with your group. Be ready to explain your answers.

	Column I	Column II
appellere	to land	appulernut
gaudere	to rejoice	gavisus est
praemium	reward	praemia
ferre	to bring, carry	ferrent
suscipere	to undertake	susceperunt
auferre	to carry away	auferre
novitas	novelty, newness	novitate
referre	to bring back	referret
ratio	method	ratione
tollere	to raise	sublatis
provehere	to carry forward	provectus
stare	to stand	stans
emittere	to send out	emisit
configere	to dash together	conflixerunt
remus	oar	remis
eripere	to snatch, rescue	erepti essent

Anticipation Guide

Facing the Harpies and the Symplegades

Organizing idea: Danger takes on many forms.

Directions: Below you will find seven statements. With your group discuss each statement related to the organizing idea above, and decide together whether you agree with it on the basis of your own knowledge and experience. Place a check on the first line if you agree with the statement. Be able to support your decision with evidence. The read "Facing the Harpies and the Symplegades" to see if the author agrees with you. If he does, place a check on the second line.

_____   _____ 1. No man deserves to die for his crimes.

_____   _____ 2. A hero can defeat any enemy.

_____   _____ 3. The promise of a reward tempts men to undertake dangerous tasks.

_____   _____ 4. Strength always determines the outcome of a battle.

_____   _____ 5. Gold (money) is the only reward worth risking your life for.

_____   _____ 6. It's best to put off facing danger for as long as possible.

_____   _____ 7. It is impossible to overcome obstacles devised by the gods.

The *Ferre* Tree

The verb *ferre* has many compounds. On the tree you will find the compounds that are used in "Jason and the Argonauts." With your group fill in the meanings of each of the listed verbs. Use your Latin dictionary if necessary.

Prefixes

ab (a, abs)—away from
ad—to, toward, near
ambi—both, around
ante—before
bene—well
bi—two, twice
circum—around
con (co, com)—with, together, deeply, completely
contra—against
de—down, from
dis (di)—apart, away
ex (e)—out
extra—outside, beyond
in—in, on, upon, into
in—not, without
inter—between
intra (intro)—within, inside

male—badly
non—not
ob—against, toward
per—through, thoroughly, very
post—after, behind
prae—ahead, before, very
praeter—by, beyond
pro—forth
quadri (quadru, quadr)—four
re (red)—back
retro—backward, back
se (sed)—apart, away
semi—half
sub (sus)—under, up from under
super—over, beyond
trans (tra)—across, over
tri—three

In the spaces below, write the principal parts of each of the verbs. Then tell which of the above prefixes was added to *ferre* to form the compound. Be ready to explain how the addition of the prefix affected the meaning of *ferre*. Use your Latin dictionary if necessary. Work with your group.

ferre, tuli, latus—to bring, bear, carry

1. sufferre _____

   _____

2. auferre _____

   _____

3. conferre _____

   _____

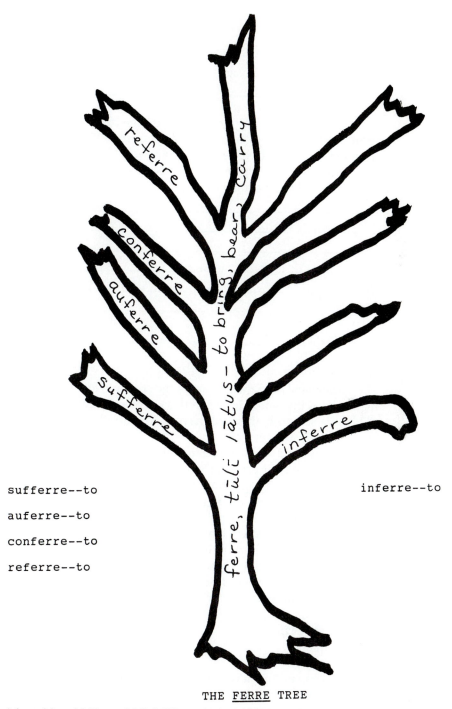

sufferre--to

auferre--to

conferre--to

referre--to

inferre--to

THE <u>FERRE</u> TREE

Adapted from McKenna, M. B. (1959) *Successful Devices in Teaching Latin*. Portland, ME: J. Weston Walch, p. 115.

4. referre _____

_____

5. inferre _____

_____

There are three empty branches on the tree. Using the list of prefixes, form compounds of *ferre* to complete your tree. Then write the verb and its meaning beside the tree. Verify your answers by checking your Latin dictionary. Work with your group. Be ready to explain how the addition of the prefix affected the meaning of *ferre*.

1. _____

_____

2. _____

_____

3. _____

_____

CHAPTER FOUR

Rationale

The vocabulary guide will prepare the students for the reading by presenting many of the words found in this chapter. By choosing the correct word to finish a sentence, they will have to identify the meaning since all words are grammatically correct.

The applied level of the three-level guide is presented first to allow students to use their previous knowledge and world experience as a context for reading. This passage contains a detailed account of Jason's ultimate test which is important to the students' understanding of how he fits the description of a hero. The literal and interpretive levels, which follow, will lead the students through this material and also help them understand the importance of Medea's part in the hero's victory.

The writing exercise based on the guide will help the students compare their own ideas to the author's ideas and will help them review either Medea's role and character or the unit organizing idea.

Content Objectives

Pupils will:

1. Understand that a hero's life is not easy.
   a. A hero continually comes up against enemies and dangers.
   b. A hero needs supernatural aid and superhuman strength to complete tasks.

2. Understand Medea's role in the hero's life.
3. Understand the vocabulary necessary for reading the Latin passage.

Process Objectives
Pupils will:

1. Determine the correct word to complete a sentence by examining the context of the sentence.
2. Use a dictionary to define and verify definitions of words.
3. Use their previous knowledge and experience as a context for reading new material.
4. Read at the literal level to identify factual information given in a selection,
5. Read at the interpretive level to recognize ideas implied in a selection.
6. Apply knowledge gained from the text to generalizations about the world of experience.

Vocabulary Guide

Sowing the Dragon's Teeth

Organizing idea: Every hero must face the ultimate test.

Directions: With your group select the Latin word(s) in parentheses that best completes each of the following sentences, and write the answer in the blank. Use your dictionary, if necessary, and be ready to give reasons for your answers.

_____ 1. It is necessary for a farmer (arare, edicere, aperire, includere) before planting.

_____ 2. The best time for an early bird to get started is (ante meridiem, sub vesperum, orta luce).

_____ 3. The man (traxit, repperit, imposuit, vidit) the heavy crate into the yard.

_____ 4. When he saw the unusal happening, the king (miratus est, praebuit, confecit, accepit).

_____ 5. Once he knew the steps he had to take, he immediately (coepit, nesciebat, sparsit) to do the work.

_____ 6. When you are tired, it's best to take time for a (dentem, draconem, quietem, galeum).

_____ 7. If he is the only volunteer, he has to do it (solus, subito, armatus, mirus).

_____ 8. A giant is by nature (ingens, reliquus, hic, nullus).

_____ 9. It's best to fight with swords (coniectis, strictis, apertis).

_____ 10. When the bomb fell on the city, many (praedicti sunt, orti sunt, occisi sunt).

Key for Vocabulary Guide

arare—to plow

1. It is necessary for a farmer (arare, edicere, aperire, includere) before planting.

orta luce—at dawn

2. The best time for an early bird to get started is (ante meridiem, sub vesperum, orta luce).

traxit—dragged

3. The man (traxit, repperit, imposuit, vidit) the heavy crate into the yard.

miratus est—wondered

4. When he saw the unusal happening, the king (miratus est, praebuilt, confecit, accepit).

coepit—began

5. Once he knew the steps he had to take, he immediately (coepit, nesciebat, sparsit) to do the work.

quietem—rest

6. When you are tired, it's best to take time for a (dentem, draconem, quietem, galeum).

solus—alone

7. If he is the only volunteer, he has to do it (solus, subito, armatus, mirus).

ingens—huge

8. A giant is by nature (ingens, reliquus, hic, nullus).

strictis—drawn

9. It's best to fight with swords (coniectis, strictis, apertis).

occisi sunt—were killed

10. When the bomb fell on the city, many (praedicti sunt, orti sunt, occisi sunt).

Sowing the Dragon's Teeth

(The Argonauts landed at Colchis and demanded the fleece from King Aeetes. He at first refused and then realized that Jason must have had the aid of the gods to arrive there. So, the king imposed labors which Jason had to complete in order to obtain the fleece: he must yoke two fire-breathing bulls and plow the field with them; he must sow dragon's teeth in this field. Medea, the king's daughter, fell in love with Jason and decided to use her magical powers to save him from certain death. She prepared a magic ointment for his protection and gave him some unusual advice.)

Ubi is dies venit, quem rex ad arandum agrum edixerat,
Iason, orta luce, cum sociis ad locum constitutum se
contulit. Ibi stabulum ingens repperit, in quo tauri
inclusi erant; tum, portis apertis, tauros in lucem traxit,
et cum summa difficultate iugum imposuit. At Aeetes, cum (5)
videret tauros nihil contra Iasonem valere, magnopere miratus est;
nesciebat enim filiam suam auxilium ei dedisse. Tum Iason,
omibus aspicientibus, agrum arare coepit; qua in re tantam
diligentiam praebuit, ut ante meridiem totum opus
confecerit. Hoc facto, ad locum, ubi rex sedebat, adiit, et (10)
dentes draconis postulavit; quos ubi accepit, in agrum quem
araverat, magna cum diligentia sparsit. Horum autem dentium
natura erat talis, ut in eo loco, ubi sparsi essent, viri
armati miro quodam modo gignerentur.

Nondum tamen Iason totum opus confecerat; imperaverat (15)
enim ei Aeetes, ut armatos viros, qui e dentibus
gignerentur, solus interficeret. Postquam igitur omnes
dentes in agrum sparsit, Iason, lassitudine exanimatus,
quieti se tradidit, dum viri isti gignerentur. Paucas horas
dormiebat; sub vesperum tamen e somno subito excitatus, rem (20)
ita evenisse ut praedictum erat, cognovit; nam in omnibus
agri partibus viri ingenti magnitudine corporis, gladiis
galeisque armati, mirum in modum e terra oriebantur. Hoc
cognito, Iason consilium, quod Medea dedisset, non
omittendum esse putabat; saxum igitur ingens (ita enim Medea (25)
praeceperat) in medios viros coniecit. Illi undique ad
locum concurrerunt, et, cum quisque sibi id saxum (nescio
cur) habere vellet, magna controversia orta est. Mox,
strictis gladiis, inter se pugnare coeperunt, et cum hoc
modo plurimi occisi essent, reliqui, vulneribus confecti, a (30)
Iasone nullo negotio interfecti sunt.

Line 12—sparsit—spargo, -ere, sparsi, sparsus, scatter

Line 14—gignerentur—gigno, -ere, genui, genitus, produce

Line 18—lassitudo, -inis, f., weariness

Line 18—exanimo, -are, exhaust

Sowing the Dragon's Teeth (Translation for teachers)

(The Argonauts landed at Colchis and demanded the fleece from King Aeetes. He at first refused and then realized that Jason must have had the aid of the gods to arrive there. So, the king imposed labors which Jason had to complete in order to obtain the fleece: he must yoke two fire-breathing bulls and plow the field with them; he must sow dragon's teeth in this field.

Medea, the king's daughter, fell in love with Jason and decided to use her magical powers to save him from certain death. She prepared a magic ointment for his protection and gave him some unusual advice.)

When the day which the king had set for plowing the field arrived, Jason went at dawn with his comrades to the appointed place. There he found a huge stable in which the bulls had been shut; then, after opening the doors, he dragged the bulls out into the light, and, with the greatest difficulty, he yoked them. But Aeetes, when he saw that the bulls were not able to prevail against Jason, greatly wondered; for he was not aware that his daughter had given him aid. Then Jason, with everybody watching, began to plow the field; he showed so much diligence in this that he accomplished the whole thing before noon. This done, he approached the place where the king was sitting and demanded the dragon's teeth; when he received them, he scattered them in the field which he had plowed with such diligence. The nature of these teeth was such that wherever they had been scattered, armed men were produced in some miraculous manner.

Nevertheless, Jason had not yet finished the whole task; for Aeetes had ordered him to kill by himself all the armed men who were produced from the teeth. Therefore, after he scattered all the teeth in the field, Jason, exhausted, rested while those men were being produced. He slept for a few hours; just before evening he was suddenly roused from his sleep, and he knew that things had happened as predicted; for in all parts of the field, huge men, armed with swords and helmet, arose in a miraculous way from the earth. When he saw this, Jason thought that the plan which Medea had given him ought not be disregarded; therefore, he threw a huge stone (for so had Medea directed) into the midst of the men. They ran from all sides to the place, and since each wished to have the stone for himself (who knows why?), a great argument arose. Soon, with swords drawn, they began to fight among themselves, and when most had been killed in this manner, the rest, worn out by their wounds, were killed by Jason with no trouble.

Three-Level Guide

Sowing the Dragon's Teeth

Organizing idea: Every hero must face the ultimate test.

Applied Level

*Directions:*Below you will find five statements. With your group discuss each statement as it relates to the organizing idea above, and decide together whether you agree with it on the basis of your own knowledge and experience. Place a check on the line if you agree with the statement. Be able to support your decision with evidence from your knowledge and experience.

_____ 1. A hero must face a challenge alone.
_____ 2. Nothing is impossible.

_____ 3. Behind every great man there is a great woman.
_____ 4. A hero must not resort to trickery or treachery to gain the prize.
_____ 5. Blood is thicker than water.

Literal Level

Directions: Below you will find fifteen statements. With your group reach each statement, and then look in the Latin passage from Chapter Four to see if it has the same information that is contained in the statement. Place a check on the numbered line if it does so. The statement may be an exact translation, or it may use different words but say the same thing. Be ready to give reasons for your choices. The numbers in parentheses tell you at which paragraph in the passage you should look.

_____ 1. At dawn Jason went to the place appointed for his tasks. (1)
_____ 2. Jason went alone to the field. (1)
_____ 3. Jason had to drag the bulls out of a huge stable. (1)
_____ 4. Jason yoked the bulls with great difficulty. (1)
_____ 5. Aeetes was amazed that Jason was able to perform the first of his tasks. (1)
_____ 6. Aeetes did not know that his daughter had aided Jason. (1)
_____ 7. Jason plowed the field with such diligence that he was done before noon. (1)
_____ 8. Jason demanded the dragon's teeth from the king. (1)
_____ 9. Jason sowed the field with the dragon's teeth. (1)
_____ 10. Jason was exhausted when the first three tasks were done. (2)
_____ 11. Jason took a nap while the dragon's teeth were producing their crop. (2)
_____ 12. Huge armed men arose from the dragon's teeth that Jason had planted. (2)
_____ 13. Medea had told Jason to throw a huge stone in the midst of the armed men. (2)
_____ 14. The armed men argued over possession of the huge stone. (2)
_____ 15. The armed men fought each other until all were dead. (2)

Interpretive Level

Directions: Below you will find eight statements. With your group read each one, and think about how it relates to the information you discussed in the Literal Level of this exercise. Place a check on the numbered line before each statement that expresses an idea you can find in the passage. Be ready to give reasons for your choices.

_____ 1. The Argonauts showed support for their leader.
_____ 2. Jason was a man of great physical strength.

_____ 3. Aeetes never expected Jason to be alive to plow the field or sow the dragon's teeth.

_____ 4. The second and third tasks were not as dangerous as the first.

_____ 5. Jason would not have been able to complete his test if he had not been able to sleep for a few hours.

_____ 6. Medea had betrayed her father.

_____ 7. The armed men were invincible because of their great size and intelligence.

_____ 8. Jason completed all the tasks Aeetes had given him, but he couldn't have done them without Medea's help.

Now go back to the Applied Level that you completed before reading "Sowing the Dragon's Teeth" and choose one of the five statements. Write a paragraph about this statement in which you tell what the author would think about it. Support your ideas with facts from the story. Write your paragraph on the back of this paper.

_____   **CHAPTER FIVE**   _____

Rationale

Chapter Five contains so many examples of indirect statement that it lends itself to a grammar lesson on this difficult construction.

The structured overview and organizing idea will help students compare two important uses of the infinitive so that they can recognize indirect statements. The two uses are neatly and concisely compared in the overview.

The three-level grammar guide helps the students review indirect statement from the ground up by analyzing the facts, implying syntax from the facts, and finally coming up with the rules which they would then summarize by completing the overview.

These strategies are perfect for reviewing this difficult construction before attempting the translation. The guide elicits the needed information, and the overview organizes it for future use.

The lesson closes with a look at the next lesson to find examples of this construction. This will allow the students to practice recognition and translation of indirect statement in the context of a paragraph.

Content Objectives

Pupils will:

1. Compare two uses of the infinitive.
2. Recognize cases and meanings of nouns, and tenses, voices, moods, and meanings of verbs.

3. Recognize indirect statement in context.
4. Translate indirect statement.

Process Objectives

Pupils will:

1. Use a structured overview to review two uses of the infinitive.
2. Read a Latin sentence at the literal level to identify cases and meanings of nouns, and tenses, moods, voices, and meanings of verbs.
3. Read a Latin sentence at the interpretive level to identify constructions, agreement, and relationships between words.
4. Read a Latin sentence at the applied level to recognize grammatical rules illustrated by the sentence.
5. Use a structured overview to analyze Latin construction before translation.

Three-Level Grammar Guide

Medea's Choice

Organizing idea: An infinitive is not always translated with *to* plus the meaning of the verb.

Literal Level

Directions: Work with your group. Check all items that correctly identify forms or meanings contained in the displayed sentence below. Be ready to explain your answers.

> At rex Aeetes, ubi cognovit Iasonem laborem propositum confecisse, ira graviter commotus est.

_____ 1. *Rex Aeetes* is nominative singular.
_____ 2. *Ubi . . . confecisse* is a subordinate clause.
_____ 3. *Ira* is ablative.
_____ 4. *Graviter* is an adverb.
_____ 5. *Commotus est* is third person singular, perfect passive indicative.
_____ 6. *Commotus* is masculine singular nominative.
_____ 7. *Ubi* can mean "where" or "when."
_____ 8. *Cognovit* is perfect active indicative, third person singular.
_____ 9. *Iasonem* is accusative.
_____ 10. *Laborem* is accusative.
_____ 11. *Propositum* is accusative singular feminine.
_____ 12. *Confecisse* is a perfect active infinitive.

Interpretive Level

Directions: Work with your group. Check all items that correctly identify the syntax of the displayed sentence above. Be ready to explain your answers.

_____ 1. *Rex Aeetes* is the subject of the sentence.
_____ 2. The subject of *cognovit* is an implied "he."
_____ 3. *Commotus* agrees with *Aeetes*.
_____ 4. *Commotus est* is the main verb.
_____ 5. *Ira* is an ablative of cause.
_____ 6. *Cognovit* introduces an indirect statement.
_____ 7. *Iasonem* is modified by *propositum*.
_____ 8. *Laborem* is modified by *propositum*.
_____ 9. *Iasonem* is the subject of the infinitive *confecisse*.
_____ 10. *Laborem* is the object of the infinitive *confecisse*.
_____ 11. *Confecisse* denotes time before *cognovit*.
_____ 12. *Confecisse* denotes the same time as *cognovit*.
_____ 13. *Confecisse* denotes time after *cognovit*.

Applied Level

Directions: Work with your group. Check all items that identify ideas about indirect statement that are suggested by the displayed sentence above.

_____ 1. Verbs of mental action and the senses generally introduce an indirect statement.
_____ 2. In Latin the verb in an indirect statement is an infinitive.
_____ 3. The subject of an indirect statement is in the nominative.
_____ 4. An indirect statement can contain a direct object in the accusative case.
_____ 5. The verb in the indirect statement expresses time in relation to the main verb.

Medea's Choice

At rex Aeetes **ubi cognovit Iasonem laborem propositum confecisse**, ira graviter commotus est; **intellegebat enim id
per dolum factum esse**, nec dubitabat quin Medea auxilium ei tulisset. Medea autem, **cum intellegeret se in magno futuram
esse periculo**, si in regia mansisset, fuga salutem petere (5) constituit. Omnibus igitur rebus ad fugam paratis, media
nocte, insciente patre, cum fratre Absyrto evasit, et quam celerrime ad locum, ubi argo subducta erat, se contulit. Eo cum
venisset, ad pedes Iasonis se proiecit et multis cum lacrimis obsecravit eum, ne in tanto periculo mulierem
dessereret, quae ei tantum profuisset. Ille, **quod memoria** (10) **tenebat se per eius auxilium e magno periculo evasisse**,
libenter eam excepit, et postquam causam veniendi audivit, hortatus est ne patrem timeret. **Promisit autem se quam
primum eam in nave sua ablaturum esse.**

Line 9—**lacrima, -ae,** f., tear

Line 9—**obsecro,** -are, beseech

(*Note:* At this point we will complete the structured overview, using information from the Applied Level.)

Now let's translate "Medea's Choice" together. You will notice that certain phrases are in darker type. These contain indirect statements. As we work through them we will refer to the structured overview for help.

Medea's Choice (Translation for teachers)

But King Aeetes, when he learned that Jason had accomplished the task he had proposed, was very angry; for he knew that this had been done through treachery, and he did not doubt that Medea had given Jason help. Medea, moreover, when she learned that she would be in great danger if she remained at the palace, decided to seek safety by flight. Therefore, she prepared all things for her escape, and in the middle of the night, without her father's knowledge, left with her brother Absyrtus and went as quickly as possible to the place where the Argo had docked. When she had come there, she threw herself at Jason's feet and beseeched him with many tears not to leave the woman who had given him so much help in so much danger. Jason, because he remembered that he had escaped great danger through her help, willingly received her, and after he heard the reason for her coming, he urged her not to fear her father. Moreover, he promised that he would take her away on the ship as soon as possible.

Using What You Know

In Chapter Six, "The Death of Pelias," there are four examples of indirect statement. With your group choose two, and write them on the lines below.

1. _____

_____

_____

2. _____

_____

_____

Escape from Colchis—A Summary

Medea led Jason to the grove where the fleece was hidden and used her magic arts to put to sleep the dragon that guarded it. They boarded the *Argo* and set sail. Aeetes pursued them. When he had almost caught up with them, Medea murdered her brother Absyrtus and cut his body up into pieces which she threw overboard. Aeetes stopped to gather up the pieces of his son's body, and the Argo escaped.

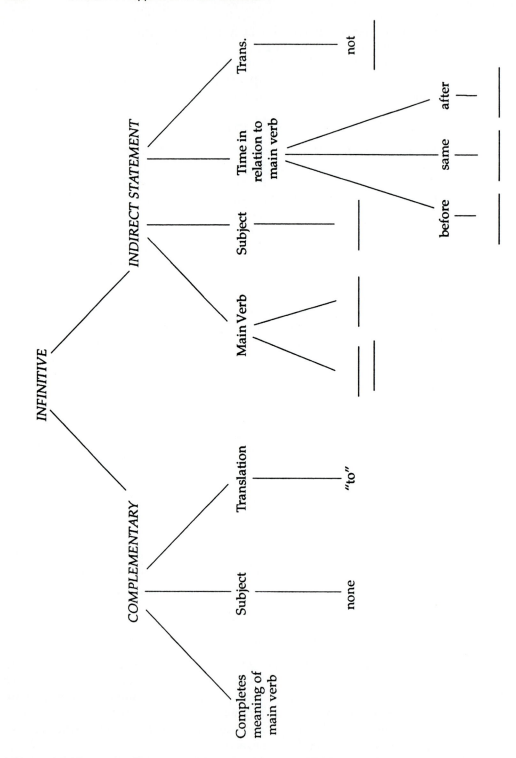

————— **CHAPTER SIX** ———————————————————

Rationale

The vocabulary guide will present students with new and review vocabulary. By categorizing it, they will be developing an understanding of words they need for comprehension of this chapter.

This passage contains several comparisons and contrasts that will be best understood with the aid of an organizational patterns guide.

The chapter closes with a word-building exercise based again on *ferre,* which is used in the reading. This guide builds on knowledge from a previous lesson to give students practice in an important skill.

Content Objectives

Pupils will:

1. Understand that a hero's life is not easy.

   a. A hero continually comes up against enemies and dangers.
   b. A hero faces family problems which threaten to be overwhelming.

2. Know the meanings of English prefixes and suffixes.
3. Recognize the English roots derived from *ferre.*
4. Understand the vocabulary necessary for reading this passage.

Process Objectives

Pupils will:

1. Identify the relationship among word in a set by deleting words that don't belong and by describing the relationship among the others.
2. Read at the literal level to recognize stated comparisons and contrasts.
3. Read at the interpretive level to recognize implied comparisons and contrasts.
4. Read at the interpretive level to recognize ideas implied in a selection.
5. Read at the applied level to recognize, explain, and illustrate the application of ideas from the text to generalization about the world of experience.
6. Apply knowledge of word parts to word building and creating definitions.
7. Use a dictionary to define words.

The Death of Pelias

(The *Argo* returned to Thessaly with the Golden Fleece. Pelias had promised Jason the throne if he successfully completed his mission, but now he asked Jason to wait until after his death to take over. He was a frail old man, so Jason agreed.)

His rebus cognitis, Meda <u>rem aegre tulit</u>, et regni
cupiditate adducta, mortem regi per dolum inferre
constituit. Hoc constituto, ad filias regis venit atque ita
locuta est: "Videtis patrem vestrum aetate iam esse
confectum, neque ad laborem regnandi perferendum satis (5)
valere. Vultisne eum rursus iuvenem fieri?" Tum filiae
regis ita responderunt: "Num hoc fieri potest? Quis enim
umquam e sene iuvenis factus est?" At Medea respondit: "Me
medicinae summam habere scientiam scitis. Nunc igitur vobis
demonstrabo, quo modo haec res fieri possit." His dictis, (10)
cum arietem aetate iam confectum interfecisset, membra eius
in <u>vas</u> aeneum coniecit, et igne supposito, aquae herbas
quasdam infudit. Tum, dum aqua <u>effervesceret</u>, carmen
magicum cantabat. Post breve tempus aries e vase desiluit
et, viribus refectis, per agros currebat. (15)

Dum filiae regis hoc miraculum <u>stupentes</u> intuentur,
Medea ita locuta est: "Videtis quantum valeat medicina.
Vos igitur, si vultis patrem vestrum in adulescentiam
reducere, id quod feci, ipsae facietis. Vos patris membra
in vas conicite; ego herbas magicas praebebo." His verbis (20)
auditis, filiae regis consilium, quod dedisset Medea, non
omittendum putaverunt. Patrem igitur Peliam necaverunt, et
membra eius in vas aeneum coniecerunt; nihil enim dubitabant
quin hoc maxime ei profuturum esset. At res omnino <u>aliter</u>
evenit <u>ac</u> speraverant; Medea enim non easdem herbas dedit, (25)
quibus ipsa usa erat. Itaque postquam diu frustra
exspectaverunt, patrem suum re vera mortuum esse
intellexerunt. His rebus gestis, Medea sperabat se cum
coniuge suo regnum accepturam esse. At cives, cum
intellegerent quo modo Pelias periisset, tantum scelus aegre (30)
tulerunt; itaque, Iasone et Medea regno explusis, <u>Acastum</u>
regem creaverunt.

Line 1—**rem aegre tulit**—was vexed

Line 12—**vas, vasis,** n. pl., **vasa, -orum,** vessel

Line 13—**effervesco, -ere, -ferbui,** boil

Line 16—**stupeo,** -ere, -un, be amazed

Lines 24–25—**aliter . . . ac,** otherwise than

Line 31—Acastus was Pelias' son.

The Death of Pelias (Translation for Teachers)

(The *Argo* returned to Thessaly with the Golden Fleece. Pelias had promised
Jason the throne if he successfully completed his mission, but now he asked

Jason to wait until after his death to take over. He was a frail old man, so Jason agreed.)

After she learned these things, Medea was vexed and driven by a desire to rule; she decided to bring about the death of the king by trickery. This decided, she came to the king's daughters and said this: "You see that your father is now worn out with age and not well enough to the job of ruling. Do you wish him to become young again?" Then the king's daughters answered in this way: "You aren't able to do this, are you? For who can ever make a young man from an old one?" But Medea answered: "You know that I have a very great knowledge of medicine. Now I will show you how this can be done." After she said this, when she had killed a ram worn out with age, she threw the parts of its body into a bronze vessel, and with a fire underneath, poured in the water certain herbs. Then, while the water was boiling, she sang a magic song. After a short time the ram jumped out of the vessel and, with its strength restored, ran through the fields.

While the king's daughters were looking at this miracle in amazement, Medea spoke in this way: "You see how powerful the medicine is. Therefore, if you want your father to become young again, you will do what I have done. Throw the parts of your father into the vessel; I will provide the magic herbs." When they heard these words, the king's daughters thought that the plan that Medea had suggested ought not to be disregarded. Therefore, they killed their father and threw the parts of his body into the bronze pot; they did not doubt that this would greatly help him. But it turned out otherwise than they hoped; for Medea did not give them the same herbs which she had used. Therefore after they waited for a long time in vain, they knew that their father was indeed dead. When these things were done, Medea hoped that she would receive the kingdom along with her husband. But the citizens, when they learned how Pelias had perished, disliked so enormous a crime; therefore, Jason and Medea were expelled, and they made Acastus king.

Vocabulary Guide

The Death of Pelias

Organizing idea: Ambition destroys those in its path.

Directions: Work with your group. For each set of words or phrases below, cross out the word or phrase that does not belong with the others. In the space provided, describe how the three words or phrases are related or why they belong together. Use your dictionary if necessary.

1. juvenis	senes	adulescentia	refectis viribus
2. mors	scientia	carmen magicum	herbae magicae
3. cupiditas	scelus	regnum	dolus
4. necari	interfici	valere	mortuus esse

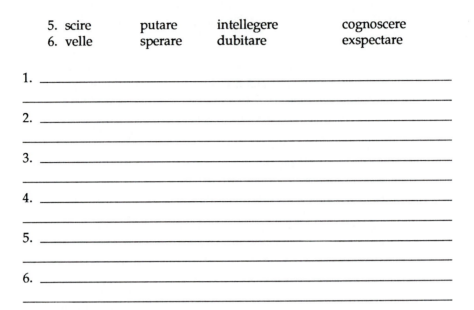

5. scire   putare   intellegere   cognoscere
6. velle   sperare   dubitare   exspectare

1. _____

_____

2. _____

_____

3. _____

_____

4. _____

_____

5. _____

_____

6. _____

_____

Key for Vocabulary Guide

The Death of Pelias

1. young man	old man	youth	with strength restored
2. death	knowledge	magic song	magic herbs
3. greed	crime	power	treachery
4. to be murdered	to be killed	to be well	to die
5. to know	to think	to understand	to learn
6. to wish	to hope	to doubt	to expect

Organizational Patterns Guide

The Death of Pelias

Organizing idea: Ambition destroys those in its path.

Part I

Directions: Listed below are nine sets of words or phrases, with the two in each set separated by a slanted line. Place a check on the numbered line if the two parts of the set represent a comparison or a contrast that can be found in Chapter Six. The comparisons or contrasts may be directly stated, or they may be implied. Work with your group and be ready to explain your answers. The numbers in parentheses tell you at which paragraph in the story you should look.

_____ 1. ambition/love (1)
_____ 2. scheming/innocent (1)

_____ 3. weakness/strength (1)
_____ 4. rich/poor (1)
_____ 5. heartless/compassionate (1)
_____ 6. expectation/reality (2)
_____ 7. truth/deception (1, 2)
_____ 8. daughters' hope/Medea's hope (2)
_____ 9. Medea's anger/citizens' anger (1, 2)

(*Note:* Number 9 may not appear to be expressed in the English, but it is very clear in the Latin.)

Part II

Directions: Place a check in front of each statement that you can support from the story *and* from your own ideas and experiences. Work with your group, and be ready to give the reasons for your choices.

_____ 1. Overwhelming desire for power can be dangerous.
_____ 2. It's hard to watch someone you care for grow old and weak.
_____ 3. A con artist takes advantage of a person's weakness.
_____ 4. A picture is worth a thousand words.
_____ 5. Things are not always what they seem.
_____ 6. The end justifies the means.
_____ 7. The best made plans often don't work out the way we expect.
_____ 8. Crime does pay.
_____ 9. One's reach can exceed one's grasp.

Building English Words from *Ferre*

Part I

Directions: Below are listed prefixes, suffixes, and the roots of *ferre.* Use these parts and assemble English derivatives of *ferre.* To assemble each word, place each word part and its meaning in the correct column and the assembled word and its meaning in its column. Then use your dictionary to find the exact English meaning, and write that in the last column also. Be ready to explain how the Latin and the English meanings are related. Work with your group.

Ferre, Tuli, Latus—to bring, bear, carry

Prefixes	*Roots*	*Suffixes*
circum—around	fer/ —bear	-ence—act of
con (co, com)—with,	carry	(t)or, -er—one who
together, completely	lat/(late)—bring	-(t)ion—act or
		result of an act

Prefixes	*Roots*	*Suffixes*

de—down from
in—in, on, upon into
ob—against, toward
prae—ahead, before,
   very
re—back
sub—under, up
   from under
trans (tra)—across,
   over

Prefix & Meaning	Root & Meaning	Suffix & Meaning	Assembled Word & Meanings
1. trans-across	late/—carry		translate—to carry across D.—to change from 1 language to another

———   **CHAPTER SEVEN**   ——————————————————

Rationale

"The Final Episode" recounts the revenge Medea takes upon Jason after he divorces her to marry another woman. I have often used this passage, and teenage students have always been familiar with the concept of a rejected woman's wrath. Some students have experienced firsthand the feelings caused by the breakup of a relationship. Others have been exposed to this theme in books or on television. *Fatal Attraction* has been so popular in the past few years that many know its plot even if they haven't seen the movie or the video. Undoubtedly, there will be some students who can call upon prior experience to help them and other group members use the anticipation guide to prepare them to read the Latin passage.

The anticipation guide is an exciting strategy for this passage. The students will have followed Jason and Medea through many adventures but will have had no clues from previous passages about the ending. The organizing idea and the statements contained in the guide should stimulate their curiosity and, at the same time, help them anticipate meaning in a passage that could otherwise prove difficult to translate.

The structured overview will help students see the relationship between the two women in Jason's life and will present new and review vocabulary that will be used in the passage to describe the character, motivation, and actions of both Medea and Glauce. Vocabulary guides are so important to prepare students for any language selection.

The reasoning guide is perfect for a character study of Medea based on her actions.

Content Objectives

Pupils will:

1. Understand that a hero's life is not easy.
    a. A hero continually comes up against enemies and dangers.
    b. A hero faces family problems that threaten to be overwhelming.
2. Understand the hero's wife's character and actions.
3. Understand the vocabulary necessary to read the passage.

Process Objectives

Pupils will:

1. Set purposes for reading.
2. Use their own experiences and knowledge as a context for reading material.
3. Use a structured overview to organize vocabulary in a selection.

4. Use a structured overview to determine relationships among characters.
5. Use their knowledge of unit content to arrive at conclusions about possible actions and statements of one characters.

Anticipation Guide

The Final Episode

Organizing idea: Hell hath no fury like a woman scorned.

Directions: Below you will find five statements. With your group discuss each statement as it relates to the organizing idea above, and decide together whether you agree with it on the basis of your own knowledge and experience. Place a check on the first line if you agree with the statement. Be able to support your decision with evidence. Then read "The Final Episode" to see if the author agrees with you. If he does, place a check on the second line.

_____   _____ 1. A hero never breaks a promise.
_____   _____ 2. People who are very nice to you have ulterior motives.
_____   _____ 3. Beautiful gifts should be enjoyed.
_____   _____ 4. Revenge is sweet.
_____   _____ 5. Justice always prevails in the end.

STRUCTURED OVERVIEW

Organizing Idea: Hell hath no fury like a woman scorned.

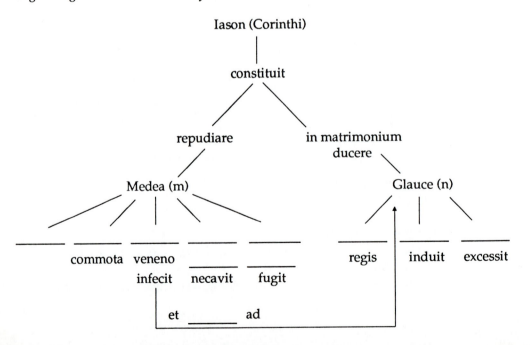

STRUCTURED OVERVIEW

Organizing Idea: Hell hath no fury like a woman scorned.

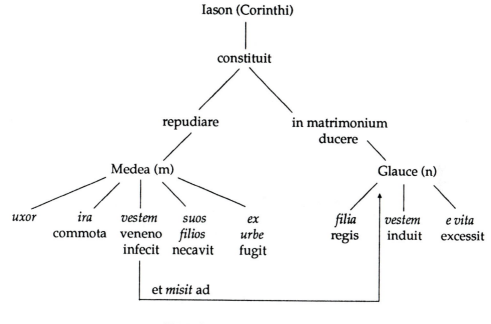

STRUCTURED OVERVIEW

Organizing Idea: Hell hath no fury like a woman scorned.

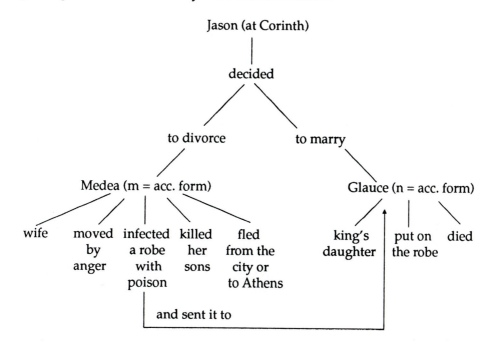

The Final Episode

Post haec Iason et Medea, e Thessalia expulsi, ad urbem
Corinthum venerunt, cuius urbis Creon quidam regnum tum
obtinebat. Erat autem Creonti filia una, nomine Glauce;
quam cum vidisset, Iason constituit Medeam uxorem suam
repudiare, eo consilio, ut Glaucen in matrimonium duceret. (5)
At Medea, ubi intellexit quae ille in animo haberet, ira
graviter commota, iure iurando confirmavit se tantam
iniuriam <u>ulturam</u>. Hoc igitur consilium cepit. Vestem
paravit summa arte <u>contextam</u> et variis coloribus <u>tinctam</u>;
hanc quodam infecit veneno, cuius vis talis erat ut, si (10)
quis eam vestem induisset, corpus eius quasi igne <u>ureretur</u>.
Hoc facto, vestem ad Glaucen misit; illa autem, nihil mali
suspicans, donum libenter accepit, et vestem novam (more
feminarum) statim induit.

Vix vestem induerat Glauce cum dolorem gravem per omnia (15)
membra sensit, et paulo post crudeli <u>cruciatu</u> affecta, e
vita excessit. His rebus gestis, Medea furore atque <u>amentia</u>
impulsa filios suos necavit; tum magnum sibi fore periculum
arbitrata, si in urbe remaneret, ex ea regione fugere
constiutit. Hoc constituto, Solem oravit ut in tanto (20)
periculo auxilium sibi praeberet. Sol autem, his precibus
commotus, currum misit, cui dracones alis instructi iuncti
erant. Medea non omittendam tantam occasionem arbitrata,
currum conscendit, itaque per aera vecta, incolumis ad urbem
Athenas pervenit. (25)

Line 8—**ulciscor, -i, ultus,** avenge

Line 9—*contexo, -ere, -textus,* weave

Line 9—**tingo, -ere, tinxi, tinctus,** dye

Line 11—*uro, -ere, ussi, ustus,* burn

Line 16—*cruciatus, -us,* m., torture

Line 17—*amentia, -ae,* f., madness

The Final Episode

After this, Jason and Medea, having been expelled from Thessaly, came to
Corinth where a certain Creon was then king. Moreover, Creon had a daughter named Glauce; when Jason had seen her, he decided to divorce his wife
Medea so he might marry Glauce. But when Medea understood what he
intended to do, she was overcome with anger, and she swore she would
avenge so great an injury. Therefore, she made this plan. She prepared a robe
woven with the greatest skill and dyed many colors; this she stained with a

certain poison, the power of which was such that if anyone had put on this robe, her body would have been burned as if by fire. When this was done, she sent the robe to Glauce; Glauce, however, suspecting nothing, willingly accepted the gift, and (as women will do) immediately put on the robe.

Scarcely had Glauce put on the robe when she felt severe pain through all her limbs, and, afflicted with excruciating torture, died a little later. Having accomplished this, Medea, overcome with madness and rage, murdered her sons; then, thinking that she would be in very great danger if she were to remain there, decided to flee. Having decided this, she begged the Sun to give her aid at this dangerous time. The Sun, moreover, moved by her entreaties, sent his dragon-pulled chariot. Medea, thinking the opportunity ought not be wasted, entered the chariot and, carried through the air, arrived safely at Athens.

Reasoning Guide

Organizing idea: Hell hath no fury like a woman scorned.

Part I

Directions: With your group read the time line of Medea's role in Jason's life.

Part II

Directions: Consider the following statements. Do you think Medea would have said them? In column I write "yes" or "no." Work with your group.

	Column I	Column II
1. Behind every great man there is a great woman.	_____	_____
2. The end justified the means.	_____	_____
3. Blood is thicker than water.	_____	_____
4. Forgive and forget.	_____	_____
5. I never get mad; I only get even.	_____	_____
6. I made you; I can break you, too.	_____	_____
7. A woman's place is in the home.	_____	_____
8. Do unto others as you would have them do unto you.	_____	_____
9. I'm a one-man woman.	_____	_____
10. My heart belongs to Daddy.	_____	_____

Timeline of Medea's Role in Jason's Life

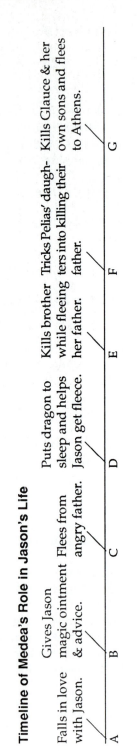

A — Falls in love with Jason.

B — Gives Jason magic ointment & advice.

C — Flees from angry father.

D — Puts dragon to sleep and helps Jason get fleece.

E — Kills brother while fleeing her father.

F — Tricks Pelias' daughters into killing their father.

G — Kills Glauce & her own sons and flees to Athens.

Part III

Directions: In Column II of Part II write a letter from the timeline of an event that supports your answer in Column I of Part II. Be ready to explain your answers. Work with your group.

Part IV

Directions: With your group consider what Medea might do now that she's in Athens. Write out two possibilities. Make sure that they reflect her character. Be ready to support your answers.

Use What You've Learned

Here are some ideas for activities that give you the opportunity to use what you have learned in this unit. Choose one that you would like to do alone or with your group.

1. We did not read about Jason's death, but it is included in the broader story. Find out how he died. Then write a story detailing Jason's life and death (as is done when a celebrity dies today) for a newspaper. (A group could produce an entire edition.)
2. Medea's death is not recorded. Write the end of her story. Begin where we last saw her on her way to Athens. Remember the past events of her life, but use your imagination as you create a story for this dynamic character. This may be written as a story or produced as a skit.
3. Interview another Greek hero. This may be written as a TV or radio script or as a newspaper story. You may even produce a tape or a video. If you work with a group, think about producing a talk show with several heroes as guests. Use what we've learned about heroes in this unit. Remember: a hero's life is not easy!
4. Be a detective. Where did those dragon's teeth come from? Find out the story of the teeth and the men who grew from them. Report your findings to the class.
5. Choose a hero, and illustrate several incidents from that person's life that prove that a hero's life is not easy.
6. Do you like to play games? Make a board game based on events in Jason's life.

Below are some books about mythology to help you:

Asimov, Issac. (1969). *Words from the Myths*. New York: New American Library.
A retelling of the Greek myths, which describes their influence on modern language and modern life.

Bulfinch, Thomas. (1965). *The Age of Fable*. New York: Airmont Publishing Company.
Our old standby; Bulfinch tells all the Greek myths.

Evans, Bergen. (1972). *Dictionary of Mythology*. New York: Dell Publishing Company.
A good reference; look up any Greek mythological name you need to know.

Graves Robert. *The Greek Myths,* vols. 1 and 2. (1969). Middlesex, England: Penguin Books.
In-depth work on the myths; everything about every story!

Hawthorne, Nathaniel. *Tanglewood Tales*. (1935). New York: Rand McNally and Company.
Interesting narrative of some of the myths.

New Larousse Encyclopedia of Mythology. (1968). New York: Putnam and Sons.
Excellent reference; contains good section on Greek myths.

Seyffert, Oskar. *Dictionary of Classical Antiquities*. (1966). Cleveland, OH: World Publishing Company.
A good place to start; brief but detailed stories of the myths.

Zimmerman, J. E. *Dictionary of Classical Mythology*. (1971) New York: Bantam Books.
Short entries to get you started; a good place to look if you are looking for a topic.

Triangular Review

You will work in groups of three to review for the unit test. There are three checklists, each covering one topic we have studied in this unit:

1. Indirect statement
2. Latin and English word building from *ferre*
3. The hero—Jason (as structured overview)

You will be working with one checklist at a time. Each of you will assume one of the following roles:

1. Speaker—will tell everything he or she knows about the topic until he or she can't respond further.
2. Interrogator—will ask leading questions.
3. Helper—will help the speaker respond when he or she can't go on.

The roles will rotate with each checklist so that each of you has a turn in each one. Place a check next to all information that the speaker recalls successfully.

Indirect Statement

A. Recognition

_____ 1. Main verb
_____ 2. Subject
_____ 3. Verb

B. Translation

_____ 1. Perfect active infinitive
_____ 2. Perfect passive infinitive
_____ 3. Present active infinitive
_____ 4. Present passive infinitive
_____ 5. Future active infinitive

Latin and English Word Building from _Ferre_

A. Latin compounds
    1. Prefixes

    _____ ab (a, abs)   ___ ex (e)   ___ pro
    _____ ad   ___ in   ___ re
    _____ circum   ___ ob   ___ sub
    _____ con (co, com)   ___ per   ___ trans (tra)
    _____ de   ___ prae

    2. Principal parts, meanings

    _____ ferre   ___ offerre
    _____ auferre   ___ perferre
    _____ afferre   ___ praeferre
    _____ circumferre   ___ proferre
    _____ deferre   ___ referre
    _____ efferre   ___ sufferre
    _____ inferre   ___ transferre

B. English derivatives
    1. Prefixes

    _____ circum   ___ prae
    _____ con   ___ re
    _____ de   ___ sub
    _____ in   ___ trans

    2. Roots

    _____ fer/
    _____ lat/ (late)

3. Suffixes

_____ -ence
_____ -(t) or, -er
_____ -(t) ion

On tomorrow's test there will be one question for which you will have to write a paragraph in which you support or argue against one of the following statements. You must support your ideas with facts from "Jason and the Argonauts." You will be given a structured overview to use during the test.

1. Heroes always defeat their enemies.
2. The gods are always on the hero's side.
3. The hero is always noble, good, and courageous.

The Hero—Jason

Organizing Idea: A hero's life is not easy.

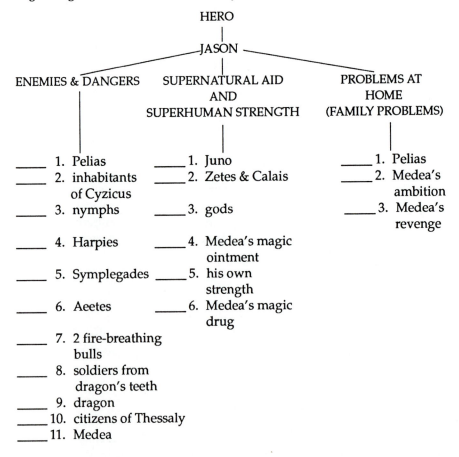

HERO
|
JASON
|

ENEMIES & DANGERS

____ 1. Pelias
____ 2. inhabitants of Cyzicus
____ 3. nymphs
____ 4. Harpies
____ 5. Symplegades
____ 6. Aeetes
____ 7. 2 fire-breathing bulls
____ 8. soldiers from dragon's teeth
____ 9. dragon
___ 10. citizens of Thessaly
____ 11. Medea

SUPERNATURAL AID AND SUPERHUMAN STRENGTH

____ 1. Juno
____ 2. Zetes & Calais
____ 3. gods
____ 4. Medea's magic ointment
____ 5. his own strength
____ 6. Medea's magic drug

PROBLEMS AT HOME (FAMILY PROBLEMS)

____ 1. Pelias
____ 2. Medea's ambition
____ 3. Medea's revenge

NAME _____

Unit Test—"Jason and the Argonauts"

Part I

Below you will find a paragraph that contains several examples of indirect statement. Underline each indirect statement. Include the verb that introduces the construction.

> *Tandem post multa pericula Iason in eundem locum pervenit, unde olim profectus erat. Tum e navi egressus, ad regem Peliam (qui regnum adhuc obtinebat), statim se contulit, et vellere aureo monstrato, ab eo postulavit ut regnum sibi traderetur; Pelias enim pollicitus erat, si Iason rettulisset, se regnum ei traditurum esse. Postuam Iason quid fieri vellet ostendit, Pelias primum nihil respondit, sed diu in eadem tristitia tacitus permansit; tandem ita locutus est: "Vides me aetate iam esse confectum, neque dubium est quin dies supremus mihi adsit. Liceat igitur mihi, dum vivam, hoc regnum obinere; cum autem ego e vita discessero, tu in meum locum venies." Hac oratione adductus, Iason respondit se id facturum esse quod ille rogasset.*

Part II

Translate each of the following sentences into English. Use the vocabulary following the sentences to help you with your translations.

1. "Videtis patrem vestrum aetate confectum esse."
2. Sciebat enim Aeetem, cum membra fili vidisset, non longius prosecuturum esse.
3. Intellexit hunc esse hominem, quem oraculum demonstravisset.
4. Intellegebat patrem suum hunc laborem proposuisse eo ipso consilio, ut Iason moreretur.

Vocabulary

aetas, aetatis, f., age

consilium, -i, n., plan

membrum, -i, n., limb

conficere, confeci, confectus, to wear out

intellegere, intellexi, intellectus, to know

scire, to know

> **proponere, proposui, propositus,** to propose
>
> **prosequi, prosecutus,** to pursue
>
> **longius,** farther
>
> **ipse, ipsa, ipsum,** an intensive pronoun, very

Part III

Give the principal parts and meanings of the following compounds of *ferre.*

1. auferre _____

_____

2. afferre _____

_____

3. sufferre _____

_____

Part IV

Below you will find four English words. Divide each into its prefix, root, and suffix (if it has one). Give the meaning of each part, and then give the meaning of the whole word by putting all the meanings together.

English	Prefix and Meaning	Root and Meaning	Suffix and Meaning	Meaning of English Word
1. relate				
2. offer				
3. circumference				
4. infer				

Part V

The next page contains a structured overview for the unit's organizing idea, a hero's life is not easy. Choose three people or things from "Enemies & Dangers," that are appropriate for the heading, two for "Supernatural Aid and Superhuman Strength," and one person or thing for "Problems at Home." Write your choices on the lines below, and then briefly explain how each one is an example of the category in which it is placed. Be sure to relate each one to Jason's life.

Organizing Idea: A hero's life is not easy.

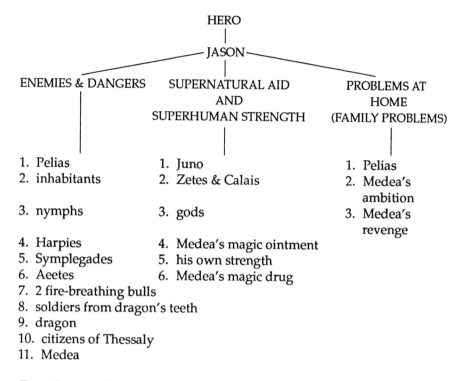

HERO
|
JASON
|

ENEMIES & DANGERS	SUPERNATURAL AID AND SUPERHUMAN STRENGTH	PROBLEMS AT HOME (FAMILY PROBLEMS)
1. Pelias	1. Juno	1. Pelias
2. inhabitants	2. Zetes & Calais	2. Medea's ambition
3. nymphs	3. gods	3. Medea's revenge
4. Harpies	4. Medea's magic ointment	
5. Symplegades	5. his own strength	
6. Aeetes	6. Medea's magic drug	
7. 2 fire-breathing bulls		
8. soldiers from dragon's teeth		
9. dragon		
10. citizens of Thessaly		
11. Medea		

Enemies and Dangers

1. _____
_____
_____
_____

2. _____
_____
_____
_____

3. _____
_____
_____
_____

Supernatural Aid and Superhuman Strength

1. _____
_____
_____

_____

2. _____

_____

_____

_____

Problems at Home (Family Problems)

1. _____

_____

_____

_____

Part VI

Write a paragraph in which you support or argue against one of the following statements. Support your ideas with facts from *Jason and the Argonauts.*

1. Heroes always defeat their enemies.
2. The gods are always on the hero's side.
3. The hero is always noble, good, and courageous.

Write your answer below.

_____

REACTIONS

Journal Entries and Discussion

In your journal, record your observations on the similarities and differences between the illustrative lesson in this chapter and the lessons you prepare for your students. What do you plan to retain? What do you plan to change?

Analysis and Discussion

Now that you have completed this chapter, consider the statements shown below. Check the numbered lines for statements you believe reflect the point of view of the authors. Circle the numbers of statements with which you agree. In writing, explore reasons for differences on any statements between your point of view and what you perceive to be the point of view of the authors. Please share and discuss your writing with colleagues who also are reading this book.

_____ 1. A structure that guides need not also inhibit.
_____ 2. Academic independence has more to do with self-sufficiency than with isolation.

_____ 3. Students do not always translate into practice what you tell them to do, a fact which suggests that telling is not teaching.

_____ 4. Some people feel the lesson is over when students move into their groups; others feel the lesson has just begun. Depending on the teacher, either can be true.

_____ 5. The structure of a reading guide can serve to structure a writing guide.

_____ 6. There is rarely a need for full-class discussion of all items on a guide if those items have been discussed effectively by students in their small groups.

_____ 7. While assumptions are implicit in the use of both declarative statements and questions to guide students' reading, the nature and substance of the assumptions are quite different for the two.

_____ 8. There is nothing more satisfying in teaching than to help students discover that their minds really can work for them.

12

Putting the Process to Work

Organizing idea: The whole is greater than the sum of its parts.

Reflections

Before reading this chapter, please record in your journal your responses to the following tasks. If possible, share your writing with other individuals who are also reading this book.

1. Using the text and your journal, review the various instructional strategies you have studied. Using the names given to the strategies, construct a semantic map that reflects appropriate interrelationships among the strategies.

2. Compare the following two ways to use the instructional strategies you have studied in this book. Consider how each would affect your teaching.

    a. Use one or two of the strategies whenever you want to give some instructional emphasis to reading, writing, or reasoning.
    b. Integrate the strategies into a unified whole for teaching content and process simultaneously.

3. Consider the differences in how your students' learning would be affected by 2a as compared with 2b.

IN THE FOLLOWING two dialogues, (Dialogues 12-1 and 12-2), we report conversations we had with two different teachers. These two conversations give focus to the purpose of this chapter.

DIALOGUE 12-1 ━━━

Teacher: How nice to have you visit our school. I've read your books and believe strongly in your philosophy about teaching reading, writing, and reasoning in content areas.

Us: Thank you so much. That's gratifying to hear. We'd love to see how you're applying the instructional strategies. Could we visit one or two of your classes while we're here?

Teacher: Oh, sorry. I'm not doing it today. Perhaps I will be the next time you are in our school—and I'd be pleased to have you visit my class if I am.

Us: Oh, . . . well, uh, . . . yes, uh . . . Thank you.

━━━

The teacher in Dialogue 12-1 had read about the use of vocabulary reinforcement materials as well as the use of levels, patterns, and reasoning guides. The "it" for him was the use of the guides and the materials. If students were not using the guides, the teacher was not doing it.

The teacher in Dialogue 12-2 was studying the instructional strategies as part of a long-term staff-development program in her district. She had not been involved in the application of the strategies long enough to perceive how they become a natural part of a person's teaching. In her mind, the instructional strategies were separate, not synthesized. Thus, her question about how frequently one used "it" was logical. Her question led to a definition of "it" and, ultimately, to her understanding of how the instructional strategies blend together to support "real teaching." Because you may have the same questions as these two teachers, we have included this chapter.

The purpose of this chapter is to show how the instructional strategies presented in this book combine to form an integrated, unified approach to teaching and learning of content and process across the curriculum.

DIALOGUE 12-2 ━━━

Teacher: The instructional strategies we're studying in this staff-development program seem helpful to my students.

Us: That's consistent with what we hear from other teachers. We're pleased that you're having a positive experience.

Teacher: Yes. Thank you. I do have a question, however. How often do you do it? Do you do it every day?

Us: Mmmmmm. Well, let's begin by defining what the "it" is about which you speak. (Extended discussion followed.)

━━━

In our conversation with the teacher in Dialogue 12-2, along with her colleagues, we defined it as "teaching by showing how." All of the strategies discussed throughout this book as well as the Instructional Framework that organizes the application of the strategies are designed to serve this purpose of showing how. This is consistent with the organizing idea that was established for this book: *The essence of good teaching is to show students how to do what is required of them to be successful.*

Synthesis for Teaching

The conversation in Dialogue 12-2 reflects a certain paradox confronted by those who study how the teaching of reading, writing, and reasoning can be integrated with the teaching of course content. On the one hand, this book stresses the importance of taking advantage of the interrelationships and interactions that take place among the processes of reading, writing, and reasoning. On the other hand each of the processes is presented in a separate chapter in order to explore it in depth. In the separate treatment of each process we include references to interrelationships with the other processes. Also, the discussion of each process is set in the context of the Instructional Framework. Even so, it may be possible to infer that teaching reading, writing, and reasoning in content areas involves just occasional applications of the instructional strategies and supporting materials. It may be possible to miss the point that all of these strategies should be integrated into a unified whole that is applied through an organized structure for teaching such as the Instructional Framework. This unified whole is not applied just on occasion. Rather, the unified whole is constantly applied in principle, that principle being that instruction involves *teaching students how to do what is required of them to be successful.*

It is important, then, to synthesize an instructional whole from the multiplicity of strategies presented in this book. The Instructional Framework provides a vehicle for this synthesis and for the teaching that applies the product of the synthesis.

Synthesis for Learning

Learning is the reciprocal of teaching. As synthesis across strategies is needed for effective instruction, so synthesis across strategies is needed for effective learning. It is helpful to point out to students that their use of information to acquire ideas through reading has a strong relationship to their use of information to express ideas through writing. The reasoning that is involved in students' analysis of resources used for learning is also involved in their creation of resources that reflect what they have learned. The vocabulary that students acquire from the teaching and presentation of words by the teacher is the vocabulary they apply through their reading and writing about organizing ideas of lessons. It is the vocabulary they apply through their conversations with other students in cooperative-learning contexts.

Instructional Framework

The Instructional Framework is a structure for teaching. Through this lesson structure, you can emphasize both the content (the substance of what is being studied) and the process (the means by which the substance is acquired) of your curriculum. The lesson structure is a vehicle for *preparing* students to study the organizing idea of a lesson, for *guiding* students in their study of that organizing idea, and for *developing students' independence* as they apply what they have learned about that organizing idea. Simultaneously, the lesson structure is a vehicle for supporting students' appropriate use of reading, writing, and reasoning as they are prepared to study the organizing idea, as they are guided in that study, and as they apply what they have learned through that study.

Reading, writing, and reasoning are applied interactively as students study the content of a lesson. This is true both within each part of the Instructional Framework and across the whole framework. As the lesson structure creates an interface between these learning processes and the content of the lesson, students simultaneously learn both content and process.

Because of the interactive relationships among reading, writing, and reasoning, many of the activities that prepare and guide students' reading, writing, or reasoning also prepare and guide their writing and reasoning or their reading and reasoning or their reading and writing, respectively. Thus, while preparing students to study an assigned topic, while guiding them as they study, and while developing their independence in the application of what they have learned from their study, you also are developing their proficiency in reading, writing, and reasoning.

It is important to remember that the preparation, guidance, and independence are always in reference to the organizing idea of the lesson. Organizing ideas drive lessons and, coupled with resources being used, dictate how reading, writing, and reasoning processes are to be applied. Remember always to apply the maxim, *content determines process*.

Preparation Revisited

The central purpose of the preparation phase of the Instructional Framework is to enable students to deal successfully with the conceptual focus of the lesson and also to deal successfully with the resources being used. Listed below are reminders of a variety of activities you have studied that support this preparation. In addition, if you are already teaching, you have tried-and-true activities that you have found successful in preparing students for the study of particular topics. In combination, these activities support students' reading, writing, and reasoning as well as their understanding of course content.

Activation of Prior Knowledge

An important component of learning is the ability to make connections between what is known and what is new. A variety of activities are available for activating students' relevant prior knowledge to provide a basis for their making connections between what is known and what is new. These activities contribute to and support the application of reading, writing, and reasoning. They also contribute to students' understanding of course content.

1. *Selection of appropriate organizing idea.* The organizing idea needs to be sufficiently general so it can be illustrated by events, conditions, actions, objects, or individuals drawn from students' prior knowledge and experience. The idea also needs to be sufficiently specific so it eventually can be illustrated by the particular content to be studied.

2. *Word association.* Students produce word lists associated with a key word drawn from the organizing idea of the lesson. Using Taba's (1967) list-group-label procedure, students perceive what they already know about the topic. They can enter this perception in their journals, share it with other students, and refer to it when the study of the topic is complete to see how their understandings were modified.

3. *Review of previous, relevant material.* Using key words from previously studied material, students can develop graphic organizers or semantic maps to portray relationships that exist between and among concepts. Using those same words, you can develop a structured overview of the previous unit and connect it with a structured overview of the upcoming unit. Students can probe specific concepts more deeply by using a semantic feature analysis. They can create group compositions that identify and discuss the most salient issues from the previous unit.

Vocabulary Development

Initiating students into the speech community of your subject area is an important purpose for your teaching. Introducing them to the technical language used in your subject area is central to that initiation. Providing opportunities for students to use the language in meaningful ways reinforces, refines, and extends their understandings of concepts represented by and communicated with that language. You have studied a variety of ways to develop your students' vocabularies. These activities contribute to and support the application of reading, writing, and reasoning. They also contribute to students' understandings of course content.

1. *Creation of word clusters.* Applying the criteria to select vocabulary for emphasis, you create word clusters that relate to concepts to be emphasized in your lesson. You draw from these clusters to create your graphic organizers, semantic maps, structured overviews, and meaning-reinforcement materials.

2. *Presentation and teaching of words.* Definitions and meanings of words are presented and taught from lists, structured overviews, semantic maps, semantic-feature analyses, and graphic organizers. Students can keep vocabulary notebooks for recording definitions and etymological information about the words. Notebooks also can be used for collecting materials that enhance students' understandings of word meanings.

3. *Reinforcement, refinement, and extension of meanings.* Students are given opportunities to manipulate words in a variety of contexts. Interrelationships they perceive through this manipulation reinforce, refine, and extend their understandings of the meanings of the words. Manipulation of words and development of meanings can be enhanced through the use of analogies, categorization, sentence completion, cloze activities, feature analyses, and matching and similar activities. Students can draw from the words to compose "possible sentences" (Moore et al. 1986) that reflect their understandings of definitions and meanings. They can write brief essays that describe concepts represented by words that are incorporated in the reinforcing materials.

Anticipation and Prediction

Learning requires assertive action on the part of learners. One form of assertion is anticipation. Learners draw on their prior knowledge and experience to create expectations with respect to concepts they are studying. In so doing, they build a sense of anticipation for what is to be learned.

Another form of assertive learning is prediction or hypothesizing. Prediction is usually grounded in more specific knowledge, whereas anticipation is usually grounded in more general knowledge. Prediction is an extension of knowledge into the unknown, asserting the probability of certain actions, conditions, or events based on that is known already. In making predictions, students build a need to know what is to be learned.

You have studied a variety of ways to promote your students' anticipation and prediction. These activities contribute to and support the application of reading, writing, and reasoning. They also contribute to students' understanding of course content.

1. *Selection of appropriate organizing idea.* Anticipation develops from what students already know about the organizing idea to be studied. A narrowly drawn organizing idea limits anticipation because it requires that students have content specific knowledge. Not having studied that specific content, students have little basis for anticipation. A broadly drawn organizing idea encourages anticipation because it allows students to use relevant

general knowledge that illustrate the idea. This relevant general knowledge provides a basis for anticipating what may be derived from the upcoming study of content-specific information.

2. *Word association.* The word-association activity facilitates students' activation of relevant general knowledge that serves as a basis of anticipation. Categories constructed out of the list-group-label (Taba 1967) procedure give focus to the anticipation. Subsequent study of content specific information allows confirmation or disconfirmation of what was anticipated. Students report results of their study in either written or oral form.

3. *Anticipation guides.* Reasoning guides can be used as anticipation guides. Statements are related to the organizing idea and allow students to draw on relevant general knowledge to support the acceptance or rejection of each. Statements do not require content specific information as the only evidence for acceptance or rejection. However, after content specific information has been studied, it is used by students to determine whether what they anticipated actually is supportable. They report on their determinations in either written or oral form.

4. *Vocabulary reinforcers.* Some vocabulary reinforcers support a blending of anticipation and prediction. Anticipation is based on relevant general knowledge. Prediction is based on relevant specific information.

After teachers have presented and taught specific vocabulary, analogies can be used to reinforce concepts. The analogies can be constructed so the first half that illustrates a relationship can be drawn from relevant general knowledge. The second half can require the use of specific information. The first half uses anticipation to speculate on what the second-half relationships should be. The second half uses prediction to hypothesize what the second-half relationship will be. Subsequent study of information sources provides the basis for confirming or disconfirming both the anticipation and the prediction.

5. *Structured overview.* Structured overviews are used to display content specific representations of organizing ideas. Content specific vocabulary is presented and taught. Definitions and meanings of words are explored.

Structured overviews can serve as a basis for students' predictions of what will be revealed during the subsequent study of the organizing idea. The predictions can be related to actions, conditions, objects, events, or whatever else might be appropriate.

6. *Prediction guides.* Reasoning guides can be used as prediction guides. The statements are related to the organizing idea but are related more to content specific information than are statements in anticipation guides.

Use of prediction guides logically follows some presentation and teaching of words, often in the context of developing a structured overview. Also, through lecture or other use of other resources, students acquire some basic information about concepts under consideration. Students use that content specific information to predict what will be revealed as a result of experiments conducted, problems addressed, resources examined, characters studied, or the like. Statements in the prediction guide shape the hypothesizing. Students draw on content specific knowledge they possess to support their acceptance or rejection of the statements. In either written or oral form, they confirm or disconfirm their predictions as part of the subsequent study.

Purpose and Direction

Each of the preparation activities contributes to a sense of purpose for studying to be done. Expectations created by the use of anticipation and prediction activities lead to purpose setting: determining the accuracy of predictions and determining the actuality of what was anticipated. The structured overview and related vocabulary work frame the tasks to be completed, and this gives purpose to subsequent study.

Direction has two meanings here. One meaning for *direction* has to do with the path to be taken. In this sense, direction is synonymous with *purpose*. Purpose and direction provide an objective to meet and a path to follow in order to meet the objective.

The other meaning for *direction* has to do with providing *guidance* for tasks to be performed. The materials you have constructed while studying this book are designed to support students' reading, writing, reasoning, and vocabulary acquisition. Their purpose is to show students how to become proficient in the use of these learning processes. The ultimate goal is for students to be able to apply these learning processes independently at levels of sophistication appropriate to what they are studying.

An important part of the independent use of the processes is understanding how they work. Directions provided with the support materials contribute importantly to that understanding.

Written directions for the supporting materials should clearly describe the task to be performed and what should be done to complete the task successfully. They should be sufficiently comprehensive that a person could complete the task successfully without intervention of another person. Even so, it is important to go over the directions with students to raise their consciousness about how they are to perform the task. This consciousness-raising contributes ultimately to students' independent performance on such tasks.

Guidance Revisited

The showing how of teaching is probably most focused in the guidance phase of the Instructional Framework. You have practiced constructing and (we hope) using levels, patterns, and reasoning guides. You have done the same with vocabulary-acquisition materials. You have practiced ways to use writing to refine students' responses to ideas explored through the application of these guide materials. If you have used your materials with students in the classroom, you have undoubtedly found that they work well.

Independence Revisited

The term *independence,* as it is used in the Instructional Framework, describes an objective more than an accomplishment. That is, the purpose of instruction is to show students how to become independent rather than to assume that they are already independent.

Students cannot function with independence when they are learning how to be independent. Students are supported in the independence phase of the Instructional Framework even as they are supported in the preparation and guidance phases.

Students are shown how to apply what they have learned about the course content, using the reading, writing, and reasoning processes they also have learned. You have seen how this can be done by having students select ideas from levels, patterns, or reasoning guides used with one set of resources and apply the ideas to different-but-related resources. Students determine agreement or disagreement between resources with respect to those ideas.

Materials and "Doing It"

While using the guide materials is important, it is more important to understand and apply the principles on which they are based, principles that can operate in the classroom whether or not such materials are in use. In this book we stress learning how to construct the materials because experience in doing so helps develop an understanding of these principles. We stress the use of the materials because the materials facilitate the application of the principles.

Comments by the teacher in Dialogue 12-1 reflect a belief in the value of the materials without an understanding of their underlying principles. Thus, because he was not using such materials, the teacher felt he was "not doing it". For him, the *it* was the materials. But for teachers (and observers) who understand the underlying principles, teachers can be "doing it" even though no such materials are in use. Applications of the underlying principles will be observable nonetheless.

Underlying Principles

Principles that provide the basis for construction and use of guide materials can be organized into four categories. You and your colleagues who are reading this book may have other principles to add to those we offer, and you may have other categories to add as well. Applications of these principles, with or without the use of guide materials, support students' integrated learning of content and relevant processes.

1. *Positive support.* Students need to be supported in their learning so they learn how to learn. This support needs to be positive in its orientation and application.

Focus should be on the probability of students' success rather than on the possibility of their failure. Your expectations influence students' outcomes. If your support is positive, their work will be also. A positive classroom provides a safe place to learn.

Teach to build on students' strengths rather than to compensate for their weaknesses. Too often we try to find out what is wrong with our students' learning and focus our attention on eliminating the problems. That leaves us with little time to build on the strengths students have in order to enhance their learning.

If we concentrate on what students do poorly, we develop a negative context that eventually dampens even what they do well. When we build on what students can do well, we develop a positive context for eventually helping them correct what they do poorly. Positive support can be applied with or without the use of guide materials.

2. *Cooperative learning.* Ideas are sometimes developed and often refined in the presence of an audience. In classes where the development and application of ideas are important, opportunities abound for students both to have an audience and to be an audience.

Being and having an audience is central to cooperative learning. Cooperative learning can occur within a small-group format or when the class operates as a committee of the whole. An audience is available in either case.

Cooperative learning can occur with or without guide materials. Guide materials do facilitate communication among participants in the cooperative learning endeavor. Statements or questions in the guide give focus to the conversation. But guide materials are not the only vehicle for facilitating cooperative learning. Students' written work stimulates conversation, particularly when teachers encourage responses to writing in progress. Also, teachers' own questions and statements serve to guide students' cooperative learning in either full-class or small-group formats.

3. *Tolerance for ambiguity.* Instruction that is oriented toward the development and application of ideas requires a tolerance for ambiguity by both teachers and students. Students need room to offer and to consider alternative explanations when they are in the process of developing ideas from information presented through single or multiple resources. Students have to be able to determine the goodness of fit between information they encounter and the ideas they construct from that information. Students need intellectual room in which to reflect on the materials and to refine the ideas

they induce. The openness that provides this intellectual room contributes to a sense of ambiguity that surrounds the work.

Also contributing to the sense of ambiguity is the willingness *not* to rush to closure when discussing ideas. When courses are organized principally to dispense information, little discussion is needed. Exploration of ideas is minimized, and discussions move rapidly closure. In contrast, when courses are organized principally to develop and apply ideas, opportunities are needed for extended manipulation of ideas. The ideas are open-ended rather than closed and restricted. Discussion of such ideas is accompanied by a sense of ambiguity and the need for tolerance for same.

4. *Rigor and discipline.* The active pursuit of ideas requires more intellectual rigor and discipline than does the memorization of information. An important part of concept development in instructional settings is an insistence that reasons be given to support proffered ideas. The question, "What's your evidence?" should be raised consistently in the development and discussion of ideas. Marshalling evidence to validate and justify positions taken on ideas requires some precision in one's thinking. Having a tolerance for ambiguity does not include having a tolerance for sloppy thinking. The ambiguity is purposeful and it is disciplined.

Intellectual discipline is the servant of intellectual rigor. Applying the processes of inference, deduction, and induction require considerably more effort than just memorizing the products of those processes. Responding positively to that effort requires intellectual discipline. Support you give students as you guide their reading, writing, and reasoning can lead to the development of this rigor and discipline.

Developing Independence

Students do not learn to become independent independently. Some showing how, some practice, and some refinement are involved—all requiring some instructional intervention. Does this mean that students can never function independently in their academic work? Not necessarily; but it is important to account for issues related to cycles of independence and strategies related to self-managed learners (Stauffer 1969) when considering just how independently students can function.

Cycles of Independence

In the teacher-learner relationship, the learner is dependent on the teacher. Learning tasks are directed by the teacher; they are under the teacher's control. Efforts to increase learners' independence require a reduction in the teacher's control and a corresponding increase in learners' control over the learning tasks.

The term fading has been used to describe this shifting of responsibility for learning from teacher to students (Moore et al. 1986) In Pearson and Leys's model (1985) of explicit instruction, instruction moves from modeling (fully under the teacher's control) through guided practice (gradually shifting responsibility from teacher to students) to practice or application (fully under the students' control). In its fully operational form, the model has students carrying 100 percent of the responsibility for their learning.

The concept of fading, with its related belief in shifting responsibility for learning from teacher to student, is supported by most educators. The problem with the concept, however, is that it is applied as though the shift of responsibility is linear and permanent. That is, in practice there appears to be an assumption that once students take control of their own learning, they no longer need teacher intervention. When this permanent shift does not occur, teachers who make this assumption become frustrated and wonder aloud when the students are ever going to be able to learn on their own.

When the assumption that students should attain a permanent state of independence in learning is challenged, most educators would agree that the assumption is unwarranted. Clearly, as students progress through the grades, they continually require varying amounts of teacher direction of their learning. Even so, the assumption persists as does the frustration it produces.

What helps clarify the issue is to assume that the shift of responsibility for students' learning from teacher to student is cyclical rather than linear. That is, at a given grade level within a given subject, teachers support students to the point where they can take responsibility for their learning. The students then function with reasonable independence. However, when those same students move to new, more complex materials that embody more abstract and sophisticated ideas, they cycle back to the need for more teacher direction for their learning. Then they develop independence at this new level of sophistication. When they move to the next level, once again they require more teacher direction.

Thus the cycles continue, building on one another with students attaining independence relative to the level of complexity of resource used and the level of abstraction and sophistication of ideas explored. If you think of the cycles as not only repeating but also expanding, the implication is that as students progress through these cycles they have longer and longer episodes of independence in learning. As students gain experience and proficiency in directing their own learning, the proportion of student-directed learning relative to teacher-directed learning increases. Students may eventually reach full independence in the use of complex resources and the exploration of sophisticated ideas.

But students' independence is constantly developing and its application to content and process is ever-expanding. Students can sustain 100 percent self-directed learning only if they remain at the levels of complexity and sopisticaiton they have already attained. When they move to higher levels, they will lose some of their independence until they attain sufficient proficiency to function with full independence again. Thus it is that our students are always *becoming* independent learners.

Self-Managed Learners

Students who progress through these cycles of independence become self-managed learners (Stauffer, 1969b). They apply strategies for learning that teachers have modeled for them, strategies for reading, writing, and reasoning. They incorporate the phases of instruction used by teachers into their own self-directed learning. That is, they prepare themselves for the study of the topic, they set up ways to guide their own thinking about resources used and ideas explored and they select means by which to demonstrate and apply what they learn.

A well-structured lesson plan, such as the Instructional Framework, serves students in two ways. First, it provides a structure for teachers to follow while teaching lessons. Second, it also provides a model of organization for students to follow in their self-managed learning. When we help students learn how to apply this structure and help them learn how to apply appropriate reading, writing, and reasoning skills to what they study, we help them become self-managed learners.

Teaching for Independence

Students' independence in learning cannot be an unintended consequence of teaching. While some highly motivated students may develop independent learning skills on their own, most independent learners have learned their independence from another person. Students do not become independent independently.

Teaching for students' independence is a conscious act. But it is not an act that is separate from regular teaching. You do not have to set aside special time to have lessons on developing independence in reading, writing, or reasoning. Teaching for independence requires particularized explanations of learning processes you are helping students to learn as a regular part of your curriculum. Teaching for independence also requires particularized explanations of lesson structures you use to help students learn both the content and process of your curriculum. These particularized explanations are grounded in your own methods for teaching and learning, in your own experiential context for teaching.

Experiential Context

The point has already been made that it takes time to internalize the instructional strategies we have explored in this book and to synthesize them into a unified whole. It takes time to adapt the Instructional Framework to your style and your needs and to use the synthesized strategies as appropriate to the framework. It takes time to perceive how the instructional strategies and supporting materials affect students' reading, writing, and reasoning. What you derive from the expenditure of all this time is an experiential context for your teaching, and it is this experiential context that allows you ultimately to teach for independence.

In this experiential context you learn that reading, writing, and reasoning can be taught functionally. You can integrate instruction in those three processes with instruction in course content. You learn to operationalize the principle that content determines process: the substance of what is studied dictates the means by which it is studied.

In this experiential context you learn that when you support students' reading, writing, and reasoning as they study your course content, you can raise the level of sophistication at which they function without having separate lessons on how to read, write, and reason. You learn that as you ask students to provide evidence to support the product of their reading, writing, and reasoning, they develop an intuitive understanding of how those processes work. Your teaching ultimately provides students with their own experiential context for learning.

Your own experiential context for teaching confirms the importance of requiring students to provide supporting evidence to buttress their decisions and ideas. You ask them to identify information they have put together to confirm predictions they have made or to support conclusions and inferences they have drawn. You also ask them how and why they put the information together as they did. As you discuss the how and the why, you raise their consciousness about the learning processes they are applying. It is this metacognitive awareness of how and why learning processes work that contributes to students' ability to become self-managed learners.

Teaching for Metacognitive Awareness

According to Brown (1980), metacognition "refers to the deliberate conscious control of one's own cognitive actions" (Brown 1980, 453). As applied to reading, this control involves several activities:

1. *Clarifying the purposes of reading, that is, understanding the task demands, both explicit and implicit*
2. *Identifying the aspects of a message that are important*
3. *Allocating attention so that concentration can be focused on the major content area rather than trivia*
4. *Monitoring ongoing activities to determine whether comprehension is occurring*
5. *Engaging in review and self-interrogation to determine whether goals are being achieved*

6. *Taking corrective action when failures in comprehension are detected*
7. *Recovering from disruptions and distractions—and many more deliberate, planful activities that render reading an efficient information-gathering activity (Brown 1980, 456).*

The objective of these activities is for students to become efficient readers of resources assigned in their classes.

Consider the various instructional strategies you have studied in the previous chapters of this book. In combination, these strategies provide contexts in which these seven activities can be exercised. Tasks given to students in the preparation phase of the Instructional Framework help to establish the purposes for work to be done. Guide materials to support students' comprehension of resources help focus attention on information that is critical to an understanding of the organizing idea of the lesson. The structure of the guides help students learn how to focus on essentials and not be distracted by trivia. Having students work in groups and consistently challenge one another with the question "What's your evidence?" encourages students to monitor the sensibleness of their interpretations of what they read. Review procedures applied in the independence phase of the Instructional Framework help students monitor their accomplishments in reference to established purposes. Interactions among students, with the careful monitoring of the teacher, reveal comprehension problems when they occur and provide an opportunity for students to deal constructively with the problems and facilitate the desired comprehension.

Awareness of Content

Metacognitive awareness includes three kinds of knowing, each of which can be related to the substance of what is being studied in a given lesson or unit of instruction:

1. Knowing when you know
2. Knowing what you know
3. Knowing what you need to know (Brown 1980)

Knowing when you know is virtually inseparable from knowing what you know. What you know is what is known in knowing when you know! Obviously, learning is aided when learners are aware when they do and don't know what is to be studied. Connecting what is known with what is new is facilitated when students become involved in knowing what they know.

Instructional strategies presented in this book include those that help students become aware of the knowledge they possess about the organizing idea of the lesson or unit. The strategies help develop students' awareness of what they know and when they know it. This awareness, in turn, develops students' awareness of what they need to know.

Knowing what you need to know is different from actually possessing the targeted knowledge. There is an awareness of gaps to be filled, of questions that cannot yet be answered, of fugitive information that is disconnected from the whole. Instructional strategies presented in this book include those that help students become aware of what they don't know and, consequently, precipitate in them a need to know.

Awareness of Process

The three kinds of metacognitive awareness just discussed also can be related to the processes by which the substance of a given lesson or unit of instruction is acquired: knowing when you know; knowing what you know; knowing what you need to know.

Knowing When You Know. Experiential context influences when students know about the reading, writing and reasoning processes they apply during the study of a concept. Students can apply the processes without knowing how they work. Guiding their use of these processes provides an experiential context for their eventual study.

For example, teachers use the levels-of-comprehension construct to guide students' reading of required resources. Students recognize that the levels aid their understanding of the text, but most do not think about how the levels work when they first start using the construct. Initial directions tell students how to do the required tasks at each of the levels. However, explanations of how the levels work are not given.

Students do not have to understand how the process works in order to be able to use it in a way that helps them understand the required readings. Repeated, successful experiences with the construct reinforces the success and establishes the value of the construct.

When students' experience with the construct is sufficiently strong to serve as a context for understanding *how the process works.* teachers provide appropriate explanations. These explanations are timely, are grounded in successful experience with the process, and enable students to know when they know about the process.

Knowing What You Know. The experiential context derived from being guided in the application of learning processes provides the basis for students to acquire knowledge and understanding about what they know through that experience. Teachers can talk with students about how they manipulate information from the text to support statements at each of the levels of comprehension. They talk about the importance of accuracy in discerning information from text, and they draw on students' experience to confirm the process. They talk about how ideas are revealed as readers put information together and draw inferences or conclusions, and they draw on students' experience to confirm the process. They talk about how ideas from previous study are synthesized with ideas derived from the text to create broader generalizations that bridge both sources, and they draw on students' experience to confirm the process.

Teachers provide the same kind of explanations about other learning processes for which students have developed an experiential context. The consequence of these explanations is that students develop an understanding of how these learning processes work. They gain knowledge about what they have experienced in applying these processes. With this understanding they are in a position to apply these processes with increasing degrees of independence.

Knowing What You Need to Know. The challenge—and delight—in the study of concepts presented in various subject areas is that they are sufficiently abstract and global that they can be studied at multiple levels of sophistication. As students progress through the grades, they encounter the same concepts but at increasing levels of sophistication. The resources used to present these concepts also become more abstract and sophisticated. Consequently, the learning processes appropriate to the study of these concepts and resources are applied with increasing sophistication and finesse.

Students need to know how to apply the learning processes at increasing levels of sophistication. Taking levels of comprehension as an example, students find the construct useful in the lower intermediate grades as well as at the college level. To get from the former to the latter requires that students be able to adapt the construct to fit the materials used at each of the intervening grade levels.

Part of developing students' metacognitive awareness of how learning processes work is to push the boundaries of that knowledge as far as one can. What students need to know is that these learning processes grow as they grow, and that they are adequate for meeting the demands made of them. Teachers can help students develop this knowledge as they show them how to use the learning processes (such as levels of comprehension) to probe ideas more deeply:

- Becoming more selective as information becomes more dense and complex
- Becoming more analytical in interpreting the information, and more probing in the search for implications
- Becoming more creative in the blending of resources, and more elaborative in the synthesis of ideas

Teachers help students develop this knowledge when they, first, develop the experiential context that comes with the successful, guided application of the learning processes (such as levels of comprehension). They continue this help when they, second, explain to students how the processes they have been applying successfully actually work. In this way, students develop an awareness of the learning processes that enables them to learn with increasing independence: knowing when they know, knowing what they know, and knowing what they need to know.

Order of Awareness

Implied in the previous discussion of metacognitive awareness is an order to what is done to develop the awareness. Reducing the issue to simple terms, one has two choices for ways to develop metacognitive awareness of learning processes:

1. Either one can explain to students how a learning process works and then show them how to apply it.
2. Or one can show students how to apply a learning process and then explain to them how it works.

We advocate the second choice. It takes advantage of everything we know about how prior knowledge influences learning. Providing students with successful experiences in the application of a learning process provides a positive knowledge base on which to build the explanations of how that process works. The initial applications of the process are not diluted or distracted by explanations of how the process actually works. Subsequently, students are able to connect what is known (an awareness of the process and a positive experience in applying it) with what is new (an understanding of the process through explanations of how it actually works). Previous success in the application of the process gives students a reason for listening to the explanations as well as a way to think about what the explanations mean. The consequence of this order is an understanding of both how and why a learning process works.

The first choice requires explanations in the abstract. Without earlier experiences in applying the learning process, students have nothing with which to connect the explanations. Even when the explanations are accompanied by applications, students may not have sufficient experience in the application to provide a knowledge base for understanding the explanations. The consequence of this order can be a limited knowledge of both how and why the learning process works.

Teaching with Metacognitive Awareness

Metacognition applies to teaching as well as to learning. In the previous section we discuss how teaching *for* metacognitive awareness can enhance students' learning. In this section we discuss how teaching *with* metacognitive awareness can enhance teachers' teaching.

In working with content-area teachers over the years, we have observed four stages in the learning and application of instructional strategies that support students' reading, writing, and reasoning. The first stage is when teachers just want practical suggestions on how to help their students learn their content more effectively. Teachers don't want to be burdened with theory at this stage. Demonstrating activities that prepare students to read, write, and reason as well as showing teachers how to construct materials that guide students' reasoning and reading provide teachers with help that has immediate and practical impact on their teaching.

The second stage is after teachers find that the instructional strategies they are applying do work with their students. That is, students are positive in their responses to the materials. The preparatory activities and the guide materials, coupled with cooperative learning, seem to facilitate students' learning and build in them an enthusiasm for pursuing the ideas being explored. With the confidence that comes with students' positive response, teachers begin to wonder why these strategies work as well as they do. Their success with the practice makes them receptive to the theory. They are interested in exploring the rationale for the strategies. Understandings derived from this exploration enable them to refine their use of the strategies.

Teachers in the third stage begin to personalize the strategies, adapting them to fit comfortably into their instructional repertoire and with their teaching styles. They understand how the strategies fit into "real teaching." Most importantly, they understand the principles that underlie the instructional strategies. This understanding of principles allows teachers to adopt, adapt, and personalize the instructional strategies in the following ways:

- Accepting the principles of preparing students to do required tasks, of showing them how to complete the tasks, and of supporting their independent applications of what they have learned, teachers find that many of the tried-and-true instructional strategies they have used heretofore follow the same principles. Thus, old and new strategies are synthesized into an expanded instructional repertoire.
- Understanding the rationale for preparation, guidance, and independence, teachers are not limited to the particular applications of these principles that they study in their preservice or in-service education experiences. Ways to prepare and guide students and to support their independent applications of what they have learned are infinite in their variability. As teachers apply their creativity and imagination to these principles, they develop a multiplicity of instructional strategies. Thus, teachers' instructional repertoires are expanded.

In the fourth stage, teachers refine and extend their expanded repertoires. They run ministudies to compare one set of materials and/or strategies with another set, and to determine the relative effectiveness of each for their students. In this manner, they develop increasing confidence in the instructional strategies they hold in their repertoires.

As teachers progress through these four stages, they move from awareness to acceptance to understanding to commitment with respect to the
instructional strategies they adopt, adapt, and refine. As they progress
through these stages, they become increasingly sensitive to how the instructional strategies work and to ways that the effectiveness of the strategies can
be enhanced.

Order of Awareness

The order of development across the four stages is important to consider.
The order moves from general to specific, from practice to theory, and from
uncertainty to confidence.

Success with functional teaching of reading, writing, and reasoning
processes (an emphasis on comprehension, for example) serves as a general
context for explicit teaching of how those processes work (an emphasis on
how inference works thus contributes to comprehension, for example). Confidence teachers derive from the functional teaching of the learning processes allows them to take time for the explicit teaching that refines
students' understanding of the processes. Without that previous success
with general, functional instruction, teachers would be less likely to take the
time to use specific, explicit instruction.

Successful practice with instructional strategies serves as a context for
studying the theories that underlie the strategies. The confidence that teachers derive from observing how well the strategies work with their students
allows them to take time to explore their rationale and to understand why
they work as they do. Without that prior, successful application of instructional strategies, teachers would be less inclined to take time for the study of
their rationale.

Success with functional teaching of reading, writing and reasoning
processes removes uncertainty and doubt from the minds of content-area
teachers. Their confidence begins to mount as they watch how students
respond to the instructional strategies. Their confidence blossoms further as
they recognize how many of the instructional strategies they have used in
the past are consistent in principle with the new strategies they are studying.
Their confidence soars as they adopt, adapt, and personalize the new instructional strategies, synthesizing them with previously known strategies
into a unified, instructional whole. Thus they move from uncertainty to
confidence.

Learning with Independence

Developing independent learners is a common goal for both curriculum and
instruction. If you examine curriculum guides for most subject areas and

grade levels, you find this goal expressed in one form or another. Talk to most subject-area teachers about their instructional goals, and you will find developing independent learners among them.

How to develop students' independence is a fascinating issue and there are many different opinions on how this can be accomplished. For example, we talked to a teacher of seniors about developing independent learners. When we asked how he dealt with the issue of developing students' independence, he said, "Well, when my students go to college, they are expected to function independently. So to get them ready for that independent work, I put them on their own in my classes so they can experience what it is like to work independently." When we asked him how he helped his student learn to function independently, he said, "by putting them on their own in my classes."

We had a similar conversation with a ninth-grade teacher who was concerned that when students moved to the high school grades they were expected to function independently. He said that he prepared his students for that independent work in high school by putting them on their own in his junior high classes.

A sixth-grade teacher said she prepared her students for junior high (where they were expected to function independently) by putting them on their own in her intermediate grade classes. We even met a third-grade teacher who prepared her students for the independent work expected of them in intermediate grades by putting them on their own in her classes.

If this experience is a reasonably accurate representation of how we prepare students for functioning independently, then a logical question to ask is "Who shows them how to function independently?" If one level prepares students for the independence required at the next level by requiring independence at that first level, one can conclude that no one shows students how.

Principles Related to Independence

Out of our work with content-area teachers over the past three decades, we have induced five principles related to developing students' independence in learning:

1. Independence in the performance of a task is a logical extension of having learned and practiced that task. The instructional strategies discussed and demonstrated in this text provide the means for showing students how to acquire learning processes. The strategies provide an opportunity for students to practice those processes as they learn and apply the organizing ideas of their lessons. Students' independent work is an extension of these processes and ideas.

2. Students' independence is developed by design, not by chance. The instructional strategies presented in this text provide a carefully orches-

trated interplay between guidance and practice. Teachers guide students' work to show them how to use particular strategies related to reading, writing, and reasoning. Teachers then provide opportunity for students to practice those learning processes by applying them to new materials; new concepts, or new purposes. Having shown students how to apply certain strategies, teachers gradually shift the control of learning tasks from themselves to their students.

3. Independence is a relative state, conditioned by the concepts being studied, the sophistication of the resources being used, and the maturity of the learner. In Chapter 1 we discuss the importance of transitional instruction and its implications for providing instruction in reading and in all subjects and at all grade levels. Given the steady increase in the complexity of ideas and in the sophistication of materials over the grades, independence attained for one level is not sufficient for the next. Independence, thus, is relative to these variables.

4. Independence does not mean isolation. Independence does not mean separation or isolation from others. Independence in learning has more to do with *who is in charge* of the learning rather than *who one is with* during the learning.

To be an independent learner does not require one to be cut off from other learners or to make use of resources without any assistance from others. Truly independent learners recognize when they need help in their learning and know how to obtain that help.

A main outcome of formal education is knowledge of what you don't know and how to educate yourself about that knowledge if you choose to do so. If you are a learner, it means you are studying something you don't know. If you are a learner studying something you don't know, you often need help in identifying and locating useful information. If you are a learner using useful information in the study of something you don't know, you often need to explain to someone what you are learning to clarify your thinking on what you are studying. Also, you often need to test the appropriateness and reasonableness of ideas you have developed in your study by talking with someone who is knowledgeable in the area of study you are pursuing.

In this operational definition of independent learning, learners clearly are not separated from others nor do they work in isolation. Such individuals are what Stauffer (1969b) calls "self-managed learners." They recognize what they don't know. They know how to use resources to obtain appropriate information. They know how to test and refine ideas. They know how to apply the product of their thinking in appropriate ways. They know when to interact with others and when to isolate themselves from others. They know the power of choice and how it effects information, ideas, processes, and products. They know how to exercise that power. In that sense, they are independent: self-reliant and self-managed.

5. Independence is never fully attained. It is important to note that independent, self-reliant, self-managed learning is never fully acquired in the absolute sense. This, of course, is because the more one learns the more one realizes what one does not know. So learning cycles continue, with information, ideas, and resources increasing in levels of sophistication and abstraction. Thus it is that we are always *becoming* independent learners.

Developing Independence

Students do not develop independence independently. They have to be shown how to use their understanding of learning processes in self-reliant, self-managed ways. The means for showing students how to develop independence in learning is instruction that shows students how to learn to read, write, and reason to learn. The instructional strategies you have studied in this text constitute the means for helping students become independent learners.

We have found three kinds of activities useful in moving students toward more self-managed learning as they apply the ideas and skills learned during the preparation and guidance phases of the Instructional Framework. We classify these activities under three headings: refining, extending, and sharing (Herber and Nelson-Herber 1987).

Refining

Refining is a fine tuning of what has been learned during the preparation and guidance phases of the lesson. Students fine-tune their understanding of concepts as they participate in discussions with their peers and as they create products that reflect their understanding. For example, these products could be multiple drafts of writing in progress or the creative applications of relevant vocabulary to demonstrate some dimension of the organizing idea of the lesson. The fine tuning is enhanced as students receive feedback on their products from their peers and their teachers.

At the same time that students fine-tune their understanding of concepts, they also fine-tune their applications of reading, writing, and reasoning. Feedback on writing in progress helps fine-tune the composing process. Revisiting particular segments of text for purposes of clarification or elaboration helps fine-tune the reading process. Synthesizing ideas across resources or analyzing materials created by other students, or analyzing resources for concepts relevant to the organizing idea of the lesson all fine-tune the reasoning process.

Implicit in the notion of fine tuning is a series of small, sometimes delicate, adjustments. The desired result is not usually obtained in a single trial. While teachers cannot do the fine tuning for their students, they can provide repeated opportunities for students to engage in refining activities and they can create an environment that accepts multiple adjustments (Herber and Nelson-Herber 1987, 587).

Extending

Extending involves new or different applications of what was learned during the preparation and guidance phases of the lesson. Students can extend their understandings of concepts by applying them to different settings or to different principles. At the same time, students can extend their understandings of learning processes by applying them to different resources or to different products. They also can extend the development of their products by using them in different contexts with different audiences.

For example, students can extend their understandings of the writing process by creating various forms of poetry: haiku, lanterne, cinquain, diamante, acrostic, or limerick. Through the application of these forms of poetry, students also extend their understandings of the concepts to which the poetry is applied.

> *Implicit in the idea of extending is the notion of utility. The concepts, processes, and products are not ends in themselves. Part of their value is in their usefulness. While teachers cannot do the extending for their students, they can provide opportunities for students to engage in extending activities and they can create an environment that supports the use of what has been learned (Herber and Nelson-Herber 1987, 587).*

Sharing

Sharing involves giving while keeping, with a focus on three outcomes of the preparation and guidance phases of the Instructional Framework:

1. Understanding of content
2. Facility with learning processes
3. Products created by the application of content and process

Students share their understandings of concepts through discussion and writing. Sharing one's understanding of a concept with others fixes the concept more firmly in one's mind—giving while keeping.

Students share their facility with processes by helping other students refine and extend their own skills. Sharing one's facility with a process with others fixes the process more firmly in one's repertoire—giving while keeping.

Students share their products by participating in feedback essential to the refining and extending activities. Sharing the product of one's mind with others enriches the context in which the mind works— giving while keeping. "While teachers cannot do the sharing for their students, they can provide opportunities for students to engage in these sharing activities and they can create an environment that promotes the spirit of giving" (Herber and Nelson-Herber 1987, 587-588).

From Answers to Questions

We have emphasized using answers rather than questions to guide students' reading, writing, and reasoning about the organizing ideas for lessons. Teachers ask themselves questions about organizing ideas for lessons and resources to be used. They answer their questions in the form of declarative statements. They give these statements to their students, who are asked to determine whether the statements are appropriate to the materials being discussed and to the ideas being explored, and why. Students construct reasons for their decisions and share their evidence through discussions in cooperative-learning groups and through written responses shared with their peers and teachers.

A natural concern related to guiding students' responses with declarative questions is whether they eventually will be able to respond successfully to questions. Questions require more independence in that students not only must find pertinent material to answer the questions, they also must create statements that accurately reflect their thinking at levels of sophistication and abstraction required by the questions.

Shifting from answers to questions as a means for guiding students' response to organizing ideas and related resources is an important issue related to helping students learn with independence. Based on Pearson and Johnson (1978) and Raphael and Pearson (1982), Raphael (1982, 1984, 1986) developed a system for constructing questions based on a question-answer relationship. This system serves particularly well as a means for helping students make the transition between statements and questions.

Question-Answer Relationships (QAR)

Pearson and Johnson (1978) present three dimensions of comprehension (discussed in Chapter 8): textually explicit, textually implicit, and scriptally implicit. In their discussion of these dimensions, they made the point that until one hears or reads the answer to a question, one cannot be certain which dimension the question reflects. For example, a question might be intended to be textually explicit but the answer reflected some inferences drawn by the respondent. The question, given the answer, was really a textually implicit question for that particular respondent. This question-answer relationship is a significant factor in judging the quality and effectiveness of students' comprehension.

Raphael took the notion of question-answer relationships and formalized it into a system for raising students' metacognitive awareness of the comprehension process. She calls the system QAR (for *question-answer* relationship). She gave more user friendly labels to each of the dimensions of comprehension: *right there* for textually explicit, *think and search* for textually implicit, *the author and me* for scriptally implicit. The labels help students think about how they should deal with information and ideas when they answer the respective questions.

1. *Right there:* Students learn that information used to answer questions with the label *right there* is right there in the text. One does not have to speculate or read between the lines. The appropriate information is clearly available. One can use it directly to answer the question.
2. *Think and search:* Students learn that information from the text has to be put together to answer questions with the label *think and search*. One has to think about implications raised by the question, search through the text for information that can be combined to answer the question, and write out a response that reflects the interpretation, inference, or conclusion derived from that thinking and searching.
3. *The author and me:* Students learn that information and ideas from the text have to be put together with information and ideas they already hold in their memory, drawn from prior knowledge and experience when they answer questions with the label *the author and me*. One has to think about the generalization or broad principle raised by the question and how ideas drawn from the two sources (author and me) provide examples of the generalization or principle. One then has to write out a response to the question that includes the examples and shows how they relate to the question.

Raphael (1986) added one more type of question to her system. She calls it "on my own." The question provides students with opportunities to refine, extend, elaborate, or expand on ideas that are stimulated by the studying they have been doing. Answers typically reveal connections with what has been studied but are not constrained by the particular representation of the organizing idea being studied. Other examples and applications of the organizing idea are encouraged.

With the addition of the label "On my own", Raphael's system for question-answer relationships now has four questions organized into two categories:

1. Text based questions

    Right there
    Think and search

2. Reader based questions

    The author and me
    On my own

Transitioning from Answers to Questions

Guides for levels of comprehension, organizational patterns, and reasoning can be used to help students make the transition between the use of answers and the use of questions to support their response to text. Statements for the three levels of comprehension reflect answers to the two text based and the two reader based QARs. You can effect the transition in three stages:

1. Create questions that match the statements in the guide so the statements really are answers to those questions. Explain to students the differences among the four kinds of questions. Have students match questions to statements, using the criteria for the four types of questions. Have them do this in groups with guides they already have discussed. Arrange the questions by level to facilitate the matching and to support students' initiation into this type of questioning.

2. Have students work together in groups to practice creating questions for statements that appear in a levels guide. Having done the work described in Number 1 above, they will be familiar with the criteria for the four different kinds of questions. You will need to monitor their work to be certain they are able to construct questions truly appropriate to each level.

3. The first two stages of this transition develop students' familiarity with the types of question-answer relationships. They are now able to judge the kind of question being asked and the kind of answer that should be given. Having matched answers to questions by type, students are familiar with different constructions of answers that are possible for each type of question. They are now ready to respond to questions as a means of both supporting and probing their comprehension.

Guides for organizational patterns can be used the same way. Part one of a patterns guide mixes both literal and interpretive type statements while part two mixes interpretive and applied. You can follow the same three stages, first preparing a mixture of right there and think-and-search questions for part one then a mixture of the-author-and-me and on-my-own (perhaps even some think-and-search) questions for part two.

Guides for reasoning also can be used the same way. In reasoning guides usually there is a mixture of think-and-search, author-and-me and on-my-own statements. Follow the same three stages as with levels and patterns. Be certain to have students do their work in groups so they can discuss the criteria and reasons for the matches they make and the questions they construct.

Cyclical Not Linear

The purpose in this transition from the use of statements to the use of questions to guide students' response to text is to support their development of independent learning. As already discussed, students are always in the process of *becoming* independent learners. As requirements, materials, concepts, and sophistication levels change, students move from dependence to independence within grades as well as across grades. It is important, therefore, to recognize that the transition from statements to questions as the means for structuring response to text is cyclical, not linear. Your sensitivity to your own students' needs will dictate how often you cycle between statements and questions as the means for supporting their response to text.

Clearly, the cycle between the two modes can become tighter as students progress through a course or across grades. The criteria for different QARs don't change. Time you spend early on explaining the criteria will not have to be repeated as fully.

QARs and Composing

Students' familiarity with the different types of question-answer relationships can facilitate their independence in learning through writing as well as in learning through reading. Once familiar with the criteria, students can be directed to write "as though you are answering a right-there (or think-and-search or the-author-and-me) question. You can use the QAR descriptors to describe different kinds of writing tasks: right-there type for informing, think-and-search type for speculation, author-and-me type for synthesis, and the on my own type for elaboration.

Study Skills

In many respects, study skills are the independently applied, logical extension of reading, writing, and reasoning skills functionally taught through formal content-area lessons. They are applied, refined, and extended as part of the independence phase of the Instructional Framework. They also are applied during homework— to the extent that you may distinguish between homework and the independence phase of the Instructional Framework.

General Study Skills

What already has been discussed in this chapter relative to developing students' independent learning is applicable to the development of study skills. What already has been discussed in previous chapters relative to vocabulary development, reading, writing, and reasoning are applicable to the development of study skills:

- What students learn about the use of context, structure, and use of reference materials for vocabulary acquisition becomes appropriate study skills that support their independent vocabulary development.

- What students learn about the use of levels of comprehension for understanding resource materials becomes appropriate study skills that support their independent acquisition of information as well as development and application of ideas.
- What students learn about the use of organizational patterns of text for understanding resource materials becomes appropriate study skills that support their independent analysis of text, acquisition of information, and application of ideas.
- What students learn about the use of writing both to prepare for reading and reasoning as well as to reflect on their reading and reasoning becomes appropriate study skills that support their independent composing for the same purposes.
- What students learn about the use of text based (closed) reasoning and reader based (open) reasoning becomes appropriate study skills that support their independent analysis of and elaboration upon ideas they study.

Specific Study Skills

Discussions of specific study skills are available in abundance in literacy related professional literature. Most of the recommendations are identified by acronyms. Once your students develop proficiency with their general study skills (based on your functional teaching of vocabulary development, reading, writing, and reasoning), you may want to help them add some of the more specific study skills. Specific study skills relate to vocabulary acquisition, use of reference tools, use of reference resources, note taking, outlining, organization of information, and the like.

Publications from the International Reading Association, National Council of Teachers of English, National Reading Conference, and College Reading Association over the past few decades have included articles on various study skills and study-skill programs. As your interests dictate, you may wish to peruse these resources and decide which of the study skills would be appropriate to teach your students.

Assessment and Evaluation

The terms diagnosis, testing, assessment, and evaluation are used to address important educational questions: How well can students learn? What have students learned? How well can they use what they have learned?

Diagnosis implies a specialized analysis of students' strengths and weaknesses with respect to learning processes. Diagnosis lies outside the purview of this book and is not discussed.

Testing typically involves formal, published tests used to measure targeted groups for change in learning over specified time periods. Of course, testing also involves examinations constructed by teachers. We do not analyze published tests or their use. Other sources are available for that purpose. We do consider teacher prepared examinations as part of our discussion of assessment and evaluation.

Functional Assessment

Assessment involves appraisal, estimation, and judgment. As applied to learning processes and course content, these terms imply an on-going determination of students' growth and development. That is, teachers observe how students respond to on-going instruction, make judgments about the progress they are making, make adjustments in instruction to maximize the progress, continue the instruction, and extend the observation.

We call this assessment of content and process functional for the same reason we call the teaching of content and process functional. Instructional strategies presented in this text support students' learning of reading, writing, and reasoning processes that are natural to and consistent with ideas being emphasized and resources being used in that teaching. This teaching of reading, writing, and reasoning is functional in that it serves to develop an understanding of the content being studied and the resources being used. Reading, writing, or reasoning skills are not taught in isolation from the content studied or the resources used for that study.

Assessment is functional when it is an integral part of instruction and when it informs instruction. As teachers provide instruction that supports students' application of reading, writing, or reasoning processes, they observe how students respond. Teachers make judgments about how subsequent instruction should be adjusted to maximize students' learning. This is functional assessment.

Notice that the purpose of functional assessment is to make adjustments in instruction to facilitate students' learning. This is because the purpose of instruction is to show students how to be successful in doing what is required of them. Implicit in that purpose is a need to know students' level of success in that instructional context. Also implicit in that purpose is the obligation to adjust instruction when students are having difficulties in order to increase the probability of their success.

Clearly, adjustments in instruction can be made only by appraising how well individual students are responding to the instruction. But the appraisal is not an end in itself; rather it is a means to an end. Therefore, the appraisal does not require that a grade be attached or even that a particular appraisal be recorded somewhere. Rather, information derived from appraisals is cumulative. Teachers gather impressions of individual student's needs and accomplishments over time. Drawing from their observations, they can provide a professional opinion of any student's progress and needs and can support this opinion with particularized information drawn from the instruction that has taken place.

So it is that as you engage in functional teaching you also engage in functional assessment. Even as you do not have to set aside time to teach skills separately from content, you do not have to set aside time to assess separately from teaching.

- When you support students' reading, you also provide the means to assess their progress and needs in reading and course content.
- When you support students' writing, you also provide the means to assess their progress and needs in writing and course content.
- When you support students' reasoning, you also provide the means to assess their progress and needs in reasoning and course content.

Time devoted to the crafting of carefully structured lessons and units is doubly well spent. What you produce supports students' learning through functional teaching as well as through functional assessment.

Feedback to Students

Students need to be informed of your beliefs about their progress and needs if your assessment is to have value to them. You can provide feedback to them as you respond to their writing in progress, a clear form of functional assessment. As you monitor the group work of students on various guide materials, you can provide feedback to the group as a whole or to individuals on changes they need to make to improve their proficiency.

As your students develop proficiency in cooperative-learning roles and responsibilities, they provide feedback to one another on work in progress. With your students working proficiently in groups, you have opportunity to hold conferences with individual students on occasion. You may also wish to hold a conference with a whole group on a special project they are conducting. Through the use of such conferences you can provide important feedback to students from your functional assessment of their work.

Contextualized Evaluation

Students' work needs to be evaluated from time to time to provide more formal records of their progress. Depending on your institution, this record of progress can be in the form of grades or anecdotal records. Whatever the form of reporting, the feedback to students and parents should be clear and unambiguous. Grades do not lessen ambiguity nor do anecdotal records increase it. Clarity, in large part, depends on the sources drawn on for data as well as the clarity of criteria by which the data are judged and reported. Data derived from contextualized evaluations contribute strongly to unambiguous reporting.

Teacher Prepared Tests

The principle governing any means of evaluating students' learning should be that the evaluation be consistent both with what was taught and with how it was taught. This is the meaning of *contextualized evaluation*.

This principle may seem so obvious that it need not be stipulated. However, one finds that the principle often is violated. Convenience or presumed ease of measurement frequently influences both the substance and format of evaluations. As a consequence, evaluation instruments sometimes require students to respond to tasks they have not been taught on material they have not studied. Such evaluation could conceivably indicate how well students can perform independently on new tasks applied to new materials. However, information derived from such evaluation contributes minimally to knowing how well students understand the content and process that was taught in a given lesson or unit.

One way to make certain that teacher prepared tests are consistent with both what was taught and how it was taught is to emphasize organizing ideas as much in the preparation of tests as in the preparation of lessons. A matrix similar in structure to a semantic-feature analysis (see Chapter 7, Example 7-2) can be used to do a content analysis of tests. Such analyses helps determine the conceptual loading of tests you construct.

Identify the major concepts emphasized and the features emphasized for each by items. In that way you can judge whether what you are testing is consistent with what you have been teaching. If it does not, you can easily change the substance of the test items.

Similarly, you can compare the level of support you provide for students' learning with the level of independence you require of them in the tests you prepare. For example, if you are supporting students' comprehension with declarative statements, your tests will be inconsistent with that level of support if students are required to respond independently to essay questions. A consistent means of evaluation would be if you were to give students a question along with different possible answers and ask them to select the most appropriate answer and to provide in writing the reasons.

Portfolios

Another means of contextualized evaluation is the use of portfolios. If you want to know how students are progressing in their writing, examine their work in progress as well as samples of work completed across time periods. Collecting students work in a portfolio or, preferably, having students keep samples of their work in a portfolio provides appropriate samples for examination and study.

Students produce a variety of materials in response to the instructional strategies presented in this text. Guide materials with associated writing provide information over time about how students are applying reading and reasoning skills. Students' collection of subject relevant vocabulary, as well as materials they create to refine, extend, and share their knowledge of the words, reveals growth and development of vocabulary-acquisition skills. Students' responses to periodic special assignments provide a spot-check record of how they are thinking about what they are studying and how the quality of that thinking is progressing.

The collection of materials that you and the students choose to place in their portfolios provides a comprehensive set of data by which to judge the quality of work being done and the growth in that quality over time. Portfolios provide a means of evaluation that is consistent with the everyday tasks in which students are engaged. Indeed, what is contained in the portfolios is material that is derived from those every-day tasks.

Periodic conferences with individual students to discuss the contents of their portfolio provide excellent means for providing feedback to students on the progress of their work. The frequency of these conferences has to be determined by your schedule and the number of students you teach. The time it takes for an individual conference may not be as long as you might think in that you will be familiar already with most of the material placed in the portfolio. The job would be to look at materials produced at different times of the year to determine the nature and quality of change.

An important aspect of using portfolios as part of contextualized evaluation is that it involves students collaboratively in deciding what should be placed in their portfolios and how the portfolios should be evaluated. Participating in establishing the criteria for evaluating their work makes students more receptive to the outcomes of the evaluation. If your circumstance is such that you need to grade the portfolios with A, B, C, and so forth, you can work out with your students a full description of the criteria for each letter grade. They, then, can participate in formulating grades for the work done.

Tierney, Carter, and Desai (1991) have written an excellent book on portfolio assessment. We recommend it if you are seriously interested in using portfolios as part of your contextualized evaluation.

Summary

Teaching in content areas involves the pursuit of ideas and the development of learning processes. It involves the instructional integration of content and process.

Teaching in content areas also involves instructional interaction among the processes of reading, writing, and reasoning. These interacting processes are used to support students' learning of course content, resulting in an instructional integration of content and process. Transitional instruction (helping students learn to read, write, and reason to learn) supports students through multiple cycles of teacher-directed, self-managed learning. As a consequence, students *are becoming* independent learners at increasingly sophisticated levels as they progress through the grades and into college.

Strategies and materials that support transitional instruction are not applied in isolation or on a whim. Rather, they are applied in a unified, synthesized whole as a natural part of on-going teaching. And the whole is greater than the sum of its parts.

REACTIONS

Journal Entries and Discussion: In your journal, record your analysis of the relationship between (1) transitional instruction and developing independent learners and (2) functional teaching and functional assessment.

Record your opinion on which of the instructional strategies contributes most significantly to students' learning. Explain your rationale for this opinion.

Analysis and Discussion: Now that you have completed this chapter (and book!), consider the statements shown below. Check the numbered lines for statements you believe reflect the point of view of the authors. Circle the numbers of statements with which you agree. In writing, explore reasons for differences on any statements between your point of view and what you perceive to be the point of view of the authors. Please share and discuss your writing with colleagues who also are reading this book.

_____ 1. Seeing is believing. No amount of talk can substitute for direct experience.

_____ 2. When it comes to teaching and learning, letting go must be balanced by taking over.

_____ 3. One needs negatives to balance positives in magnetic environments but not in instructional environments.

_____ 4. Few achievement tests can provide information about students that their positively oriented, observant teachers have not already discovered through their teaching.

_____ 5. Even as the content in curriculum areas increases in sophistication through the grades, so does the process by which that content is learned; and students need to be taught how to handle both.

_____ 6. Lesson structure should be sufficiently firm to give a sense of purpose and direction yet sufficiently loose to allow for individuality and divergence.

_____ 7. All instruction should remain simple unless it would serves students better to make the instruction more complicated.

_____ 8. A profitable teacher-education course does not replace old methods with new; rather, it promotes a synthesis of compatible new and old methods and ideas.

Credits

Chapter two: Practice 2-2/Sand Art, On a Deadline, *New York Times,* August 13, 1989, Section 4, p. 22. Copyright © 1989 by The New York Times Company. Reprinted by permission.

Chapter three: Practice 3-2/Changing Angle of Attack, *Private Pilot Manual,* copyright 1988 by Jeppsen Sanderson, Inc. Reproduced with permission; Practice 3-3/Predicting performance, *Private Pilot Manual,* copyright 1988 by Jeppsen Sanderson, Inc. Reproduced with permission; Practice 3-4/Ignorance, Ignorantly Judged by Roald Hoffmann, *New York Times,* September 14, 1989. Copyright © 1989 by the New York Times Company. Reprinted by permission; Practice 3-5/Passing Down Murphy's Law by Ray Recchi, *Syracuse Herald American,* August 27, 1989. Reprinted with permission of the *Ft. Lauderdale Sun-Sentinel;* Practice 3-6/The Blunderers of June by Vincent G. Dethier, *Yankee,* June 1985. Reprinted by permission; Practice 3-7/Graphic organizers, *Teaching Reading in Content Areas,* 1978. Reprinted by permission of Prentice-Hall, Inc.

Chapter six: Practice 6-1/When to lie to yourself by Nick Jordan, *Psychology Today,* June 1989, Vol. 23, No. 6. Reprinted with permission from *Psychology Today Magazine* copyright © 1989 (Sussex Publishers, Inc.); Practice 6-2/Bedtime Story by Russel Baker, August 24, 1990, Copyright © 1989 by The New York Times Company. Reprinted by permission.

Chapter seven: Example 7-3/Carl Greve; Example 7-4/Maria Lourdes L. Ladrido; Example 7-5/Renee Dewald; Example 7-6/Renee Dewald; Example 7-8/Jennifer Connor; Example 7-9/Jane Wickens; Example 7-10/Jane Wickens; Example 7-11/Linda Tait; Example 7-12/Linda Tait; Example 7-13/David J. Wray; Example 7-15/Denise Micek; Example 7-16/Linda Tait; Example 7-17/Kathy Klein; Example 7-18/Patti Franks; Example 7-20/Dan Swanberry; Practice 7-1/Maria Lourdes Ladridos; Practice 7-2/Jacqueline A. Morgia.

Chapter eight: Practice 8-1/Now, there's a kinder, gentler argument in favor of a free press by R. J. Rummel, *The Bulletin of the American Society of Newpaper Editors,* February 1989, #711. Reprinted from the Bulletin of the American Society of Newspaper Editors; Practice 8-2/*Verbal jabs don't have equal punch* by Zorika Petic Henderson, *Human Ecology Forum,* Winter 1989, Vol. 17: No. 2, p. 28. Reprinted from *Human Ecology Forum,* published by Cornell University; Practice 8-3/*Never mind your number—They've got your name* by Stephen Phillips. Reprinted from September 4, 1989 issue of *Business Week* by special permission, copyright © 1989 by McGraw-Hill, Inc.; Practice 8-4/The Future of Pennies, No, let's keep them. © 1989, by Cullen Murphy. Reprinted from the December, 1989, issue of *The Atlantic Monthly;* Practice 8-6/*Women in architecture* by Ann Mackin & Ingrid Strong, *Art New England,* March 1989, p. 14. Reprinted by permission.

Chapter ten: Practice 10-2b/Leap second to put clocks in sync with heavens, *Syracuse Herald American* Sunday, December 31, 1989, page B4. Reprinted by permission; Practice 10-3/Chayet, Neil (1986) Law and morality. In D. Gavitch (Ed.), *Life Studies: A Thematic Reader.* New York: St. Martin's Press. (p. 540) 175 Fifth Avenue, New York, NY 10010. Reprinted by permission of Neil Chayet; Example 10-1/Jean Arnold; Example 10-2/Jean Arnold; Example 10-3/Jean Arnold; Example 10-5/Jane Klausmeier Janis; Example 10-7/Vel Chesser.

Chapter 11: Latin unit, *Jason and the Argonauts:* Diane Mannix.

Appendix A: Practice 7-1/Maria Lourdes Ladridos; Practice 7-2/Jacqueline A. Morgia.

Appendix B: Material drawn from a unit in life science: Ann Pangburn; materials drawn from a unit on propaganda: Patricia Schmidt; materials drawn from a unit in geometry: Janet Zerfas.

REFERENCES

Alvermann, D. (1987a). Discussion strategies for content area reading. In D. Alvermann, D. R. Dillon, and D. G. O'Brien, (Eds.), *Using discussion to promote reading comprehension* (pp. 34–42). Newark, DE: International Reading Association.

Alvermann, D. (1987b). Integrating oral and written language. In D. Alvermann, D. Moore, and M. Conley (Eds.), *Research within reach: Secondary school reading* (pp. 109–129). Newark, DE: International Reading Association.

Alvermann, D. E., and Boothby, P. R. (1983). A preliminary investigation of the differences in children's retention of "inconsiderate" text. *Reading Psychology, 4,* 237–246.

Alvermann, D. E.; Dillon, D. R.; and O'Brien, D. G. (1987). *Using discussion to promote reading comprehension.* Newark, DE: International Reading Association.

Anderson, C. W., and Smith, E. L. (1984). Children's preconceptions and content-area textbooks. In G. G. Duffy, L. R. Roehler, and J. M. Mason (Eds.), *Comprehension instruction: Perspectives and suggestions* (pp. 187–201). New York: Longman.

Anderson, R. C. (1985). The role of the reader's schema in comprehension, learning and memory. In H. Singer and R. B. Ruddell (Eds.), *Theoretical models and processes of reading* (3rd ed.), (pp. 372–384). Newark, DE: International Reading Association.

Anderson, R. C., and Freebody, P. (1981). Vocabulary knowledge. In J. T. Guthrie (Ed.), *Comprehension and teaching: Research perspectives.* Newark, DE: International Reading Association.

Anderson, R. C.; Heibert, E.; Scott, J.; and Wilkinson, I. (1984). *Becoming a nation of readers.* Washington, D. C.: The National Institute of Education.

Anderson, R. C., and Pearson, P. D. (1984). A schema-theoretic view of basic processes in reading. In P. D. Pearson (Ed.), *Handbook of reading research.* New York: Longman.

Anderson, R. C.; Reynolds, R. E.; Schallert, D. L.; and Goetz, E. T. (1977). Frameworks for comprehending discourse. *American Educational Research Journal, 14,* 367–382.

Anderson, T., and Armbruster, B. (1984). Content area textbooks. In R. C. Anderson, J. Osborn, and R. J. Tierney (Eds.), *Learning to read in American schools: Basal readers and content texts.* (pp. 193–226). Hillsdale, NJ: Erlbaum.

Applebee, A. N. (1981). *Writing in the secondary school.* Urbana, IL: National Council of Teachers of English.

Applebee, A. N. (1986). Problems in process approaches: Toward a reconceptualization of process instruction. In A. R. Petrosky and D. Bartholomae (Eds.), *The teaching of writing.* Chicago, IL: National Society for the Study of Education.

Applebee, A. N., and Langer, J. A. (1983). Instructional scaffolding: Reading and writing as natural language activities. *Language Arts, 60,* 168–175.

Armstrong, D. P.; Patberg, J. P.; and Dewitz, P. (1988). Reading guides: Helping students understand. *Journal of Reading, 31,* 532–541.

Au, K. H. (1979). Using the experience-text-relationship method with minority children. *The Reading Teacher, 32,* 678–679.

Ausubel, D. (1963). *The psychology of meaningful learning.* New York: Grune and Stratton.

Ausubel, D. (1968). *Educational psychology: A cognitive view.* New York: Holt, Rinehart and Winston.

Ausubel, D. (1978). *Educational psychology: A cognitive view* (2nd ed.). New York: Holt, Rinehart and Winston.

Ausubel, D. P. (1960). The use of advance organizers in the learning and retention of meaningful verbal material. *Journal of Educational Psychology, 51,* 267–272.

Babbs, P., and Moe, A. (1983). Metacognition: A key for independent learning from text. *The Reading Teacher, 36,* 422–426.

Bader, L., and Pearce, D. (1983). Writing across the curriculum 7–12. *English Education, 15,* 97–106.

Baker, L., and Brown, A. L. (1984). Metacognitive skills and reading. In P. D. Pearson (Ed.), *Handbook of reading research* (pp. 333–394). New York: Longman.

Baldwin, R. S.; Ford, J. C.; and Readance, J. E. (1981). Teaching word connotations: An alternative strategy. *Reading World, 21,* 103–108.

Baldwin, R. S.; Luce, T. S.; and Readence, J. E. (1982). The impact of subschemta on metaphorical processing. *Reading Research Quarterly* 17 (4), 528–543.

Barron, R. F. (1969). The use of vocabulary as an advance organizer. In H. L. Herber and P. L. Sanders (Eds.), *Research in reading in the content areas: First year report* (pp. 29–39). Syracuse, NY: Syracuse University, Reading and Language Arts Center.

Barron, R., and Stone, F. (1973). The effect of student constructed graphic post organizers upon learning of vocabulary relationships from a passage of social studies content. Paper presented at the meeting of the National Reading Conference, Houston, TX.

Bartlett, F. C. (1932). *Remembering.* Cambridge: Cambridge University Press.

Bean, T. W. et al. (1986). The effect of metacognitive instruction in outlining and graphic organizer construction on students' comprehension in a tenth-grade world history class. *Journal of Reading Behavior,* 18, 153–169.

Bean, T. W., and Pardi, R. (1979). A field test of a guided reading strategy. *Journal of Reading.* 23, 144–147.

Beck, I. L.; Perfetti, C. A.; and McKeown, M. G. (1982) Effects of long-term vocabulary instruction of lexical access and reading comprehension. *Journal of Educational Psychology,* 74 (4), 506–521.

Berget, E. (1973). Two methods of guiding the learning of a short story. In H. L. Herber and R. F. Barron (Eds.), *Research in reading in the content areas: Second year report* (pp. 53–57). Syracuse, NY: Syracuse University, Reading and Language Arts Center.

Berliner, D. C. (1981). Academic learning time and reading achievement. In J. T. Guthrie (Ed.), *Comprehension and teaching: Research reviews.* Newark, DE: International Reading Association.

Beyer, B. (1984). Improving thinking skills—Defining the problem. *Phi Delta Kappan,* 65, 486–490.

Beyer, B. K. (1983). Common sense about teaching thinking skills. *Educational Leadership,* 41, 44–49.

Bormuth, J. R. (1963). Cloze as a measure of readability. In J. A. Figurel (Ed.), *Reading as an intellectual activity. International Reading Association Conference Proceedings,* 8 (pp. 131–134). Newark, DE: International Reading Association.

Bormuth, J. R. (1965). Validities of grammatical and semantic classifications of cloze test scores. In J. A. Figurel (Ed.), *Reading and inquiry. International Reading Association Conference Proceedings,* 10 (pp. 283–286). Newark, DE: International Reading Association.

Bormuth, J. R. (1966). Readability: A new approach. *Reading Research Quarterly,* 1 (3), 79–132.

Bormuth, J. R. (1967). Comparable cloze and multiple choice comprehension test scores. *Journal of Reading,* 10, 291–299.

Bormuth, J. R. (1968). Cloze test readability: Criterion reference scores. *Journal of Educational Measurement,* 5, 189–196.

Bransford, J. D., and Johnson, M. K. (1972). Contextual prerequisites for understanding: Some investigations of comprehension and recall. *Journal of Verbal Learning and Verbal Behavior,* 11, 717–726.

Bransford, J. D., and Stein, B. S. (1984). *The idea problem solver: A guide for improving thinking, learning, and creativity.* New York: W. H. Freeman.

Bromley, K. D. (1985). Precis writing and outlining enhance content learning. *The Reading Teacher,* 38, 406–411.

Brookover, V.; Schweitzer, J.; Scheider, J.; Beady, C.; Flood, P.; and Wisenbarker, J. (1978). Elementary school social climate and school achievement. *American Educational Research Journal,* 15, 301–318.

Brown, A. L. (1980). Metacognition development and reading. In R. J. Spiro, B. C. Bruce, and W. F. Brewer (Eds.), *Theoretical issues in reading comprehension* (pp. 453–481). Hillsdale, NJ: Erlbaum.

Brown, A. L.; Campione, J. C.; and Day, J. D. (1981). Learning to learn: On training students to learn from texts. *Educational Researcher*, 10 (2), 14–21.

Brown, R. G. (1991). *Schools of Thought.* San Frncisco: Jossey-Bass, Publishers.

Brozo, W. G., and Simpson, M. L. (1991). *Readers, teachers, learners: Expanding literacy in the secondary schools.* New York: Macmillan.

Bruner, J. S.; Goodnow, S. J.; and Austin, G. A. (1956). *A study of thinking.* New York: Wiley.

Bruner, J. S. (1960). *The process of education.* Cambridge, MA: Harvard University Press.

Bruner, J. S. (1965). The act of discovery. In *On knowing.* New York: Atheneum.

Calkins, L. (1986). *The art of teaching writing.* Portsmouth, NH: Heineman.

Carr, E. M.; Dewitz, P.; and Patberg, J. P. (1989). Using cloze for inference training with expository text. *The Reading Teacher,* 42, 380 385.

Carr, E. M., and Ogle, D. (1987). K-W-L Plus: A strategy for comprehension and summarization. *Journal of Reading,* 30, 626–631.

Casale, U. P., and Kelly, B. W. (1980). Problem-solving approach to study skills (PASS) for students in professional schools. *Journal of Reading,* 24, 232–238.

Chall, J. (1947). The influence of previous knowledge on reading ability. *Educational Research Bulletin,* 26, 225–230.

Chall, J. S. (1983a). *Learning to read: The Great Debate* (updated ed.). New York: McGraw-Hill.

Chall, J. S. (1983b). *Stages of reading development.* New York: McGraw-Hill.

Chandler, T. A. (1975). Locus of control: A proposal for change. *Psychology in Schools,* 12, 334–339.

Clary, L. M. (1977). How well do you teach critical reading? *The Reading Teacher,* 31, 142–146.

Colby, B. N., and Cole, M. (1973). Culture, memory, and narrative. In R. Horton and R. Murray (Eds.), *Modes of thought.* (pp. 63–91). London: Faber and Faber.

Collins, C. (1987). Content mastery strategies aid class discussion. *The Reading Teacher,* 40, 816–818.

Conley, M. (1985). Promoting cross-cultural understanding through content area reading strategies. *Journal of Reading,* 28, 600–605.

Conley, M. W. (1986). Teachers' conceptions, decisions, and changes during initial classroom lessons containing content reading strategies. In J. A. Niles and R. V. Lalik (Eds.), *Solving problems in literacy: Learners, teachers, and researchers. Thirty-fifth yearbook of the National Reading Conference* (pp. 120–126). Rochester, NY: National Reading Conference.

Cooper, E. J. (1989). Toward a new mainstream of instruction for American schools. *Journal of Negro Education*, 58 (1), 102–116.

Cooper, J. D. (1986). *Improving reading comprehension*. New York: Houghton Mifflin.

Cowan, G., and Cowan, E. (1980). *Writing*, New York: Wiley.

Crafton, L. K. (1983). Learning from reading: What happens when students generate their own background information? *Journal of Reading*, 26, 586–592.

Crist, R. (1981). Learning concepts from contexts and definitions: A single subject replication. *Journal of Reading Behavior*, 13 (3), 271–277.

Crist, R., and Petrone, J. M. (1977). Learning concepts from contexts and definitions. *Journal of Reading Behavior*, 9 (3), 201–301.

Cunningham, D., and Shablak, S. L. (1975). Selective Reading Guide-O-Rama: The content teacher's best friend. *Journal of Reading*, 18, 280–382.

Cunningham, J. W.; Cunningham, P. M.; and Arthur, S. V. (1981). *Middle and secondary school reading*. New York: Longman.

Cunningham, P. M., and Cunningham, J. W. (1976). SSSW, better content-writing. *The Clearing House*, 49, 237–238.

Cushman, Jr., J. H. (1990). 'Smart' cars and highways to help unsnarl gridlock. *The New York Times*. April 12, A-16.

Davey, B. (1987). Team for success: Guided practice in study skills through cooperative research reports. *Journal of Reading*, 30, 701–705.

Davey, B., and McBride, S. (1986). Effects of question-generation training on reading comprehension. *Journal of Educational Psychology*, 78, 256–62.

Davis, F. (1944). Fundamental factors of comprehension in reading, *Psychometrika*, 9, 185–190.

Davis, F., (1968). Research in comprehension in reading. *Reading Research Quarterly*. vol. 3, no. 4, pp. 499–545.

Dechant, E. (1970). *Improving the teaching of reading*. Englewood Cliffs, NJ: Prentice-Hall.

Derby, T. (1987). Reading instruction and course-related materials for vocational high school students. *Journal of Reading*, 30, 308–316.

Dewey, J. (1933). *How we think*. Boston: Heath.

Dewitz, P.; Carr, E. M.; and Patberg, J. P. (1987). Effects of inference training on comprehension and comprehension monitoring. *Reading Research Quarterly*, 22, 99–121.

Draper, A. G., and Moeller, G. (1971). We think with words (Therefore, to improve thinking, teach vocabulary). *Phi Delta Kappan*, 52, 482–484.

Dreyer, L. G. (1984). Readability and responsibility. *Journal of Reading*, 27, 334–338.

Drum, P. A., and Konopak, B. (1987). Learning word meanings from written context. In M. G. McKeown and M. E. Curtis (Eds.), *The Nature of Vocabulary Acquisition*. Hillsdale, NJ: Erlbaum.

Duffelmeyer, F. A.; Baum, D. D.; and Merkley, D. J. (1987). Maximizing reader-text confrontation with an extended anticipation guide. *Journal of Reading.* 31, 146–150.

Duffy, G. G., and Roehler, L. R. (1982). Direct instruction of comprehension: What does it really mean? *Reading Horizons.* 23, 35–40.

Duffy, G. G.; Roehler, L. R.; and Mason, J. M. (1984). *Comprehension instruction: Perspectives and suggestions.* New York: Longman.

Duffy, G. G.; Roehler, L. R.; Meloth, M. S.; Vavrus, L. G.; Book, C.; Putnam, J.; and Wesselman. R. (1986). The relationship between explicit verbal explanations during reading skill instruction and student awareness and achievement: A study of reading teacher effects. *Reading Research Quarterly,* 21, 237–252.

Duin, A. H. (1984). *The effects of intensive vocabulary instruction on a specific writing task.* ERIC Document Reproduction Service No. Ed 239222.

Duke, C. R. (1987). Integrating reading, writing, and thinking skills into the music class. *Journal of Reading,* 31, 152–157.

Durrell, D. D. (1966). *Improving reading instruction.* New York: Harcourt Brace Jovanovich.

Eanet, M. G., and Manzo, A. V. (1976). REAP-A strategy for improving reading/writing/study skills. *Journal of Reading,* 19, 647–652.

Earle, R. (1969). The use of the structured overview in mathematics classes. In H. L. Herber and P. L. Sanders (Eds.), *Research in reading in the content areas: First-year report.* Syracuse, NY: Syracuse University, Reading and Language Arts Center.

Earle, R., and Barron, R. F. (1973). An approach for teaching vocabulary in content subjects. In H. L. Herber and R. F. Barron (Eds.), *Research in reading in the content areas: Second year report* (pp. 84–100). Syracuse, NY: Syracuse University, Reading and Language Arts Center.

Eeds, M., and Cockrum, W. A. (1985) Teaching word meanings by expanding schemata vs. dictionary work vs. reading in context. *Journal of Reading,* 28, 492–497.

Ennis, R. H. (1962). A concept of critical thinking. *Harvard Educational Review,* 32, 81–111.

Ennis, R. H. (1981). Rational thinking and educational practice. In J. Soltis (Ed.), *The philosophy of education* (pp. 143–183). Chicago: University of Chicago Press.

Ennis, R. H. (1989). Critical thinking and subject specificity: Clarification and needed research. *Educational Researcher,* April, 18 (3), 4–19

Ericson, B.; Hubler, M.; Bean, T. W.; Smith, C. C.; and McKenzie, J. V. (1987). Increasing critical reading in junior high classrooms. *Journal of Reading,* 30, 430–439.

Estes, T. H. (1969). Use of prepared guide material and small group discussion in reading ninth grade social studies assignments: Pilot study report. In H. L. Herber and P. L. Sanders (Eds.), *Research in reading in the content areas: First year report* (pp. 64–70). Syracuse, NY: Syracuse University, Reading and Language Arts Center.

Estes, T. H. (1973). Guiding reading in social studies. In H. L. Herber and R. F. Barron (Eds.), *Research in reading in the content areas: Secondary year report* (pp. 58–63). Syracuse, NY: Syracuse University, Reading and Language Arts Center.

Estes, T. H., and Vaughan, J. L., Jr. (1978). *Reading and learning in the content classroom.* Boston: Allyn & Bacon.

Estes, T. H., and Vaughan, J. L. (1986). *Reading, writing, and reasoning beyond the primary grades.* Boston: Allyn and Bacon.

Farr, R.; Tuinman, J.; and Rowls, M. (1975). *Reading achievement in the United States: Then and now.* Report for Educational Testing Service. (Contract OEC-71-3715 USOE), Washington, D.C.: U.S. Government Printing Office.

Farr, R.; Fay, L.; and Negley, H. (1978). *Then and now: Reading achievement in Indiana.* Bloomington: Indiana University.

Farr, R., and Blomenberg, P. (1979). Contrary to popular opinion. *Early Years,* 52–53, 68.

Feathers, K. M., and Smith, F. R. (1987). Meeting the reading demands of the real world: Literacy based content instruction. *Journal of Reading,* 30, 506–511.

Fitzgerald, J. (1989). Research on stories: Implications for teachers. In K. D. Muth (Ed.), *Children's comprehension of text.* (pp. 2–36). Newark, DE: International Reading Association.

Forgan, H. W., and Mangrum, C. T. (1985). *Teaching content area reading skills.* Columbus, OH: Merrill.

Foucault, M. (1977). *The archaeology of knowledge.* (A. M. S. Smith, translation) New York: Random House.

Frager, A. M., and Thompson, L. C. (1985). Conflict: The key to critical reading instruction. *Journal of Reading,* 28, 676–683.

Frayer, D. A.; Fredrick, W. C.; and Klausmeier, H. J. (1969). *A schema for testing the level of concept mastery* (Working Paper No. 16). Madison, WI: RandD Center for Cognitive Learning.

Fry, E. (1968a), A readability formula that saves time. *Journal of Reading,* 11, 513–516, 575–578.

Fry, E. (1968b). The readability graph validated at primary levels. *The Reading Teacher,* 3, 534–538.

Fry, E. (1977). Fry's readability graph: Clarification, validity, and extension to level 17. *Journal of Reading,* 21, 242–252.

Fry, E. (1987). The varied uses of readability measurement today. *Journal of Reading,* 30, 338–343.

Gagne, R. (1965). *The conditions of learning.* New York: Holt, Rinehart and Winston.

Gardner, H. (1983). *Frames of mind.* New York: Basic Books.

Gebhard, A. (1983). Teaching writing in reading and the content areas. *Journal of Reading, 27,* 207–211.

Gere, A. (1985). *Roots in the sawdust—Writing to learn across the disciplines.* Urbana, IL: National Council of Teachers of English.

Gerhard, C. (1975). *Making sense: Reading comprehension improved through categorizing.* Newark, DE: International Reading Association.

Gipe, J. P. (1979). Investigating techniques for teaching word meanings. *Reading Research Quarterly, 14* (4), 624–644.

Gipe, J. P. (1980). Use of a relevant context helps kids learn new word meanings. *The Reading Teacher, 33,* 398–402.

Goodlad, J. (1984). *A place called school.* New York: McGraw-Hill.

Goodman, K. (1970). Behind the eye. In *Reading process and program.* Urbana, IL: National Council of Teachers of English, 25–26.

Goodman, K. S. (1984). Unity in reading. In A. Purves and O. Niles (Eds.), *Becoming readers in a complex society. Eighty-third yearbook of the National Society for the Study of Education. Part 1* (pp. 79–114. Chicago: University of Chicago Press.

Gordon, W. J. (1961). *Synectics.* New York: Harper and Row.

Gordon, W. J. (1973). *The metaphorical way of learning and knowing.* Cambridge, MA: Porpoise Books.

Graves, D. (1983). *Writing: Teachers and children at work.* Portsmouth, NH: Heinemann.

Graves, M. F. (1985). *A word is a word . . . or is it!* New York: Scholastic.

Graves, M. F. (1987a). Vocabulary learning and instruction. *Review of Research in Education, 18.*

Graves, M. F. (1987b). The roles of instruction in fostering vocabulary development. In M. G. McKeown and M. E. Curtis (Eds.), *The nature of vocabulary acquisition.* Hillsdale, NJ: Lawrence Erlbaum.

Graves, M. F.; Slater, W. H.; and White, T. G. (1989). Teaching content area vocabulary. In D. Lapp, J. Flood, and N. Farnan (Eds.), *Content area reading and learning: Instructional strategies* (pp. 214–224). Englewood Cliffs, NJ: Prentice-Hall.

Gray, D. J. (1988). Writing across the college curriculum. *Phi Delta Kappan, 69* (10), 729–733.

Gray, W. (1960). The major aspects of reading. In H. Robinson (Ed.), *Development of reading abilities.* Supplementary Educational Monographs No. 90. Chicago: University of Chicago Press.

Guszak, F. J. (1967). Teacher questioning and reading. *The Reading Teacher, 21,* 227–234.

Guthrie, J. (1974). The maze technique to assess, monitor reading comprehension, *Reading Teacher, 28,* 161–168.

Hafner, L. (1967). Using context to determine meanings in high school and college. *Journal of Reading, 10,* 491–498.

Hafner, L. E. (1977). *Developmental reading in middle and secondary schools: Foundations, strategies, and skills for teaching.* New York: Macmillan.

Haggard, M. R. (1978). The effect of creative thinking-reading activities (CT-RA) on reading comprehension. In P. D. Pearson and J. Hansen (Eds.), *Reading: Disciplined inquiry in process and practice. Twenty-seventh yearbook of the National Reading Conference* (pp. 233–236). Clemson, SC: National Reading Conference.

Haggard, M. R. (1982). The vocabulary self-collection strategy: An active approach to word learning. *Journal of Reading, 27*, 203–207.

Hanf, M. B. (1971). Mapping: A technique for translating reading into thinking. *Journal of Reading, 14*, 225–230, 270.

Hansen, J. (1981). The effects of inference training and practice on young children's comprehension. *Reading Research Quarterly, 16*, 391–417.

Harker, W. J. (1972–1973). An evaluative summary of models of reading comprehension. *Journal of Reading Behavior, 5*, 26–34.

Harris, T., and Hodges, R. (1981). *A dictionary of reading.* Newark, DE: International Reading Association.

Hayes, D. A., and Tierney, R. J. (1982). Developing readers' knowledge through analogy. *Reading Research Quarterly, 17*, 256–280.

Head, M. H., and Readence. J. E. (1986). Anticipation guides: Enhancing meaning through prediction. In E. K. Dishner, T. W. Bean, J. E. Readence, and D. W. Moore (Eds.), *Reading in the content areas: Improving classroom instruction* (2nd ed.), (pp. 229–234). Dubuque, IA: Kendall/Hunt.

Heimlich, J. E., and Pittelman, S. D. (1986). *Semantic mapping: Classroom applications.* Newark, DE: International Reading Association.

Heller, M. (1986). How do you know what you know? Metacognitive modeling in the content areas. *Journal of Reading, 29*, 415–422.

Hennings, D. G. (1984). A writing approach to reading comprehension— Schema theory in action. In J. M. Jensen (Ed.), *Composing and Comprehending* (pp. 191–200). Urbana, IL: National Conference on Research in English.

Henry, G. H. (1974). *Teach reading as concept development: Emphasis on affective thinking.* Newark, DE: International Reading Association.

Herber, H. L. (1970). *Teaching reading in content areas.* Englewood Cliffs, NJ: Prentice-Hall.

Herber, H. L. (1978). *Teaching reading in content areas* (2nd ed.). Englewood Cliffs, NJ: Prentice-Hall

Herber, H. L. (1985). Levels of comprehension: An instructional strategy for guiding students' reading. In T. L. Harris and E. J. Cooper (Eds.), *Reading, thinking, and concept development.* New York: The College Board.

Herber, H. L. (1987). Foreword. In D. Alvermann, D. Moore, and M. Conley, (Eds.), *Research within reach/Secondary school reading.* Newark, DE: International Reading Association.

Herber, H. L., and Nelson, J. (1975). Questioning is not the answer. *Journal of Reading, 18* (7), 512–517.

Herber, H. L., and Nelson-Herber, J. (1984). *Final report: Network of demonstration centers for teaching reading in content areas.* (ED 282 176).

Herber, H. L., and Nelson-Herber, J. (1987). Developing independent readers. *Journal of Reading,* 30 (7), 584–588.

Hillocks, G., Jr. (1987). Synthesis of research on teaching writing. *Educational Leadership,* 44 (8), 71–76, 78, 80–82.

Hinchman, K. (1987). The textbook and three content-area teachers. *Reading Research and Instruction,* 26, 247–263.

Hittleman, D. (1978). Readability, readability formulas, and cloze: Selecting instructional materials. *Journal of Reading,* 22, 117–122.

Hoffman, J. V. (1986). *Effective teaching of reading: Research and practice.* Newark, DE: International Reading Association.

Hogan, R. (1971). You'll like it. It's caneloni. *Phi Delta Kappan,* April, 468–470.

Holbrook, H. T. (1984). Prereading in the content areas. *Journal of Reading,* 27, 368–370.

Holmes, B., and Roser, N. (1987). Five ways to assess readers' prior knowledge. *Reading Teacher,* 40, 646–649.

Huey, E. (1908). *The psychology and pedagogy of reading.* New York: Macmillan, Cambridge, MA: MIT Press 1968.

Irwin, J. W., and Baker, I. (1989). *Promoting active reading comprehension strategies.* Englewood Cliffs, NJ: Prentice-Hall.

Jenkins, J. R.; Stein, M. L.; and Wysocki, K. (1984). Learning vocabulary through reading. *American Educational Research Journal,* 211 (41), 767–787.

Johnson, D. D., and Pearson, P. D. (1978). *Teaching reading vocabulary.* New York: Holt, Rinehart and Winston.

Johnson, D. D.; Pittelman, S. E.; and Heimlich, J. E. (1986). Semantic mapping. *The Reading Teacher,* 39, 778–783.

Johnson, D. W., and Johnson R. T. (1987). *Learning together and alone: Cooperative, conjunctive, and individualistic learning.* Englewood Cliffs, NJ: Prentice-Hall.

Johnston, P., and Pearson, P. D. (1982). *Prior knowledge, connectivity, and the assessment of reading comprehension. Technical Report 245.* Urbana, IL: University of Chicago, Center for the Study of Reading.

Kaneenui, E. J., Carnine, D. W., and Freschi, R. (1982). Effects of text construction and instructional procedures for teaching word meanings on comprehension and recall. *Reading Research Quarterly.* vol. 17, no. 3, 367–388.

Kameenui, E. J.; Dixon, R. C.; and Carnine, D. W. (1987). Issues in the design of vocabulary instruction. In M. G. McKeown and M. E. Curtis (Eds.), *The nature of vocabulary acquisition.* Hillsdale, NJ: Erlbaum.

Karlin, R. (1984). *Teaching reading in high school: Improving reading in content areas* (4th ed.). New York: Harper & Row.

Kintsch, W. (1977). *Memory and cognition.* New York: Wiley.

Kirby, D., and Liner, T. (1988). *Inside out: Developmental strategies for teaching writing.* Portsmouth, NH: Boynton/Cook.

Kirsch, I., and Guthrie, J. T. (1977–1978). The concept and measurement of functional literacy. *Reading Research Quarterly, 13,* 485–507.

Kirsch, I., and Jungeblut, A. (1986). *Literacy: Profiles of American's young adults.* Princeton, NJ: National Assessment of Educational Progress.

Klare, G. (1974–1975) Assessing readability. *Reading Research Quarterly, 10,* 62–102.

Klein, M. L. (1988). *Teaching reading comprehension and vocabulary.* Englewood Cliffs, NJ: Prentice Hall.

Konopak, B. C. (1988). Using contextual information for word learning. *Journal of Reading, 31,* 334–338.

Konopak, B. C.; Martin, M. A.; and Martin, S. H. (1987). Reading and writing: Aids to learning to the content areas. *Journal of Reading, 31,* 109–115.

Kozol, J. (1985). *Illiterate America.* Garden City, NY: Anchor Press/Doubleday.

Langer, J. A. (1981). From theory to practice: A prereading plan. *Journal of Reading, 25,* 152–156.

Langer, J. A., and Nicolich, M. (1981). Prior knowledge and its relationship to comprehension. *Journal of Reading Behavior, 13,* 373–379.

Langer, J. A., and Purcel-Gates, V. (1985). Knowledge and comprehension: Helping students use what they know. In T. L. Harris and E. J. Cooper (Eds.), *Reading, thinking, and concept development.* New York: The College Board.

Lapp, D.; Flood, J.; and Farnan, N. (1989). *Content area reading and learning: Instructional strategies.* Englewood Cliffs, NJ: Prentice-Hall.

Larson, C., and Dansereau, D. (1986). Cooperative learning in dyads. *Journal of Reading, 29,* 516–520.

Lehr, R. (1984). Cooperative learning. *Journal of Reading, 27,* 458–460.

Leu, D. J., Jr., and Kinzer, C. K. (1991). *Effective reading instruction in the elementary grades.* Columbus, OH: Merrill.

Lipson, M. Y. (1982). Learning new information from text: The role of prior knowledge and reading ability. *Journal of Reading Behavior, 14,* 247–261.

MacGinitie, W. H., and MacGinitie, R. K. (1986). Teaching students not to read. In S. De Castell, A. Luke, and K. Egan (Eds.), *Literacy, society, and schooling.* Cambridge: Cambridge University Press

McGonigal, E. (1988). Correlative thinking: Writing analogies about literature. *English Journal, 77* (1), 66–67.

McKeown, M. G.; Beck, I. L.; Omanson, R. C.; and Perfetti, C. A. (1983). The effects of long term vocabulary instruction on reading comprehension: A replication. *Journal of Reading Behavior, 15* (1), 3–18.

McKeown, M. G. and Curtis, M. E. (Eds.), (1987). *The nature of vocabulary acquisition.* Hillsdale, NJ: Erlbaum.

McPeck, J. (1981). *Critical thinking and education.* New York: St. Martin's.

Maimon, E. P. (1988). Cultivating the prose garden. *Phi Delta Kappan,* June 1988, vol. 69 (10), 734–739.

Mandler, J. M., and Johnson, M. S. (1977). Remembrance of things parsed: Story structure and recall. *Cognitive Psychology,* 9, 111–115.

Manzo, A. V. (1969a). The request procedure. *Journal of Reading,* 11, 123–216.

Manzo, A. V. (1969b). Improving reading comprehension through reciprocal questioning (Doctoral dissertation, Syracuse University, Syracuse, NY, 1968). *Dissertation Abstracts International,* 30, 5344A.

Manzo, A. V. (1969c). The request procedure. *Journal of Reading,* 13, 123–216.

Manzo, A. V. (1975). The guided reading procedure. *Journal of Reading,* 18, 287–291.

Manzo, A. V., and Manzo, U. C. (1990). *Content area reading.* Columbus, OH: Merrill.

Marzano, R. J., and Marzano, J. S. (1988). *A cluster approach to elementary vocabulary instruction.* Newark, DE: International Reading Association.

Mason, J. M. (Ed.) (1989). *Reading and writing connections.* Boston: Allyn & Bacon.

Maxon, G. A. (1979). An investigation of the relative effectiveness between questions and declarative statements as guides to reading comprehension for seventh grade students. In H. L. Herber and J. D. Riley (Eds.), *Research in reading in the content areas: Fourth year report* (pp. 66–78). Syracuse, NY: Syracuse University, Reading and Language Arts Center.

Meyer, B. J. F. (1977). The structure of prose: Effects on learning and memory and implications for educational practice. In R. C. Anderson, R. J. Spiro, and W. E. Montague (Eds.), *Schooling and the acquisition of knowledge.* Hillsdale, NJ: Erlbaum.

Meyer, B. J. F. (1979). Organizational patterns in prose and their use in reading. In M. L. Kamil and A. J. Moe (Eds.), *Reading research: Studies and applications.* (pp. 109–117). Clemson, SC: National Reading Conference.

Meyer, B. J. F., and Rice, G. E. (1984). The structure of text. In P. D. Pearson, R. Barr, M. L. Kamil, and P. Mosenthal (Eds.), *Handbook of reading research* (pp. 319–349), New York: Longman.

Miceli, D. (1980). Using levels guides to support students' written composition. *Conversations, demonstrations, observations.* Bronx, NY: School District No. 11.

Micklos, J. (1980). The facts, please, about reading achievement in American schools. *Journal of Reading,* 24, 44–45.

Micklos, J. (1982). A look at reading achievement in the United States. *Journal of Reading,* 25 (8), 760–762.

Mikulecky, L. (1982). Job literacy: The relationship between school preparation and workplace actuality. *Reading Research Quarterly,* 17, 440–419.

Miles, M. B. (1967). *Learning to work in groups.* New York: Teachers College Press.

Miller, G. R., and Coleman, E. B. (1967). A set of 36 prose passages calibrated for complexity. *Journal of Verbal Learning and Verbal Behavior*, 6, 851–854.

Misulus, K. (1988). Application of instructional strategies across subjects, grades, and teaching styles. Research paper, Syracuse University.

Moore, D.; Moore, S. A.; Cunningham, P.; and Cunningham, J. (1986). *Developing readers and writers in the content areas.* New York: Longman.

Moore, D. W.; Readence, J. E.; and Rickelman, R. J. (1982). *Prereading activities for content area reading and learning.* Newark, DE: International Reading Association.

Moore, D. W.; Readence, J. E.; and Rickelman, R. J. (1983). An historical exploration of content area reading instruction. *Reading Research Quarterly.* 18 (4), 419–438.

Moore, W. E.; McCann, H.; and McCann, J. (1981). *Creative and critical thinking* (2nd ed.). Boston: Houghton Mifflin.

Mosenthal, J. (1989). The comprehension experience. In K. D. Muth (Ed.), *Children's comprehension of text.* Newark, DE: International Reading Association.

Muth, K. D. (1987). Structure strategies for comprehending expository text. *Reading Research and Instruction,* 27, 66–72.

Muth, K. D. (Ed.) (1989). *Children's comprehension of text.* Newark, DE: International Reading Association.

Nagy, W. E. (1988). Teaching vocabulary to improve reading comprehension. Urbana, IL: ERIC/RCS.

Nagy, W. E., and Herman, P. A. (1987). Breadth and depth of vocabulary knowledge: Implications for acquisition and instruction. In M. G. McKeown and M. E. Curtis (Eds.), *The Nature of Vocabulary Acquisition* (pp. 19–36). Hillsdale, NJ: Erlbaum.

Nagy, W. E.; Herman, P. A.; and Anderson, R. C. (1985). Learning words from context. *Reading Research Quarterly,* 20, 233–253.

National Assessment of Educational Progress. (1986). *Mathematics report card.* Princeton, NJ: Educational Testing Service.

National Assessment of Educational Progress. (1988). *Reading report card.* Princeton, NJ: Educational Testing Service.

Nelson, J. (1978). Readability: Some cautions for the content area teacher. *Journal of Reading,* 21, 620–625.

Nelson-Herber, J. (1985). Anticipation and prediction in reading comprehension. In T. L. Harris and E. J. Cooper (Eds.), *Reading, thinking, and concept development.* New York: The College Board.

Nelson-Herber, J. (1986). Expanding and refining vocabulary in content areas. *Journal of Reading,* 29, 626–633.

Nelson-Herber, J., and Herber, H. L. (1984). A positive approach to assessment and correction of reading difficulties in middle and secondary schools. In J. Flood (Ed.), *Promoting reading comprehension.* Newark, DE: International Reading Association.

Nelson-Herber, J., and Johnston, C. S. (1989). Questions and concerns about teaching narrative and expository text. In K. D. Muth (Ed.), *Children's comprehension of text.* (pp. 263–279). Newark, DE: International Reading Association.

Newman, A. P., and Beverstock, C. (1990). *Adult literacy: Contexts and challenges.* Newark, DE: International Reading Association.

Niles, O. (1965). Organization perceived. In H. L. Herber (Ed.), *Developing study skills in secondary schools* (pp. 57–76). Newark, DE: International Reading Association.

Noyce, R. M., and Christie, J. F. (1989). *Integrating reading and writing instruction.* Boston: Allyn & Bacon.

Omanson, R. C.; Beck, I. L.; McKeown, M. G.; and Perfeti, C. A. (1984). Comprehension of texts with unfamiliar versus recently taught words: Assessment of alternative models. *Journal of Educational Psychology, 76* (6), 1253–1268.

Otto, W.; Wolf, A.; and Eldridge, R. G. (1984). Managing instruction. In P. D. Pearson, R. Barr, M. L. Kamil, and P. Mosenthal (Eds.), *Handbook of reading research* (pp. 799–828), New York: Longman.

Palincsar, A. S., and Brown, A. L. (1984). Reciprocal teaching of comprehension-fostering and comprehension-monitoring activities. *Cognition and Instruction, 1,* 117–175.

Palincsar, A. S., and Brown, A. L. (1986). Interactive teaching to promote independent learning from text. *The Reading Teacher, 39,* 771–777.

Parker, C. J., and Rubin, L. J. (1966). *Process as content: Curriculum design and the application of knowledge.* Chicago: Rand McNally.

Pauk, W. (1974). *How to study in college.* Boston: Houghton Mifflin.

Paul, R. W. (1984). Critical thinking: Fundamental to education for a free society. *Educational Leadership, 42* (1), 4–14.

Pearce, D. (1983). Guidelines for the use and evaluation of writing in content classrooms. *Journal of Reading, 17,* 212–218.

Pearce, D. (1987). Group writing activities: A useful strategy for content teachers. *Middle School Journal, 18,* 24–25.

Pearce, D., and Bader, L. (1984). Writing in content area classrooms. *Reading World, 23,* 234–241.

Pearson, P. D. (1974–1975) The effects of grammatical complexity on children's comprehension, recall, and conception of certain semantic relations. *Reading Research Quarterly, 10* (2), 155–192.

Pearson, P. D. (1984). Direct explicit teaching of comprehension. In G. G. Duffy, L. R. Roehler, and J. Mason (Eds.), *Comprehension instruction: Perspectives and suggestions* (pp. 222–233). New York: Longman.

Pearson, P. D. (Ed.). (1984). *Handbook of reading research.* New York: Longman.

Pearson, P. D.; Hansen, J.; and Gordon, C. (1979). The effect of background knowledge on young children's comprehension of explicit and implicit information. *Journal of Reading Behavior, 12,* 201–209.

Pearson, P. D., and Johnson, D. D. (1978). *Teaching reading comprehension.* New York: Holt, Rinehart and Winston.

Pearson, P. D. and Leys, M. (1985). "Teaching" comprehension. In T. L. Harris and E. J. Cooper (Eds.), *Reading, thinking, and concept development* (pp. 3–20). New York: College Entrance Examination Board.

Pearson, P. D., and Spiro, R. (1982). The new buzz word in reading is schema. *Instructor,* May, 46–48.

Perkins, D. N., and Salomon, G. (1989) Are cognitive skills context-bound? *Educational Researcher,* January-February, 19 (1), pp. 16–25.

Peters, C. W. (1982). The content processing model: A new approach to conceptualizing content reading. In J. P. Patberg (Ed.), *Reading in the content areas: Application of a concept* (pp. 100–109). Toledo, OH: University of Toledo, College of Education.

Petrosky, A. R., and Bartholomae, D. (Eds.) (1986). *The teaching of writing.* Chicago: National Society for the Study of Education.

Phelps, S. (1979). The effects of integrating sentence combining activities and guided reading procedures on the reading and writing performance of eighth grade students. In H. L. Herber and J. D. Riley (Eds.), *Research in reading in the content areas: Fourth year report* (pp. 99–112). Syracuse, NY: Syracuse University, Reading and Language Arts Center.

Phelps, S. (1984). A first step in content area reading instruction. *Reading World,* 23, 265–269.

Piaget, J. (1952). *The language and thought of the child.* London: Routledge and Kegan Paul.

Pittelman, S. D.; Heimlich, J. E.; Berglund, R. L.; and French, M. P. (1991). *Semantic feature analysis.* Newark, DE: International Reading Association.

Raphael, T. E. (1982). Teaching children question-answering strategies. *The Reading Teacher,* 36, 186–191.

Raphael, T. E. (1984). Teaching learners about sources of information for answering comprehension questions. *Journal of Reading,* 27, 303–311.

Raphael, T. E. (1986). Teaching question-answer relationships, revisited. *The Reading Teacher,* 39, 516–522.

Raphael, T. E.; Kirschner, B. W.; and Englert, C. S. (1988). Expository writing program: Making connections between reading and writing. *The Reading Teacher,* 41, 790–795.

Raphael, T. E., and Pearson, P. D. (1982). The effect of metacognitive awareness training on children's question answering behavior. Technical Report No. 238. Urbana, IL: Center for the Study of Reading.

Ratekin, N.; Simpson, M. L.; Alvermann; D. E.; and Dishner, E. K. (1985). Why teachers resist content area reading instruction. *Journal of Reading,* 28, 432–437.

Reynolds, R. C.; Taylor, M. A.; Steffensen, M. S.; Shirey, L. L.; and Anderson, R. C. (1983). Cultural schemata and reading comprehension. *Reading Research Quarterly,* 17 (3), 353–356.

Richardson, J. S., and Morgan, R. F. (1990). *Reading to learn in the content areas.* Belmont, CA: Wadsworth.

Rieck, B. J. (1977). How content teachers telegraph messages against reading. *Journal of Reading,* 20, 646–648.

Riley, J. D. (1979a). The effect of reading guides upon students' literal, interpretive, and applied level comprehension of word problems. In H. L. Herber and J. D. Riley (Eds.), *Research in reading in the content areas: Fourth year report* (pp. 113–131). Syracuse, NY: Syracuse University, Reading and Language Arts Center.

Riley, J. D. (1979b). The effects of reading guides and a directed reading method on word problem comprehension, problem solving ability, and attitude toward mathematics. In H. L. Herber and J. D. Riley (Eds.), *Research in reading in the content areas: Fourth year report* (pp. 79–98). Syracuse, NY: Syracuse University, Reading and Language Arts Center.

Robinson, F. P. (1961). *Effective Study* (Rev. ed.). New York: Harper & Row.

Roehler, L. R., and Duffy, G. G. (1984). Direct explanation of comprehension processes. In G. Duffy, L. R. Roehler, and J. M. Mason (Eds.), *Comprehension instruction: Perspectives and suggestions* (pp. 265–280). New York: Longman.

Rogers, D. B. (1984). Assessing study skills. *Journal of Reading,* 27, 346–354.

Rosenshine, B., and Berliner, D. (1978). Academic engaged time. *British Journal of Teacher Education,* 4, 3–16.

Rosenshine, B., and Stevens, R. (1984). Classroom instruction in reading. In P. D. Pearson, (Ed.). *Handbook of reading research.* New York: Longman.

Rosenthal, R. (1968). Self-fulfilling prophesy. *Psychology Today,* II, September, 44–52.

Rosenthal, R., and Jacobson, L. (1968). *Pygmalion in the Classroom.* New York: Holt, Rinehart and Winston.

Rosler, N. (1984). Teaching and testing reading comprehension: An historical perspective on instructional research and practices. In J. Flood (Ed.), *Understanding reading comprehension: Cognition, language, and the structure of prose* (pp. 48–60). Newark, DE: International Reading Association.

Rothkopf, E. (1970). The concept of mathemagenic activities. *Review of Educational Research,* 40, 325–336.

Ruddell, R. A. (1964). A study of the cloze comprehension technique in relation to structurally controlled reading material. *Proceedings of the International Reading Association,* 9, 298–303.

Rumelhart, D. E. (1975). Notes on a schema for stories. In D. B. Bobrow and A. M. Collins (Eds.), *Representation and understanding.* New York: Academic Press.

Rumelhart, D. E. (1977). Toward an interactive model of reading. In S. Dornic (Ed.), *Attention and performance, VI: Proceedings of the Sixth International Symposium on Attention and Performance, Stockholm, Sweden, July 8–August 1, 1975* (pp. 573–603). Hillsdale, NJ: Erlbaum Associates.

Rumelhart, D. E. (1980). Schemata: The building blocks of cognition. In R. J. Spiro, B. C. Bruce and W. F. Brewer (Eds.), *Theoretical issues in reading comprehension*, (pp. 33–58). Hillsdale, NJ: Erlbaum.

Rumelhart, D. E. (1981). Schemata: The building blocks of cognition. In J. Guthrie (Ed.), *Comprehension and teaching: Research review*. Newark, DE: International Reading Association.

Rumelhart, D. E. (1984). Understanding understanding. In J. Flood (Ed.), *Understanding reading comprehension: Cognition, language, and the structure of prose* (pp. 1–20). Newark, DE: International Reading Association.

Sanacore, J. (1984). Metacognition and the improvement of reading: Some important links. *Journal of Reading, 27,* 706–712.

Santa, C. M.; Isaacson, L.; and Manning, G. (1987). Changing content instruction through action research. *The Reading Teacher, 40,* 434–438.

Santeusanio, R. (1983). *A practical approach to content area reading*. Reading, MA: Addison-Wesley.

Schatz, E. K., and Baldwin, R. S. (1986). Context clues are unreliable predictors of word meanings. *Reading Research Quarterly, 21,* 439–453.

Schell, L. M. (1988). Dilemmas in assessing reading comprehension. *The Reading Teacher, 42,* 12–16.

Schön, D. A. (1983). *The Reflective Practitioner*. New York: Basic Books.

Shablak, S. L., and Castallo, R. (1977). Curiosity arousal and motivation in the teaching/learning process. In H. L. Herber and R. T. Vacca (Eds.), *Research in reading in the content areas: Third year report* (pp. 51–65). Syracuse, NY: Syracuse University, Reading and Language Arts Center.

Shanahan, T. (1986). Predictions and limiting effects of prequestions. In J. A. Niles and R. V. Lalik (Eds.), *Solving problems in literacy: Learners, teachers, and researchers. Thirty-fifth yearbook of the National Reading Conference* (pp. 92–98). Rochester, NY: National Reading Conference.

Shepherd, D. (1982). *Comprehensive high school reading methods* (3rd ed.). Columbus, OH: Merrill.

Shoemaker, M. (1977). Mediating effect of guide materials. Personal conversation.

Simpson, M. L. (1986). PORPE: A writing strategy for studying and learning in the content areas. *Journal of Reading, 29,* 407–414.

Simpson, M. L. (1987). Alternative formats for evaluating content area vocabulary understanding. *Journal of Reading, 30,* 20–27.

Simpson, M. L.; Hayes, C. G.; Stahl, N. A.; Connor, R. T.; and Weaver, D. (1988). An initial validation of a study strategy system. *Journal of Reading Behavior, 20,* 149–180.

Sinatra, R. (1986). *Visual literacy connections to thinking, reading and writing*. Springfield, IL: Charles C. Thomas.

Singer, H., and Bean, T. (1988). Three models for helping teachers to help students learn from text. In S. J. Samuels and P. David Pearson (Eds.), *Changing school reading programs* (pp. 161–183). Newark, DE: International Reading Association.

Singer, H., and Dolan, D. (1980). *Reading and learning from text.* Boston: Little, Brown.

Singer, H., and Donlan, D. (1985). *Reading and learning from text.* Hillsdale, NJ: Erlbaum.

Slater, W. H., and Graves, M. F. (1989). Research on expository text: Implications for teachers. In K. D. Muth (Ed.), *Children's comprehension of text* (pp. 140–166). Newark, DE: International Reading Association. 140–166.

Smith, D. E. P. (1967). *Learning to learn.* New York: Harcourt Brace Jovanovich.

Smith, F. (1971). *Understanding reading.* New York: Holt, Rienhart and Winston.

Smith, F. (1973). *Psycholinguistics and reading.* New York: Holt, Rinehart and Winston.

Smith, F. (1978). *Understanding reading: A psycholinguistic analysis of reading and learning to read* (2nd ed.). New York: Holt, Rinehart & Winston.

Smith, F. (1979). *Reading without nonsense.* New York: Teachers College Press.

Smith, F. (1984). Reading like a writer. In J. M. Jensen (Ed.), *Composing and comprehending* (pp. 47–56). Urbana, IL: National Conference on Research in English.

Smith, N. B. (1965). *American reading instruction.* Newark, DE: International Reading Association.

Squire, J. R. (1984). Composing and comprehending: Two sides of the same basic process. In J. M. Jensen (Ed.), *Composing and comprehending* (pp. 23–32). Urbana, IL: National Conference on Research in English.

Stahl, S. (1983). Differential word knowledge and reading comprehension. *Journal of Reading Behavior,* 14 (4), 33–55.

Standal, T. C., and Betza, R. E. (1990). *Content area reading: Teachers, texts, students.* Englewood Cliffs, NJ: Prentice-Hall.

Stauffer, R. (1969a). *Directing reading maturity as a cognitive process.* New York: Harper & Row.

Stauffer, R. (1969b). *Teaching reading as a thinking process.* New York: Harper and Row.

Stein, N. L., and Glenn, C. G. (1979). *New directions in discourse processing.* Norwood, NJ: Ablex.

Sternberg, R. J. (1985). Teaching critical think, Part I. Are we making critical mistakes? *Phi Delta Kappan,* November, 194–198.

Stevens, K. C. (1982). Can we improve reading by teaching background information? *Journal of Reading,* 25, 326–329.

Taba, H. (1967). *Teacher's handbook for elementary social studies.* Reading, MA: Addison-Wesley.

Taylor, W. L. (1953). "Cloze procedure": A new tool for measuring readability. *Journalism Quarterly,* 30, 415–433.

Thelen, J. N. (1977). Use of advance organizers and guide material in viewing science motion pictures in ninth grade. In H. L. Herber and R. T.

Vacca (Eds.), *Research in reading in the content areas: Third year report* (pp. 179–189). Syracuse, NY: Syracuse University, Reading and Language Arts Center.

Thompson, G., and Morgan, R. (1976). The use of concept formation study guides for social studies reading materials. *Reading Horizons*, 17, 132–136.

Thorndike, E. L. (1917). Reading and reasoning. *Journal of Education Psychology*, 8, 323–332.

Thorndyke, P. W. (1977). Cognitive structures in comprehension and memory of narrative discourse. *Cognitive Psychology*, 9, 77–110.

Tierney, R. J.; Carter, M. A.; and Desai, L. E. (1991). *Portfolio assessment in the reading-writing classroom*. Norwood, MA: Christopher Gordon Publishers.

Tierney, R. J., and Pearson, P. D. (1984). Toward a composing model of reading. In J. M. Jensen (Ed.), *Composing and comprehending* (pp. 33–46). Urbana, IL: National Conference on Research in English.

Tierney, R. J.; Readence, J. E.; and Dishner, E. K. (1985). *Reading strategies and practices: A compendium* (2nd ed.). Boston: Allyn & Bacon.

Tonjes, M. J. (1991). *Secondary reading, writing, and learning*. Boston: Allyn & Bacon.

Tonjes, M. J., and Zintz, M. V. (1981). *Teaching reading/thinking study skills in content classrooms*. Dubuque, IA: William C. Brown.

Tonjes, M. J., and Zintz, M. V. (1987). *Teaching reading, thinking, study skills in content classrooms* (2nd ed.). Dubuque, IA: William C. Brown.

Uttero, D. A. (1988). Activating comprehension through cooperative learning. *The Reading Teacher*, 41, 390–395.

Vacca, R. T. (1973). An investigation of a functional reading strategy in seventh-grade social studies classes (Doctoral dissertation, Syracuse University, Syracuse, NY). *Dissertation Abstracts International*, 34, 6278A.

Vacca, R. T., and Vacca, J. L. (1986). *Content area reading* (2nd ed.). Boston: Little, Brown.

Vacca, R. T., and Vacca, J. L. (1989). *Content area reading,* Glenview, IL: Scott, Foreman.

Valeri-Gold, M. (1987). Previewing: A directed reading-thinking activity. *Reading Horizons*, 27, 123–216.

Vaughan, J., and Estes, T. (1986). *Reading and reasoning beyond the primary grades*. Newton, MA: Allyn & Bacon.

Vygotsky, L. S. (1962). *Thought and Language*. Cambridge, MA: MIT Press.

Vygotsky, L. S. (1978). *Mind in Society*. Cambridge, MA: Harvard University Press.

Wassermann, S. (1987). Teaching for thinking: Louis E. Raths revisited. *Phi Delta Kappan*, 68 (6), 460–466.

Weaver, P. (1978). *Research within reach*. Washington, D. C.: National Institute of Education.

Weinstein, C. E. (1987). Fostering learning autonomy through the use of learning strategies. *Journal of Reading, 30,* 590–595.

Williams, J. D. (1989). *Preparing to teach writing.* Belmont, CA: Wadsworth.

Wixson, K. K.; Peters, C. W.; Weber, E. M.; and Roeber, E. D. (1987). New directions in statewide reading assessment. *The Reading Teacher, 40,* 749–754.

Wood, K. D. (1985). Free associational assessment: An alternative to traditional testing. *Journal of Reading, 29,* 106–111.

Wood, K. D. (1987). Fostering cooperative learning in middle and secondary level classrooms. *Journal of Reading, 31,* 10–18.

Yager, R. E. (1983). The importance of terminology in teaching K–12 science. *Journal of Research in Science Teaching, 20* (6), 577–588.

—— Appendix A ——————————

Sand Art, on a Deadline

Practice 2-2
Chapter 2

Conceptual analysis: An artist creates beauty out of fragile material, deliberately doing so within the environment that is both the source of the material and the inevitable cause of its destruction.

Organizing idea: The essence of creativity lies more in its process than in its product.

Calculations on Fry Readability Graph

Practice 3-1
Chapter 3

Average number of sentences = 7
Average number of syllables = 144
Grade-level estimate = 7

Content Reading Inventory: Predicting Performance

Practice 3-3
Chapter 3

1. **What performance is discussed in this reading selection?**
   The reading selection discusses the ability to predict the performance of an airplane.
2. **What factors determine whether an airplane is flying at its maximum level flight speed?**
   Maximum level flight speed is computed from engine power compared against total drag.
3. **The acronym *FAR* appears in the third paragraph of the reading selection, but without its definition. What do you think the initials might stand for, and why?**

FAR probably stands for Federal Aviation Regulations. The third paragraph refers to regulations (R). The regulations deal with the operation of airplanes or the control of aviation (A). Most forms of interstate transportation are controlled by federal agencies (F).

4. **What is the difference between service ceiling and absolute ceiling for an airplane?**

   Service ceiling is the altitude at which a single-engine airplane is able to maintain a maximum climb of only 100 feet per minute. Absolute ceiling is reached when a plane is unable to climb any further.

5. **What is the difference between maximum endurance speed and maximum range speed?**

   Maximum endurance speed allows a plane to remain aloft while using the least amount of power and the lowest rate of fuel consumption in order to sustain level flight. This differs from maximum range speed, which is based on the speed attained and the rate of fuel consumption for any given power setting in order to produce the greatest distance traveled per gallon of fuel consumed.

6. **If a pilot has to clear obstacles at the end of the runway on takeoff, should he or she use the best angle-of-climb airspeed or the best rate-of-climb airspeed? Why?**

   To clear obstacles on takeoff, a pilot should use best angle-of-climb airspeed because this airspeed provides the greatest lift over a given distance traveled upon takeoff.

7. **Which works better when a plane is at absolute ceiling, best angle-of-climb airspeed or best rate-of-climb airspeed? Why?**

   Neither type of climb works at absolute ceiling because further climbing is not possible at absolute ceiling.

8. **If a pilot is low on fuel and over territory unsuitable for landing, should he or she be concerned more about maximum endurance speed or maximum range speed? Why?**

   The pilot in this circumstance should be more concerned about maximum range speed in order to travel the greatest distance possible to search for a suitable landing site.

9. **How do the factors of thrust and drag contribute to the flight of an airplane?**

   The power source for an airplane provides the thrust that gives it forward motion. The drag of an airplane provides resistance to forward motion. When thrust exceeds drag, the plane accelerates. When thrust balances drag, the plane maintains level flight.

10. **What knowledge comes from being able to predict the performance of an airplane?**

    Predicting the performance of an airplane allows pilots to determine length of runway needed for takeoff, probability of clearing obstacles in the departure path, time needed for reaching the planned destination, fuel required for the planned flight, and the length of runway needed for landing.

Ignorance, Ignorantly Judged

Practice 3-4
Chapter 3

Organizing idea: What you don't know may hurt you.

Organizational pattern: Comparison/contrast

Passing Down Murphy's Law

Practice 3-5
Chapter 3

Organizing idea: What inevitably is will eventually be.

Organizational pattern: Cause/effect

The Blunderers of June

Practice 3-6
Chapter 3

Organizing idea: Taking a long run for a short slide

Organizational pattern: Time order

Declaration Against PCs

Practice 3-7
Chapter 3

Organizing idea: Mental ideas can be represented in physical form.

Organizational pattern: Simple listing

Activity I: Reinforcement of Definitions of Words

Practice 7-1
Chapter 7

Magic Square: How well do you know these terms?

Directions: Select from the numbered statements the best answer for each of the terms related to food and its uses. Put the number in the proper space in the magic-square box. The total of the numbers will be the same across each row and down each column.

Terms	*Statements*
A. secretions	1. Essential food substances that are needed for proper growth and health of the body.
B. digestion	2. The living materials of the cell.
C. albumin	3. Sugar produced in living organisms from starch and other sugars.
D. excretion	4. The process by which waste materials are removed from the body.
E. protoplasm	5. The process in which food is changed to soluble forms for use in the body.
F. amino acid	6. Organic substance that is needed for the normal growth and regulation of the body.
G. molecule	7. The smallest particle of a substance that can exist and still show the properties of the substance.
H. hemoglobin	8. Nutrient that furnishes materials for growth and repair of cells in the body.
I. glucose	9. Any of a large group of simple, water-soluble proteins found in all living matter.
J. energy	10. The ability or capacity to do work.
K. vitamin	11. One of a group of compounds of which proteins, present in all living tissues, are composed.
L. minerals	12. Any of a class of compounds of carbon, hydrogen, and oxygen, which are manufactured by plants and are the ultimate source of animal food.
M. fats	13. Nutrients that furnish heat and energy in the body.
N. protein	14. A red protein substance in the red blood cells needed to carry oxygen.
O. carbohydrates	15. Nutrients that furnish materials for growth and regulation of the body.
P. nutrients	16. Substances produced by glands in the body.

Answer Box for Magic Square

A	B	C	D
E	F	F	H
I	J	K	L
M	N	O	P

Magic number =

Answers to Magic Square

A	B	C	D
16	5	9	4
E	F	G	H
2	11	7	14
I	J	K	L
3	10	6	15
M	N	O	P
13	8	12	1

Magic number = 34

Activity II: Reinforcement of Definitions of Words

Hidden Word Puzzle: Terms related to food and its uses

Directions: This is a hidden word puzzle involving terms related to food and its uses. Listed below are brief statements about the hidden words. As you figure them out, write the word or words on the blank before the number. Then circle the word or words in the puzzle. These words may appear diagonally, horizontally, or vertically, and they may be printed from top to bottom or from bottom to top.

C	O	M	P	L	E	X	S	U	G	A	R	S
A	A	E	R	O	B	I	C	N	U	R	S	U
R	I	L	S	T	O	L	I	D	M	T	U	C
B	L	A	C	K	N	E	T	E	A	D	A	R
O	F	T	U	I	N	G	A	R	I	E	V	O
H	Y	E	R	I	U	U	C	N	L	R	E	S
Y	O	D	V	R	E	M	A	O	G	E	O	E
D	B	O	Y	E	K	I	M	U	S	P	L	N
R	Z	E	R	B	A	N	O	R	M	P	R	E
A	N	E	M	I	A	H	Y	I	W	O	N	T
T	U	R	F	R	N	I	E	S	A	C	A	U
E	C	O	L	E	D	I	T	H	N	O	M	L
S	O	L	E	B	E	R	N	E	G	R	E	G
B	A	L	A	N	C	E	D	D	I	E	T	A

Hidden Word Puzzle

_____ 1. A disease common in Oriental countries and prevented by Vitamin B_1.

_____ 2. Supplied with less than the minimum amount of foods essential for sound health and growth.

_____ 3. When the foods you eat supply the body with the essential minerals and vitamins as well as with the necessary nutrients.

_____ 4. They have the chemical formula $C_{12}H_{22}O_{11}$.

_____ 5. A sugar that occurs in ordinary table sugar and in many fruits and vegetables.

_____ 6. The chief source of energy in the body.

_____ 7. A mineral that is needed for tissue respiration and enzyme activities.

_____ 8. A condition resulting from lack of iron in the diet.

_____ 9. A protein found in milk and milk products.

_____ 10. A severe condition affecting the joints that results from lack of vitamin C.

_____ 11. A mineral needed for building bones and teeth, clotting blood, and the regulation of heart and muscles.

_____ 12. A protein found in peas and beans.

_____ 13. A protein found in all cereals, such as wheat, rice, and barley.

_____ 14. A mineral needed for the formation of hemoglobin and for tissue respiration.

Answer to hidden word puzzle:

```
C O M P L E X S U G A R S
A A E R O B I C N U R S U
R I L S T O L I D M T U C
B L A C K N E T E A D A R
O F T U I N G A R I E V O
H Y E R I U U C N L R E S
Y O D V R E M A O G E O E
D B O Y E K I M U S P L N
R Z E R B A N O R M P R E
A N E M I A H Y I W O N T
T U R F R N I E S A C A U
E C O L E D I T H N O M L
S O L E B E R N E G R E G
B A L A N C E D D I E T A
```

1. beriberi
2. undernourished
3. balanced diet
4. complex sugars
5. sucrose
6. carbohydrates
7. copper
8. anemia
9. casein
10. scurvy
11. calcium
12. legumin
13. gluten
14. iron

Word Puzzle: Energy for the Body

Directions: Fill in the blanks below using the definitions given after the puzzle to identify some of the vocabulary words we have been working on in the unit. Work together in your groups. When you have completed the puzzle, read the letters in parentheses downward to see what word has been created.

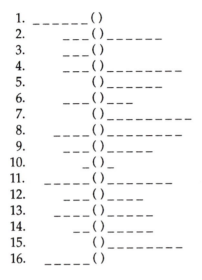

```
 1.  _ _ _ _ _ _ ( )
 2.        _ _ _ ( ) _ _ _ _ _ _
 3.        _ _ _ ( )
 4.        _ _ _ ( ) _ _ _ _ _ _ _ _
 5.            ( ) _ _ _ _ _ _
 6.        _ _ _ ( ) _ _ _
 7.            ( ) _ _ _ _ _ _ _ _ _
 8.       _ _ _ _ ( ) _ _ _ _ _ _ _ _
 9.        _ _ _ ( ) _ _ _ _ _
10.          _ ( ) _
11.     _ _ _ _ _ ( ) _ _ _ _ _ _ _
12.        _ _ _ ( ) _ _ _ _
13.       _ _ _ _ ( ) _ _ _ _ _
14.         _ _ ( ) _ _ _ _ _
15.            ( ) _ _ _ _ _ _ _ _
16.     _ _ _ _ _ ( )
```

Definitions

1. The unit used to measure the heat energy in foods.
2. The more simple units of which all proteins are composed.
3. A brownish fluid necessary for the proper breakdown of fat molecules.
4. The contractions of muscles that move through the digestive system.
5. A substance produced in the complete digestion of carbohydrates.
6. Chemical substances that speed up chemical changes in the cells.
7. Substances produced in the complete digestion of fats.
8. A substance produced in the respiration cycle of glucose.
9. The essential substances in food needed by the body for proper health.
10. The chemical compound that stores energy in a cell.
11. Nutrients that furnish most of the energy in the body.
12. Nutrients that furnish materials for growth and regulation in the body.
13. The sum of the activities in the body necessary to life.
14. Nutrients that furnish materials for growth and repair of the body.
15. The process in which food is changed to soluble forms in the body.
16. A severe condition which affects the joints and is the result of the lack of vitamin C.

Pollution, Man, and Technology Analogies

Practice 7-2
Chapter 7

Directions: Read the following sentences, and complete the analogies, or comparisons, by using the words from the list shown below. Remember, the first pair of words have a definite relationship, and you are looking for the same type of relationship in the second pair of words. Fill in the blanks with the best word or words. Be ready to give reasons for your choices.

1. Pollution problems are to technology as _____ are to technology.
2. Toxic substances are to PCBs as _____ are to insect and weed killers.
3. An open dump is to the land as _____ is to the atmosphere.
4. An explosive charge is to a gun as a _____ is to an aerosol container.
5. A sanitary landfill is to a land-pollution solution as a _____ _____ is to a water pollution solution.
6. A railroad track is to a train as a _____ is to wastewater.
7. Toxic materials are to chemical wastes as _____ are to hazardous wastes.
8. Pounds are to weight as _____ are to noise.
9. A reporter is to the news as the _____ is to air quality.
10. Sanitary landfills are to the land as _____ are to the air.
11. Safe disposal is to hazardous wastes as _____ is to plastics, papers, containers, and garbage.
12. Cigarettes are to cancer as _____ is to heart disease.

pump button sprays	radioactive materials
wastewater treatment plant	sewer
noise	acid rain
decibels	organic wastes
pollution solutions	pesticides
PSI	propellant
recycling	stationary
ozone layer	crop destruction
primary sewage treatment	health problems
air pollution	

Pollution Analogies Answer Key

1. pollution solutions
2. pesticides
3. acid rain
4. propellant
5. wastewater treatment plant
6. sewer
7. radioactive materials
8. decibels
9. PSI
10. pump button sprays
11. recycling
12. noise

Pollution Categorizing

Directions: Below is a list of words from your pollution lesson, followed by the names of four categories. Write each word under one or more of the categories, depending on what meaning or understanding you have of them. You must be able to back up your choices with reasons. You will be placed in groups to discuss your responses in order to compare and resolve any differences. We will discuss all of your lists as a class when the activity is completed.

toxic substances	aerosols	sludge
sanitary landfill	health problems	thermal inversion
acid rain	hazardous wastes	pollution controls
PSI	open dumps	PCBs
pesticides	ozone layer	rock music
organic wastes	smog	recycle
nuclear waste	decibels	wastewater treatment plants

Air Pollution	*Water Pollution*	*Noise Pollution*	*Land Pollution*

Pollution Categorizing Answer Key

The key provided most closely fits the text readings; however, the lists provided by the students might very well vary. This activity was designed to provide for student interaction and may result in different, and of course, equally acceptable lists. In addition to class discussion and textbook readings, the individual student will bring his own past experiences and personal schema of the subject to the assignment. Their responses will be legitimate provided the students use sound reasoning and examples, and are able to convince the teacher and classmates of their responses.

Air Pollution	Water Pollution	Noise Pollution	Land Pollution
toxic substances	toxic substances	decibels	sanitary landfill
	chemical wastes	rock music	chemical wastes
health problems	health problems	pollution controls	nuclear waste
acid rain	recycle		toxic substances
PSI			
PCBs			
pesticides	pesticides	health problems	
chemical wastes			
thermal inversion	sludge		recycle
acid rain	wastewater treatment plants		PCBs
aerosols			pesticides
ozone layer			acid rain
pollution controls	acid rain		pollution controls
hazardous wastes	pollution controls		hazardous wastes
smog	hazardous wastes		health problems
nuclear waste	nuclear wastes		open dumps

Verbal Jabs Don't Have Equal Punch

Practice 8-2
Chapter 8

The conceptual analysis for the article "Verbal Jabs Don't Have Equal Punch" is given below, followed by the organizing idea for a lesson based on this article.

We identified the level of comprehension reflected by each of the twelve statements. We identified four statements at each of the three levels. Each statement is listed below under the heading reflecting its level. Each statement retains its original number from Chapter 8.

Conceptual analysis: Teasing and ridicule differ in intention and effect. Teasing is positively correlated with self-esteem; also with paranoia. High self-esteem people accept teasing as a sign of their inclusion in a group. Low self-esteem people covet teasing in their desire for acceptance by a group.

Organizing idea: No pain, no gain

Level One

1. The teasing and ridicule adolescents engage in are distinct behaviors and have very different relationships with self-esteem.
2. The results show that those who perceive that they are frequently teased have high self-esteem.
4. Teasing was reported to occur much more often than ridicule.
9. Kids like teasing because it shows they're connected to others and are accepted. If they aren't teased they feel isolated.

Level Two

3. A single comment can be interpreted as teasing by persons of high self-worth and as ridicule by persons of low self-worth.
5. A research study revealed that teasing and ridicule are not the same behavior.
7. Teasing that is forced or unnatural may be misinterpreted by the recipients.
11. Teasing is used to express positive feelings or to educate, while ridicule is used to express anger or to hurt.

Level Three

6. Adversity may be essential to progress.
8. People not skilled in receiving usually are not skilled in giving.
10. How people feel about themselves may influence their beliefs about how others feel about them.
12. Commonly held beliefs, even by experts, can be proven wrong through research.

Never Mind Your Number—They've Got Your Name

Practice 8-3
Chapter 8

The conceptual analysis for the article "Never Mind Your Number—They've Got Your Name" is given below, followed by the organizing idea for a lesson based on this article.

We identified the level of comprehension reflected by each of the twelve statements. We identified four statements at each of the three levels. Each statement is listed below under the heading reflecting its level. Each statement retains its original number from Chapter 8.

Conceptual analysis: Private business is no longer private. Social Security numbers once were private and confidential. Now they are open to government and to virtually all manner of businesses. Because of wide accessibility of social security numbers, ease of tracking people has advanced from numbers to names. Social, psychological and economic implications are vast.

Organizing idea: Personal rights once lost are rarely regained.

Level One

1. Social security numbers are available to government agencies, educational and financial institutions, and credit bureaus.
5. There is no way to avoid being listed in credit reports and other data bases.
6. Credit bureaus eventually may be able to anticipate purchases and influence how decisions are made.
8. Once credit bureaus needed a social security number to find a name; now they can use a name to find the number.

Level Two

3. Appearance on one consumer list increases the probability of appearance on multiple lists.
7. The utility of a unique number for each person in the country made inevitable the use of social security numbers by governmental, social, and business institutions and agencies.
10. Living a normal life requires some compromise on a desire for privacy.
12. Targeted marketing owes its existence to ease in tracking people by name.

Level Three

2. Beware the camel getting his nose in your tent!
4. You can run but you cannot hide.
9. Patterns of past behavior validate predictions of future behavior.
11. Personal rights once lost are rarely regained.

The Future of Pennies

Practice 8-4
Chapter 8

Organizing idea: The value of an object may be in its service as well as in its substance.

Level One

Directions: Listed below are five statements. Place a check on the numbered line of each statement that presents information found in the article "The Future of Pennies." Be ready to provide evidence from the text to support your decisions. Discuss your decisions and supporting evidence with other members of your group.

_____ 1. The proposal to eliminate the penny in the United States should be treated with disdain.
_____ 2. Inflation consistently threatens the value of the penny.
_____ 3. Pennies serve important social functions.
_____ 4. Pennies contribute to our cultural development.
_____ 5. Eliminating the penny would be penny-wise and pound-foolish.

Level Two

Directions: Listed below are five statements. Place a check on the numbered line for each statement that can be supported by combinations of information found in the article "The Future of Pennies." Be ready to cite evidence from the article to support your decisions. Discuss your decisions and supporting evidence with other members of your group.

_____ 1. Currency requires both upper and lower denominational limits.
_____ 2. Pennies serve social purposes, ranging from history lessons to the instigation of casual conversation.
_____ 3. Financial security contributes to contentment.
_____ 4. Saving pennies contributes to a person's sense of thrift.
_____ 5. Social costs should not exceed physical convenience.

Level Three

Directions: Listed below are five statements. Place a check on the numbered line for each statement that you can support with ideas derived from the article "The Future of Pennies" *and* from your own knowledge and experience. Be ready to provide evidence from *both* sources to support your decisions. Discuss your decisions and supporting evidence with other members of your group.

_____ 1. The very existence of a least common denominator usually assures its use.

_____ 2. Common good may be served better by multiple contributions than by a single contribution.

_____ 3. Security can be measured by what one discards as well as by what one keeps.

_____ 4. The whole is greater than the sum of its parts.

_____ 5. The value of an object may be in its service as well as in its substance.

Women in Architecture

Practice 8-5
Chapter 8

Organizing idea: What is is better than what was but not as good as *what will be.*

Part One

Directions: On each of the following numbered lines there is a pair of words or phrases separated by a slanted line. As you read the article "Women in Architecture," decide whether what the first word or phrase stands for is being compared with what the second word or phrase stands for in a pair, according to the text. If you believe it does, place a check on the numbered line. Follow this procedure with each of the pairs. Be ready to support your decisions with information and ideas from the text.

_____ 1. Women's interests/men's interests

_____ 2. Women's ability/men's ability

_____ 3. Women's professional opportunity/men's professional opportunity

_____ 4. Women's professional accomplishments/men's professional accomplishments

_____ 5. Older generation's awareness/younger generation's understanding

_____ 6. Effort by women/effort by men

_____ 7. Stress/satisfaction

_____ 8. Unperceived slights/exposed prejudices

_____ 9. Educational philosophy of the 1970s/educational philosophy of the 1980s

_____ 10. Virtue/hindrance

_____ 11. Difference as variability/difference as inferiority

_____ 12. Denying differences/accepting differences

Part Two

Directions: Listed below are five statements. Place a check on the numbered line for each statement that expresses an idea that can be supported by the article "Women in Architecture" *and* by your knowledge and experience. Be ready to share the reasons for your decisions.

_____ 1. Measurement of social progress requires an extended set of benchmarks.

_____ 2. *What is* is better than *what was* but not as good as *what will be.*

_____ 3. One person's obstacle is another person's opportunity.

_____ 4. Expectation creates reality out of imagination.

_____ 5. Vive la différence!

Reasoning Guide for "Law and Morality"

Practice 10-3
Chapter 10

Organizing idea: True obligation is driven more internally than externally.

Directions: Before you read the article "Law and Morality," respond to each of the following statements and decide whether it seems reasonable to you. That is, does a statement fit well in your mind? Do you possess knowledge or have you had experiences that support the idea as it is expressed here? If so, place a check on the numbered line. If not, leave the numbered line blank. Be ready to discuss the reasons for your decisions.

_____ 1. What's yours is mine; what's mine is my own.

_____ 2. One cannot have freedom without responsibility.

_____ 3. Cast your bread upon the waters.

_____ 4. Do unto others as you would have them do unto you.

_____ 5. Am I my brother's keeper?

_____ 6. When parts dominate excessively, there can never be a whole.

_____ 7. True obligation is driven more internally than externally.

Directions: Now that you have read "Law and Morality," respond again to each of the statements. Decide whether the author of the article would agree with your decisions on whether the statements are reasonable. Circle the number(s) of the statement(s) on which you and the author agree. Be ready to provide evidence from the article to support your decisions.

Appendix B

Materials Drawn from a Unit in Life Science

Organizing Idea: They share a similarity of dissimilars.

Class: Seventh-grade accelerated science class.

Vocabulary:

Words to Present	Words to Teach
Monerans	protists
chlorophyll	euglenas
photosynthesis	dinoflagellates
vacuole	diatoms
enzymes	protozoans
amoebas	flagellates
paramecia	sporozoans
reproduction	sarcodines
asexual	ciliates
fission	cysts
	pseudopods
	conjugation
	foraminiferans
	tripanosomes

Materials: Paul Jantzen and Judith Michel, *Life Science*, New York: Macmillan Publishing Company, 1986, pp. 92–99.

Structured Overview: One-Celled Organisms

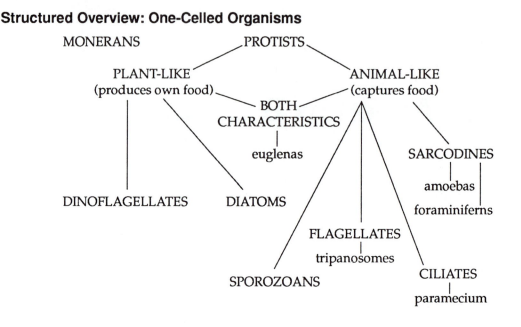

Levels Guide

Level One

What did the author say?

Directions: In this exercise you will be working in groups. Together you will decide which of the following statements you believe say what the author said. The wording may be exactly the same or it may be a paraphrase. Be prepared to defend your choices with evidence from the text. Place a check on the numbered line for each of your choices.

_____ 1. Plantlike protists are a source of food and oxygen for other organisms.
_____ 2. Cyst formation helps protists survive.
_____ 3. The contractile vacuole removes excess water and wastes from the organism.
_____ 4. Sporozoans cannot move around on their own.
_____ 5. Paramecia are an example of a protist that can reproduce by conjugation.
_____ 6. Enzymes are special proteins that speed up the processes in living things.

Level Two

What did the author mean?

Directions: Place a check on the line before each statement which expresses an idea that can be reasonably supported with information from the text. Be ready to discuss the supporting evidence with others in your group.

_____ 1. Deposits of protists are useful to human beings in several ways.
_____ 2. The normal cell activities of the protist cease temporarily during cyst formation.
_____ 3. There are two kinds of vacuoles serving different functions.
_____ 4. Flagella, cilia, and pseudopods are examples of ways in which protists move.
_____ 5. Some organisms can reproduce both sexually and asexually.

Level Three

How do you apply the ideas?

Directions: Place a check on the numbered line for each statement that you can support with ideas from the text and from our own experience and knowledge. Be ready to share the evidence you have used to support your decisions.

_____ 1. The seemingly insignificant can have a significant impact on our daily lives.
_____ 2. The function of enzymes in a food vacuole is similar to the effect of caffeine and nicotine in the human body.
_____ 3. The need for conjugation in paramecia is similar to the need for legislation forbidding brothers and sisters and first cousins to marry.
_____ 4. Several features of protists are characteristic of human beings.
_____ 5. Adapt or perish.

How Is the Organism's Food Obtained?

Directions: If any of the organisms listed below possess chlorophyll and make their own food, write their names under the category heading *Plantlike Organisms*. If any of the organisms capture their food, write their names under the category heading *Animallike Organisms*. If any of the organisms possess both plantlike *and* animallike characteristics, write their names under the category heading *Both*. Be ready to discuss the reasons for your responses.

dinoflagellates, flagellates, sarcodines, diatoms,
euglenas, sporozoans, ciliates

Plantlike Organisms   *Animallike Organisms*   *Both*

How Does the Organism Move About?

Directions: If any of the organisms listed below move on their own, write
their names under the appropriate category headings (*Pseudopod, Flagella,
Cilia*) to indicate how they move. If any of the listed organisms cannot move
on their own, write their names under the category heading *Parasitic.* Be
ready to discuss the reasons for your responses.

amoebas, foraminiferans, sporozoans, paramecium,
dinoflagellates, diatoms, ciliates, flagellates

Pseudopod   *Flagella*   *Cilia*   *Parasitic*

Materials Drawn from a Unit on Propaganda

Grade five reading class

Unit organizing idea: Propaganda persuades

Lesson organizing idea: Propaganda persuades us politically, economically
and socially

NAME _____ DATE _____

Matching Activity

Directions: Match each word with its definition. Write the letter for each
definition on the numbered line of the word it defines.

Words   *Definitions*

_____   1. Propaganda   a. Information deliberately spread
                                              to help or harm a person, idea,
                                              product or group.

_____   2. Disguise   b. Influence someone to something.
_____   3. Sinister   c. Capable of producing a result.
_____   4. Psychological   d. Dealing with the mind and what
                                              it does.

_____   5. Rumor   e. Evil.
_____   6. Propagandist   f. Hide, cover-up or lie.
_____   7. Economic   g. Having to do with government.
_____   8. Consumer   h. Gossip.
_____   9. Political   i. A person who spreads helpful or
                                              harmful information about an
                                              idea, product, person or group.

_____   10. Persuade   j. A person who uses goods and
                                              services.

_____   11. Social   k. Production, distribution and
                                              consumption of goods and ser-
                                              vices.

_____   12. Effective   l. The health, education and wel-
                                              fare of the people.

_____   13. Media   m. The radio, newspapers, maga-
                                              zines, television and any other
                                              means of spreading propaganda.

NAME _____ DATE _____

Word Pairing

Directions: For each pair of words, you must decide whether a similarity or
difference exists betw4en the words. On the numbered lines put an "S" if the
words in the pairs are nearly the same, and "D" if the words are different.
Discuss reasons for your decisions with your group.

_____   1. Psychological - - - - - - - - - - - - - - - - - - - Support
_____   2. Rumor - Information
_____   3. Sinister - Evil
_____   4. Public - Consumers
_____   5. Political - Social
_____   6. Disguise - False
_____   7. Truth - Belief

_____	8. Persuade -----------------------	Influence
_____	9. Propaganda ---------------------	Opinion
_____	10. Economic -----------------------	Commercials
_____	11. Economic -----------------------	Advertisement
_____	12. Propagandist --------------------	Gossip
_____	13. Effective -----------------------	Can do
_____	14. Media -------------------------	Communication

NAME _____ DATE _____

Cause/Effect Pattern Guide

Directions: The following CAUSE/EFFECT ideas were taken from your reading assignment concerning economic propaganda. Select from the column at the left the causes which led to the effects in the column at the right. Put the letter of each effect on the numbered line next to the appropriate cause.

Causes	_Effects_
_____ 1. Advertise America	a. the taxing of colonial newspaper advertising by the British.
_____ 2. Because the young country grew	b. when they emigrated and built America.
_____ 3. Because consumers are unprotected	c. then the free competition and American economy could be hurt.
_____ 4. Early America was a lonely and hostile place	d. in order to see a country.
_____ 5. People responded to American's propaganda	e. industries grew and competition increased.
_____ 6. Franklin's successful advertising to protest taxes caused	f. so colonizers had to use propaganda to get people to settle in America.
_____ 7. If propaganda is strictly controlled	g. they must learn to detect propaganda devices.

NAME _____ DATE _____

Writing Activity

1. Read silently and follow along as the teacher reads the first paragraph advertising "Nova Britannia". List the reasons or causes why many

people decided to sail to the American wilderness and discuss them in your group.
2. Discuss the second paragraph in this excerpt and list the possible effects or results when the settlers discovered the realities of America.
3. Discuss the lists in your group and then write an advertisement which would encourage people to live in Fayetteville, New York.
4. Finally, read the advertisements for the cola and the automobile. List the causes or reasons why these examples of economic propaganda were effective.

NAME _____ DATE _____

Cause/Effect Pattern Guide

Directions: Read the following statements from th articles about social propaganda. Decide which part of the statement is the ause or reason and which part is the effect. Write the answers on the lines provided. Share your answers with your group and help each other understand the cause/effect relationships.

1. Effective social propaganda causes a change in beliefs.
   CAUSE _____
   EFFECT _____
2. A story written by a thirty-nine-year-old housewife changed the course of human history.
   CAUSE _____
   EFFECT _____
3. Harriet Beecher Stowe wrote *Uncle Tom's Cabin* so she could convince the American people that the abolitionist cause was right.
   CAUSE _____
   EFFECT _____
4. Mrs. Stowe wrote her book because she wanted to make the whole nation feel what a terrible thing slavery was.
   CAUSE _____
   EFFECT _____
5. Mrs. Stowe's book sold more than 300,000 copies the first year, so it was translated into many European languages.
   CAUSE _____
   EFFECT _____
6. Many Northern, Eastern and Midwestern people who didn't care about black people and slavery became furious with Southern slaveholders after reading the book, *Uncle Tom's Cabin.*
   CAUSE _____
   EFFECT _____

Writing Activity

In your group, study the picture taken from the book, *Uncle Tom's Cabin*. List all the reasons why this picture might have helped change beliefs about slavery.

Materials from a Unit on Geometry

Organizing Idea: The world around us is filled with lines, shapes, and figures.

Intended Class: For use in a unit on geometry for a general mathematics eighth-grade class. (average- and low-level students)

Source Material: Siegfried Haeniseh. *Riverside Mathematics, Level 8*, Chicago, Illinois, Riverside Publishing Company, 1987.

Rationale: Attached are three different reasoning activities that reinforce the material covered in class and in the book. These guides will help students learn how to think through mathematical information and through word problems.

For this unit on geometry, I would first generate a general discussion about geometry from which students can share their ideas about the topic through personal experience. I feel that my organizing idea encourages such a discussion. Then, I will work with students in presenting all the new vocabulary and concepts that they would be encouraged to record in their notebooks. Then, the enclosed three reasoning activities would be used (at various points in the presentation of the unit) to guide students' reasoning and to reinforce the new concepts, materials, and processes. All activities invite and encourage students to use and understand their notes.

Activity One is an excellent way for students to reason through the large quantity of vocabulary that is in a geometry unit and to understand the relationships and differences among the new concepts. It is also an excellent opportunity for students to begin to learn how to use and study from their math notes and their textbooks. (This is a necessary tool that even many freshmen college students have not learned.) I constructed several declarative statements that would cause major group discussion and lead to a thorough understanding of the meaning of new concepts. I am excited for students to be active and to be discussing the material.

Activity Two is an exploratory activity in which students will learn how to reason through the process of classifying triangles. I am pleased that the latter part of this activity has several declarative statements that will require a higher level of comprehension and reasoning than the earlier statements. I believe that the groups will enjoy this activity because they will be working with manipulatives to help reinforce new concepts. I was extremely selective in the wording and clarity of my directions, working through several revisions before I was content. I am confident that students will experience success and a positive feeling from this group activity.

Activity Three first presents students with a choice of possible solutions to a rather challenging word problem on angles in a polygon. Then, the students must reason through why they chose a particular solution.

For all three activities, students would be placed in a cooperative-learning situation in which a wide variety of ability is apparent in each group. I will be careful not to bore students by a thorough review of all items on the sheet. Only statements that are particularly important or challenging will be discussed. I feel that students will benefit greatly from the group discussions that these activities will generate.

Reasoning Activity One

Directions: Read each statement. Put a check on the line if you *agree* with the statement. Leave it blank if you *disagree.* Be prepared to use the text or your class notes to support youranswers.

_____ 1. Parallel lines never intersect.
_____ 2. An acute angle and an obtuse angle together could never be complementary angles.
_____ 3. Vertical angles are only congruent when the intersecting lines form right angles.
_____ 4. All right angles are congruent.
_____ 5. A scalene triangle has two congruent sides.
_____ 6. All trapezoids are quadrilaterals.
_____ 7. All squares are rectangles.
_____ 8. Every rhombus is a square.
_____ 9. The opposite angles of a parallelogram are congruent, and the adjacent angles are supplementary.
_____ 10. If a parallelogram has a right angle, then it is classified as a rectangle and as a square.
_____ 11. An acute triangle has acute angles only.
_____ 12. The sum of the angles of an acute triangle is greater than the sum of the angles of an obtuse triangle.
_____ 13. To find the number of degree in each angle of a regular hexagon, divide the angle sum by 6.
_____ 14. The sum of the angles of any polygon can be determined by subdividing the figure into triangles.
_____ 15. When two lines are parallel to a third line, they are parallel to each other.

Directions: Open the group's envelope containing three different paper triangles. Your task is to classify each of the three triangles by both sides and angles by completing the activities in Parts 1 and 2. You may use a ruler (to check the measurements of the sides) and a protractor (to check the measurements of the angles). Use your paper triangles, your measurements, and the corrections from the preactivity to complete parts 1 and 2.

Part 1.

Look at Triangle 1, and consider the measurements of its angles and sides. Check off each of the conditions below that are true for Triangle 1 and the column labeled *TRI 1*. When you have finished with all eight statements for Triangle 1, proceed in the same manner with Triangle 2 and then Triangle 3.

TRI 1	*TRI 2*	*TRI 3*	
_____	_____	_____	1. two sides congruent
_____	_____	_____	2. three sides congruent
_____	_____	_____	3. no congruent sides
_____	_____	_____	4. one right angle
_____	_____	_____	5. two congruent angles
_____	_____	_____	6. three congruent angles
_____	_____	_____	7. all acute angles
_____	_____	_____	8. one obtuse angle

Reasoning Activity Three

Directions: The Pentagon Building outside Washington, D.C., is in the shape of a regular polygon. Below are six number sentences. Place a check on the line before each one that you can use to find the number of degrees in an angle at each corner of the Pentagon Building.

_____ 1. $(5 - 2) \times 180° \div 5 = ?$
_____ 2. $180° \times 5 \div 5 = ?$
_____ 3. $1/5 \times 3 \times 180 = ?$
_____ 4. $5 \times 180° + 5) - (2 \times 180° \div 5) = ?$
_____ 5. $5 \times (5 - 2) \times 180° = ?$
_____ 6. $(5 \times 180 - 2 \times 180°) \div 5 = ?$

Now place a check on the line before each statement that gives a reason for your choices or for any part of your choices.

_____ 1. To find the sum of the angles of any polygon
_____ 2. In a regular polygon
_____ 3. To find the number of dgrees in each angle of a polygon
_____ 4. A pentagon has 5 sides.
_____ 5. To find the number of degrees in each angle of a regular polygon

Reasoning Activity Two

Preactivity Directions: Discuss in your group the statements below. Place a check before a statement if the entire group agrees with that statement. If a statement is not correct, cross out the incorrect part and write the correct word(s) above it. The part(s) that may need changing are underlined. Then, check that statement off once the entire group agrees with the correction(s). Go through the process for all the fifteen statement below. Use your notes and textbook to support your decisions.

_____ 1. Triangles can *only be classified by their sides.*
_____ 2. *Scalene* triangles have no equal sides.
_____ 3. An *isosceles* triangle has two congruent sides.
_____ 4. All three sides of an *equilateral* triangle are congruent.
_____ 5. The sum of the angles of a triangle is *360 degrees.*
_____ 6. An acute angle measures less than *90 degrees.*
_____ 7. A right angle measures *approximately* 90 degrees.
_____ 8. An obtuse angle measures *between 90 and 270 degrees.*
_____ 9. A triangle with *three acute angles* is an isosceles triangle.
_____ 10. A triangle with *one or two* obtuse angles is an obtuse triangle.
_____ 11. A triangle with a right angle is a *right triangle.*
_____ 12. A triangle can be classified as both *scalene* and right.
_____ 13. A triangle can be classified as both isosceles and *obtuse.*
_____ 14. A triangle can be classified as both *obtuse* and right.
_____ 15. A triangle can be classified as both *obtuse* and equilateral.

Part 2

You now have enough information to classify each triangle by its sides and by its angles. Look at the information from Part 1 and from the Preactivity that describe Triangle 1. Place a check in every blank below in the column under TRI 1 if the name is a correct classification for Triangle 1. Next to the check, write the numbers of the statements from the preactivity that support your decision. When the group has finished classifying Triangle 1, continue with this classification process for Triangle 2 and then Triangle 3.

TRI 1   *TRI 2*   *TRI 3*

_____   _____   _____   A. Scale triangle
_____   _____   _____   B. Isosceles triangle
_____   _____   _____   C. Equilateral triangle
_____   _____   _____   D. Acute triangle
_____   _____   _____   E. Obtuse triangle
_____   _____   _____   F. Right triangle

AUTHOR INDEX

── SUBJECT INDEX ──